English Grammar: Theory and Use

Hilde Hasselgård, Stig Johansson and Per Lysvåg

English Grammar: Theory and Use

Universitetsforlaget
Oslo

ISBN 82-00-12693-5

Henvendelser om denne boka kan rettes til

Universitetsforlaget
Postboks 2959 Tøyen
0608 Oslo

Omslag: Anneli Skaar
Sats: Tekstflyt as, Larvik
Skrift: Times 10,5/12,5
Trykk: PDC Grafisk Produksjon, Aurskog
Innbinding: Refsum A/S, Oslo

Preface

This book is addressed to university and college students of English at the undergraduate level. For these students, grammar should not just be a tool in learning the language; it should also give insight into how the language works. As indicated by the title, our aim is to provide both practice and theoretical insight.

The emphasis on practice distinguishes this book from *Understanding English Grammar* (by Stig Johansson and Per Lysvåg), which focuses more on discussion and explanation. Although there are similarities in both content and presentation, the present publication is a new book and not just a revised and abbreviated version of the previous work.

The present book is also new in the sense that it has been produced by a team of three authors. The overall plan was worked out by the whole team, but the main responsibility for individual chapters was divided as follows:

Hilde Hasselgård: Chapters, 1, 8, 9, 10, 12, 13
Stig Johansson: Chapters 4, 5, 11, 14, 16
Per Lysvåg: Chapters 2, 3, 6, 7, 15

Although our book cannot be placed within a particular theoretical camp, it reflects some central concerns in recent linguistic theory. One of these is the importance of lexis and the interplay between lexis and grammar (Chapter 3). Another has to do with the use of grammatical structures in context. Throughout the book, we are concerned with the meaning and effect of grammatical choices, and two chapters focus specifically on grammar in written and spoken discourse (Chapters 15 and 16). Ample illustrations are given of English in use, with examples drawn from a variety of texts.

To increase the practical utility of the book, we frequently draw attention to differences between Norwegian and English that are likely to cause difficulties for Norwegians, and we provide a great deal of exercise material. There is also useful reference material in appendices at the end of the book. A *Key to Exercises* is provided in a separate volume.

We would like to express our gratitude to our consultants, Leiv Egil Breivik, Kjell Eirheim, and Glenn Martin, whose comments on the manuscript for this book have certainly improved the final version.

We hope that our book will satisfy the practical needs of university students of English and at the same time provide stimulation, and perhaps even enjoyment, for those who want to explore the workings of the English language.

Oslo, November 1997

Hilde Hasselgård   Stig Johansson   Per Lysvåg

Contents

1 Introduction

1.1 What is grammar?

There are several answers to this question. Most people's idea of grammar will probably include elements of grammar instruction at school, such as correcting mistakes, drilling structures, and memorizing irregular verbs in a foreign language. We may also hear people say such things as 'the grammar of Russian is very difficult', or 'there is a lot of grammar in German'. The word *grammar* can mean different things to different people, partly depending on what they need it for. Let us take a look at how one dictionary defines *grammar*.

> **Grammar** is 1.1 the rules of a language, concerning the way in which you can put words together in order to make sentences. EG *I need some books to be able to look up the grammar ... Is there enough grammar taught in schools? ... I hear you've abandoned teaching grammar lessons.*
>
> 1.2 the way someone either obeys or does not obey the rules of grammar when they write or speak a language. EG *I'm constantly having to correct their grammar ... take off a full point for any errors in grammar.*
>
> 2 A **grammar** is 2.1 a book that describes the rules of a language. EG *... an old French grammar.* 2.2 a theory that is intended to explain the rules of a language. EG *the theory of Case Grammar.*
>
> (From *Collins COBUILD English Language Dictionary*)

According to the first definition in the dictionary entry (1.1), these rules are properties of a language, that is, the language is such that its elements must be combined according to certain patterns. Combinations that are not allowed by these rules result in ungrammatical sentences (such as **I is a expert*, which is not an English sentence, in that *I* cannot be combined with *is*, and *a* cannot be combined with *expert*, a word beginning with a vowel sound).

The second definition (1.2) suggests that the rules of language can be either obeyed or violated. We saw that the sentence **I is a expert* violates rules of English grammar, while all the other sentences on this page are formed according to those rules. (The * marks the structure as ungrammatical.)

The last definition (2.2), defining grammar as a theory of language, belongs to theoretical linguistics, and is not relevant to our grammar book. We do not aim to present any particular theory of language. The grammatical framework, as well as the terminology used, is relatively traditional, and draws on various sources with a view to giving a balanced presentation of the essentials of English grammar.

The book is thus concerned with 'the way in which you can put words together in order to make sentences' (definition 1.1). This is an area of **syntax**. Furthermore, we focus on the choice of linguistic forms in individual sentences (for example the choice of verb form, as shown above). Finally, we view grammar in a wider perspective, in seeing the grammar of a sentence as part of a larger text structure, and as an important component in expressing meaning.

1.2 Prescriptive and descriptive grammar

A word which occurs in all dictionary definitions of *grammar* is *rules*. Rules of grammar are of at least two different kinds: prescriptive and descriptive. A descriptive rule is an attempt to describe a feature of language use; it is a statement about how linguistic elements actually behave in a certain language. Prescriptive (or normative) rules, on the other hand, are rules formulated by grammarians about how a language should be spoken or written. They are meant as advice on how to speak or write good English, or, in other words, as rules for linguistic behaviour. Prescriptive grammar is concerned with 'right' and 'wrong', and is often relatively conservative in its nature, that is, it does not usually welcome new developments in the language system. A prescriptive grammarian might, for example, say that example (1) below should be corrected to (2) because one should avoid ending a sentence with a preposition, and in addition use the form *whom* rather than *who* (because it is not the subject of the sentence). A descriptive grammarian would not say that (1) is 'wrong', but that it illustrates a construction which occurs quite commonly in present-day English, and which is less formal in style than (2).

1 Who did you give the money to?
2 To whom did you give the money?

Descriptive grammar is thus about working out the structure of language as it is used in speech and writing by its native speakers. There are rules for combining linguistic elements that native speakers use consciously or unconsciously when they speak or write, and these rules are what descriptive grammarians try to formulate. The analysis of language is thus an attempt to create order out of chaos. It involves breaking down chunks of text into sentences, phrases, and words, which may in turn be assigned to a category and given a name. It is important to note that the naming of linguistic categories is only a tool for describing the structure of a language; it is not an aim in itself. However, the description of the bits and pieces of language is probably a necessary step for understanding how these bits and pieces combine to express meaningful messages.

This book by and large takes a descriptive approach to grammar. However, we sometimes make recommendations for language use. Since this is a book for learners of English, we feel that such recommendations are necessary. Learners, even at an advanced stage, are likely to make mistakes that no native speaker of a language would make, and which would be rejected according to prescriptive and descriptive rules alike. Besides, it is an important feature of linguistic competence to know the level of formality of some grammatical structures, as well as to know that certain ways of expressing oneself can raise eyebrows in some circles.

1.3 Knowing how vs. knowing about

'Knowing the grammar of a language' can mean at least two different things. You have to know the grammar of English in order to be able to speak it. Of course, this does not mean that everyone who can speak English has read grammar books and learnt all the rules in it by heart. Knowing a language means mastering the rules of that language, and this knowledge need not be conscious. As a matter of fact, it seldom is in people's first language, unless they have studied grammar at school. This leads us to the second way in which one can know the grammar of a language, which means being able to talk about linguistic structures and how the language is built up.

1.4 Grammar and meaning

An important issue in this book is the inseparability of grammar and meaning. The meaning of a sentence is made up by a combination of the words and the grammatical structures that are used. Let us look at some examples.

1 They found the paper easy.
2 They found the paper easily.

The only difference between (1) and (2) is the ending of the last word. This may seem to be merely a grammatical difference. But the two sentences have completely different meanings, namely, 'they read the paper and thought it was easy', and 'they were looking for the paper and found it without any great effort'.

3 I've been reading *Hamlet*.
4 I've read *Hamlet*.

Examples (3) and (4) have different verb phrases. This grammatical difference signals that the speaker of (3) has recently been reading (part of) the play, but is not likely to have finished it, whereas the speaker of (4) has read the whole play at some unspecified point in the past.

1.5 Grammar and discourse effect

The same basic meaning can often be expressed in a number of different ways, involving different grammatical structures. In such cases, grammatical choices are highly relevant to the effect the sentence has on the hearer or reader. For example, word order usually signals what the speaker or writer wants to focus on, as illustrated by (1) and (2). Another grammatical distinction which can change the perspective of a message is that between the active and the passive voice, as shown in (3) and (4).

1 In the kitchen Mama was wiping the cupboards.
2 Mama was wiping the cupboards in the kitchen.
3 'America', the most widely sung of the patriotic songs, was written by a New England Baptist clergyman, Samuel Francis Smith.
4 A New England Baptist clergyman, Samuel Francis Smith, wrote 'America', the most widely sung of the patriotic songs.

1.6 Grammar and style

Grammar is also closely linked with style. Different genres of English, for example newspaper reports, poems, personal letters, telegrams, political speeches, and informal chats, all have their typical features which make us recognize the genre. Some of these features are linked to the choice of words, while others are linked to grammar. For example, in (1) we recognize the newspaper style, because of its rather long and complex structures. This is different from the style of (2), a poem by Langston Hughes. Of the many features that mark the latter off from ordinary prose, we note the omission of *are* after *so* in lines 2 and 4, and the unusual placement of *beautiful* in the last two lines.

1 A magazine publisher is claiming £5 million compensation after being given drugs that he claims greatly increased his sex drive and sent him temporarily mad.

Richard Davis, 50, says two drugs he took to combat nasal congestion led to his bankruptcy. He claims that they caused him to make irrational business decisions, live an over-extravagant lifestyle and commit fraud and assault for which he was jailed.

(From *The Times*)

2 **My people**

The night is beautiful,
So the faces of my people.

The stars are beautiful,
So the eyes of my people.

Beautiful, also, is the sun.
Beautiful, also, are the souls of my people.

(From Langston Hughes, *The Dream Keeper and other Poems*)

1.7 Grammar and medium

Spoken language is sometimes characterized as 'ungrammatical'. This is a far cry from the truth. Spoken English clearly has rules for how words and phrases can be combined; otherwise it would be impossible to interpret the meaning of utterances. However, the grammar of spoken English differs in some respects from the grammar of written English. The example below represents spoken English, and it contains several features that we would not expect to see in writing. Of those that belong to grammar we can mention the use of *like* in the first line, *gonna* in lines 4 and 6, and *innit* in the last line. There are also examples of hesitation (marked by *erm*) and some self-correction (line 8). Besides, the way in which sentences are joined together, mostly by means of *and* and *then*, is typical of spoken English.

And erm, I'm supposed to do a show for like her birthday, which is easy cos kids are easy actually, you just exaggerate like this is my opening routine I got this out of a book actually, you come on okay? and go, I'm a bit shy you see, erm, well I'm a bit shy, and tell the truth, I have to admit I'm a bit shy, so, I when I come on I'm gonna say hello, and then you say hello back to me, okay? and then, no one has to be shy, then I go off okay and I come on, and basically they're all gonna shout hello, right, yeah, no, no, that's not right no, I say hello first here I'll show you, go off I come on, I go ... and wait about for a min= half a sec= ha= you know just wait for about ten seconds, I've forgotten what I'm supposed to say wha= can you remind me? and they all shout hello, so I, erm, one more time, I go off I come on, hello, and they say hello, and that's that. It's good innit?

(From the British National Corpus)

1.8 Grammar and register

Speakers and writers have a range of registers at their disposal, which means that they vary their language according to the needs and the conventions of a particular situation. Differences between registers are perhaps most conspicuous in the choice of words, but there may also be grammatical differences. Sports broadcasters speak in a quite distinct style when they are commenting on, say, a football match, but they will express themselves differently when speaking to friends over a cup of coffee. Here is an example of the football commentary style. The # sign has been used instead of punctuation.

It's coming this way towards us # and towards Willy Morgan # the ball now # with Willy Morgan # on this near side # Willy Morgan taking it up # turns the ball infield to Gowling # Gowling to Bobby Charlton # Charlton # working his way # on the left foot # towards the edge of the area # flicks it out to John Aston # Aston now # getting inside the area # chips the ball in this is a good one for Kydd # Kydd goes up # gets a head to it #

(From the London–Lund Corpus)

1.9 Which English?

1.9.1 Regional and social variation vs. Standard English

For any language, the speech habits of individual native speakers vary quite a lot. For one thing, language varies across regions. There are some noticeable differences between British and American English. Other countries where

English is the first language also have their own national varieties. Within each country there are further differences in language use. People from Texas, California, and Massachusetts speak very differently, and so do people from London, Cardiff, and Edinburgh. The greatest differences are found in the spoken language; they mostly have to do with pronunciation, and to a certain extent the choice of words (lexis). The list below shows some well-known lexical differences between British and American English.

British English	**American English**
autumn	fall
biscuit	cookie/cracker
film	movie
ground floor	first floor
pavement	sidewalk
public school	private school
lift	elevator
tap	faucet

The grammatical differences between British and American English are not equally conspicuous. On the whole there is a remarkable similarity between these two varieties of English. There is general agreement about a standard for written English which transcends national borders. This agreement can be summed up in the term **Standard English**. This is a form of the language which is prestigious enough to be the norm for educated spoken and written English. It is not linked to any region, in contrast to the written English of the Middle Ages, which could be strongly coloured by the local dialect of the writer. After that time, English was standardized through a long process. Some important landmarks of this process were the spread of printing in the late 15th century, the publication of Shakespeare's (1564–1616) works and King James's Authorized Version of the Bible (1611), and the writing of dictionaries and grammars of English in the 17th and 18th centuries.

The term 'Standard English' suggests the existence of other types of English which are non-standard. This is indeed the case. Spoken colloquial English may have many features which disagree with the standard language. Consider the following sentences.

1 She never done it.
2 I ain't got no money.

Both sentences are fully acceptable in some regional varieties of English. The most noticeable non-standard feature of (1), typical of southern British English, is the use of *done* where Standard English would have *did*. Also, *never* is often used instead of *not*. In Standard English the sentence might thus be *She did not do it*. Example (2) has so-called double negation (*not* in combination with *no*) as well as the form *ain't* for *have not*. Such forms are found in many regional varieties on both sides of the Atlantic. A corresponding standardized version is *I haven't (got) any money*. Consider also (3), which gives an example of (American) Black English Vernacular as represented by Toni Morrison in *Sula*. This is a variety which is dependent on a person's social and/or ethnic group rather than on region.

3 "Sho he all right. Everybody all right. 'Cept Mamma. Mamma the only one ain't all right. Cause she didn't *love* us."
"Awww, Mamma."
"Awww, Mamma? Awww Mamma? You settin' here with your healthy-ass self and ax me did I love you? Them big old eyes in your head would a been two holes full of maggots if I hadn't."

(From Toni Morrison, *Sula*)

1.9.2 Historical development

So far we have looked at variation across regions and social groups. As indicated above, the English language has evolved and changed over time. The history of the language is no concern of this grammar. Examples (1) to (4) – all variations on the same sentences from the gospel according to St Luke – will have to suffice as illustrations of the development from Old English up to present-day English.

1 Sōþlicē his yldra sunu wæs on æcere; an hē cōm, and þā hē þām hūse genēalǣhte, hē gehȳrde þæne swēg and þæt wered. þā clypode hē ānne þēow, and āscode hine hwæt þæt wǣre. (Old English, early 11th century)
2 Forsoth his eldere sone was in the feeld, and whanne he cam and neiȝede to the hous, he herde a symfonye and a crowde. And he clepide oon of the seruanuntis, and axide what thingis thes weren. (Middle English, 1384)
3 Now his elder sonne was in the field, and as he came and drew nigh to the house, he heard musicke & dauncing, and he called one of the seruants, and asked what these things meant. (Early Modern English, 1611)
4 Now his older son was in the field, and when he came and approached the house, he heard music and dancing. And he summoned one of the servants and began inquiring what these things could be. (From New American Standard Bible, 1960)

1.9.3 The English in this grammar

The main concern of this book is thus the grammar of present-day Standard English, not social or regional varieties. Where British and American English are known to differ from each other, we state the difference explicitly. We do not, however, deal with other national standards, nor with social or regional varieties.

A note on the language used in this book may also be in order. The main body of the text is written in British English. However, all authentic examples have been reproduced in their original form. Many of these are thus in American English, and some of the British ones may follow slightly different spelling conventions from those we have chosen.

1.10 Special features of this grammar

As stated above, this is a grammar which aims at describing the structure of English words, phrases, and clauses. In addition it takes a look at how clauses combine to form texts. The text (or discourse) perspective is also present in the discussion of smaller units, in that we show how, and to what effect, the different constructions are used in actual texts. These texts can be spoken or written. There is a separate chapter devoted to the grammar of spoken English (16), but differences between speech and writing are commented on in other chapters as well.

The examples are an essential part of this book. Most of the examples are authentic, and thus reflect actual language use. They are an important part of our approach to grammar, not merely as illustrations, but as evidence of the relationship between form, function, and meaning.

Vocabulary is discussed in Chapter 3. Vocabulary does not traditionally have a place in grammar books, but we feel that it is important for any student of a language to have some insight into the linguistic building blocks – words.

Bearing in mind that this is primarily a grammar book for learners of English, we have given it a contrastive dimension. Points of English grammar which are known to be difficult for Norwegians are given special treatment, and examples are sometimes translated in order to show differences between Norwegian and English. There are frequent comparisons of the two languages throughout the book.

1.11 Why study grammar?

The study of the grammar of English as a foreign language should have a double aim. One is to improve your own command of English. Knowledge about the structure of words, phrases, and sentences will be useful in speaking, writing, hearing, or reading English. The second aim is to discover, and learn how to describe, the complex interrelationship between meaning and linguistic form. It is our hope that the study of grammar may heighten your interest in the fascinating structure of language, our most important tool for expressing thoughts and ideas. Linguistic analysis is the process by which we can get acquainted with the bits and pieces of a language and discover how it works. Knowledge about how language is built up may in turn enable us to appreciate shades of meaning created by linguistic variation.

Terms

descriptive grammar
prescriptive grammar
regional variation
register
social variation
Standard English
syntax

Exercises

1 Are the following rules descriptive or prescriptive? Justify your answers. **(1.2)**

a A preposition must not occur at the end of a sentence.
b A verb phrase can contain only one modal auxiliary (*may, can, will,* etc.).
c An uncountable noun (*sand, music, idealism,* etc.) cannot occur with numerals.
d A sentence should not begin with *and* or *but*.

2 Rewrite this text in a style which is more appropriate in writing. Comment on the changes you make. (The example is repeated from **1.7**.)

And erm, I'm supposed to do a show for like her birthday, which is easy cos kids are easy actually, you just exaggerate like this is my opening routine I got this out of a book actually, you come on okay? and go, I'm a bit shy you see, erm, well I'm a bit shy, and tell the truth, I have to admit I'm a bit shy, so, I when I come on I'm gonna say hello, and then you say hello back to me, okay? and then, no one has to be shy, then I go off okay and I come on, and basically they're all gonna shout hello, right, yeah, no, no, that's not right no, I say hello first here I'll show you, go off I come on, I go ... and wait about for a min= half a sec= ha= you know just wait for about ten seconds, I've forgotten what I'm supposed to say wha= can you remind me? and they all shout hello, so I, erm, one more time, I go off I come on, hello, and they say hello, and that's that. It's good innit?

3 Identify non-standard features in this excerpt from Sue Townsend's *The Queen and I*. Explain how these features differ from Standard English. What are the Queen's thoughts about her own accent? (**1.9.1**)

The queue shuffled in until the Queen was sufficiently far forward to be able to see inside the large room where a menacing clock with black hands and a hurrying second hand told her that it was twelve minutes past five. A baby began to cry and was given an unopened packet of crisps to suck.

'S no good givin' him a actual *crisp*, they're salt and vinegar,' said the young mother – number thirty-eight. 'E don't like salt 'n vinegar.'

The Queen nodded, reluctant to open her mouth and advertise her class. Her accent was proving to be rather a bother. Should she try to modify it? And her grammar was a nuisance. Should she throw in a few double negatives? It was terribly difficult to work out where she *belonged* any more – except as a number between thirty-eight and forty.

4 Correct any mistakes in the following sentences. Try to explain what is wrong and why the corrections have to be made.

a Once upon a time it lived a vain emperor.
b He loved to show his clothes off to his peoples.
c Word of the Emperors refined habits spread over his kingdom and beyond.
d Two scoundrels decided taking advantage of the Emperor's vanity.
e They were introducing themselves at the gates of the palace with a scheme in mind.
f After many years of research have we invented a method of weaving a cloth so light and fine that it looks invisibly.
g In fact the cloth are invisible to anyone who is too stupid for to appreciate its quality.
h The Prime Minister ran to the Emperor and disclosed these terrible news.
i Besides to be invisible this cloth will be woven in colours and patterns created special for you.

2 Levels of Description

2.1 Introduction

Language has a fascinating structure. One characteristic feature is that a limited set of smaller units combine into a set of units at a higher level, which in turn combine into still larger units. Language is thus **hierarchical**. The main levels are:

The phoneme level:	/b/ + /e/ + /d/ + /z/
The morpheme level:	{bed} + {plural}
The word level:	beds
The phrase level:	the new beds from IKEA
The clause level:	The new beds from IKEA are made of birch.
The sentence level:	The new beds from IKEA, which we bought before Christmas, are made of birch.
The discourse level:	The new beds from IKEA, which we bought before Christmas, are made of birch. We like them a lot. They have a lovely finish, and besides they remind us of the bed that our grandparents used to sleep in the 20s and 30s.

The object of grammar is to describe the structure of language. Grammarians do this by means of a special language, often referred to as a **metalanguage**, which includes all the specific terms that are needed to make the description precise and consistent. This chapter introduces the various levels and the terms we will use in the book.

2.2 The phoneme level

On the phoneme level English has some 44 distinctive consonant and vowel units. Each of these is made up of a number of features from the limited inventory of **distinctive features** of English sounds; for example, /b/ has the features bilabial, lenis stop. So, below the phoneme level, we could have added a level of distinctive features which combine to yield the phonemes of English. In addition to the segmental features, there are **prosodic features** like stress and intonation which extend over more than one segment.

The phoneme level will not be dealt with in this book, but there will be comments on intonation in Chapters 14 and 16.

2.3 The morpheme level

A morpheme consists of one or more phonemes. It is the minimum unit of meaning. We distinguish between **free morphemes**, which can occur alone with an independent meaning (e.g. *bed*) and **bound morphemes**, which are tacked on to free morphemes, either at the beginning (prefixes) or the end (inflectional and derivational suffixes).

Inflectional suffixes are the grammatical endings that nouns, verbs, adjectives, and adverbs have. The *s* in *beds* is a realization of the plural morpheme. Inflectional endings have no effect on the word class the free morpheme belongs to. Both *bed* and *beds* are nouns. The inflections of the main word classes are dealt with in **4.4.1–4.4.5** and **5.5.1** (nouns), **6.3.1** (verbs), **8.2** (adjectives), and **8.13** (adverbs). Some pronouns also have inflectional endings (**5.8**).

Derivational suffixes often bring about a change in word class membership, e.g. *friend* (noun) – *friendly* (adjective); *sharp* (adjective) – *sharpness* (noun); *clever* (adjective) – *cleverly* (adverb). They may be followed by inflectional suffixes, e.g. in *friendlier*, where the comparative ending is added to *friendly*.

Prefixes are also used to derive new words, though they do not usually bring about a change of word class (e.g. *de-*, *re-*, and *ex-* in *delimit*, *reopen*, and *ex-director*). Prefixes and suffixes may combine in the same word, as shown in the last example (*ex-*, *-or*). An extreme case is *anti-disestablishmentarianism*, with two prefixes (*anti-*, *dis-*) and three suffixes (*-ment*, *-arian*, *-ism*).

Some common derivational patterns of the main word classes are taken up in **4.8.2** (nouns), **6.3.5–6.3.6** (verbs), **8.1** (adjectives), and **8.12** (adverbs).

2.4 The word level

Words consist of one or more morphemes. They are marked by a certain degree of independence. Most obviously, they can stand alone and are written as separate entities. The spelling of **compound words** ('sammensatte ord') is often very tricky, however. A recent dictionary lists *school board* and *school friend* written as two words, but *schoolday* and *schoolboy* as one word, and it hyphenates *school-leaver*. See also the discussion of what is meant by a word in Chapter 3.

2.4.1 Lexical words and function words

We distinguish between **lexical words** such as *bed* and **function words** such as *the*, *or*, and *during*. Lexical words have meanings that we can look up in a dictionary. They code the concepts we have in our minds, for example the thing we sleep on at night, which we arbitrarily code as *bed*. Grammatical words have little meaning, although some, e.g. *during*, have more than others, e.g. *the*. In this they are similar to the bound morphemes we mentioned in **2.3**. The dictionary will describe function words in terms of how they are used, rather than what they mean.

Most people have an intuitive ability to distinguish between lexical words and function words, although the dividing line may sometimes be difficult to draw. These are the main classes:

Lexical words:
- nouns (e.g. *bed, birch, Tom*; see Chapter 4)
- verbs (e.g. *make, take, buy*; see Chapter 6)
- adjectives (e.g. *lovely, old, white*; see Chapter 8)
- adverbs (e.g. *here, tomorrow, quickly*; see Chapter 8)

Function words:
- determiners (e.g. *the, a, some*; see Chapter 5)
- pronouns (e.g. *I, you, somebody*; see Chapter 5)
- auxiliary verbs (e.g. *be, must, could*; see **6.4.2–6.4.4**)
- prepositions (e.g. *at, in, during*)
- co-ordinating conjunctions (e.g. *and, but, or*; see **12.2**)
- subordinating conjunctions (e.g. *that, if, when*; see **12.7.1**)
- existential *there* (see **11.7**)
- dummy *it* (see **11.8–11.10**)
- the negator *not* (see **8.15.3**)
- the infinitive marker *to* (as in *to go, to see*)

Lexical words have the following characteristics:

- They have a meaning that can be looked up in a dictionary. They have inherent sense (see Chapter 3).
- Each lexical class consists of a large number of words.
- Any one lexical word occurs infrequently across a range of discourse types.
- New lexical words can be coined. Lexical words are open classes.
- Lexical words can be long or short. They are often complex (containing prefixes and/or suffixes), and most can take inflectional endings.

Function words have the following characteristics:

- They have little inherent meaning. Dictionaries will explain them in terms of how they function, rather than in terms of what they mean.
- Each class has few members. Existential *there*, dummy *it*, the negator *not*, and the infinitive marker *to* constitute classes of their own.
- Any one function word occurs relatively frequently across a range of discourse types.
- New function words cannot be coined at will. The function words are closed classes.
- Function words are typically short, simple words. Some pronouns, however, take inflectional endings.

We can sum up these distinguishing characteristics by saying that function words belong to the grammar of the language. They are the grammatical glue that binds the lexical words together.

There is an important qualification to make here. In many cases two or more words together constitute one lexical unit, a lexeme (see **3.2.1C**). A combination like *have a chip on one's shoulder* ('have a grievance') is a lexical unit, an idiom. *Be supposed to* is a modal unit, which we classify as an auxiliary equivalent (see **6.4.3B**).

There are two additional classes which do not fit neatly into the classes of lexical words and function words: numerals and interjections. Numerals consist of a limited number of simple forms that can be used to build an indefinite number of more complex forms (see Appendix 3). Syntactically, they generally behave like determiners or nouns. Interjections are words which do not combine with other words to build phrases or clauses, nor do they combine with prefixes or suffixes. Traditionally, interjections were defined as words used to express feelings (e.g. *oh, gosh*), but spoken interaction contains many other forms with similar grammatical characteristics (e.g. *yes, no, OK*). For this reason, we prefer the new term **insert** (see **16.3.2**).

2.4.2 How to distinguish between the lexical word classes

The lexical word classes can be distinguished with reference to a number of criteria, as illustrated below:

	Morphological	Syntactic	Semantic
Nouns	bed – beds	the dirty cup	denote people, things,
	John – John's	I found the cup	substances, and abstract entities
Verbs	ask – asks ask – asked ask – asking	have asked was asking I asked him	denote processes, actions, and states
Adjectives	hard – harder – hardest	awfully hard hard of hearing	denote qualities of people, things, and abstract entities
Adverbs	soon – sooner – soonest carefully	very soon drives carefully	denote time, place, manner, degree, etc.

By morphological criteria we mean the typical endings that the lexical word classes take. Syntactic criteria include both the way the words are used to build phrases (phrase syntax) and the typical functions at the clause level (clause syntax). For example, nouns are inflected for number and case, can be the head of a noun phrase, and can function as subject, direct object, etc. in the clause.

Semantic criteria define the types of meanings that are characteristic of the classes, in terms of the entities, processes, or qualities that make up our experience of the world. When we list these features, we focus on the **prototypical** members of the classes, i.e. the most typical members.

Practically all grammatical categories have fuzzy edges, so there may well be members of a word class which do not have all the features in our list. The crucial thing is how the word is used. No occurrence of a word can belong to more than one word class at a time.

2.4.3 Membership in more than one class

It is characteristic of English that the same form can often belong to more than one class and is then used in different contexts. For example, *no* can be both a determiner and an insert; *to,* both a preposition and an infinitive marker. More extreme examples are:

a *round* table (adjective)	a cup of sugar and a *like* amount of flour (adjective)

a *round* of golf (noun)	I've never seen the *like* (noun)
to *round* the corner (verb)	I *like* it (verb)
to dance *round* a tree (preposition)	he died *like* a hero (preposition)
to turn *round* (adverb)	do *like* I say (conjunction, non-standard)

English words can jump word class boundaries easily. The following example is based on a humorous parody of the language allegedly used by former US Secretary of State Alexander Haig. On the discourse level, as a parody, it may well be quite effective, but the result is a piece of non-standard language, although it conforms to some rules of English word formation. Note, for example, in the last part of the sentence that *noun* is used as a verb, *verb* is used as a verb, and *adverb* is made into the verb *adverbize*.

> Alexander Haig, in Congressional hearings before his confirmatory, paradoxed his auditioners by abnormalling his responds so that verbs were nouned, nouns verbed, and adjectives adverbized.

2.5 The phrase level: introduction

A phrase consists of one or more words. Corresponding to each of the lexical word classes there is a phrase type, with the lexical word as **head** (the head is italicized in the examples below):

noun phrase:	the new *bed* from IKEA
verb phrase:	will have *gone*
adjective phrase:	very *good* indeed
adverb phrase:	as *soon* as possible

The phrases are built up according to the rules of English phrase syntax. A noun like *bed* expands into a noun phrase like *the new bed from IKEA*, but not into **the bed new from IKEA* or **the from IKEA new bed*. The head is the only obligatory element. Verb phrases differ from the other types in that the head (the main verb) is always at the end.

Multi-word phrases can be recognized by substitution and movement tests:

1 *The new beds from IKEA* are made of birch.
2 *They* are made of birch.
3 We bought *the new beds from IKEA* yesterday.
4 *The new beds from IKEA* were bought yesterday.

The entire noun phrase in (1) is replaced by a pronoun in (2). In (3) and (4) we see that the same phrase is moved as a unit.

Prepositional phrases differ from the types above in that they consist of two obligatory elements: a preposition and a complement (usually in the form of a noun phrase). In (5) below neither the preposition *at* nor the noun phrase *the local rate* can stand for the whole phrase:

5 Such calls are charged *at the local rate.*

2.5.1 Modification and complementation

Noun phrases, adjective phrases, and adverb phrases may contain **premodifiers** and **postmodifiers** (see the examples in **2.6**). There is a relationship of modification between these and the head. The notion of modification is usually not applied to verb phrases, however.

The term **complementation** is used about expressions of various types which complement the meaning of a preceding adjective or verb. Modifiers are optional; complements ('utfyllinger') frequently are not. We can leave out *new* and *from IKEA* in (1) and *awfully* in (2), but not *of horses* in (3) or *to wait a while* in (4):

1 We've got *the new beds from IKEA.* (noun phrase with pre- and postmodifier)
2 I'm *awfully tired.* (adjective with premodifier)
3 He's *fond of horses.* (adjective phrase with prepositional complement)
4 She *prefers to wait a while.* (verb phrase with infinitive complement)

Note that in our syntactic analysis we do not analyse complements of verbs as parts of verb phrases. They are rather analysed in terms of clause elements (usually as objects, as in example 4 above).

2.5.2 Expansion by co-ordination

Elements of phrases can be expanded by co-ordination:

1 this shock and despair (co-ordinated heads in noun phrase)
2 red and blue flowers (co-ordinated premodifiers in noun phrase)
3 to and from the station (co-ordinated prepositions)
4 from Oslo and Bergen (co-ordinated complements in prepositional phrase)

As phrases can be built up through a combination of modification, complementation, and co-ordination, we may get long and complex phrases: *a thick thumb and an index finger brown from tobacco* (noun phrase), *happy and willing to run errands* (adjective phrase).

2.6 The structure of the phrase types

2.6.1 The structure of noun phrases

Noun phrases (often referred to by the abbreviation NP) range from simple one-word phrases to very complex ones, which we typically find in written English. The overall structure is:

determiner + premodifier + head + postmodifier

The head may also be accompanied by a phrase in **apposition (4.10)**. Table 2a gives some examples of different types of noun phrases. Noun phrases are dealt with in detail in Chapter 4.

Table 2a: Examples of full noun phrases

Determiner	Premodifier	Head	Postmodifier
		water	
a		student	
some	new	books	
many	new	books	from Collins
its	rapid	discoveries	of oil
	foreign	companies	established in China
the		shock and despair	which he felt
several	quite distinct	approaches	involving the use of x
all my	persuasive	power	
no other	satisfactory	way	to stop this

2.6.2 The structure of pronoun-headed noun phrases

Pronouns replace full noun phrases. Compare:

1 *The already strict rules on conflict of interest* are being tightened.
2 *They* are being tightened.

As pronouns are used in the same positions as phrases headed by nouns, we include both among the category of noun phrases. If there is a need to distinguish the two, we speak about noun-headed noun phrases vs. pronoun-headed noun phrases.

Pronouns normally function alone as noun phrases, but indefinite and interrogative pronouns in particular can take modifiers. See the examples in Table 2b. Pronouns are dealt with in detail in Chapter 5.

Table 2b: Examples of pronoun-headed noun phrases

Head	**Postmodifier**
anybody	
anybody	with normal intelligence
anybody	else
anything	costing more than 100 dollars
everybody	over twelve
nothing	important
nothing	to worry about
somebody	else with friends in high places
something	mentioned in the paper
who	in this picture

2.6.3 The structure of verb phrases

Verb phrases differ from noun phrases, adjective phrases, and adverb phrases in that they contain verb forms only (apart from the infinitive marker *to*), whereas the other phrase types combine words from quite different classes. The head of a verb phrase, which is usually referred to as the **main verb**, is a lexical verb. This may be preceded by **grammatical auxiliaries** (*be, have, do*), **modal auxiliaries** (*can, may, must*, etc.), **auxiliary equivalents** (*be able to, be allowed to*, etc.), and a group which we have chosen to call **catenatives** (*get, keep*, etc.). The last are lexical verbs which have a function that is close to that of auxiliaries (**6.4.4**). Table 2c gives examples of verb phrases of different types. Verb phrases are dealt with in detail in Chapter 6.

Notice that verb phrases as defined in our book consist of a main verb, potentially preceded by one or more of the elements mentioned above. Other grammars often use the term verb phrase (VP) for the clause element verb plus complements. For example, a sequence such as *has taken many prisoners* is often referred to as a VP, whereas we analyse it as a sequence of verb phrase and noun phrase on the phrase level, and as verb plus direct object on the clause level. See further **2.7**.

Table 2c: Examples of finite verb phrases

Modal auxiliary	Grammatical auxiliary	Auxiliary equivalent	Catena-tive	Main verb
				flies
	are			added
	do			feel
	have			gone
will				follow
must	be			going
may	have			gone
	have			heard and seen
will		be able to		leave
	has	been allowed to		drive
			kept	reminding
will			get	going
	do		happen to	prefer

2.6.4 Finite and non-finite verb phrases

Finite verb phrases are distinguished by having a **finite verb** as their first (or only) word, i.e. a verb which varies for tense and person. Accordingly, the present and past tense form of verbs are finite. In addition, modal auxiliaries and imperative verb forms are always finite:

writes	has written
am writing	has been writing
may write	may have been writing
write!	etc.

Verbs have three non-finite forms: the **infinitive** (e.g. *to write*), the *-ing* **participle** (e.g. *writing*), and the **past participle** (e.g. *written*). A non-finite verb phrase contains non-finite forms only:

to write	to have written
writing	to have been writing
written	having been writing
to be writing	having been written
to be written	etc.

The distinction between finite and non-finite verb phrases is of special importance in connection with subordinate clauses (**2.9**). As regards finite and non-finite verbs, see also **6.4.1**.

2.6.5 The structure of adjective phrases

The head of an adjective phrase is an adjective or a participle form of a verb. This can be accompanied by premodifiers (as in *very good*) and, more rarely, by postmodifiers (as in *good enough*) or split modifiers (as in *more difficult than I thought*). Modifiers are typically adverbs and denote degree or some combination of degree and attitude (as in *sweetly oblivious*). When the head is a participle form, the premodifier frequently specifies the manner of the action denoted by the verb (as in *carefully built, quickly rising*).

The adjective head may be followed by complements (**2.5.1**), in the form of prepositional phrases or clauses. Table 2d gives examples of adjective phrases of different types. Adjective phrases are dealt with in more detail in **8.3**.

Table 2d: Examples of adjective phrases

Premodifier	Head	Complement
	thin	
	friendly and open	
very	odd	
extremely	charming	
	fond	of horses
	hard	to convince
rather	slow	to realize
quite	certain	that he's wrong
very	busy	marking papers

2.6.6 The structure of adverb phrases

The structure of adverb phrases is normally quite straightforward. The head is an adverb, which may be premodified for degree, postmodified, or surrounded by a split modifier. Table 2e illustrates the most common types.

Table 2e: Examples of adverb phrases

Premodifier	Head	Postmodifier
	fast	
	however	
extremely	fast	
	amazingly	enough
so	fast	that he fell
too	slowly	to attract any interest
more	convincingly	than his wife

2.6.7 The structure of prepositional phrases

A prepositional phrase consists of a preposition and a complement, usually in the form of a noun phrase (1). In (2) the preposition is followed by an *-ing* clause. Note that English does not allow a preposition to be followed by an infinitive or a *that*-clause (**12.8.1** and **13.4.1**).

1 I met him *in Paris*.
2 She became a different person *after turning her hand to politics*.

In interrogative sentences and indirect questions, the preposition and its complement may be separated (3, 4). A formal variant of (3) is to move the entire prepositional phrase to front position (5). In relative clauses we have the same choice between a version with a stranded preposition (6) and a formal variant (7).

3 *Who* did you get it *from*?
4 I don't know *where* he comes *from*.
5 *From whom* did you get it? (formal)
6 The girl (*who/whom*) she gave the money *to* had disappeared.
7 The girl *to whom* he gave the money had disappeared. (formal)

As regards stranded prepositions, see further **11.3.1**.

2.7 The clause level

When we move on from the phrase to the clause level, we move from the level which codes our mental concepts to the level which codes information into messages which may be true or false. It does not make sense to ask whether *the new bed from IKEA* is true, but it does make sense to ask whether it is true that *the new beds from IKEA are made of birch*.

Clauses are made up of combinations of phrases following the rules of English clause syntax. In the following example we have our noun phrase (*the new beds from IKEA*), a verb phrase (*are made*), and a prepositional phrase (*of birch*), in that order. However, on the clause level another grammatical dimension becomes all-important, namely, the analysis into **clause elements**:

|-------------S---------------| |----V----| |---A----|
The new beds from IKEA are made of birch.

The main clause elements are:

• Subject (S):	*I*'ll pay you the money tomorrow.
• Verb (V):	I'*ll pay* you the money tomorrow
• Direct object (dO)	I'll pay you *the money* tomorrow.
• Indirect object (iO)	I'll pay *you* the money tomorrow.
• Subject predicative (sP)	The door was *open*.
• Object predicative (oP)	She left the door *open*.
• Adverbial (A)	I'll pay you the money *tomorrow*.

Each clause element, except the verb, can be **realized** by more than one phrase type. The most common relationships between clause elements and phrase types are summarized in **2.8.6**. In addition, most clause elements can also be realized by subordinate clauses. The clause elements and their combinations are dealt with in detail in Chapter 9.

2.8 The syntactic functions of phrases

Phrases function as clause elements or are used to build up other phrases. The functions most typical of the phrases with a lexical word as the head are usually referred to as:

noun phrase	nominal function
verb phrase	verbal function
adjective phrase	adjectival function
adverb phrase	adverbial function

The main functions of each phrase type will be listed below.

2.8.1 The syntactic functions of noun phrases

The most typical nominal functions are: subject, direct and indirect object, subject and object predicative on the clause level, and complement of preposition on the phrase level.

A Clause level

Subject:	*Many of the new and interesting books from Collins* are over-priced.
Direct object:	We bought *an elegant, old, Swiss oak table.*
Indirect object:	I gave *those students* a piece of my mind.
Subject predicative:	It is *water.*
Object predicative:	We considered them *reliable systems for separating X from Y.*
Adverbial:	I'll meet him *the day after tomorrow.*

B Phrase level

Complement of preposition:	I refuse to be impressed by *such clearly overused words and phrases from the language of advertising.*
Premodifier in noun phrase:	The *Patriotic Front land nationalization* proposals were not accepted.
Apposition:	John Henry, *the Mayor of York*, has been included in the Queen's list.

As regards the **embedding** of noun phrases within other phrases, see further **4.11**.

2.8.2 The syntactic functions of verb phrases

A Clause level

Whereas the noun phrase has a number of functions at the clause level, a finite verb phrase always has the same function. We will use the term **verb** for this clause element. There is no need to introduce a new term, as there is a one-to-one correspondence between the phrase type verb phrase and its syntactic function on the clause level. The syntactic analyses below make this clear.

```
  |---------S---------| |----V----| |-----------A------------|
1 Some new books are added at the end of the year.

  S  |-------V------| |-------------dO-----------------|
2 We tend to forget the shock and despair he felt.
```

S |---------V---------| |----------------------dO-----------------------|

3 Joan happens to prefer such clearly overused words and phrases.

It is important that students are aware of whether reference is made to phrase syntax or clause syntax.

As regards the syntactic function of non-finite verb phrases, see further **6.4.1** and Chapter 13.

B Verb forms on the phrase level

The participle forms of verbs (**2.6.4**) may have non-verbal functions, e.g. as premodifiers in noun phrases (4, 5). In our grammar we treat such participles as a group of adjectives (**6.3.1**, **8.4.3**).

4 The most *moving* passage mourns the extinction of folk music.
5 The *proposed* co-operation should start immediately.

Many forms in *-ing* and *-ed* have become regular adjectives and nouns, and they are treated as such in dictionaries and grammars. Compare:

6a The old *building* will be demolished.
6b *Building* a new house will take a year.

7a She was very *surprised* to hear the news.
7b She was *surprised* by the detective stopping at her door.

Example (6a) contains the regular noun *building*, which can be pluralized and can take the same determiners and modifiers as other nouns. In (7a) *surprised* is an adjective; it is used as a subject predicative and is preceded by the adverb *very*, which can only modify adjectives. In the other examples, the verb phrases are used in their regular function at the clause level. *Building* is the verb in a non-finite clause in (6b); in (7b) the verb is realized by the complex verb phrase *was surprised*. As regards the borderline between adjective and verb, see also **8.10.2**.

2.8.3 The syntactic functions of adjective phrases

The most typical adjectival functions are: subject and object predicative on the clause level, and pre- and postmodifier in noun phrase on the phrase level.

A Clause level

Subject predicative:	She is *extremely charming*.
Object predicative:	We found him *friendly and open*.

B Phrase level

Premodifier in noun phrase:	It was a *very odd* reaction.
Postmodifier in noun phrase:	People *interested in things Indian* should buy the book.
Split modifier:	He is a *hard* person *to convince*.
Head of noun phrase:	I accept the reward in the name of the *homeless and the poor*.
	The *proud and defiant* remained.

The syntactic functions of adjective phrases are dealt with in detail in **8.6**. Note especially that adjectives can function as the head of a noun phrase and can then be used in typically nominal functions (**8.9**).

2.8.4 The syntactic functions of adverb phrases

The most typical adverbial functions are: adverbial on the clause level, and modifier in an adjective or adverb phrase on the phrase level.

A Clause level

Adverbial:	She was treated *fairly*.
	Amazingly enough, nobody had heard of him.
	However, there is no reason to panic.

B Phrase level

Modifier in adjective phrase:	He is *very* old.
Modifier in adverb phrase:	They work *irritatingly* slowly.
Modifier in noun phrase:	The table *below* shows the possible combinations.
	All the *upstairs* rooms are clean, Madam.

The syntactic functions of adverb phrases are dealt with in detail in **8.15** and Chapter 10.

2.8.5 The syntactic functions of prepositional phrases

The main functions are: adverbial on the clause level and postmodifier in noun phrase.

A Clause level

Adverbial:	It was written *by Frank Smith.*
	We met our man *in Seattle.*
	In short, nobody has any reason to complain.
Subject:	*From Oslo to Moss* is no more than 60 km.
	After sunset is a good time to record city lights.

B Phrase level

Postmodifier in noun phrase:	This is the topic *of the next chapter.*
	We met our man *in Seattle.*
Premodifier in noun phrase:	*Under-the-counter* sales were not uncommon.
Complement in adjective phrase:	He is guilty *of a serious crime.*
	I wasn't quite sure *of his opinion.*

If a prepositional phrase occurs in a postverbal position, say, after a direct object, there is potentially a structural problem. We see this in our second example above. If the sentence answers a *where*-question, then *in Seattle* functions as an adverbial. If, however, the sentence answers a questions about *who* we met, then *in Seattle* is a postmodifier in the noun phrase *our man in Seattle*. As regards the problems of distinguishing between postmodifier and adverbial, see further **9.9**.

2.8.6 The functions of phrases on the clause level: summary

The main functions of the phrase types on the clause level are summarized in Figure 2a. No distinction is made between direct and indirect objects, nor between subject and object predicatives.

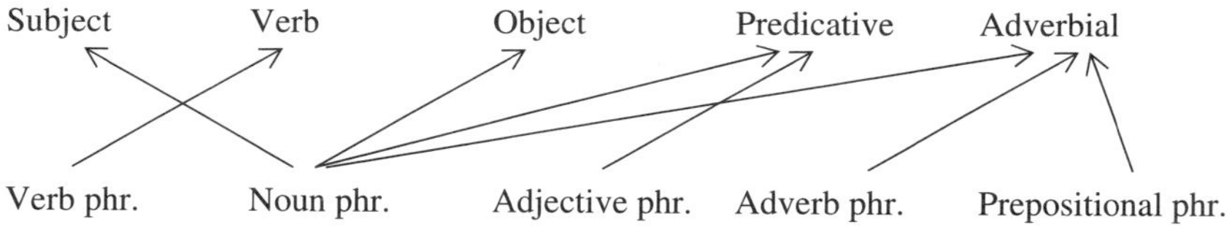

Figure 2a: Phrase type and syntactic functions on the clause level

2.9 The sentence level

A single clause which occurs on its own is called a **simple sentence**. Two or more clauses may combine in two main ways. Example (1) shows co-ordination of clauses into a **compound sentence**. If one clause is subordinated to another, we talk about a **complex sentence** (2). Here, *which we bought before Christmas* is a **subordinate clause**. Its subordinate status is shown by the fact that it cannot stand alone. A **main clause**, on the other hand, is independent. Example (1) consists of two main clauses. All of (2) is a main clause. See further **12.2.**

1 The new beds from IKEA are made of birch, but the table is made of pine.
2 The new beds from IKEA, which we bought before Christmas, are made of birch.

Subordinate clauses function as clause elements in the superordinate clause or as parts of phrases. In (2) the relative clause is a postmodifier of the noun phrase with the head *beds*.

Subordinate clauses can be **finite** (2) or **non-finite** (3), containing finite and non-finite verbs phrases (**2.6.4**), respectively. Note that the non-finite clause *made of birch* can easily be expanded to a finite clause *which are made of birch*.

3 Beds made of birch are beautiful.

It is important to realize that the subordination of clauses allows us to draw conclusions about the discourse relation between the statements in the various clauses. For example, in (4) the initial non-finite clause allows us to draw the conclusion that it was because they were familiar with birch furniture from IKEA that they bought the bed there. We see here that the logical relations between the statements in simple clauses are expressed through grammatical means, namely, subordination.

4 Having taken a fancy to birch furniture from IKEA, we bought our new beds there.

The structure of clause combinations is dealt with in detail in Chapters 12 and 13.

2.10 Application: analysis on the word, phrase, clause, and sentence levels

In Figure 2b below we analyse the structure of a complex sentence by means of a **tree diagram**, followed by an analysis on the word class level. Figure 2c analyses a complex noun phrase in a corresponding manner. The clause elements are abbreviated as shown in **2.7**. The realization of the clause elements and most of the phrase elements is specified after a colon. Lower-case *p* is an abbreviation for a phrase, *Mv* stands for main verb, and the abbreviation *c* represents the connector that links phrases and clauses (as regards clause connectors, see **9.8.6**). The other abbreviations should be self-explanatory.

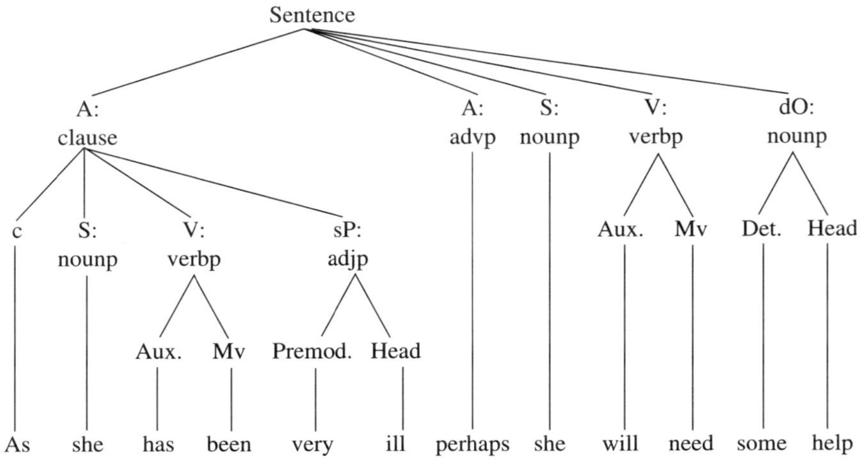

Figure 2b: Tree diagram: sentence structure

Analysis in terms of word class:

		lexical word	function word
As	subordinating conjunction		x
she	personal pronoun		x
has	grammatical auxiliary		x
been	*be* used as a lexical verb	x	
very	adverb	x	
ill	adjective	x	
perhaps	adverb	x	
she	personal pronoun		x
will	modal auxiliary		x
need	lexical verb	x	
some	quantifying determiner		x
help	noun	x	

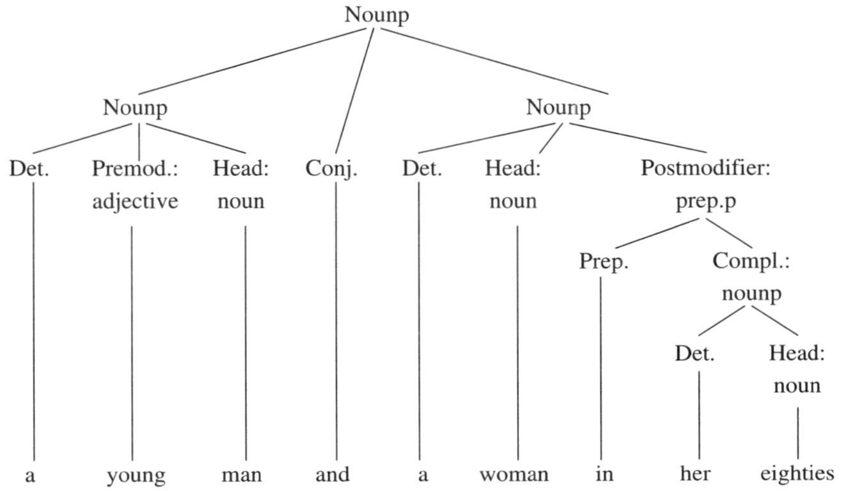

Figure 2c: Tree diagram: phrase structure

Analysis in terms of word class:

		lexical word	function word
a	indefinite article		x
young	adjective	x	
man	noun	x	
and	co-ordinating conjunction		x
a	indefinite article		x
woman	noun	x	
in	preposition		x
her	possessive determiner		x
eighties	noun	x	

2.11 The discourse level

Discourse is a common term used about any piece of language – long or short, spoken or written – which is produced by a speaker/writer on a certain occasion with a communicative purpose and addressed to some hearer/reader. When we adopt this perspective on language, we become concerned with how real people use language in real life. The ability to adapt one's language to the needs of a multitude of different situations is often referred to as **communica-**

tive competence or **discourse competence**. This ability is clearly different from **linguistic competence** in a narrow sense, which can be defined as the ability to put together bits and pieces of language according to the formal rules of grammar.

Both answers to (1) below are correct as far as the formal rules of English grammar are concerned, but only (2b) orders the elements in such a way that the answer feels natural.

1 Where did you buy that jacket?
2a In a shop in Stonegate I bought it.
2b (I bought it) in a shop in Stonegate.

When we think of language in terms of purposeful human behaviour, a whole set of new questions arise. We may ask: why did somebody say X, why did he or she put it in one way rather than in some other way, who was X intended for, how was X understood by the receiver, does X conform to the stylistic conventions of this type of discourse, etc.? Providing answers to such questions is normally far more difficult than, for example, describing the structure of an English clause. We need to have access to all the variables in the speech situations, and even then we cannot really be sure what motives the speaker/hearer has.

Here are a few more examples of language at the discourse level. The first is an example of the many silly jokes based on the difference between form and discourse function. Speaker B interprets A's question literally to mean: 'Can you say this sequence of words?'

3 A: Can you say if this is enough?
B: If this is enough.
A: ???

If a friend comes into your house and utters (4), the normal response would not be to say *Really?* or *Are you?*, but to choose one of the alternatives in (5). After all, the most likely reason why your friend says (4) is that he/she wants to make a request for a drink.

4 I'm dying for something to drink.
5 Can I offer you a beer from the fridge?
Do you want something hot or cold?
Help yourself to some tea/coffee.

In the next example there are three versions of a piece of discourse taken from the preface of a book. We feel that (6a) introduces an unmotivated switch from the active to the passive, whereas the alternatives in (6b) and (6c) are better. This is a matter of the better or more appropriate grammatical choice on the discourse level. We are talking about stylistic effect. The elliptical active versions in (6b) and (6c) read better, and may furthermore be less dismissive.

6a I have taken advantage of some of the comments I have been offered, whereas they have been disregarded in other cases. The responsibility for the present text is therefore mine.
6b I have taken advantage of some of the comments I have been offered, but disregarded others. The responsibility for the present text is therefore mine.
6c I have taken advantage of some of the comments I have been offered, but not all. The responsibility for the present text is therefore mine.

If a friend of yours utters (7), your response in (8) may be intended not only as neutral information, but as advice or a suggestion, and may be perceived as such.

7 We're thinking of buying new beds.
8 You know, the new beds which we bought from IKEA before Christmas are made of a lovely birch.

When we focus on such things as the purpose, meaning, and effect of a piece of discourse, no matter whether it is a lexical or a grammatical choice, grammarians use terms like the **discourse function**, **pragmatic function**, or **communicative function** of the expression in question. In this book we use the term *communicative function* in talking about the communicative purposes of sentences, and *discourse function* in referring more generally to the function and effect of forms in context.

Matters of discourse organization are taken up particularly in Chapters 15 and 16, but are also dealt with in other places throughout the book, e.g. lexical choices in Chapter 3, noun phrases in discourse in **4.12** and **5.14–5.16**, adverbials in **10.10**, word order and related choices in Chapter 11, clause combinations in **12.11** and **13.12**, and sentence form and communicative function in Chapter 14.

Terms

levels:	morpheme	lexical words:	nouns
	word		lexical verbs
	phrase		adjectives
	clause		adverbs
	sentence		
	discourse		

function words:	determiners pronouns auxiliary verbs prepositions co-ordinating conjunctions subordinating conjunctions existential *there* dummy *it* the negator *not* the infinitive marker *to*
other word classes:	numerals inserts
relations:	modification complementation co-ordination subordination
clauses:	subordinate main clause finite non-finite
sentences:	simple compound complex

metalanguage
prototypical member
discourse function
pragmatic function
communicative function

phrase types:	noun phrases verb phrases adjective phrases adverb phrases prepositional phrases
phrase functions:	nominal verbal adjectival adverbial
structure of noun phrases:	determiner premodifier head postmodifier
structure of verb phrases:	auxiliary main verb finite non-finite
structure of adjective phrases:	premodifier head postmodifier split modifier complement
structure of adverb phrases:	premodifier head postmodifier split modifier
structure of prepositional phrases:	preposition complement
clause elements:	subject verb direct object indirect object subject predicative object predicative adverbial

Exercises

1 Place the words in the following sentences in their appropriate word classes. Lexical words as well as function words should be classified. (**2.4**)

a It was a relief when the record ended and the young man took his hand from her wrist.
b Some conflicts are long-standing and won't be easily papered over.
c Vietnam has just authorized cheque-writing – a new concept in a country where cash is king.
d A 20-minute drive lands you in a still-rural landscape.
e But mostly, the CIA stonewalls.
f His constant 'don't know' irritated me immensely.

2 Go back to the material in question 1 and identify one prototypical member of each lexical word class. Give your reasons why you think they are prototypical. (**2.4**)

3 What word class does the italicized item belong to? Give subclass membership of both lexical words and function words. (**2.4**)

a 1 We could turn that vacant *lot* into a playground.
2 Andrea always had a *lot* of money.
b 1 *Some* couldn't even spell their names.
2 There was *some* confusion as to what had happened.
c 1 *Can* you help with these dishes?
2 All I've got is a couple of *cans* of soup.
3 We need to *can* the meat immediately.
d 1 I have lived *there* for more than a year.
2 *There* was some confusion about what had happened.
e 1 *What* did you buy for your brother?
2 I didn't know *what* book he was talking about.
f 1 We gave *each* a small prize.
2 She kept a record for *each* child.
g 1 *No* country can insulate itself from the affairs of others in our ever-smaller world.
2 '*No*', he said, 'I can't allow you to refer to me.'
h 1 *His* is nothing but a copy of what he handed in last time.
2 He kept *his* hands in his pockets and looked as if he couldn't care less.

4 Identify noun phrases, verb phrases, adjective phrases, and adverb phrases in the sentences below. (**2.5**)

a In America, such prophecies are frightening indeed.
b Everything in our background has prepared us.
c These politicians have been seeing each other quite regularly.
d Carefully, very carefully, the patient was lifted on to the bed.

5 Identify the noun phrases in the sentences below. Remember that a noun phrase may occur inside another noun phrase. (**2.6.1**)

a Boris is turning out to be a rather nice chap, by the way.
b It is the easiest thing in the world to make a will.
c This general election landslide is the biggest victory in Britain this century.
d The man refuses to condemn Labour campaign workers who have been telling elderly people that the Tories might take their money.
e Roger had mussels and some infinitely messed-about steak.
f She has got the best deal possible from a Congress that might otherwise have appointed a city manager.

6 Give the internal structure of the following noun phrases. Disregard noun phrases embedded inside the main noun phrases. (**2.6.1**) In the case of pronoun-headed noun phrases, you should identify what type of pronoun heads the phrase. (**2.6.2**)

a any attack on his family
b huge areas of urban sprawl
c the analogy troubling many loyal Tory voters
d a constantly growing fear that their majority will shrink
e a right-wing populist, Carl I. Hagen, whose Progress Party won 7 per cent of the vote and 10 of the parliament's 165 seats in 1993
f somebody in authority
g we, who have grown up in a world of free trade

7 Analyse the structure of the italicized noun phrases in terms of determiners, premodifiers, and heads. How can such analyses explain the difference in meaning between the two members of each pair?

a 1 Mary had *a little grilled lamb.*
2 Mary had *a little white lamb.*
b 1 We had *many good students* this year.
2 We had *a good many students* this year.
c 1 There are *an awful lot of Swedes* in London.
2 There is *an awful group of Swedes* in London.

8 Identify the finite verb phrases in the examples below and give their internal structure. That means finding the main verb, any modal or grammatical auxiliaries, any auxiliary equivalents, and catenatives. (**2.6.3**)

a Nothing's like a good lie-down after dinner.
b The latest example of this kind has come from the cricket field.
c What can be done to avoid a repeat of past embarrassments?
d Two factors are combining to produce this increase.
e She must have been having a lot of trouble with her car.
f We were supposed to leave before the rest of the family.
g The brothers claim to feel '100 per cent British'.
h Don't you be clever with me!
i I should be able to finish it by next Friday.

9 Identify finite and non-finite verb forms in the italicized verb phrases below. Give the correct name of any non-finite forms. (**2.6.4**)

a This is a lucid discussion of how public discourse *has been degraded*.
b The Archbishop *was* merely *repeating* the Church's position on remarriage.
c Their equipment can *be replaced* by more efficient technology.
d *Should* you *feel* like a cup of tea, just help yourself.
e The Church *did* in fact *face* a deep crisis.
f I*'ll take* her away and marry her, or else I*'ll stop seeing* her. Either way I *shan't be going on* like this.

10 Identify the adjective phrases in the following sentences and give their internal structure. (**2.6.5**)

a Did you find anything interesting?
b He's totally convinced that he is right.
c A horrible, modern, sixteen-foot-long, flower-pot-pink structure that everybody wants down.
d It was based on a cleverly crafted piece of writing.
e Washington's political theatre is suddenly vivid, loud, and local.
f It's terribly over-priced.
g She's got as blameless a reputation as any politician in the city.
h She is too polite to add that the cause of the problem is the mayor himself.
i He is likely to be accused of fraud.
j Those lines of demarcation, once generous-looking, feel throttling now.

11 Identify the adverb phrases in the following examples and give their internal structure. (**2.6.6**)

a I know it all too well.
b Such initiatives are badly needed in this area.
c It's only the tip of the iceberg, but it glistens alarmingly.
d Because of this impediment, he spoke so indistinctly that most people had great problems understanding him.
e Oddly enough, when asked about his row with Mr B, he praised him for treating him so fairly.
f The instinct for suppression went much too far.

12 Identify the prepositional phrases in the sentences below and explain what type of structure realizes the complement, whether a noun-headed phrase, a pronoun-headed phrase, or a clause. (**2.6.7**)

a Today, in reality, about half of the members come from abroad.
b Since last Friday, nobody has been allowed into the house.
c Mr C had invited a wealthy business executive from whose coffers he had received considerable sums of money.
d These were the same woods that he used to play in when he was a boy of 10.
e It is expected of everybody that they stick to the rules of the game.
f In April President Clinton followed that up by issuing a special executive order.

13 Analyse the following sentences in terms of clause elements and then explain what type of phrase realizes the various clause elements. That means stating what type of phrase constitutes the subject, what type of phrase constitutes possible subject predicatives, adverbials, direct objects, etc. (**2.7–2.8**)

a John made his remark with an impassive face.
b Nobody else had made remarks like those.
c What nationality is your friend?
d At the end of the day, nothing is going to change much.
e It is a modest attempt to bring peace to the region.
f But Mr N has made Palestinian aspirations unrealizable.
g After the meeting, he introduced himself to the audience in his inimitable, almost arrogant style.
h John handed me his notes from the lecture.
i Where on earth did you come across this rare book?

14 What phrase type has been italicized in the pairs below? Describe its syntactic function at phrase or clause level in each sentence. (**2.8**)

a 1 He saw the man *with the stick.*
2 He hit the man *with the stick.*
b 1 Everybody agreed that he had been treated *fairly.*
2 It was *fairly* obvious that he was going to lose.
c 1 *From my house to the station* is not more than a mile.
2 I can walk the distance *from my house to the station* in less than 15 minutes.
d 1 There is no doubt that he is *highly qualified.*
2 Some *highly qualified* applicants were short-listed for interviews.
e 1 *One piece of evidence* seemed crucial.
2 I couldn't think of *one piece of evidence* in support of this view.
f 1 *The next day* was a Sunday and all the shops were closed.
2 We set off for Bangkok *the next day.*
g 1 *However* we cut the costs, some people will be disappointed.
2 *However*, we cut the costs and still managed to run a very efficient operation.
h 1 This *satisfied* even his strongest critics.
2 *Satisfied*, he got up from the chair and left the room.
i 1 We the unwilling have done the *impossible* for the *ungrateful.*
2 It is, understandably, *impossible* for them to help such *ungrateful* people.

15 What clause type has been italicized in the pairs below? Describe its syntactic function at phrase or clause level in each sentence. (**2.6.4**)

a 1 *That he will disagree* is pretty obvious.
2 I'm positive *that he will disagree.*
b 1 By *leaving the door open*, he hoped to be able to overhear their conversation.
2 I very much regret *leaving the door open.*
c 1 Beds *made of solid birch* are sturdier than those made of pine.
2 *Made of solid birch*, these beds will probably last the rest of our lives.
d 1 I hope *to pass the grammar exam.*
2 *To pass the grammar exam*, you have to practise analysing sentences.

3 Words and Their Meaning

3.1 Introduction

Traditionally, a distinction has been made between grammar and vocabulary. The grammar of English can be described in terms of a limited set of rules, while its vocabulary is huge and open-ended. The best source of information on the words of English is a standard, comprehensive, reliable, and up-to-date monolingual dictionary (see **3.9**). Why then talk about words in this book? There are many reasons why the study of words is important. Here are some:

A The words we use normally carry most of the meaning of our messages. Not only that, often they carry more or less insidious connotations as well as their literal meanings. Consider the word *housewife* in the innocent-looking *She's a housewife*. A speaker who says this may intend to make a judgement rather than give a neutral description. There is a famous book by Dwight Bolinger called *Language – The Loaded Weapon*, most of which is devoted to the power of words. An awareness of this powerful weapon is essential.

B The meaning of many common words is in a sense slippery, because it varies with the particular **co-text** (= linguistic context) and **context** (= extra-linguistic context) in which it occurs. Learners need to be aware of such variation.

1 The people on the *course* are really nice.
2 We traced the *course* of the Ganges on our map.
3 The first *course* was soup with delicious crusty rolls.
4 Of *course*, nobody knows for sure.

C In countries where English is a foreign language, the learners' English will always benefit if they use a rich, varied, precise, and stylistically appropriate vocabulary. Obviously, this applies equally to a native speaker's English.

The main reason why a chapter on words is included in our grammar book is that there is an obvious interrelationship between words and grammar (**3.4.4B**). This is becoming increasingly recognized in both the theory and practice of English language studies. For example, once you select the verb *enjoy*, its clausal object must appear in the form of an *-ing* participle clause: *I enjoyed reading his memoirs*. The noun *information* is uncountable, which means that it cannot pattern with any grammatical elements which imply countability, e.g. **an information, *these informations*. In other words, there is no clear cut-off point between grammar and vocabulary.

3.2 What is a word?

If we ask an apparently simple question like 'How many words does the sentence below contain?', we realize that the answer depends on what we mean by *word*.

> This can't be swept under the carpet because we don't have a carpet to sweep it under.

If your answer is 17, you have probably relied on orthography and counted words separated by spaces. That is what we call an **orthographic definition** of *word*. There are no hyphenated words here, but two or more words combined by hyphen(s) count as one orthographic word. Obviously, spelling applies only to the written language. A count of orthographic words in spoken English is both impossible and irrelevant.

If your answer is 15, you may have disregarded the second instance of *carpet* and *under*. Clearly, the word *carpet* occurs twice, and so does *under*. We can say we have one word **type**, *carpet*, with two word **tokens** and one word type, *under*, with two word tokens. This argument implicitly depends on the assumption that both tokens have the same meaning, which we shall see later is not at all obvious.

Informal written English allows a number of auxiliaries and the word *not* to be reduced and combined with the preceding word. In our example we have *can't* and *don't*. In more formal English they will be written *can not* (or *cannot*) and *do not*. They appear as one orthographic form, but clearly consist of two distinct meaning elements. So it is possible to say that the example above has 19 words (tokens).

3.2.1 Lexeme

A **lexeme** can be defined as a unit of meaning which underlies a number of **word forms** that are grammatically related through inflections. For example, *sweep, sweeps, swept,* and *sweeping* are different forms of one lexeme: SWEEP. The same goes for the plural *-s* and genitive *-s* of nouns, and the *-er* and *-est* endings of adjectives. *Man, man's, men, men's* are all word forms of the lexeme MAN (an irregular noun); and *quick, quicker, quickest* are word forms of the lexeme QUICK. Most dictionaries are alphabetical lists of lexemes, and the headword, i.e. the word that guides our search, is the **base form** of the lexeme.

A Are function words lexemes?

Although the notion of lexeme is useful, it is by no means unproblematic. If we go by the definition above, we cannot include function words such as *under, the, because, to,* and *a* in the example above as lexemes, because they do not have any inflected forms. However, some function words vary in form, e.g. *this - these, he - him.* Moreover, there are lexical words which cannot be inflected, e.g. *tomorrow* and *meanwhile.* This means that we have to relax our definition above and accept different types of lexemes. As regards lexical words and function words, see **2.4.1**.

B Polysemy or homonymy

A further complication is the fact that the same form may have two or more meanings. *Fair* (n. 'an outdoor event') and *fair* (adj. 'light in colour') are obviously two separate lexemes. Not only do they belong to different word classes, but their meanings are widely different. When one form, *fair*, has two distinct meanings, *fair* (n.) and *fair* (adj.) are **homonyms**. The solution is not so obvious in other cases. Are *man* (n. 'male person') and *man* (n. 'human being') the same lexeme? The answer is probably yes, since the two meanings are fairly close. *Man* shows **polysemy**, i.e. one form with two or more related meanings. The criterion we go by is the extent to which the meanings are related, though that in itself is a pretty vague yardstick.

C Multi-word lexemes

We must also include among our examples of lexemes combinations of elements whose meaning is different from the sum of the meanings of the elements in the combination. The idiomatic multi-word verbs *sail through* (v. 'succeed') and *run out of* (v. 'have nothing left') are single lexemes. So are combinations like *go Dutch* (v. 'split the cost'), *be in the red* (v. 'owe money'), and *roll out the red carpet* (v. 'give an official welcome'). English has a huge number of such idiomatic phrases, often with a metaphorical meaning. To the extent that one can identify a single unitary meaning, they are lexemes.

As a case in point, our example sentence in **3.2** contains *sweep under the carpet.* The first occurrence can have the idiomatic meaning 'keep something secret', but the co-text excludes this meaning in favour of the literal meaning in the second part of the sentence. This clearly complicates our word count based on lexemes.

Where to enter such idiomatic combinations is always a problem for dictionary makers. Although dictionaries are typically arranged by lexemes, multi-word lexemes are generally listed under one of the component elements, e.g. *sweep under the carpet* under the entry for the verb *sweep*.

D Compounds as lexemes

There is also the question of the lexemic status of compounds. Many compounds have a literal meaning, e.g. *bus conductor* (n.), *sit-in* (n.), *nose job* (n.), *have-nots* (n.), *sun-bathe* (v.), *sleep-walk* (v.), *well-argued* (adj.), *overpriced* (adj.). Others have an idiomatic meaning, e.g. *nose-dive* (n. 'a sudden steep drop'), *soft-pedal* (v. 'to make things seem less important'), *run-down* (adj. 'tired, bad condition'). In either case the compound would be considered one lexeme because it has a combined meaning which is different from the meanings of the components that make up the compound.

E Forms with double word class membership

Finally, many forms can belong to more than one word class (**2.4.3**). For example, many nouns can be used as verbs, and very many verbs can be used as nouns in English (**6.2**). It is common practice to regard such forms as representing different lexemes, e.g. *shop* (v.) and *shop* (n.), *sweep* (v.) and *sweep* (n.). However, practice varies in different dictionaries. Some list them as different headwords, whereas others include both in the same entry.

F Summing up

In cases where the question of the number of words in a piece of writing does crop up, for example in essays or abstracts of scholarly articles, it is probably best to use a practical count based on orthographic words (see the comparison in **16.3.1**). However, a student of English needs to know a little more about the theoretical problems connected with our everyday use of the word *word*. It is in this context that the concept of the lexeme is useful.

3.3 Form – sense – referent

So far we have talked about the meaning of a word (or lexeme) without really discussing what we mean by 'meaning'. In this section we will explore the interrelationship between the **form**, the **sense**, and the **referent** of a lexeme, commonly illustrated in the semiotic triangle in Figure 3a. It is easy to slip into the habit of using *word* instead of *lexeme*, but we will try to be consistent and use the latter. Semiotics is the study of sign systems of all possible types. Language is one type within this field, which investigates the connection between signs and meaning.

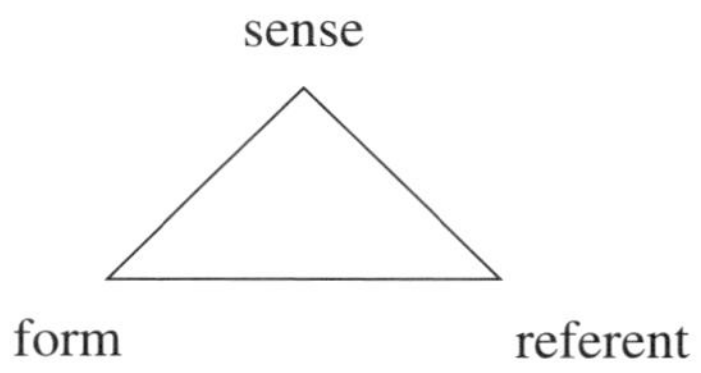

Figure 3a: The semiotic triangle

3.3.1 Form

The form side of an English lexeme is relatively easy to describe. That is because both the written form and the spoken form of any lexeme are made up of a limited number of units: 26 letters in the alphabet and some 44 segmental phonemes in the phonemic inventory of English. The correlation between letters and sounds is notoriously problematic in English, but that is a different matter.

If we take the lexeme MILK (n.), its written form is a combination of four letters, *m* + *i* + *l* + *k*, in that order. Its spoken form is a combination of four segmental phonemes. In both its spoken and written form MILK has a form with a concrete manifestation, which makes it easy to study. Although MILK happens to consist of four letters and four phonemes, spoken and written forms are in principle entirely different. Compare, for example, the five letters in THING and the three phonemes in /θɪŋ/.

3.3.2 Sense

The sense of MILK, on the other hand, is a mental concept which is far more difficult to investigate. We have a mental category of MILK in our mind. We have no good method of investigating mental concepts. The sense of MILK can best be explained by means of the paraphrase a standard dictionary gives. The *Longman Dictionary of Contemporary English* provides several related senses, but the first is 'a white liquid produced by cows or goats that is drunk by people'.

3.3.3 Referent

The referent, the third point in the triangle above, can be appreciated only if we use MILK in actual discourse.

1 A: Where did you put the milk?
B: It's in the fridge.

This dialogue presupposes a real situation involving two people where A wants to know where a particular amount of milk is. This amount of milk is called the referent of MILK in this specific situation. In general, the referent of a lexeme is that thing/person, that activity/state, or that quality that a noun, verb, or adjective respectively is used to refer to in actual discourse. The abstract relationship between sense and referent is called **reference**. Below we see three different uses of MILK.

2 'Milk' has four letters.
3 Milk is good for you.
4 The milk is in the fridge.

In (2) we talk about the form side and appropriately use a citation form with inverted commas. In (3) we talk about milk in general, and in (4) we talk about a particular referent.

The form–sense–referent relationship is fundamental in language, so we need to explore it in some more detail.

3.4 How to define the sense of lexemes

3.4.1 The sense of nouns with concrete referents

From time to time we find ourselves in arguments about what lexeme to use for a particular referent, e.g. whether to call something *red* or *orange*, whether to call a specific plant *a bush* or *a shrub*, whether to call a particular drinking vessel *a mug, a cup,* or *a bowl.* Essentially the same problem crops up in discussions about whether the penguin is a bird or the whale a fish.

Speakers of any language have a **mental lexicon** in their heads. This can be thought of as a storehouse for the lexemes in the language. It contains the sense of the lexemes as well as their grammatical, collocational (cf. **3.4.4C**), and stylistic properties. A good dictionary gives reliable information on the collective mental lexicon of a language community.

A Fuzzy categories

It is difficult to investigate our mental lexicon, but a few well-known experiments have brought some results. One classic example involves the nouns *cup, mug, bowl,* and *vase.* The result of this experiment showed that the informants' conception of the sense of the four lexemes was not fixed and discrete. They had **fuzzy boundaries**. What also became clear was that the informants agreed on what was typically a mug, a cup, etc. These typical members are sometimes referred to as **prototypes**.

The reason why the sense of many lexemes is fuzzy is that there are no clear cut-off points between their potential referents in the external world. Not all Norwegians would agree where the referent of *høydedrag* becomes *ås* and where *ås* becomes *fjell*. It is a different matter that an Englishman would probably draw the lines differently.

The concept of a prototypical member of a class has proved useful in linguistics. In a way *cup, mug, bowl,* and *vase* are trivial, uncomplicated lexemes in the huge inventory which we have called the mental lexicon. It is far more difficult to establish the sense of abstract nouns like *hate, patience,* and *socialism.*

B Precise categories

In special contexts there may be good reason to operate with precise sense categories. This is, for example, the case in courts of law or in scientific investigations. We once overheard a discussion between two teenagers. One, whom we will call Emil, could not accept that there was water in milk; the other, Frank, claimed there was. The difference seemed to be that Emil had in mind the everyday sense of *milk* (which is quite distinct from that of *water*), whereas Frank knew that milk contains a fair amount of water. Both were right, but had different senses of *milk* in mind.

As ordinary language users, we employ both fuzzy categories and more precisely defined categories, depending on the situation. Obviously, the precise categories require exact, specialized knowledge. One typical feature of specialized language is that it contains a terminology with well-defined categories.

In a very general sense we can say that nouns refer to things, adjectives to qualities, and verbs to actions and states. Whereas qualities may come and go, and actions and states stop, things have an existence and permanence not shared by qualities and actions. So if a speaker refers to something by means of a noun, the language invests its referent with a stable, undisputed existence. The language of advertising often includes nouns which refer to mysterious substances that are supposed to be good for the consumer, for example *toothpaste with irium* (whatever that is).

3.4.2 The sense of verbs – some examples

It is exceedingly difficult to describe the sense of lexemes in an objective and consistent way. The reason is that it means trying to impose some system on human experience in all its multi-faceted complexity. In **6.3** we distinguish between several classes of verbs on the basis of form. Other classes can be established on the basis of a broad semantic classification. In **7.5.4** we distinguish between **stative** and **dynamic** verbs. The second type includes verbs which refer to actions over which human beings have some control. There is syntactic correlation between type of verb and aspect. Dynamic verbs allow the progressive aspect; stative verbs do not. Other semantically based classes include:

- verbs of communication: *speak, talk, say, claim, assert, maintain, write*, etc.
- verbs of perception: *see, hear, feel, sense, observe, notice*, etc.
- verbs of cognition: *think, believe, know, realize, understand, assume, suppose*, etc.

Here as well, there is some degree of correlation between semantics and syntax. Most of the verbs above take *that*-clauses as complements.

If we select a set of near-synonyms of the verb *look at*, we can show that their senses differ in terms of how and for what purpose the action of looking takes place; see Table 3a. A plus sign (+) marks the distinguishing feature for each verb. *Look at* is the more general, **superordinate** verb. It has none of these features.

Table 3a: Features distinguishing a set of near-synonyms of the general, superordinate verb look at

	fixedly	angrily	quickly	with mouth open	through opening	carefully	very thoroughly	with strong sexual implications	with sexual implications
look at									
stare	+								
peek			+						
peep					+				
ogle								+	
examine						+			
gape				+					
glare		+							
leer									+
scrutinize							+		

We assume that most native speakers, if given these sense components to choose among, would mark the verbs in the same way. Note that a degree component plays a part in differentiating between the senses of some of the verbs, namely, 'carefully/very thoroughly' and 'sexual implications/strong sexual implications'. There is something arbitrary about this selection of verbs and the selection of sense components we have made. If we had included verbs like *see, watch, observe, eye, notice,* our table would have become more complex. Also, a different set of verbs would have had to be differentiated along other dimensions. But this is the nature of sense.

Finally, although we may well agree in the abstract on the sense of these verbs, we can easily fall out over their use in real situations, as in the following example. This takes us into the treacherous ground of reference (**3.7.2**).

Plaintiff: Your honour, he clearly leered at me.
Defendant: I certainly did not. I just looked at her.

3.4.3 The sense of adjectives – some examples

Adjectives typically denote qualities that can be graded. With some we can establish **objective standards**. Once that is done, we can agree on the sense of adjectives of shape, such as *round, square, triangular*; of size, such as *tall, medium-sized, small, short*; and colour, such as *red, orange, yellow*. However, such adjectives are also used without reference to a standard, in which case they have fuzzy boundaries.

Other gradable adjectives are selected on the basis of the speaker's subjective value judgements of a person or situation, e.g. *firm, headstrong, stubborn, obstinate, pig-headed*. These vary along an **evaluation scale** from positive to negative. However, the important point is that the same referent, for example a characteristic shown by somebody, can be referred to by five different people by five different adjectives. This is the basis of the famous conjugation suggested by Bertrand Russell (1). Example (2) is modelled on the same kind of 'conjugation'.

1 I am firm.
You are obstinate.
He is a pig-headed fool.

2 I am beautiful.
You are quite nice.
She isn't bad-looking, if you like that type.

The sense of other adjectives differs along the **intensity scale**. The strong–weak dimension is suitable for gradable adjectives. Of the adjectives in the list *annoyed-miffed-angry-furious-irate-livid,* the first two are weak, *angry* occupies a middle position, and the others are strong. In addition, *miffed* is informal (**3.5.1**), while *irate* and *livid* are more formal. This illustrates how dimensions intersect.

It is a fact that the sense of a lexeme is in no small part determined by the words that this lexeme tends to co-occur with, or, to use a technical term, by its **collocations** (**3.4.4C**). This is illustrated in Table 3b. *False, spurious, counterfeit, artificial, mock,* and *fake* all have a core sense of 'not real, genuine or true', but they cannot be used interchangeably. *False* is a fairly general word, a **core** word; the others have different collocational tendencies. The vertical column in the table lists the adjectives we want to focus on, whereas the horizontal line includes typical **collocates** of the adjectives, i.e. words with which they tend to co-occur, or collocate.

Table 3b: Collocations of the core word false and a set of near-synonyms (based on B. Rudska et al., The Words You Need)

	teeth	argument	money	flowers	jewellery	exam
false	+	+				
spurious		+				
counterfeit			+			
artificial				+	+	
fake					+	
mock						+

The point is that the native speaker's knowledge of the sense of each of these words rests on what other, related lexemes there are in the language (the vertical column above) and on what words each lexeme tends to collocate with (the horizontal line).

3.4.4 Other complications

A Polysemy

In many examples above we were able to distinguish, however fuzzily, one lexeme from another on the basis of different meaning components, for example *cup* vs. *bowl*, *stare* vs. *glare*. It is an important aspect of the sense make-up of many lexemes that they have two or more related senses (**3.2.1B**). These are some senses of two polysemous words:

Social

- 'related to human society and organizations': *Such social ills have been ignored.*
- 'related to friendly, non-business activity': *It was just a social gathering.*
- 'inclined to or fond of being in the company of others': *I'm not very social tonight.*

Paper

- 'material made from wood or cloth used for writing and printing': *It is made of paper.*
- 'newspaper': *Do you take that paper?*
- 'a set of printed questions used for examination in a subject': *The English paper was difficult.*
- 'a talk on a specialist topic for a group of specialists': *He gave a paper on polysemy.*

In real discourse even a sub-sense like 'newspaper' can be used with different referents (specified in parentheses below). However, these special applications are a matter of **pragmatics**, of language use in real situations where people can infer the exact referents from the context. They should not be considered part of the sense of *newspaper*. Compare the following examples, which have been taken from Georgia M. Green, *Pragmatics and Natural Language Understanding*:

- *The newspaper raised the price per inch for its classified advertising.* (the board of the newspaper)
- *The newspaper fell from my lap.* (the sheets of the newspaper)
- *'Dear Abby' is not in that newspaper on Saturdays anymore.* (the columns of the newspaper)
- *The printer's union wants to buy that newspaper.* (the stocks of the newspaper)
- *The newspaper has always supported a Republican candidate for president.* (the editorial policy of the newspaper)

Instead of talking imprecisely about the meaning of a word, we are now in a position, if the need arises, to refer to a particular sense of a polysemous lexeme.

B Grammatical differences

Lexemes also have grammatical properties. In the set *shake, tremble,* and, *quiver,* only *shake* can be used as a transitive verb: *He shook the tree.* The following near-synonyms with the meaning 'say no to' differ in the type of object they combine with: *refuse* is followed by an infinitive object, *deny* by an *-ing* participle clause, and *reject* and *turn down* by regular noun phrases.

When the adjective *capable* ('have the skill, power, or intelligence necessary to do something') is used as a subject predicative, it tends to be followed by an *of*-construction: *He is perfectly capable of handling this. Able*, on the other hand, is followed by a *to*-infinitive: *He is able to do it.* In premodifying position before a noun, no *of*-construction or infinitive is possible. This is part of the grammar of the two adjectives.

The nouns *proof* and *evidence* can both mean 'information that proves something', but only *proof* can be used in the plural in this sense. *Evidence* is an uncountable noun. Incidentally, the same form is listed as a verb in the *Longman Dictionary of Contemporary English* with the extra grammatical information 'usually passive': *The volcano is still active, as evidenced by the recent eruption.*

All this goes to show that lexemes are invested with grammatical properties. Good dictionaries include such information in a condensed, often cryptic form under each entry (see **3.9**). Knowing the sense of these lexemes also means knowing how to use them in correct grammatical constructions.

C Collocations

When we discussed the sense of adjectives (**3.4.3**), we talked about collocational tendencies. *False teeth* and *counterfeit money* are good collocations; *false* and *teeth, counterfeit* and *money* collocate. We should note the use of the word **tendency**. We cannot categorically rule out other combinations. Nevertheless, such tendencies are an important aspect of idiomatic English.

When we speak or write, language comes to us to a large extent in 'prepackaged units'. This applies to:

- sequences involving two or more grammatical words such as *I am, there is, did you,* where a grammatical rule may allow little or no choice;
- collocations of grammatical and lexical words such as *sure enough, in the meantime, for a while,* which likewise allow little choice;
- collocations consisting of two or more lexical words, such as *false teeth.*

Overuse of lexical collocations may easily turn them into predictable clichés. The last two in the following list are clichés, while the first three are rather common collocations: *vicious circle, hugely popular, attract attention, proudly present* (show business language), *desirable residence* (real estate language).

D Connotations

Often language users have more or less subjective associations connected with individual lexemes. Such associations are called connotations. We mentioned *housewife* in **3.1**. Another fairly uncontroversial example would be *woman* and *lady.* Both have the sense 'female human being', but whereas *woman* is neutral, *lady* has connotations of 'high class, elegance', etc. The phrase *old boy* as a form of address is associated with high-class users. The vocabulary of English is almost infinitely rich. It is therefore very difficult to distinguish between a lexeme's objective components of sense and its subjective connotations. The first type is recorded in dictionaries.

A quick check among a few native speakers of English on the sense of the verbs in the following set, all with the core sense of 'work hard', revealed the following:

toil	'work hard, over a period of time, no pleasure'
slave away	'work hard, over a period of time, like a slave' (i.e. boring work decided by others)
beaver away	'work hard, over a period of time, like a beaver' (i.e. repeated, diligent action)
work at	'work hard, over a period of time, in order to become better'
labour	'work hard, physical work'
push oneself	'work hard, harder than normal capacity'

One informant associated *toil* with 'farming, work on the land'; another said that *labour* conjured up associations of pick and shovel. These are fairly clear connotations. Some said that *work at, toil,* and *labour* implied 'lack of intelligence/skills'. Is this a connotation, or part of the sense of the verbs? At least for *toil* and *labour*, it is probably closer to the first. All this goes to show how immensely difficult it is to draw a clear line between sense and connotations.

Connotations tend to vary. They may vary from one individual to the next, from one English-speaking community to the next, from one period of time to another, and from one culture to another. Despite this variation, there is often considerable agreement on the connotations of words. That is why they are so important in real communication.

3.5 Type of discourse

3.5.1 Formality

The total knowledge we have about individual lexemes also includes knowledge about their appropriate use in real discourse, i.e. in what situations a lexeme would be suitable and in what situations it would be unsuitable.

1 It was said that a great poet had *resided* here.
2 It was said that a great poet had *lived* here.

Reside (1) is a verb which definitely belongs to formal written English. *Live* (2), on the other hand, is neutral. That means that it is appropriate in many types of spoken English and in many types of written English, e.g. in personal letters, in business letters, and in formal inquiries to official agencies. Consider the words in set (3) below:

3 *eager, gung-ho, zealous*

Gung-ho is informal, *zealous* is more formal, whereas *eager* is neutral. A word like *gung-ho*, although it may occur in respectable newspapers, should not be used in official contexts.

In sets like (3) we are generally able to pick out the **core** word, i.e. the word which is most neutral. This means neutral not only in formality, but also in terms of positive and negative components of meaning, and in the sense that it has the widest collocational range.

The vocabulary of English consists of words of two main origins: French or other Romance, and Germanic. Phrasal and prepositional verbs based on Germanic words like those in (4) are informal/neutral as compared with the roughly corresponding more formal words of Romance origin in (5).

4 *put off, run into, put out, talk into*
5 *postpone, encounter, extinguish, persuade*

We have made a broad distinction with respect to formality: formal, informal, and neutral. This is a crude, but useful, three-way split. On the informal side, we can make more distinctions. Consider the words in (6).

6 *cool, dandy, groovy, neat, swell*

There are many more such **slang** words for 'excellent'. They are often short-lived and tend to belong to the spoken language of a restricted group of speakers. They should be avoided in serious writing.

There are no clear cut-off points between the categories below, which have been arranged according to degree of formality. Our classification is subjective.

taboo	slang	colloquial	informal	neutral	formal
shit	go to the can (AmE)	go to the loo (BrE)/john (AmE)	go to the gents/ladies (BrE)	go to the toilet/bath-room	defecate

3.5.2 Regional variation

English is spoken by hundreds of millions of people around the world. There are obvious differences between the vocabularies of British English, American English, and Australian English to mention three huge English-speaking communities. According to the *Longman Dictionary of Contemporary English*, *garbage* ('søppel') is AmE for BrE *rubbish.* The general English word *friend* has informal, regional alternatives, such as *cobber* (AustrE), *mate* (BrE and AustrE), and *crony* (AmE). Good dictionaries contain information on such examples of **regional variants.**

3.5.3 Register

Register, or field of discourse, is the term generally used for language varieties associated with particular social situations. For example, we may speak of the specialized register of the different professions and sciences. *Lexeme* belongs to linguistics; *chloroform,* to chemistry or medicine. If the language becomes too difficult to understand for ordinary people, we often speak about

jargon. Jargon gone too far may become almost impenetrable gobbledygook. This example hits our own profession, linguistics:

1 In traditional linguistics it has been assumed that the analysis of sentences can be performed upon examples isolated from the process of interaction within which they naturally emerge.

This simply means that 'traditional linguists thought that sentences could be analysed out of context'. Compare also:

2 Child: You see, Gran'ma, before you suck this egg, or more properly speaking, before you extract the matter contained within the shell by suction, you must make an incision at the apex and a corresponding aperture at the base.
Gran'ma: My dear, how very clever! They only used to make a hole at each end in my time. Well, I declare, they are making improvements in everything.

3.5.4 Other differences in use

Some dictionaries use terms like *archaic* or *obsolete* for words which are dated or have gone out of use, e.g. *half-crown* ('coin used in the UK before 1971'), and *poetic* or *literary* for words that typically occur in literature, e.g. *flaxen* ('fair colour of hair').

3.6 Sense relations

If we want to describe the relationship between different lexemes from within the language as it were, we can do so in terms of sameness of sense (**synonymy**), oppositeness of sense (**antonymy**), and inclusiveness of sense (**hyponymy**).

3.6.1 Synonymy

On the basis of what we have said above, it should be clear that it is very difficult to find two lexemes which are completely synonymous. The test would be if they can be used interchangeably in all contexts. That is hardly ever the case; compare (1) and (2) below.

1 I'm afraid Mr X is busy/occupied at the moment.
Is this seat occupied/*busy?
2 The restaurant is particularly/especially popular with young people.
Do you want to come to the party? Not particularly/?especially.

There is nearly always some element that is different. There may be a difference in formality (*live* - *reside*), a difference in grammatical potential (*shake* - *tremble*), a difference in connotation (*woman* - *lady*), a difference in collocation (*false* - *fake*), etc. However, from a practical point of view, it is useful to talk about synonyms or near-synonyms (see **15.4.1**).

Books of synonyms and thesauruses are essential if one wants to avoid the repetitive, imprecise use of lexemes with a fairly broad meaning which learners are comfortable with (sometimes called 'lexical teddy bears' (A. Hasselgren 1994)). Thesauruses are collections of words arranged in lists or groups according to sense. Some publishers use the term *word finder*, which avoids the technical implications of *synonym* and *thesaurus*.

As an illustration, we include the entries for *interesting*, a lexeme which is overused by many learners, from three different word finders: *Roget's Student Thesaurus, The Macmillan Dictionary of Synonyms and Antonyms*, and the Longman *Language Activator – The World's First Production Dictionary*. The *Language Activator* contains a wealth of information. It includes not only alternative adjectives, but also other expressions with roughly the same sense as *interesting*. We have reduced and simplified all the material in the *Activator* into a list of near-synonymous expressions.

The Macmillan Dictionary of Synonyms and Antonyms:

interesting adj. attractive, fascinating, absorbing, engrossing *That was one of the most interesting books I have ever read.* Ant. uninteresting, boring, tedious, wearisome.

Roget's Student Thesaurus:

interesting: **Interesting** means making you feel like paying attention and knowing more. *To a chameleon, any insect is interesting.*

Intriguing means interesting because it makes you curious. *The ads for the new movie were intriguing, but the movie itself was boring.*

Fascinating means so interesting that it's hard to stop. *Damien finds computer programming so fascinating that he'll sit at his keyboard for hours.*

Absorbing means extremely interesting. *Naoko enjoys crossword puzzles if they are hard enough to be absorbing.*

Spellbinding means so interesting that it is impossible to stop paying attention. *Both pitchers have no-hitters going into the eighth inning of this spellbinding game.*

Engrossing means so interesting that it makes you forget other things. *'When I'm painting,' Frazier wrote to his pen pal, 'it's so engrossing I don't think of anything else'.*

Antonyms: dull, boring, uninteresting.

Language Activator:
interesting: fascinating, intriguing, be of interest, interestingly, stimulating, hold your attention, absorbing, riveting, gripping, compelling, couldn't put it down, eventful, colourful, never a dull moment, unusual, have character, be a character, liven up, jazz up, add variety.

3.6.2 Antonymy

Antonymy is a tricky notion. If we ask native speakers to give antonyms for *male* and *dead,* the answers are likely to be *female* and *alive*. A lexeme like *cold* would be given the antonym *hot.* In their normal literal sense these words differ along a single dimension. However, when asked about the antonym of *boy*, natives might answer *girl* or *man*. If asked about antonyms of *artificial,* they might suggest *real, genuine,* or *natural.* A verb like *permit* might trigger antonyms like *forbid, disallow,* and *prohibit*. The point we are trying to make is that, once we choose lexemes which differ along many different dimensions, the answer is not obvious.

Lexemes like *dead* and *alive* are called binary antonyms. They represent the only two points along that dimension. Lexemes like *hot* and *cold* are called gradable antonyms. They represent the extremes at either end of a scalar dimension. There are others along the same dimension, e.g. *warm, lukewarm, tepid, chilled.* In **15.4.4** we show how lexemes whose senses are loosely antonymous can create variety and cohesion on the discourse level.

3.6.3 Hyponymy

This term refers, for example, to the relationship between *flower* and *rose.* The sense of *rose* includes the sense of *flower.* There is no rose which is not also a flower. We say that *rose* is a **hyponym** of *flower* and *flower* is the **superordinate term**. A specialist in botany will be able to list sub-types of roses, which would then be hyponyms of *rose*. We can set up a hierarchy of relations, part of which is shown in Figure 3b.

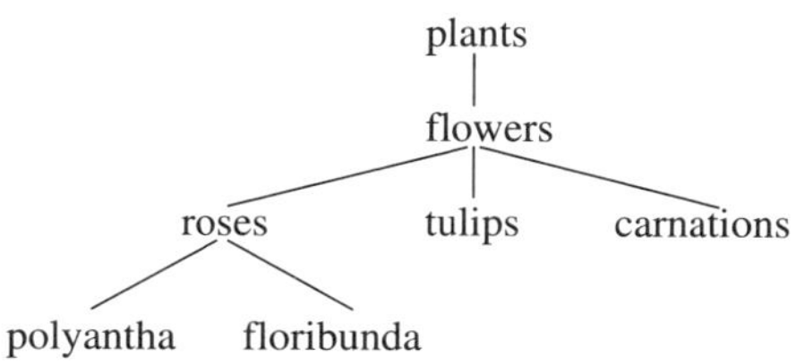

Figure 3b: A hierarchy of sense relations: plants

Classifications of this kind are used, for example, in the natural sciences. The superordinate term is the lexeme with the most general sense, and further down in the hierarchy we find lexemes with a more precise, specialized sense. *Vehicle - car, dwelling - cottage, book - novel, play - comedy, crime - murder/burglary/embezzlement, vessel - boat/tanker/ship* relate to each other in much the same way. Lexical variation in discourse depends in part on the ability to make use of such relations, as in (1). See also **15.4.1–15.4.2**.

1 I bought a yellow rose for my girlfriend the other day. She was really taken by surprise. She immediately decided where she wanted the plant to go in her garden. It's touching to see how she cares about it. Roses are beautiful flowers.

The examples given so far have illustrated some rather uncomplicated relations. Figure 3c shows a hierarchy with the abstract noun *emotion* as the most general term. The words grouped under *hatred* are only a few of those listed in *Roget's Thesaurus*. The relationships in this hierarchy are similar to those above, but we would hesitate to talk about hyponyms and superordinate terms. *Hatred, love, anger, relief, disappointment* are all types of emotion and can be used in sentences such as (2). It is more difficult to claim that the lexemes listed on the lowest level in Figure 3c are sub-types of *hatred.* They have different, specialized senses.

2 There was obviously a lot of disappointment there, but he managed to conceal his emotion.

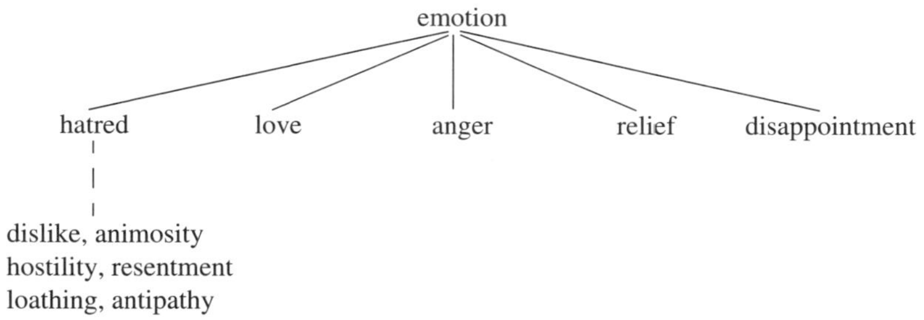

Figure 3c: A hierarchy of sense relations: emotions

3.7 Applications in discourse

3.7.1 Exploitations of the form–sense–referent relationship

A Word-play based on the form–sense relationship

Some lexemes are identical in spoken and written form, e.g. *bear* (v. 'carry') and *bear* (n. 'large animal'), but obviously different in sense. They are **homonyms**. Others are identical in written form but pronounced differently, e.g. *bow* /baʊ/ (v. 'bend forward') and *bow* /bəʊ/ (n. 'curved stick used to shoot arrows'). These represent a sub-type of homonyms called **homographs** (= identity in spelling). Still others are pronounced the same way but spelt differently, e.g. *place* (n.) and *plaice* (n. 'type of flat fish'). These represent another sub-type of homonyms, namely, **homophones** (= identity in pronunciation). Homonymy is often exploited by creative users, and the English seem to be particularly fond of such word-play. We see this, for example, in advertisements, graffiti, and newspaper headlines.

1 I'm on a seafood diet – whenever I see food I eat it.
2 A Puritan is a man who 'noes' what he wants. (to *no* = 'to say no to something')
3 Van Gogh was ear. (near-homonym of *here*)
4 I still miss my ex-wife. I must improve my shooting.
5 The Mourning After (newspaper headline the day after Princess Diana's funeral)

Literary devices such as alliteration and rhyme capitalize on the fact that lexemes have formal similarities. Edgar Allan Poe's 'The Raven' cleverly exploits both. This is the opening stanza:

6 Once upon a midnight dreary, while I pondered, weak and weary,
Over many a quaint and curious volume of forgotten lore,
While I nodded, nearly napping, suddenly there came a tapping,
As of some one gently rapping, rapping at my chamber door.
" 'Tis some visitor," I muttered, "tapping at my chamber door –
Only this, and nothing more."

B Word-play based on polysemy

The fact that many words have several related senses can likewise be exploited for special effect. The obvious double meaning of *sleep* ('die' and 'go to sleep') in Robert Frost's poem 'Stopping by Woods on a Snowy Evening' is a case in point (7). Compare also the word *light* in the invocation of Book iii in Milton's *Paradise Lost* (8), where *light* has both a physical sense and a divine sense.

On a more mundane level, (9) and (10) appeared on the package of a breakfast cereal. Example (9) trades on the two senses of *wake up* ('to awaken' and 'to become aware'). In (10) the sense of the first occurrence of *heart* implies 'we are kind and generous', while the sense of the second is quite literally 'your blood pump'. (This must be understood against the background of the wider co-text which mentions oat bran and cholesterol level.)

7 The woods are lovely, dark and deep,
But I have promises to keep,
And miles to go before I sleep.
And miles to go before I sleep.

8 Hail, holy Light, offspring of heaven first-born,
Or of the eternal, co-eternal beam
May I express thee unblamed? Since God is light …

9 Wake up to the crunchy goodness of natural whole grains and fruit
10 From our heart – for your heart

C Word-play based on sense paraphrases

In (11) and (12) the sense of some rather learned word has been given a special twist by being illustrated in a humorous way. Example (12) is patterned on the well-known graffiti form.

11 I like to reminisce with people I don't know, but it takes such a long time.
12 Cowardice rules, if that is OK with you.
Procrastination will rule one day, OK?
Sceptics may or may not rule one day, OK?
Synonyms govern, all right.
Amnesia rules, O.
Dyslexia rules, KO.

D Same referent – different sense expressions

The expressions *the Morning Star* and *the Evening Star*, although obviously different in sense, have the same star as referent. Similarly, the possible referents of the expressions *featherless biped* and *rational animal* are the same. Any creature that is a featherless biped is also a rational animal (we may dislike being called animals). This is not just of theoretical interest; it can be related to real language use. In some types of writing it is not uncommon to use different expressions with the same referent and in that way build up a picture of a person or a thing. The danger is that readers may be lulled into thinking that there is no question that Mr X has these characteristics.

13 *Mr X* seemed to be quite at ease in the company of his radical hosts. *The former student leader* joked about his student days and no amount of hectoring or criticism seemed to stop *the beer-loving politician* from enjoying his pint in the student pub. *The famous war-wounded hero* has a flair for establishing good rapport with people from all walks of life. *He* ...

E Sense and reference: some additional points

The sense of some lexemes is so general that they can be used appropriately with a huge number of different referents. This is the case with nouns like *thing, device,* and *gadget,* which are often used to refer to concrete objects that the speaker cannot think of a more precise name for, as in *Give me that thing.* Nouns like *point* and *problem* can be used similarly with more abstract referents. The verbs *do* and *make* have little sense when they are used as delexical verbs (**6.3.4**), for example in *to do a song, to do one's hair.* Such lexemes approach the status of pro-forms (**15.3.1H**).

Postmodifiers of nouns typically help clarify the exact referent of noun phrases. From our perspective in this chapter we can say that nominal expressions which consist of many lexemes have single (group) referents; compare *the book I got yesterday, the chair by the window, people who fancy that sort of thing.*

Some forms have imaginary referents. There are probably no *trolls* and no *Loch Ness Monster* or *Xanadu* in the real world. Still, the forms can be used to refer to such creations of human imagination in just the same way as if they were real.

3.7.2 Reference – a minefield!

A Imaginative and non-imaginative language

It is important first to distinguish between imaginative language, as in fiction and poetry, and non-imaginative language. The former type creates imaginary people in imaginary situations. We appreciate such language because of its literary qualities. Whether or not it is factually correct is irrelevant. The latter type includes all those types of discourse which involve real situations with real people. In such contexts language must reflect reality in an accurate, truthful, and balanced way. If not, the people concerned have good reason to feel offended, hurt, or misrepresented. It is this relationship that we have called a minefield. It takes us into the essence of language use in real discourse.

B Emotive or biased language

In **3.3.3** we defined the relationship between the sense of a lexeme and its intended referent in the external world as reference. *Milk* in our example is straightforward, but the same principle applies to the reference of abstract nouns, and to verbs and adjectives. If somebody talks at length in a childish way about unimportant matters, the appropriate lexeme to use might be *prattle*. This verb, however, clearly has derogatory connotations. Two people might choose different adjectives to characterize a person who never yields an inch in discussions. One might choose *firm*, the other *stubborn*. But the choice is certainly not inconsequential, and it reflects the attitude and motives of the users.

Nobody is always able to use completely neutral and unbiased language. Communication would be dead boring if we did. We get carried away by our emotions and use **emotive language**, sometimes openly and aggressively when we use swear-words and taboo words, at other times in a more calculated way when we use taunts and sarcasms or select biased vocabulary full of positive or negative meaning. Here are some examples.

Euphemism: neutral and positive words used to gloss over unpleasant or painful facts

> *to go to the bathroom* or *to wash one's hands* for what one does in the toilet bowl
> *pass away, sleep, kick the bucket* for 'die'
> *terminological inexactitude* for a 'lie'
> *developing countries* for 'undeveloped' or 'underdeveloped countries'
> *underachievers / special needs children* for 'those who fall behind at school'
> *the underprivileged* for 'the poor'
> *family life education* for 'sex education'

Dysphemism: neutral or negative words used to make people or things appear in an unfavourable light

> *creatures* for 'Jews' in Hitler's propaganda
> *Castro Hordes Swarm Globe* (headline of article when Fidel Castro sent Cuban troops to Third World countries; *horde* and *swarm* clearly have negative connotations)

Epithet: a special type of dysphemic language involving nouns or adjectives used as 'labels' to categorize and often brand people, especially when blaming them; epithets are full of connotations

X is a true *fascist.*
Don't be such an *alarmist!*
You sound like a real *ayatollah.*
This is *middle-suburban, semi-detached-and-privet-hedge, gin-and-golf, tax-hating* England.

Political rhetoric: a negatively loaded term for the language used by politicians to promote their own or their party's interest. Example (1) contains some extracts from an analysis of the rhetoric of New Labour (election campaign 1997) – also referred to as *Blairspeak.* The lexeme *Blairspeak* is a new creation, but it clearly alludes to the *Newspeak* in George Orwell's political novel *1984.*

1 We grew up linking Labour rhetoric with the terminology of Marxist socialism. The 'working class', the 'means of production', the language of the Manifesto. What is new about Blairspeak is not so much what it includes, but what it omits. 'Socialism' gives way to 'social cohesion', 'the working class' to the 'people' …

There's an old-fashioned air about the new political terminology: 'mutualism' (the concept that the people and the state both share rights and responsibilities); the linguistic links are with the old mutual societies (building homes for the future, trust, shared resources); a non-threatening -ism: communitarianism … [contrasted with communism]

The latest buzzword is stakeholder, contrasted cunningly with shareholder …

Tony Blair is noted for remarks such as *the public is not daft. Daft* seems to be an acceptable, non-aggressive adjective. The public, Labour strategists seem to think, likes to be spoken to in its own language.

(Based on a newspaper article)

Example (2) must be understood in the context of an inquiry made by a citizen to her MP about the serious consequences of the cut-back in funding for higher education. It is a brief extract from a letter by the then (Tory) Minister of State in the Department for Education and Employment.

2 I acknowledge that universities have made impressive efficiency gains in recent years in terms of the unit of resource per student. Our spending plans reflect further efficiency gains of 3% in 1996–97 and 1997–98 and 1998–99. These are in line with what the sector has achieved in the last few years without quality being compromised. It is reasonable to expect higher education, along with other publicly funded programmes, to improve efficiency.

What is noteworthy here is the choice of the positively loaded phrase *efficiency gains* and the claim that these have been achieved *without quality being compromised*, which some people at least might feel is debatable. In the rhetoric of Tory politics both were opportune in 1996.

Obfuscation is a formal word with a clearly negative meaning. It is sometimes used about the type of language which is deliberately made difficult in order to prevent readers and listeners from understanding the truth. Such language may sound impressive and convincing, but can easily lack substance. Example (3) is a parody of the type of rambling language that a politician may be guilty of when his associations run freely. Note the accumulation of words with positive sense content: *democracy, strength, responsibility, practical, effective, sound, common sense,* etc. This is at the same time the language of persuasion, but it is carried to its extreme, thereby defeating its own purpose. That is the intention here.

3 There will always be arguments and it is right that there should be arguments because it is the strength and the essence of democracy that people should be free to say what they feel and express those very real concerns which affect us all as we go about our daily lives and try and try again to find the right way and the just way and above all the responsible way to face the often difficult decisions and they are difficult, they are a matter of judgement and sound common sense and they must moreover be practical and effective, for unless they are effective and practical then they will surely be seen as mere empty words of biased and dogmatic emptiness and hopelessness, which is honestly not the way, it is honestly not, you know ...

3.8 The vocabulary of English and Norwegian

It is of course impossible to do justice to the heading above within the framework of this book. A good Norwegian–English (or English–Norwegian) dictionary is the only source that allows us to compare the vocabulary of the two languages. However, the information we find only allows a comparison of specific lexemes and their translation equivalents in the other language. There is very little that can be said in general, apart from such obvious points as the fact that the English lexicon consists of both Germanic and Romance words, whereas the basic vocabulary of Norwegian is overwhelmingly Germanic in origin. Still, a few points are worth making on vocabulary problems facing Norwegian learners of English.

The examples below contain words which result in wrong, awkward, inappropriate, or inadvertently funny English. We will return to these examples later. The question marks suggest that the sentences, although not ungrammatical, are more or less awkward because of the choice of a lexeme.

?1 I have a vision of my personal heaven, and I will try to tell about it.
?2 The chairman's orientation was surprising.
?3 I'm afraid this is wholly impossible.
?4 Ladies are requested not to have children in the bar. (sign in a cocktail lounge)
?5 The police had ransacked the room very carefully.
?6 Today we combine Viking to being tough and strong.
?7 The sofa has a base made of tree.
?8 He's bought himself a new and extremely rapid car.
?9 Referring to your recent advertisement in the Yorkshire Evening Press, I must say I sort of fancy working in a record shop, and would be ...
?10 You are invited to take advantage of the chambermaid. (sign in a hotel)
?11 Since there is only one world, it's important to remember that we must share this clode.
?12 Have you seen the new wall-carpet in lobby downstairs?
?13 Most people want the Church itself to decide what to mean in such matters.
?14 This was the time to start getting a family.

In discussing the examples, we will refer to English as 'the target language', or L2, and Norwegian as 'the source language', or L1.

3.8.1 False friends

A false friend, or a deceptive cognate, is a lexeme in L2 whose form (typically, written form) is similar to the form of a lexeme in L1, but differs from it in meaning. We have such well-known examples as *fabrikk* ('factory') vs. *fabric, konsekvent* ('consistent') vs. *consequent, simpel* ('coarse, vulgar') vs. *simple, kinn* ('cheek') vs. *chin, permisjon* ('leave of absence') vs. *permission, eventuelt* ('possibly') vs. *eventually, halte* ('limp') vs. *halt.*

If a learner goes wrong here, the result is most often a very odd English sentence – odd because it becomes unintelligible, misleading, or funny, as when a Norwegian claimed: *We often go skiing in knickers.*

There is something odd about (?5) above, where the verb *ransack* has presumably been chosen under the influence of Norwegian *ransake*. But while the latter implies an action done by the police, *ransack* in English is a search (by somebody, not the police) which leaves a place in a mess. *Search* would have been a better verb in (?5).

It is not uncommon for Norwegians to produce bloomers based on false friends like those mentioned above. Other words with similar written forms, such as *anger* ('repentance') - *anger* or *plaster* ('adhesive bandage') - *plaster,* probably cause fewer problems.

The greatest problems are caused by lexemes which are similar in their written form but have senses which partially overlap. These are the real troublemakers because the learner does not know how the senses diverge. Some examples are *tre - tree/wood/wooden, salat - lettuce/salad, mene - mean/think, bein - bone/leg, plass - place/room, ferdig -ready/finished.*

Example (?7) is odd because *tree* cannot be used about the material that something is made of; *wood* or *wooden* is correct (*a base made of wood* or *a wooden base*). However, when we refer to what we find in the woods, *tre* and *tree* correspond. In (?13) *mean* is a wrongly chosen lexeme. Although *Hva mener du?* corresponds to *What do you mean?*, *mean* does not have the sense 'think, believe' in English.

Example (?2) caused considerable amusement on a particular occasion because *orientation* tends to be understood as 'sexual orientation'. The intended meaning should have been rendered as *the chairman's statement/report.* It is only in the sense 'training or preparation for a new job or period of study' that *orientation* corresponds to *orientering.* In the sense 'give information about', English uses, for example, *make a statement* or *give a report.*

3.8.2 The creation of non-existent lexemes in L2

Low-level learners may even create L2 lexemes that do not exist. The word *clode* (?11), based on *klode*, is hopeless. Whereas the friends that we talked about metaphorically in **3.8.1** do actually exist in L2, **clode* and **crete* (for Norwegian *valgkrets*) do not. To carry on the metaphor, they are no friends at all.

3.8.3 The overuse of lexical favourites

Languages carve up reality differently. Generally, the English grid is finer, since it often has two or more lexemes for a single Norwegian one. Compare:

ta eksamen	vs.	*sit for an exam, pass an exam*
se på TV/TV'n	vs.	*watch television, look at the (television) set*
vekke barna/interesse	vs.	*wake the children, arouse interest*
samle familien/på frimerker	vs.	*gather the family, collect stamps*

There is a tendency among Norwegians to overuse more general core lexemes, so-called lexical teddy bears. This may lead to imprecision (*he never managed to take the exam*), wrong collocations (*this didn't wake any interest*), or the overuse of lexical teddy bears. *Getting* in (?14) is a lexical teddy bear. The sentence would improve if *raising* was used instead. The use of *have* in (?4) was probably meant to mean 'ha med seg', for which *bring* is much better. *Have children* means 'give birth to'. In (?6) *combine* is probably intended to mean 'forbinde noen med noe', for which English has the better alternative *associate somebody with.*

Two teddy bears within the class of adjectives are *nice* and *interesting* (note the alternatives in **3.6.1**). *Very* and *a lot* are often overused as intensifying adverbs.

3.8.4 Awkward collocations

We have seen examples of unidiomatic collocations previously in this chapter. When a Norwegian student writes:

> The Prime Minister thinks that the disagreement within the party is to blame for the humiliating disappointment in the local election on Thursday.

it is as if the adjective *humiliating* cries out for a better collocate, namely, *defeat.*

The combination *wholly impossible* in (?3), corresponding to *helt umulig*, is unidiomatic. If we want to intensify how impossible something is, we should use intensifiers like *totally, absolutely, quite. Wholly* collocates with adjectives like *dependent, inadequate, inappropriate, unacceptable.*

The sense of *rapid* (?8) is 'done or happening quickly or over a short period'. It collocates with *change, growth*, etc., but not with *car. Fast* and *quick* are better in combination with *car.*

The unintended humour in (?10) also has to do with collocations. One can *take advantage of a unique offer* ('benytte seg av et enestående tilbud'), but *take advantage of a chambermaid* has a different sense.

To conclude, unidiomatic English can to a great extent be put down to the fact that the learner does not know enough about the collocations of lexemes.

3.8.5 Translation loans

This term refers to the process of breaking down a word or phrase in one language and using it as the basis for a new form in another language. For example, *froskemann* in Norwegian is a translation loan based on English *frogman.* In this context we are concerned with incorrect English which arises from breaking down an expression in Norwegian and translating it bit by bit into English. An example is **wall-carpet* for *veggteppe*; the correct English form is *wall-hanging* (?12). Another candidate is **expedition office*, or even worse

expeditionoffice*, for *ekspedisjonskontor*. In Norwegian we can string together two or more bits into one long orthographic word. This is not possible in English, unless the compound is well established (cf. **4.8.1). And what about this: **Near the centre of Oslo you'll find the biggest used market* ('bruktmarked') *in Norway*.

We see the same process in the translation of the phrase 'en alvorlig splittelse i egne rekker' as **a serious split in own queues*. There are many examples of hilarious translations of L1 idioms, e.g. **suddenly he started rowing* ('begynte å ro'), where *backtrack* is a better L2 choice; **be completely gone* ('helt gå'en'), where *exhausted* is better; **they may be well off* ('de kan ha det så godt'), where something like *that serves them right* is better in L2. Translations of proverbial expressions in L1 may likewise lead to unidiomatic English, as in **sleep like a stone* for *sleep like a log*.

3.8.6 Wrong grammar

We have seen that lexemes have grammatical properties. Example (?1) is wrong because the writer did not realize that *tell*, unlike the Norwegian *fortelle,* requires an object when followed by a *that*-clause or prepositional phrase. The verb *ønske* allows a finite nominal clause as an object in Norwegian. The English equivalent *want* does not; compare **I want that you keep this a secret.*

3.8.7 Inappropriate style

Native English speakers show tolerance of lexical errors made by foreign speakers as long as they can make out the intended meaning. If, however, a lexeme is chosen which belongs to the wrong stylistic range, resentment may result. This has to do with things like conventions in writing, respect for the addressee, etc. Slang or too colloquial lexemes may upset the relationship to the addressee if the occasion requires more formal language. On the other hand, language which is too formal may sound pompous in situations which require a less formal style, and a native speaker may feel put down.

The use of the lexeme *fancy* and the phrase *sort of* (?9) is inappropriate in a job application. Moreover, they are incongruous given the formal opening: *Referring to your …*

An academic essay on Salinger's *The Catcher in the Rye* must not be written in Holden Caulfield's own adolescent language.

3.9 Dictionaries

An authoritative monolingual, i.e. English–English, dictionary is an indispensable tool for anyone studying the English language. If Norwegian is the source language, bilingual Norwegian–English and English–Norwegian dictionaries are obviously also very useful. A well-known British lexicographer once said that the average Englishman would spend hours asking questions about and checking the car he was considering buying. However, the same person, if he ever needed a dictionary, would gladly walk into a bookshop and pick the first one he happened to find on the shelf. It is a shame that people generally do not think too much about their needs when they buy a dictionary. Dictionaries differ in many important ways, and only somebody who has weighed his or her needs against the qualities of various dictionaries can make a sound choice.

In the section below we ask a series of questions which focus on different features of dictionaries. Then, at the end, we include some entries from four different books. This makes it possible to compare the dictionaries and check if and in what way they include the information asked for in **3.9.1**.

3.9.1 What you should look for in a dictionary

- What type of dictionary is it?
  - a monolingual dictionary
  - a bilingual dictionary
  - a learner's dictionary (beginner, intermediate, or advanced learner), as opposed to a dictionary for native speakers
  - a special-variety dictionary (e.g. slang, American English, technical English)
  - a dictionary of phrasal verbs or a dictionary of idioms
  - a special corpus dictionary (one exclusively based on data from one corpus)
  - a dictionary of synonyms or a thesaurus
  - a pictorial dictionary (which relies heavily on pictures)
- How many entries does it have?
- Does it give information on the frequency of lexemes?
- Does it contain encyclopaedic information (such as information on geographical names, names of famous people, etc.)?
- Does it contain reference material (such as standard abbreviations, a list of irregular verbs, surveys of measurements, etc.)?
- Does it give information on etymology (i.e. the origin of words)?
- Does it have information on pronunciation (phonetic transcription), and, if so, what transcription system is used?
- Does it tell you where to put in hyphens?

- Is it an encoding dictionary (i.e. a dictionary which helps you produce correct English)? If so, what type of grammatical information is given, and how is it presented?
- How are the various forms of a lexeme presented?
- How are derived forms (e.g. *friendship* from *friend*) presented?
- How is the sense of a lexeme explained?
  - in lexicographese (i.e. using short, condensed phrases often containing words which are more difficult than the one we are looking up)
  - by using a defining vocabulary (i.e. in a language with a limited number of words)
  - in full sentences with an authentic ring (e.g. *a lynx is a wild animal of the cat family*)
- How are polysemy and homonymy handled?
- Is there any information on possible synonyms and autonyms of entries?
- Does it have information on text varieties (formal/informal, British/American, etc.)?
- How is usage illustrated?
  - by means of full sentences or just phrases
  - by genuine attested examples
  - by modified attested examples
- Do the examples give enough information on collocations?
- Are idiomatic expressions included? If so, where are they placed?
- Does the dictionary have extra boxes with information on usage, grammar, etc.?
- How user-friendly is the dictionary?
- How detailed is the introduction (which helps you understand the organization of the dictionary and explains abbreviations, special symbols, etc.)?

You will understand from this list of questions that dictionary makers have some hard thinking to do before they can decide on what are the best solutions for their book.

3.9.2 Examples from four dictionaries

In the examples below, we have drawn special attention to grammatical information in the dictionaries. Note especially the information on type of noun (countable or uncountable), type of adjective, and verb patterns.

Collins COBUILD English Language Dictionary

stagger /stægə/, **staggers, staggering, staggered**. 1 If you **stagger**, you walk or stand very unsteadily, as if you are about to fall. EG *I staggered to the nearest chair... We managed to stagger back up to the deck.*

V: USU+A — verb usually followed by an adverbial
= lurch

2 If something **staggers** you, it makes you feel surprised and shocked, usually because it is so unexpected that you can hardly believe it; an informal use. EG *...an event that staggered the world.*

V+O — verb plus direct object
↑ amaze
= astound

◇ **staggered**. EG *We were staggered to learn they would be closing down the college.* ◇ **staggering**. EG *Its estimated cost has climbed to a staggering £35 billion... The effects are staggering.* ◇ **staggeringly**. EG *...staggeringly high prices.*

◇ ADJ QUALIT — qualitative adjective (gradable)
◇ ADJ QUALIT
= stunning
◇ ADV+ADJ/ADV

3 If things such as people's holidays or hours of work are **staggered**, they are arranged so that they do not all happen at the same time. EG *The summer holidays are staggered so that we can keep the factory running... They staggered their church-going hours.*

V+O: USU PASS

stagnant /stægnənt/. 1 If something such as a situation is **stagnant**, it is unsuccessful or dull because it is not changing or developing in any way. EG *...a stagnant society... British shipbuilding output remained stagnant at around one million tons a year.*

ADJ CLASSIF — classifying adjective (non-gradable)
= sluggish, stale

2 **Stagnant** water is not flowing or moving, and therefore often smells unpleasant. EG *The White Volta dries up into a string of stagnant pools in the summer.*

ADJ CLASSIF
↑ still
= brackish, stale

stagnate /stægneɪt, stægneɪt/, **stagnates, stagnating, stagnated**. If a situation **stagnates**, it is unsuccessful or dull because it is not changing or developing in any way. EG *The economy stagnated as a result of these tax measures... The party's membership has stagnated and its electoral performance has declined.* ◇ **stagnation** /stægneɪʃən/. EG *Industrial stagnation inevitably leads to the loss of jobs.*

V — intransitive verb
◇ N UNCOUNT — uncountable noun

utter /ʌtə/, **utters, uttering, uttered**. 1 When you **utter** sounds or words, you say them in order to communicate ideas and feelings. EG *Sam opened his mouth, then quickly shut it again without uttering a sound... She had never been known to utter an unkind word to anyone... He seldom uttered, but when he did everyone listened.*

V OR V+O

2 You use **utter** to give emphasis to the noun which follows it by indicating that the quality or emotion mentioned is total and without any limits. EG *To my utter amazement I was made managing director... Most of my friends believe that Judith is a complete and utter fool... Only now can I say with utter conviction that I do believe in God... He laboured in the service of his country with utter disregard of his own well-being.*

ADJ CLASSIF
ATTRIB — attributive-only adjective
= absolute

utterance /ʌtərəns/, **utterances**; a fairly formal word. 1 An **utterance** is something which is expressed in speech or in writing, such as a word, a sentence, or a number of sentences. EG *The children watched and copied every act and utterance of the older men... May I suggest that in your public utterances you should emphasize the things the Government has achieved.*

N COUNT — countable noun
↑ expression

2 Utterance is the expression in words of ideas, thoughts, and feelings. ■G *He was now ready to give utterance to his intentions... The mere utterance of the word 'Rogers' seemed to frighten my aunt.* — N UNCOUNT

utterly /ʌtəli¹/. You use **utterly** to give emphasis to the adjective or verb with which it is being used, in order to indicate that the quality mentioned is complete and total. ■G *I am utterly convinced of your loyalty to your colleagues... On the other side of the island, the view was utterly different... My thirteen-year-old niece was standing at the door trying to look like a young lady but failing utterly.* — ADV = absolutely, totally, completely — adverb

The grammatical information is placed in a separate column, and the abbreviations can easily be interpreted. Note that it is possible to look up all the grammatical abbreviations in the actual dictionary. A special feature of this dictionary is that all uses of a word are included in the same entry (whereas most dictionaries normally have separate entries for each word class).

Longman Dictionary of Contemporary English

verb — intransitive + adverb or preposition

stag·ger¹ /ˈstægəʳ/ *v* **1** [I+*adv/prep*] to walk or move unsteadily and with great difficulty, almost falling: *The drunken man staggered towards us/away.* | *He staggered to the door, bleeding from his wounds.* | (*infml*) *I finally staggered into bed at 3 o'clock in the morning.* —compare TOTTER **2** [T] to cause to feel shocked disbelief; seem almost unbelievable to: *Her incredible story staggers the imagination.* | *I was staggered by his outrageous suggestion.* **3** [T] to arrange (esp. working hours, holidays, etc.) not to begin and end at the same time — transitive

noun — **stagger²** *n* an unsteady movement of a person having trouble walking or standing

adjective — **stag·ger·ing** /ˈstægərɪŋ/ *adj* almost unbelievable; very surprising and shocking: *It cost a staggering £30,000!* —~**ly** *adv*

noun — **stag·ing** /ˈsteɪdʒɪŋ/ *n* **1** [C;U] the action or art of performing a play: *an imaginative modern-dress staging of "Hamlet"* **2** [U] movable boards and frames for standing on; SCAFFOLDING — countable uncountable

staging post /ˈ·· ·/ *n* a place at which regular stops are made on long journeys: *Bahrain is a staging post on the flight from Britain to Australia* —compare STOPOVER

adjective — **stag·nant** /ˈstægnənt/ *adj* **1** (esp. of water) not flowing or moving, and often bad-smelling: *a stagnant pond covered with scum* **2** not developing or growing; inactive; STATIC: *Due to low investment, our industrial output has remained stagnant.* —~**ly** *adv* —**-nancy** *n* [U]

stag·nate /stægˈneɪt‖ˈstægneɪt/ *v* [I] to become stagnant; stop moving or developing: *a stagnating economy* | *She didn't want to stagnate in her dull office job until she retired.* —**-nation** /stægˈneɪʃən/ *n* [U]: *economic stagnation*

adjective — **ut·ter¹** /ˈʌtəʳ/ *adj* [A] (esp. of something bad) complete: ABSOLUTE: *It was an utter waste of time.* | *What utter rubbish he talks!* | *an utter moron* —see LANGUAGE NOTE: Intensifying Adjectives — attributive only

verb — **utter²** *v* [T] *esp. fml or lit* to make (a sound) or produce (words), sometimes with difficulty: *The wounded man uttered a groan.* | *She didn't utter a word all night.* — transitive

ut·ter·ance /ˈʌtərəns/ *n esp. fml or tech* **1** [U] the act of speaking: *She has not yet* **given utterance to** (= expressed) *her opinion.* **2** [C] something that is said: *Politicians have to be very careful in their public utterances.* — uncountable; countable

adverb — **ut·ter·ly** /ˈʌtəli ‖ -ər-/ *adv* completely: *You're utterly crazy!* | *He was utterly charmed by her.* —see LANGUAGE NOTE: Gradable and Non-gradable Adjectives

The grammatical coding is fully explained in the preface to the dictionary. There are special language notes on particular grammatical points (see *utter* above).

Oxford University Press, *Oxford Advanced Learner's Dictionary*

intransitive verb; transitive verb — verb pattern 2A: no complement needed; verb pattern 2C: with adverbial

stag·ger /ˈstægə(r)/ *vi, vt* **1** [VP2A,C] walk or move unsteadily (from weakness, a heavy burden, drunkenness, etc): *The man* ~*ed along/to his feet/across the room/from side to side of the road.* **2** [VP6A] (of a blow or shock) cause to walk or move unsteadily; (of news, etc) shock deeply; cause worry or confusion to: *receive a* ~*ing blow.* *I was* ~*ed to hear/on hearing/when I heard that the firm was bankrupt.* **3** [VP6A] arrange (times of events) so that they do not all occur together: ~ *office hours,* so that employees are not all using buses, trains, etc, at the same time; ~ *the annual holidays.* □ *n* **1** (*sing*) ~ing movement. **2 the** ~**s**, giddiness; nervous disease of cattle and horses, marked by ~ing. ~**er** *n* — verb pattern 6A: with direct object

noun — **stag·ing** /ˈsteɪdʒɪŋ/ *n* **1** [C,U] stage(6); (platform or working area on) scaffolding for men on constructional work, e g building. **2** [U] (method of) presenting a play on the stage of a theatre. — countable; uncountable

adjective — **stag·nant** /ˈstægnənt/ *adj* **1** (of water) without current or tide; still and stale: *water lying* ~ *in ponds and ditches.* **2** (fig) unchanging; inactive: *Business was* ~ *last week.* **stag·nancy** /-nənsɪ/ *n*

stag·nate /stægˈneɪt *US:* ˈstægneɪt/ *vi* [VP2A] be stagnant; (fig) be or become dull or sluggish through disuse, inactivity, etc. **stag·na·tion** /stægˈneɪʃn/ *n* [U].

adjective — **ut·ter¹** /ˈʌtə(r)/ *adj* complete; total: ~ *darkness; an ~ scoundrel. She's an ~ stranger to me.* **~·ly**

adverb — *adv* **1** completely. **2** to the depths of one's being: *She ~ly detests him.*

transitive verb — **ut·ter²** /ˈʌtə(r)/ *vt* [VP6A] **1** make (a sound or sounds) with the mouth: ~ *a sigh/a cry of pain.* **2** say: *the last words he ~ed.* **3** put (false money, etc) into circulation. **~·ance** /ˈʌtərəns/ *n* **1** (*sing only*) way of speaking: *a clear/defective/very rapid ~ance.* **2** [C] sth said; spoken word or words. **3** [U] *give ~ance to* (*one's feelings, etc*), express in words.

ut·ter·most /ˈʌtəməʊst/ *adj, n* = utmost: *the ~ ends of the earth.*

The grammatical coding is fully explained in the preface to the dictionary.

Merriam-Webster's Collegiate Dictionary

verb — **¹stag·ger** \ˈsta-gər\ *vb* **stag·gered; stag·ger·ing** \-g(ə-)riŋ\ [alter. of earlier *stacker,* fr. ME *stakeren,* fr. ON *stakra,* freq. of *staka* to push; perh. akin to OE *staca* stake — more at STAKE] — information on etymology

vi (15c) **1 a :** to reel from side to side : TOTTER **b :** to move on unsteadily **2 :** to waver in purpose or action : HESITATE **3 :** to rock violently ⟨the ship ~*ed*⟩ ~

transitive verb — *vt* **1 :** to cause to doubt or hesitate : PERPLEX **2 :** to cause to reel or totter **3 :** to arrange in any of various zigzags, alternations, or overlappings of position or time ⟨~ work shifts⟩ ⟨~ teeth on a cutter⟩ — **stag·ger·er** \-gər-ər\ *n*

²stagger *n* (1577) **1** *pl but sing or pl in constr* **:** an abnormal condition of domestic mammals and birds associated with damage to the central nervous system and marked by incoordination and a reeling unsteady gait **2 :** a reeling or unsteady gait or stance **3 :** an arrangement in which the leading edge of the upper wing of a biplane is advanced over that of the lower — noun, with information on grammar

³stagger *adj* (1875) **:** marked by an alternating or overlapping pattern — adjective

stag·ger·bush \ˈsta-gər-ˌbu̇sh\ *n* (1847) **:** a shrubby heath (*Lyonia mariana*) of the eastern U.S. that is poisonous to livestock — encyclopaedic information

staggering *adj* (1530) **:** so great as to cause one to stagger : ASTONISHING, OVERWHELMING ⟨a ~ feat⟩ ⟨~ medical bills⟩ — **stag·ger·ing·ly**

adverb — \ˈsta-g(ə-)riŋ-lē\ *adv*

stag·gery \ˈsta-g(ə-)rē\ *adj* (1778) **:** UNSTEADY

stag·gy \ˈsta-gē\ *adj* (1918) **:** having the appearance of a mature male — used of female or castrated male domestic animals — date shows earliest recorded use

stag·horn coral \ˈstag-ˌhȯrn-\ *n* (1884) **:** any of several large branching corals (genus *Acropora* and esp. *A. cervicornis*) that somewhat resemble antlers

staghorn sumac *n* (ca. 1868) **:** a sumac (*Rhus typhina*) of eastern No. America that is a shrub or small tree with velvety-pubescent branches and flower stalks, leaves turning brilliant red in fall, and dense panicles of greenish yellow flowers followed by hairy crimson fruits

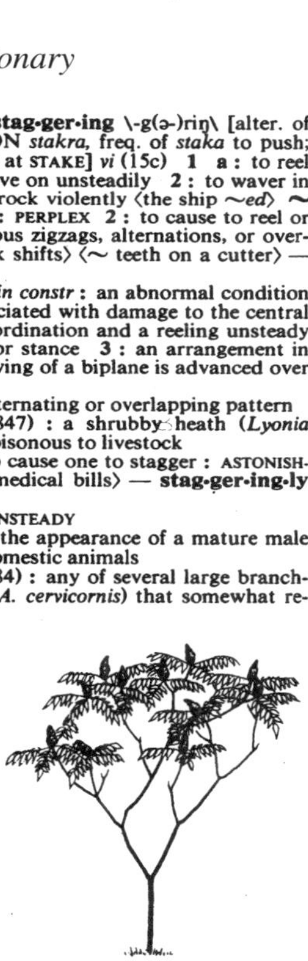

staghorn sumac

stag·hound \ˈstag-ˌhau̇nd\ *n* (1707) **:** a hound formerly used in hunting the stag and other large animals; *specif* **:** a large heavy hound resembling the English foxhound

stag·ing \ˈstā-jiŋ\ *n* (14c) **1 :** SCAFFOLDING **2 a :** the business of running stagecoaches **b :** the act of journeying in stagecoaches **3 :** the putting of a play on the stage **4 a :** the moving of troops or matériel forward in several stages **b :** the assembling of troops or matériel in transit in a particular place

staging area *n* (1943) **:** an area in which participants in a new operation or mission are assembled and readied

Stag·i·rite \ˈsta-jə-ˌrīt\ *n* [Gk *Stagiritēs,* fr. *Stagira,* city in ancient Macedonia] (ca. 1620) **:** a native or resident of Stagira ⟨Aristotle the ~⟩

stag·nant \ˈstag-nənt\ *adj* (1666) **1 a :** not flowing in a current or stream ⟨~ water⟩ **b :** STALE ⟨long disuse had made the air ~ and foul —Bram Stoker⟩ **2 :** not advancing or developing — **stag·nan·cy** \-nən(t)-sē\ *n* — **stag·nant·ly** *adv*

stag·nate \ˈstag-ˌnāt\ *vi* **stag·nat·ed; stag·nat·ing** [L *stagnatus,* pp. of *stagnare,* fr. *stagnum* body of standing water] (1669) **:** to become or remain stagnant — **stag·na·tion** \stag-ˈnā-shən\ *n* — intransitive verb

[1]**ut·ter** \'ə-tər\ *adj* [ME, remote, fr. OE *ūtera* outer, compar. adj. fr. *ūt* out, adv. — more at OUT] (15c) : carried to the utmost point or highest degree : ABSOLUTE, TOTAL ⟨~ darkness⟩ ⟨~ strangers⟩ — **ut·ter·ly** *adv*

[2]**utter** *vb* [ME *uttren,* fr. *utter* outside, adv., fr. OE *ūtor,* compar. of *ūt* out] *vt* (15c) **1** *obs* : to offer for sale **2 a** : to send forth as a sound **b** : to give utterance to : PRONOUNCE, SPEAK **c** : to give public expression to : express in words **3** : to put (as currency) into circulation; *specif* : to circulate (as a counterfeit note) as if legal or genuine ⟨~ false tokens⟩ **4** : to put forth or out : DISCHARGE ~ *vi* : to make a statement or sound ***syn*** see EXPRESS — **ut·ter·able** \'ə-tə-rə-bəl\ *adj* — **ut·ter·er** \'ə-tər-ər\ *n*

[1]**ut·ter·ance** \'ə-tə-rən(t)s, 'ə-trən(t)s\ *n* [ME *uttraunce,* modif. of MF *outrance* — more at OUTRANCE] (15c) *archaic* : the last extremity : BITTER END

[2]**ut·ter·ance** \'ə-tə-rən(t)s *also* 'ə-trən(t)s\ *n* (15c) **1** : something uttered; *esp* : an oral or written statement : a stated or published expression **2** : vocal expression : SPEECH **3** : power, style, or manner of speaking

[1]**ut·ter·most** \'ə-tər-ˌmōst\ *adj* [ME, alter. of *uttermest,* fr. [1]*utter* + *-mest* (as in *utmest* utmost)] (14c) **1** : OUTERMOST **2** : EXTREME, UTMOST

[2]**uttermost** *n* (14c) : UTMOST ⟨to the ~ of our capacity —H. S. Truman⟩

cross-reference to synonyms

obs=obsolete; usage note

syn=synonym; usage note

archaic; usage note

The dictionary has both an explanatory chart and 13 pages of explanatory notes.

Terms

word:	orthographic definition	collocation
	type and token	connotation
lexeme:	polysemy	evaluation scale
	homonymy	intensity scale
sense:	fuzzy category	emotive/biased language
	prototype	euphemism, dysphemism, epithet
	precise category	obfuscation
		false friend
		translation loan
		'lexical teddy bear'
	synonymy	
	antonymy	mental lexicon
	hyponymy	
	superordinate term	
	core word	
referent/reference		
text variety:	formality	
	register	
	regional variation	
	jargon	

Exercises

1 Try to determine how many words there are in the following sentences. Discuss any problem you may have. (**3.2**)

a He caught sight of Gloria sitting on the floor in the darkest corner of the room.
b He's said he's going to help us fix the vacuum cleaner.
c He's been known to sail close to the wind on several occasions.

2 The following verbs can all have the core sense 'express something in words', but they differ in their finer shades of meaning. Explain how they differ. (**3.4.2**)

say, claim, allege, maintain, assert, declare, state

3 Put in the most appropriate verb from the list of near-synonyms below in the open spaces in the following sentences. Choose the correct form of the verb as required by the co-text.
Each verb should be used only once. (**3.4.2**, **3.6.1**)

reach, attain, gain, achieve, accomplish

a He was really pleased with what he had ______ in life.
b When they ____ the shore on the other side of the lake, they made a fire.
c I am relatively new in the job, but I'm already _____ experience.
d Rod _____ good results in the test.
e After several years of clever political manoeuvring, he _____ the position of junior minister.

4 Put in the most appropriate adjective from the list of near-synonyms below in the open spaces in the following sentences. Each adjective should be used only once. (**3.4.3**, **3.6.1**)

apt, liable, prone, subject, susceptible

a Foreigners are _____ to be stopped by the police.
b People from hot climates are ______ to the cold.
c The road is _____ to flooding.
d His cousin is _____ to fits of depression.
e These shoes are ____ to slip on wet ground.

5 The word *game* occurs in all the examples below. Does it have the same sense in all cases? If not, in which cases can we talk about homonymy?

Are there examples of multi-word idiomatic lexemes in these data? If yes, what do they mean? (**3.2.1B**, **3.4.4A**)

a You need two people to play this game.
b I was always hopeless at games.
c I always give the game away – you've only got to look at my face.
d Mary plays a good game of tennis.
e The men had gone to hunt wild game.
f Stop playing silly games, Jeremy!
g 'Would you like to join us?' I said. 'Of course, I'm game for anything.'
h Do I look like easy game?
i The Japanese were beating the West at its own game.

6 The text below is partly written in the jargon used in sports reports. Identify words which belong to this type of professional register. Can you find features of informal spoken English in this piece of discourse? (**3.5.1**, **3.5.3**)

Godwinson slams fixture pile-up

King Harold Godwinson last night lashed out at the fixture snarl-up which threatens the England team's chances when they take on the Norman French at Hastings later this month.

The gruelling battle the team fought with the Norwegians at Stamford Bridge on the 21st September leaves Godwinson with injuries to several key members of his squad.

'The whole thing's crazy', said Godwinson. 'At Stamford Bridge the boys done wonderful. Afterward we were over the comet. But how can we build up our national side playing so many battles in a season? The Normans have had their squad together for months now; yet we are supposed to get together in a few days.'

(From *The Lavishly Tooled Smith & Jones*)

7 Arrange the following sentences in terms of level of formality. (**3.5.1**)

a Hats off, please.
b Patrons are kindly requested to doff their hats.
c Please, take off your headgear.
d Customers are asked to remove their hats.

8 The two extracts below are from J. D. Salinger, *The Catcher in the Rye*. Identify examples of informal, colloquial language (slang, swear-words, etc.) in both grammar and lexis in these two extracts. (**3.5.1**)

Anyway, the corridor was all linoleum and all, and you could hear his goddam footsteps coming right towards the room. I don't even remember where I was sitting when he came in – at the window, or in my chair or his. I swear I can't remember.

He came in griping about how cold it was. Then he said, 'Where the hell is everybody? It's like a goddam morgue around here.'

'God damn it.' He was sore as hell. He was really furious. 'You always do everything backasswards.' He looked at me. 'No wonder you're flunking the hell out of here,' he said. 'You don't do one damn thing the way you're supposed to. I mean it. Not one damn thing.'

9 The following sentences contain italicized dialect words from Scotland and northern England. They are probably related to Old Norse words etymologically. (**3.5.2**) Guess what they mean.

a We'll just *rive* it out of the ground.
b I feel fit as a *lop*.
c Your side can't *laik* football.
d She'd *flitted* to Bridlington.
e There's a *beck* down in the valley.
f The *kirk* is on yon side.
g They've got their *bairns* visiting.

10 This text is an ironic description of a once-thriving coastal village. Most of its old cottages have been turned into second homes for the city-rich, who visit the village only during weekends, their small boats hitched on to trailers. Identify examples of literary words in this text. Does it contain any literary allusions? (**3.5.4**)

It's lonely in Tresoddit when the fleet's away. The little hamlet holds its breath and gazes out to sea and waits for the safe return of its wayfaring ones. And those remaining sons and daughters of Tresoddit, who also watch and wait, eke out a doleful existence. The streets are silent and the hostelries bereft of the regulars; oilskinned, sea-booted, filling the bar with salty chat. Only the wind howls down the chimneys of all those depleted hearths – Crab's Pots, Thrift Cottage, Ocean Spray. And then one day, the first sail is spotted. Soon the fleet blows into its haven for a sojourn, which must be all too brief. But for a short while, the streets are full of merry mariners and all the tills ring.

(Adapted from Posy Simmonds, *Very Posy*)

11 Give (near-)synonyms of the following words. Discuss any problems you may have. (**3.6.1**)

answer, component, rationale, punishment, leave out, evaluate, get acquainted with, give up, postpone, quit, remember

12 The language of advertising often depends on word-plays, where the written and spoken forms of two lexemes are identical or similar although their senses are different. Explain the word-plays in these examples. (**3.7.1**)

a People who can. Not people who con. (political slogan for Labour)
b Labour isn't working. (political slogan for the Tory party)
c I think therefore IBM. (ad for IBM)
d I think more carefully therefore I Amstrad. (follow-up ad from Amstrad)
e Better late than the late (road safety campaign)
f The Loan Arranger (ad for a credit institution)
g We won't stand alone. (student slogan in campaign to keep their grants)
h Better in jams than strawberries (ad for a small car)

13 Identify cases of lexical dissonance in these Norwegian-produced examples. Suggest improvements and try to determine what type of lexical dissonance each case exemplifies. (**3.8**)

a As children we often heard that we would come to heaven when we died.
b Personally, if I could choose over again, I would take modern languages and history.
c Some people still believe that you can be attacked by icebears in the northern parts of Norway.
d We really enjoyed the party last night. Your friends were so cosy.
e There was a leakage in one of the water pipes.
f The family moved to our village some months ago and they seem to be thriving here.
g This will always remind me of my fatherland and what it has to offer me.
h But at least one thing is sure.
i My vision is of people walking around, smiling and laughing, eating grapes and generally being enormously happy.
j These Vikings are believed to have attacked everything they came over.
k Could you ring me when you come there?
l During the Olympics at Lillehammer the world saw Norway at its best; plenty of snow and cold degrees.
m This was a punch in the face for our EU-friendly government.
n He showed tremendous engagement in his work for the homeless.
o The poor little boy had been mobbed by his classmates for more than a month.

p They have been consequent in opposing the plan for a bridge across the strait.
q The two bothers looked very elegant in their smokings.
r The police had received a number of tips before the murder.
s You see only the top of the iceberg. That's what makes them so dangerous.
t The meat is very salt.
u What a genial idea!
v Some guests held beautiful speeches on the occasion of his 60th anniversary.
w He draws a regular salary, and on top of that he gets a nice provision.
x John works very effectively.
y We are thinking of a garden party, but can, eventually, go indoors if the weather is not good.

14 Compare the entry for *stagger* below, taken from the *Cambridge International Dictionary of English,* with the corresponding entry in the *Longman Dictionary of Contemporary English* as shown in **3.9.** What are the most noticeable differences?

stag·ger [MOVE] /£ˈstæg·əʳ, $-ɚ/ *v* [I] to walk or move in a way that shows a lack of balance as if you are going to fall • *After he was attacked, he managed to stagger* **to** *the phone and call for help.* • *As we went into the bar, a drunken man staggered* **out of** *the door.* • *Every morning she would wake up at 7a.m. and stagger half-awake* **into** *the bathroom to get washed.* • *(fig.) The company is staggering* **under** *a $15 million debt and will almost certainly collapse by the end of the year.*

stag·ger /£ˈstæg·əʳ, $-ɚ/ *n* [C usually sing] • *He left the pub with a drunken stagger.*

stag·ger *obj* [SHOCK] /£ˈstæg·əʳ, $-ɚ/ *v* [T] to cause (someone) to feel shocked or surprised because of something unexpected or very unusual happening • *They'd only known each other for two weeks so I was staggered to hear that they'd decided to get married.* • *He staggered all his colleagues by suddenly announcing that he was leaving the company at the end of the month.*

stag·ger·ing /£ˈstæg·ᵊr·ɪŋ, $ˈ-ɚ-/ *adj* • *She won the race by a staggering seven seconds.* • *It costs a staggering $50 000 per week to keep the museum open to the public.*

stag·ger·ing·ly /£ˈstæg·ᵊr·ɪŋ·li, $ˈ-ɚ-/ *adv* • *The bank charged me a staggeringly high rate of interest on my £5000 loan.* • *She gave a staggeringly good performance in the TV programme as a police officer investigating a murder.*

stag·ger *obj* [ARRANGE] /£ˈstæg·əʳ, $-ɚ/ *v* [T] to arrange, esp. hours of work, holidays or events, so that they begin at **different times from those of other people** • *Lunch breaks for shop workers are often staggered so that shops can stay open over lunchtime.* • *Travellers are being advised to stagger their journeys this weekend as long delays are expected on main roads.* • *Many countries have introduced a system of staggered holidays in schools so that roads and holiday resorts do not become overcrowded.* • If a race has a staggered **start** the competitors start at different times or in different positions: *The official starter's gun set the seven all-women teams off on a staggered start.* • *(Br) A* **staggered junction** *is a place where several roads meet a main road at a slight distance apart so that they do not all come together at the same point.*

stag·ing /ˈsteɪ·dʒɪŋ/ *n* [C] See at STAGE [THEATRE]

stag·nant [NOT FLOWING] /ˈstæg·nənt/ *adj* not flowing or moving and smelling unpleasant • *There is a stagnant* **pool** *at the bottom of the garden.* • *Disease is a serious threat in the region because food is in short supply and the water is stagnant.* • *People who live in crowded cities often experience breathing problems during the summer when high temperatures combine with stagnant polluted air.*

stag·nant [NOT BUSY] /ˈstæg·nənt/ *adj* not growing or developing • *The stagnant property* **market** *is making it very difficult for many people to sell their houses.* • *In 1991, while the* **economies** *of industrialized countries were stagnant, the economies of many developing countries were growing rapidly.*

stag·nate /£stægˈneɪt, $ˈstæg·neɪt/ *v* [I] • *The electronics industry is showing signs of stagnating after 15 years of tremendous growth.*

stag·na·tion /stægˈneɪ·ʃᵊn/ *n* [U] • *A fear of unemployment is one of the main factors behind the current stagnation in the property market.* • *If the* **economic** *stagnation in many countries is to be overcome, trade needs to be increased between industrial and developing nations.*

4 Nouns and Noun Phrases

4.1 Some characteristics of noun phrases

4.1.1 Noun phrases are referring units

Noun phrases are abundant in any text. The noun phrases are enclosed within square brackets in the following text (adapted from a visitor's guide to Liverpool):

> [Liverpool] is [a vibrant and exciting place to visit] and [a warm welcome] is always guaranteed. [The centre] is alive with [theatres, clubs, restaurants and attractions that are able to provide something for everyone]. [It] is [one of the world's most famous and historic cities] and [its distinguished life as a centre for world trade and commerce] is clearly reflected in [its rich culture and architectural heritage].

If we take away the noun phrases from this text, there is very little left:

> [-] is [-] and [-] is always guaranteed. [-] is alive with [-]. [-] is [-] and [-] is clearly reflected in [-].

If instead we keep only the noun phrases, the result is quite different:

> [Liverpool] - [a vibrant and exciting place to visit] - [a warm welcome] - [The centre] - [theatres, clubs, restaurants and attractions that are able to provide something for everyone]. [It] - [one of the world's most famous and historic cities] - [its distinguished life as a centre for world trade and commerce] - [its rich culture and architectural heritage].

Here most of the meaning is preserved. This is because noun phrases are referring units: they identify what we are talking or writing about.

4.1.2 Noun phrases vary in complexity

Noun phrases vary from single words to long and complex structures. Often a single word (e.g. a proper noun like *Liverpool* or a pronoun like *it*) or a determiner and a noun (e.g. *the centre*) are sufficient to clarify what we are referring to. To express new information, which is the purpose of the sample text above, we normally need to use more complex noun phrases. The overall structure of the noun phrase is summarized in Table 4a.

Table 4a: The overall structure of the noun phrase

Determiner	**Premodifier**	**Head**	**Postmodifier**
		Liverpool	
		it	
the		centre	
its	distinguished	life	as a centre for world trade and commerce
a	vibrant and exciting	place	to visit

Noun phrases may also be co-ordinated (e.g. *its rich culture and architectural heritage*). Above all, the complexity of noun phrases arises from the embedding of noun phrases within noun phrases (e.g. in the postmodifier *as a centre for world trade and commerce*). See **4.11**.

4.1.3 Types of noun phrase

Noun phrases are of two main types: noun-headed phrases (or full noun phrases) and pronoun-headed phrases. This chapter focuses on nouns; pronouns are dealt with in the next chapter.

4.2 What is a noun?

Most typically, nouns are characterized by the following features:

A They are inflected for number and, less consistently, for case: *a **girl** - some **girls**, the **girl's** parents, the two **girls'** parents.*

B They can occur as the head of a noun phrase: *the new* ***girls*** *in my class*. Noun phrases in their turn can be used in a range of positions to build up larger structures. See **2.8.1**.

C They commonly denote concrete entities, such as persons, things, and places (*a girl*, *a book*, *Liverpool*), but may also designate substances (*air*, *sand*, *water*) and abstract notions (*advice*, *kindness*, *warmth*).

These features are morphological (A), syntactic (B), and semantic (C), respectively.

4.3 Types of nouns

Not all nouns behave in the same way. We distinguish between **common nouns** and **proper nouns**. Common nouns can be **countable** or **uncountable**. See Table 4b.

Table 4b: The main classes of nouns

Class	Number		Articles	
	Singular	Plural	Indefinite	Definite
Countable	girl	girls	a girl	the girl
Uncountable	advice	-	-	the advice
Proper	Sally	-	-	-

Countable nouns vary in number and combine with both the definite and the indefinite article. Uncountable nouns do not vary in number and combine only with the definite article. Proper nouns generally do not vary in number, nor do they normally combine with articles.

The relationship between the classes is, however, more complicated. Many nouns can be both countable and uncountable (**4.5.3**). Moreover, there is not always a clear borderline between common nouns and proper nouns (**4.7.2**).

4.4 Countable nouns

Countable nouns denote entities that can be counted. They have both singular and plural forms, and combine with determiners that imply countability (numerals, the indefinite article, *every* and *each*, etc.). Countable nouns may be both concrete and abstract:

Concrete: bird, body, book, car, house, monkey, part, pupil, teacher, town, etc.
Abstract: action, difficulty, event, idea, pleasure, problem, result, etc.

In monolingual English dictionaries, countable nouns are generally given the label **C**.

4.4.1 Regular plurals

The regular plural ending is *-(e)s*, which is pronounced:

/s/ after voiceless consonants except /s, ʃ, tʃ/: *book - books, cat - cats, step - steps*;

/z/ after vowels and voiced consonants except /z, ʒ, dʒ/: *bed - beds, dog - dogs, toe - toes*;

/ɪz/ after /s, z, ʃ, ʒ, tʃ, dʒ/: *case - cases, size - sizes, wedge - wedges.*

The normal written form of the plural ending is *-s*, but if the word ends in /s, z, ʃ, ʒ, tʃ, dʒ/ and is not spelt with a final *-e*, the ending takes the form *-es*: *boss - bosses, bush - bushes, match - matches.* Note especially:

A If the word ends in a consonant plus *-y*, the ending is *-ies*: *baby - babies, spy - spies.* But: *day - days, essay - essays.* Note also the plural of names: *the Hardys, the Brodskys.*

B Some words ending in *-o* have plural forms ending in *-oes*: *echo - echoes, hero - heroes, Negro - Negroes, potato - potatoes, tomato - tomatoes, tornado - tornadoes, torpedo - torpedoes, veto - vetoes.* Most words ending in *-o*, however, simply add an *-s*: *avocado - avocados, disco - discos, Eskimo - Eskimos*, etc.

NB! Do not confuse the spelling of the regular plural ending with the genitive suffix (**5.5.1**). The plural is only exceptionally spelt with an apostrophe, notably in cases like: *A's and B's, mind one's p's and q's* ('be careful and polite about about what one says or does', *Oxford Advanced Learner's Dictionary*). Although there is variation, it is preferable to omit the apostrophe in referring to decades, e.g. *the 1960s.*

4.4.2 Irregular plurals

A small number of native words have irregular plural forms. The most common types are listed below.

A Vowel change

man - men	foot - feet
woman - women	goose - geese
louse - lice	tooth - teeth
mouse - mice	

Compounds ending in *-man* and *-woman* behave like the simple forms: *postman - postmen, policewoman - policewomen*. But: *German - Germans, Roman - Romans, Walkman - Walkmans. Mouse* may be treated as a regular noun when it refers to the hand-held device used to operate a computer. *Foot* takes a zero plural in some contexts (**4.4.4B**).

B Adding -(r)en

child - children	ox - oxen

The plural *brethren* (of *brother*) is archaic except when used about or by certain religious groups.

C Consonant change

calf - calves	scarf - scarves
half - halves	sheaf - sheaves
knife - knives	shelf - shelves
leaf - leaves	thief - thieves
life - lives	wife - wives
loaf - loaves	wolf - wolves

The majority of words ending in *-f*, however, are regular: *belief - beliefs, chef - chefs, handkerchief - handkerchiefs, proof - proofs, roof - roofs*, etc. All words ending in *-ff* are regular: *cliff - cliffs, puff - puffs*, etc. There is variation with: *dwarf - dwarfs/dwarves, hoof - hoofs/hooves, turf - turfs/turves, wharf - wharfs/wharves* ('brygge, kai').

4.4.3 Foreign plurals

Some words borrowed from Latin and Greek keep their foreign plural, or there may be alternation with regular plural forms. Where there is variation, the regular forms are preferred in everyday language.

A Latin nouns ending in *-us*

alumnus - alumni nucleus - nuclei

But: *focus - foci/focuses, cactus - cacti/cactuses, crocus - crocuses, syllabus - syllabuses.*

B Latin nouns ending in *-um*

maximum - maxima
minimum - minima
spectrum - spectra
stratum - strata

But: *aquarium - aquaria/aquariums, curriculum - curricula/curriculums, memorandum - memoranda/memorandums, stadium - stadia/stadiums.* The foreign plurals *data* and *media* have been dissociated from the original singular forms and are treated as singular or plural:

1 We analysed *these data* carefully.
2 *This data* is presented in Figure 1.

3 *The media are* to blame.
4 *The media seems* to ignore the problem.

The foreign learner is advised to treat the forms as plural (as in examples 1 and 3).

C Latin nouns ending in *-a*

alga - algae
antenna - antennae/antennas
formula - formulae/formulas

D Latin nouns ending in *-ex/-ix*

appendix - appendices/appendixes
index - indices/indexes

E Greek nouns ending in *-is*

analysis - analyses
crisis - crises
diagnosis - diagnoses
hypothesis - hypotheses
oasis - oases
thesis - theses

F Greek nouns ending in *-on*

automaton - automata
criterion - criteria
phenomenon - phenomena

4.4.4 Zero plurals

Some nouns have no overt plural endings. These are called zero plurals. The most important groups are:

A Words for some animals

cod, perch ('åbor'), pike ('gjedde'), plaice ('rødspette'), salmon, trout ('ørret'), deer, reindeer, moose ('elg'), sheep, grouse ('rype')

1 This *sheep* is black. Those *sheep* are white.
2 I caught two *salmon*.

Some other nouns are found with both a regular plural and a zero plural: *fish – fish(es), buffalo – buffalo(es).*

3 These *fishes* are nice, aren't they?
4 We caught a lot of *fish*.
5 They were hunting for *buffalo*.

The zero plural is preferred where the reference is not to specific entities, but is more general (as in the context of fishing or hunting).

B Quantifying nouns

dozen	thousand
hundred	million

The zero plural is used in examples with a preceding numeral: *two dozen eggs, two hundred dollars, twenty thousand pounds, 50 million people*. But: *dozens of times, hundreds of people, thousands of dollars, millions of viewers. Foot* and *pound* take the zero plural in examples like:

6 She is five *foot* ten. (= five feet and ten inches)
7 The floor is ten *foot* square.
8 He gave me a five-*pound* note.

Note also the zero plural *stone* (British unit of measurement = 14 pounds), as in: *She weighs ten stone.*

C Other zero plurals

aircraft, hovercraft ('luftputebåt'), spacecraft
Chinese, Japanese, Portuguese, etc.; Swiss
series, species ('art')
barracks, blues, crossroads, dice ('terning'), headquarters, means, works ('verk, fabrikkanlegg')

9 This animal belongs to an endangered *species*.
10 We should do more to save these endangered *species*.

4.4.5 Plural-only nouns

Some plural nouns have no corresponding singular form, e.g. *clothes* (cf. Norwegian 'klær'). In other cases, there is a singular form with a different meaning, e.g. *arm - arms*. When it refers to a limb, *arm* is a regular countable noun with the plural *arms*. But *arms* in the sense of 'weapons' has no corresponding singular form and is best treated as a plural-only noun. Plural-only nouns do not normally combine with numerals: **two scissors*, **two pants*. In monolingual dictionaries, plural-only nouns may be identified by the label **n plural**.

A Words referring to things consisting of two equal parts

binoculars ('kikkert')	pliers ('nebbtang')
briefs ('herretruse')	pyjamas, pajamas (AmE)
compasses ('passer')	scissors
denims/jeans	shorts
glasses ('briller')	spectacles ('briller')
knickers (BrE 'dametruse')	tongs ('tang')
panties (AmE 'dametruse')	trousers
pants (AmE 'bukser')	trunks ('badebukse')

1 These *binoculars* are good. *They* were made in Japan.
2 How much are those *trousers*?

Ordinary countable reference can be achieved by the use of the noun *pair*: *a pair of binoculars, a pair of pyjamas*.

B Cattle, clergy, crew, people, police, staff

3 How many *people* were arrested?
4 The *police* are appealing for help from the public.
5 The *staff* in this office are very polite.

- *People* combines with numerals (*ten people*). For reference to a single individual it is necessary to use another noun: *a man/woman/person*. It is more common to say *ten people* than *ten persons* for the Norwegian 'ti personer'. *People* can also be a regular countable noun in the sense of 'folkeslag': *a peace-loving people, the peoples of the world*.

- *Police* may be used with numerals (*twenty police*), but more commonly we find forms like *policemen* or *police officers*. With reference to a single individual, it is necessary to use a related word, e.g. *a policeman/police-woman/police officer*.

- *Staff* and *crew* combine with numerals (*ten staff/crew*), but reference to an individual requires a form like *a member of staff/the crew* or *a staff/crew member*. When the reference is collective, we may find *staff* and *crew* treated as singular: *a staff/crew of ten*.

C Other plural-only nouns

arms ('våpen')
belongings ('eiendeler')
congratulations
contents
customs ('toll')
damages ('erstatning')
earnings ('inntekt')
goods ('varer')
guts ('innvoller; mot')
looks ('utseende')
manners ('oppførsel')
minutes ('møtereferat')
overheads ('faste utgifter')
premises ('område')
regards ('hilsen')
savings
spirits ('alkohol, humør')
stairs ('innvendig trapp')
steps ('utvendig trapp')
surroundings ('omgivelser')
thanks
troops ('tropper')
valuables
wages

Stair and *step* are used in the singular in the sense of 'trappetrinn'. The singular of *wages* is found in set phrases such as: *living wage*, *minimum wage*, *subsistence wage*. Note the difference between English and Norwegian in (6) and (7), and between *content* and *contents* in (8) and (9):

6 I would like to thank our chairman in particular.
Jeg vil rette en spesiell takk til formannen vår.
7 I would like to offer my warmest thanks to our chairman.
Jeg vil framføre min varmeste takk til formannen vår.
8 the contents of the box; the list of contents
9 the content of the essay; the silver content

D Some special cases

Some nouns which end in *-s* and look like plural nouns behave like singular uncountable nouns (as regards *news*, see **4.5.1**).

- Words for games: *billiards*, *checkers* (AmE) and *draughts* ('dam'), *dominoes*.

10 *Billiards* is a popular game.

- Words for diseases: *measles* ('meslinger'), *mumps* ('kusma').

11 *Measles* is an infectious disease.

- Nouns denoting academic disciplines: *mathematics*, *physics*, *statistics*, etc.

12 *Mathematics* is my favourite subject.

Note that nouns ending in *-ics* may behave like plural nouns in other senses (see dictionaries):

13 The *acoustics* of the concert hall are excellent.
14 The accident *statistics* are depressing.

4.5 Uncountable nouns

Uncountable nouns commonly refer to substances (*air*, *sand*), emotional and other states (*love*, *ownership*), qualities (*importance*, *strength*), and abstract concepts (*peace*, *time*). Grammatically, they are characterized by the lack of plural forms and by not combining with determiners that imply countability (the indefinite article, *each* and *every*, etc.). In monolingual English dictionaries, uncountable nouns are generally given the label **U**.

4.5.1 Differences between English and Norwegian

There are uncountable nouns in both English and Norwegian (e.g. *grass* and 'gress', *courage* and 'mot'), but the distinction is sometimes drawn differently in the two languages. Note especially the following uncountable nouns in English:

advice ('råd')
bread ('brød')
cash ('kontanter')
change ('vekslepenger')
damage ('ødeleggelser')
evidence ('bevis')
furniture ('møbler')
homework ('lekser')
income ('inntekter')
information ('opplysninger')
interest ('renter')
jewellery ('smykker')
knowledge ('kunnskaper')
money ('penger')
news ('nyheter')
progress ('framskritt')

1 She gave me *some good advice*, but I didn't follow *it*.
Hun ga meg et godt råd, men jeg fulgte det ikke.

2 We have bought *some new furniture*. – How much did *it* cost?
Vi har kjøpt noen nye møbler. – Hvor mye kostet de?

3 According to *the information* we have received, the meeting has been postponed.
Ifølge opplysningene vi har fått, er møtet utsatt.

4 Where's *the money*? – I've lost *it*.
Hvor er pengene? – Jeg har mistet dem.

5 This is *the news*.
Her er nyhetene.

6 We have made *a lot of progress*.
Vi har gjort store framskritt.

4.5.2 Unit nouns

Countable reference of uncountable nouns can be achieved by the addition of a unit noun. The most common ones are *bit* and *piece*, which combine with a wide variety of nouns. *Bit* is colloquial.

bits of paper, a bit of help, a bit of luck
a piece of advice, a piece of bread, two pieces of toast

Some unit nouns are much more restricted in use:

a bar of chocolate/soap/gold	a scrap of paper
a loaf of bread	a slice of cake/pie
a lump of sugar	a sliver of glass
a rasher of bacon	(not) a speck of dust

Many uncountable nouns allow combinations with a variety of unit nouns:

advice:	piece, word
bacon:	pack(age), piece, rasher, slice, strip
furniture:	item, piece, set
news:	bit, item, piece
paper:	bit, heap, piece, roll, scrap, strip, wad
stone:	chip, chunk, piece, slab

By choosing different unit nouns, the speaker can bring out different qualities of the entity (size, shape, etc.).

4.5.3 Countable vs. uncountable uses of nouns

A great many nouns can be used both as countables and uncountables, with a difference in reference. The uncountable use is when we refer to something viewed as substance or material; the countable use when we refer to separate things or individual instances. Note that monolingual English dictionaries often mark senses of nouns as countable (**C**) or uncountable (**U**). Some examples are:

1 I'd like *some tea*, please. (U: the drink)
2 *Two teas*, please. (C: cup of tea)
3 This is *an odd-tasting tea*. (C: brand of tea)
4 I need *some writing-paper*. (U: paper for writing letters)
5 Did you remember to buy *a paper*? (C: newspaper)
6 Have you promised to read *a paper*? (C: conference paper)
7 *How many chickens* do you have? (C: the animal)
8 Do you like *chicken*? (U: the meat)
9 There were *four eggs* in the nest. (C: the object)
10 She had *egg* all over her face. (C: the contents of the egg)
11 We don't do *much business* with that company. (U: trade)
12 She wants to set up *a grocery business*. (C: firm, shop)
13 We must have freedom of *thought*. (U: thinking)
14 Keep your *thoughts* to yourself. (C: idea, opinion)

Note how the difference in countability is reflected in the form of the noun phrases (number, determiners).

Just as uncountable nouns may have countable uses, we find typically countable nouns used as uncountables, particularly after quantifying expressions:

15 She looked across the great plain of *floor*.
16 You get a lot of *car* for your money, sir.

Here *car* and *floor* do not denote discrete entities, but are viewed as representing a mass without precise limits.

4.6 Collective nouns

Collective nouns refer to groups of people: *army*, *committee*, *government*, etc. An army consists of soldiers, a committee has a number of members, a government consists of ministers, etc. Most collective nouns vary for number and definiteness: *army - armies, an army - the army*. However, they have some characteristics which set them apart from ordinary countable nouns.

4.6.1 Syntax and semantics

A singular collective noun may be treated as singular or plural from the point of view of verb concord and co-referent pronouns (see also **9.10.5**). Compare:

1 The committee *has* ten members. *It* is too large.
2 The committee *are* in agreement. *They* did not need to take a vote.
3 Her family *is* old. *It* can be traced back to the 13th century.
4 All the family *enjoy* cooking. But *they* hate washing up.

Examples (1) and (3) illustrate the **unit** reading of these nouns, while (2) and (4) show the **distributive** reading, where the focus is on the members making up the group. The unit reading is by far the more common use and is almost universal in American English, at least as far as verb forms are concerned. Plural pronouns are more commonly used than plural verb forms:

5 The family *is* in the waiting room. *They* are all quite anxious.

Note the plural use of names referring to sports teams:

6 England *have* beaten Germany.
7 Where *are* Liverpool in the league?

This use is characteristically British.

4.6.2 Group nouns

Group nouns are in a way the opposite of unit nouns. While unit nouns serve to split up a mass and make it possible to refer to individual instances, group nouns provide a collective reference for separate entities. Like unit nouns, they are commonly followed by an *of*-phrase:

a crowd of protesters, a crowd of students
a group of children, a group of dancers
a set of alternatives, a set of instructions

Group nouns vary with respect to the combinations they typically enter into:

a bouquet of flowers
a bunch of kids
a clump of trees
a flock of sheep
a gang of bandits
a herd of cattle
a shoal of fish ('stim')
a swarm of bees

Group nouns may be used metaphorically to suggest how the group is viewed: *a flock of messages*, *a bouquet of pencils*, *a herd of station-wagons*, *a swarm of panicked men*.

4.7 Proper nouns

Proper nouns differ from common nouns in a number of ways:

- They are spelt with an initial capital letter: *Bob*, *Laura*, *Rome*, etc.

- They do not vary for number and definiteness (see **4.3**). They refer uniquely to persons, places, etc., without the need for determiners. Common nouns, on the other hand, must be accompanied by determiners to clarify who or what is being referred to. Compare: *Bob - that man*, *my friend*.

- The most typical proper nouns are arbitrary labels which have no lexical meaning. There are no defining characteristics for those who carry the name *Bob*, except that they are male. By contrast, a common noun like *boy* can be defined as 'a young male human being', i.e. it has a sense which can be stated in a dictionary.

Proper nouns are, however, not always easy to identify. Note that an initial capital is not alone sufficient to identify a proper noun. Many nouns spelt with an initial capital letter behave in other ways like common countable nouns, in particular words derived from proper nouns: *a/the Norwegian*, *(the) Norwegians*, *a/the Marxist*, *(the) Marxists*. Note also the words for days of the week, months, and holidays: *Monday*, *Tuesday*, etc.; *January*, *February*, etc.; *Christmas*, *Easter*, etc.

In addition, many proper nouns are derived from ordinary nouns or noun phrases: *the Times*, *the British Library*, *the Rocky Mountains*, etc. Grammatically, these forms are proper nouns in that they do not vary for number and definiteness.

4.7.1 Proper nouns with the definite article

Some types of proper nouns are regularly preceded by the definite article. Often they are derived from descriptive noun phrases.

A Plural geographical names (mountain ranges, groups of islands, and some countries):

> the Alps, the Bahamas, the United States, the Netherlands

B Other geographical names, such as rivers, seas, and canals:

the Atlantic (Ocean), the Panama Canal, the Black Sea

C Public institutions, such as hotels, restaurants, pubs, theatres, museums, libraries, etc.:

the Grand Hotel, the Swan, the Old Vic, the British Museum, the Tate (Gallery), the Library of Congress, the White House

D Names of ships, particularly those which are well known in history:

the Queen Elizabeth, the Mayflower, the Titanic

E Many newspapers and some periodicals:

the Guardian, the Independent, the New York Times, the Washington Post, the New York Review of Books, the New Statesman, the Spectator (but without an article: Newsweek, Time, Punch)

F Organizations:

the BBC, the European Union, the United Nations

The great majority of proper nouns are *not* preceded by an article: personal names (*Paul*, *Margaret*); place-names (*New York*, *Canada*); names of mountains and lakes (*Mount Everest*, *Lake Windermere*); names of streets and buildings (*Fleet Street*, *Buckingham Palace*).

4.7.2 Proper noun vs. common noun

Just as common nouns may provide material for proper nouns, the latter in their turn may be used grammatically as common nouns. They then lose their unique reference and acquire meanings like:

A A person or family called X:

a Mary Malone, a Kennedy, the Clintons

B A person like X:

a Caesar, a Napoleon, a Jefferson, a real Peer Gynt

he proved to be a real Kennedy (with the qualities associated with this family)

C A product of X:

a Ford, two Chryslers, a Picasso

There is little lexical content in such examples, and the initial capital letter indicates that these are not ordinary common nouns. In some cases, however, the connection with the original bearer of the name is lost, and the word is spelt with a lower-case initial. This is true of *quisling*, which has become a common noun meaning 'traitor, especially one who helps an enemy occupying his country' (*Oxford Advanced Learner's Dictionary*).

4.8 Noun formation

Many nouns are complex. New nouns can be created by compounding or by the use of derivational suffixes.

4.8.1 Compounds

Compounds are made up of combinations of independent words. Examples:

- noun + noun: boyfriend, raindrop, roadside, schoolteacher
- noun + *ing*-form: air-conditioning, namedropping, sightseeing, sleep-walking
- *ing*-form + noun: driving school, reading-room, sleeping-pill, writing-paper
- verb + noun: crybaby, driftwood, pickpocket, wash-basin
- noun + particle: black-out, lock-out, sit-in, sit-up, walk-over

Compounds vary from examples with a transparent meaning (e.g. *raindrop*) to idiomatic combinations with a meaning that is not predictable from the individual words (e.g. *namedropping*, 'the practice of casually mentioning the names of important people (as if they were friends) to impress people', *Oxford Advanced Learner's Dictionary*). There is a wide range of compounds in both English and Norwegian. Note the following differences between English and Norwegian.

A Spelling and pronunciation

While Norwegian compounds are consistently spelt as single words, there is a great deal of variation and vacillation in English (see also the examples above): *school age*, *schoolboy*, *school-leaver*; *flowerpot*, *flower-pot*, *flower pot*. If in doubt, consult a dictionary! But note that dictionaries do not include full lists of compounds.

Norwegian compounds are pronounced with a single stress on the first element. This is also true of most English compounds (such as the examples given above), but there are many noun + noun combinations that are pronounced in the same way as phrases. Compare:

Single stress:	Double stress:
headache	headquarters
girlfriend	girl student
gold rush	gold medal
iceberg	ice-cream
paperknife	paper bag
silverfish	silver ring
weekday	weekend
womankind	woman writer

It is hard to formulate rules for stress in these cases, but note the regular use of double stress in combinations where the first element denotes some kind of material (*paper bag*, *silver ring*, etc.).

Because of the irregularity in spelling and stress, there is no clear borderline between compounds and noun phrases with premodifying nouns.

B Correspondences

Norwegian compounds very often correspond to other types of structures in English. Examples:

- adjective + noun:

  skolefilm - educational film
  statsminister - prime minister
  statsbudsjett - national budget
  statsvitenskap - political science

- noun + *of*-phrase:

  arbeidsdeling - division of labour
  produksjonsmidler - means of production

skoledirektør - superintendent of schools
streikevarsel - notice of a/the strike

- single words:

arbeidsgiver - employer
skolepenger - tuition
statsborger - citizen
streikevakt - picket

- other forms:

arbeidsro - opportunity to work undisturbed
skoleplikt - compulsory school attendance
skolevei - way to and from school
streikerett - right to strike

It is not possible to lay down rules in this area. If in doubt, consult a bilingual dictionary!

4.8.2 Some common derivational patterns

Many English nouns are made up of a base and a suffix. In the list below, the word class of the base is identified by A (adjective), N (noun), and V (verb).

-al ('action/instance of V-ing'): arrival, burial, denial

-an, *-ian* ('person who lives in N', 'language of N'): American, Bostonian, Korean; ('person associated with N'): Darwinian, Victorian

-ation ('action/instance of V-ing'): alteration, hesitation, nationalization

-cy ('state or quality of being A/N'): accuracy, adequacy, infancy

-dom ('state of being A/N'): boredom, freedom, stardom

-ee ('person who has been or is to be V-ed'): employee, evacuee, trainee

-er, *-or* ('person who V-s'): advertiser, driver, governor; ('something used for V-ing'): computer, filler, silencer

-ese ('person who lives in N', 'language of N'): Burmese, Japanese, Vietnamese; ('the style of N', usually derogatory): journalese, officialese

-ette ('small N'): kitchenette, novelette

-ful ('amount that fills N'): bucketful, handful, teaspoonful

-hood ('state of being A/N'): childhood, falsehood, widowhood

-ician ('person concerned with N'): mathematician, politician

-ie, *-y* ('diminutive or pet name for N'): daddy, doggie, Johnny

-ing ('action of V-ing'): bullying, reading, singing; ('something that one V-s or has V-ed'): building, painting, recording

-ism ('doctrine of N'): Buddhism, Marxism, Thatcherism; ('movement characterized by A/N'): impressionism, realism, Romanticism

-ist ('person believing in or following *-ism*'): Buddhist, Marxist; impressionist, realist; ('person concerned with N'): biologist, physicist, violinist

-ite ('person following N', often derogatory): Thatcherite

-ity ('state or quality of being A'): ability, purity, similarity

-let ('small N'): booklet, leaflet, piglet

-ment ('action/instance of V-ing'): development, encouragement, punishment

-ness ('state or quality of being A'): blindness, darkness, preparedness

-ship ('state of being N'): citizenship, friendship, partnership; ('skill in N'): craftsmanship, statesmanship

4.9 Complex noun phrases

Noun phrases are very often complex, particularly in informative prose ('sakprosa'). The complexity is due to the modifiers which precede or follow the head noun. The main types of modifiers are illustrated below. Note that pre- and postmodifiers frequently co-occur in the same noun phrase. Co-ordination of both head and modifiers may cause additional complexity.

A Premodification

The most typical premodifiers are adjectives and adjective phrases (1), including phrases with a participle as head (2), and nouns and noun phrases (3). Less frequent premodifiers are adverbs and prepositional phrases (4).

1 some *new* books
the *new and glossy* books from Collins
an *unusually interesting* book
2 its *rapidly growing* discoveries of oil
such *clearly overused* words and phrases from the language of advertising
3 an elegant, old, Swiss *oak* table
the British *secondary school* system
a *five-day* visit
4 the *then* Prime Minister, a *nearby* village
an *off-duty* policeman, *on-the-spot* inquiries

The ordering of the elements before the head noun can to a large extent be interpreted in terms of **scope** or layers of modification:

5 [the [recent [Tokyo [economic summit]]]]

This means that *economic* modifies *summit* (for type), *Tokyo* modifies *economic summit* (for place), and *recent* modifies *Tokyo economic summit* (for time). Note the difference between:

6 a *current affairs* programme
7 the *current* wage scale

In (6) the head noun *programmes* is modified by the noun phrase *current affairs*. In (7) there is a compound head noun, *wage scale*, modified by the adjective *current*. For more information on premodification, see **8.7–8.8**.

B Postmodification

Postmodifiers are typically longer and more complex than premodifiers, and their meaning is in general more explicitly expressed. Compare (5) and a version with a combination of pre- and postmodification:

8 the economic summit which was held recently in Tokyo

The degree of explicitness of postmodification varies, however:

9 the woman *who is standing in the corner there*
the woman *standing in the corner there*

the woman *in the corner there*
the woman *there*

The most typical postmodifiers are prepositional phrases (10), relative clauses (11), and non-finite clauses (12). Less frequent types of postmodifiers are adjectives and adjective phrases (13), and adverbs (14). Where several postmodifiers co-occur, the more complex ones tend to be placed later in the phrase.

10 the woman *in the corner*, the man *in the street*, the picture *on the wall*
the flat rejection *of their proposals by the party leader*
the murder *in Istanbul on Friday of an American servicewoman*
11 the woman in the corner *who is wearing a black dress*
the book on biology *which I mentioned last week*
12 students *living at home*
the experiment *described in this paper*
the way *to do it*
13 the members *present*, a politician *popular in the 1970s*
14 the woman *there*, the account *below* of these new experiments

For more information on postmodification, see **8.6.4A**, **12.6.1**, and **13.2**.

C Discontinuous modification

Discontinuous modifiers are found with degree expressions (15) and some types of infinitive constructions (16):

15 a *richer* man *than John*
in *as simple* a fashion *as possible*
16 a *hard* man *to convince*
the *easiest* people *to talk to*

Notice that these discontinuous modifiers can be rephrased as relative clauses: *a man who is richer than John*, *the people who are easiest to talk to*, etc.

4.10 Apposition

A noun phrase can also be expanded by apposition. The most typical examples consist of a proper noun plus a phrase indicating the role or occupation of the person referred to:

1 George Washington, the first president of the United States
Jostein Gaarder, the author of *Sophie's World*
George, my cousin in Chicago

The role or occupation can be given more prominence by being placed before the name:

2 the Prime Minister, Tony Blair
the author Erica Jong
my uncle George

There are also appositional clauses, particularly *that*-clauses (**12.8.1**) after abstract nouns like *fact*, *hope*, *idea*, *news*, *report*, *rumour*, etc.

3 The news that she will resign has upset everybody.
We have to face the fact that we made a serious mistake.

4.11 Embedding

The complexity of noun phrases is to a large extent due to the fact that modifiers are themselves complex. Noun phrases are often embedded within other noun phrases, usually as parts of clauses or prepositional phrases. Example (noun phrases are identified by brackets):

1 [The next mention of [the dream]] came in [a report written [the following day]].

Comments:

- *The next mention of the dream* is a noun phrase in subject position; this noun phrase contains a postmodifying *of*-phrase, with *the dream* as complement of the preposition.
- *A report written the following day* is a complement in a prepositional phrase with adverbial function (because it answers the question *when did it come?*); *a report* has a postmodifying non-finite clause which includes a noun phrase as adverbial: *the following day*.

The following is an analysis of the noun phrases in the text passage quoted in the opening of the chapter. Brackets identify the noun phrases, and the head of each phrase (a noun or a pronoun) is given in bold-face type.

2 [**Liverpool**] is [a vibrant and exciting **place** to visit] and [a warm **welcome**] is always guaranteed. [The **centre**] is alive with [**theatres**, **clubs**, **restaurants** and **attractions** that are able to provide [**something**] for [**everyone**]]. [**It**] is [**one** of [[the **world**'s] most famous and historic

cities]] and [its distinguished **life** as [a **centre** for [**world trade** and **commerce**]]] is clearly reflected in [its rich **culture** and architectural **heritage**].

4.12 Complex noun phrases in discourse

Complex noun phrases form convenient ways of compressing information. The need for compression is especially great in newspaper headlines, where long and complex noun phrases are commonly found:

1 **Shire's $186m Kentucky derby**
SHIRE Pharmaceuticals, the biotechnology group, signed its second transforming acquisition in six months yesterday, with the takeover of Richmond Pharmaceuticals, of Kentucky, for up to $186m (£113m).

(From *The Daily Telegraph*)

Apart from the compression, note the use of the horse-racing image.

Within a running text we characteristically find that longer and more complex phrases are used at first mention, and are referred to later by shorter and less complex forms:

2 Bulgarian defector Georgi Markov was walking from his car to his night-shift commentator's job at the British Broadcasting Corp. in London when he was jostled by *a heavyset man carrying an umbrella* ... *The umbrella man* could have been an assassin.

(From *Newsweek*)

See the comments on chains of reference in **5.16**.

Terms

types of nouns: common
countable
uncountable
proper

plural-only nouns
unit nouns
collective nouns (unit and distributive reading)

compound nouns
derived nouns

premodification
postmodification
discontinuous modification
apposition
embedding

Exercises

1 Give the plural form of the following singular nouns. In each case state the relevant rule for plural formation. (**4.4.2–4.4.5**)

analysis	MP
bagful	ox
bookshelf	potato
crisis	sheep
criterion	snowman
forum	university
mother-in-law	wife

2 Give the singular form of the following plural nouns. (**4.4.2–4.4.5**)

binoculars	media
formulae	phenomena
galleries	series
geese	statistics
lice	stimuli

3 Irregular singular – plural correspondences:
In the following list of words, the plural form has two meanings. Write one sentence for each meaning, making sure that each sentence is unambiguous. (**4.4.5**)

arm – arms	look – looks
brain – brains	pool – pools
direction – directions	premise – premises
glass – glasses	

4 Expand these uncountable nouns by means of unit nouns, so that each noun phrase implies countability. (**4.5.2**)
Example: art – a work of art

bread	knowledge
coffee	luck
furniture	news
information	poetry

5 The following nouns can be used as countable and uncountable nouns. Write two sentences for each word, showing both uses. (**4.5.3**)

air	iron
environment	marriage
experience	religion
grammar	sugar
hair	wine
interest	work

6 Are the italicized nouns used as common or proper nouns in the following sentences? (We have used capitals all the way through in order to make the exercise more difficult!) (**4.7**)

a *VANESSA* ARRIVED WITH HER *MOTHER*.
b HE LOOKS LIKE A GREEK *GOD*.
c MY *FRIEND* DREAMS OF OWNING A *JAGUAR*.
d THEY WANTED TO GO TO *ROME* BECAUSE THEY THOUGHT THEY WOULD MEET THE *POPE* IN THE *VATICAN*.
e I'LL SEE YOU IN *COURT*.
f HAVE YOU REALLY MET THE *PRESIDENT*?
g *PETER* IS UNLIKELY TO BECOME THE *EDISON* OF THE 21ST CENTURY.
h NOTHING COMES BETWEEN ME AND MY *CALVINS*.
i THESE *CUPS* ARE MADE OF *CHINA*.
j WHILE I DROVE ALONG THE *M4* I LISTENED TO THE *NEWS* FROM THE *BBC*.
k THE WORST *FEATURE* OF THE *WEATHER* IS THE *MISTRAL*, A *NORTH WIND* THAT SWEEPS DOWN THE *RHÔNE VALLEY*.

7 Translate the following sentences into idiomatic English.

a Alle pengene er borte.
b Kan du skaffe flere opplysninger?
c Kan jeg få låne en saks av deg?
d Mesteparten av gjengen har kommet.
e Lavere rente vil bidra til økt boligetterspørsel.
f Penger betyr ikke så mye for meg.
g Susan kjøpte en ny shorts til broren sin.
h De hadde med seg altfor mye bagasje.
i Vi trenger to brød og fire liter melk.
j Dette er et godt råd til alle som studerer engelsk.
k Jeg liker ikke denne tv-serien.

l Presidentvalget i USA finner sted på den første tirsdagen etter den første mandagen i november.
m FN har sitt hovedkvarter i New York City.
n Det britiske imperiet var på sitt største i 1890-årene, under dronning Victorias regjeringstid.
o Japanerne spiste rundt 2500 tonn hvalkjøtt i 1991.
p Antikvitetene ble solgt hos Sotheby's i London for to millioner pund.

8 Suggest English translations of the following compound nouns. (**4.8.1**)

attenhundretallet
diktsamling
hermetikkboks
hukommelsestap
kaffekopp
litteraturhistorie
livsfare
meningsutveksling
miljøverndepartement
morgenavis
Norgeskart
parlamentsmedlem
privatetterforsker
romanforfatter
stemmeseddel
sydenturist
synonymordbok
søvnmangel
telefonsvarer
tobindsleksikon
yrkesmusiker

9 Discuss whether the following phrases are compound nouns or combinations of premodifier + head noun. Give reasons for your answers. (**4.8.1**, **4.9A**)

a amateur performance
b best-selling author
c blue jeans
d chewing gum
e compact disc
f salad bowl
g tabloid paper
h washing machine

10 Identify the head of the following noun phrases. (**4.9**)

a the simple, good things in life
b an idealist who thrives on competition
c clever and ambitious business people in their mid-thirties
d all Volvo safety features
e the foundation of today's superpower
f two highly successful television adverts for toothpaste

11 Show the structure of the following noun phrases in tree diagrams (see Figure 2c in **2.10**).

a our simple philosophy
b my new jacket in mock suede
c a very good sense of business strategies
d new and improved bus services between Edinburgh and Glasgow

12 Complex noun phrases versus finite clauses:
Rephrase the following sentences. Begin each paraphrase in the way indicated below the sentence. (**4.9**)

Example: Van Gogh painted sunflowers in a vase.
I like Van Gogh's painting of sunflowers in a vase.

a Then we can discuss who is going to contribute what.
Then we can have a ...
b The book will be published next spring.
We look forward to the ...
c They're interested in a poet who catches murderers.
They expressed their ...
d His sense of smell had failed.
He reported the ...
e They failed to notice anything unusual about their daughter.
Doctors wondered at their ...
f Subsequently, they discussed the merits of Kafka.
There followed a ...

13 What is wrong here? Rewrite the following sentences in such a way as to convey the meaning that must have been intended. Explain the changes you make. (**4.9**, **4.12**)

a Special cocktails for the ladies with nuts.
b Squad helps dog bite victim.
c Two sisters were reunited after 18 years at a checkout counter.
d We sell unique tables for children with adjustable legs.
e The hotel has special rooms for women that cost $100 a night.

14 Identify the noun phrases in the following sentences and state their syntactic function. Then give the internal structure of each noun phrase. Note that noun phrases may be embedded in other phrases. (Text from *Yes Minister*) (**4.9–4.11**)

a At last I'm a Cabinet Minister.
b And today I had my first encounter with the Civil Service, and I must say I am very impressed.
c I got the call from Number Ten at about 9 a.m., after a sleepless night, and immediately Frank Weisel and I caught the London train.
d I got a taxi to Number Ten, where I was asked by the PM to take over the Department of Administrative Affairs.
e A moment later Sir Humphrey Appleby arrived.
f He is the Permanent Secretary of the DAA, the Civil Service Head of the Department.

15 Comment on the difference in form and meaning between the members of the following sentence pairs.

a 1 I like coffee.
  2 I'd like two coffees, please.
b 1 In the hall was a painting of her father.
  2 In the hall was a painting of her father's.
c 1 She has some business in London tomorrow.
  2 She has some businesses in London.
d 1 Leo was looking for a girl in a red dress.
  2 Leo was looking for a girl in Uptown New York.
e 1 I thought his work was wonderful.
  2 I thought his works were wonderful.
f 1 We support democracy.
  2 We support these new democracies.

5 Determiners and Pronouns

5.1 The role of determiners

When we use a common noun like *car*, there is a need for **specification** to indicate whether we are talking about one or more cars, about a particular car or about cars in general, and so on. The specification is provided by the choice of a singular or a plural form and by the use of **determiners**. The determiners are italicized in the passage below (repeated from **4.1.1**):

> Liverpool is *a* vibrant and exciting place to visit and *a* warm welcome is always guaranteed. *The* centre is alive with theatres, clubs, restaurants and attractions that are able to provide something for everyone. It is one of *the* world's most famous and historic cities and *its* distinguished life as *a* centre for world trade and commerce is clearly reflected in *its* rich culture and architectural heritage.

The main groups of determiners are the articles (**5.2**), the demonstrative determiners (**5.3**), possessive determiners (**5.4–5.5**), and quantifying determiners (**5.6**). In addition, there are *wh*-determiners, which are used to build special clause structures (**5.13**): *the girl whose mother is coming to see us*, *which way shall we go*, etc. Note also the determiner-like adjectives dealt with in **8.4.5**.

Proper nouns do not need determiners, as they have unique reference. *Liverpool* is normally sufficient by itself, unless we want to distinguish between different places with the same name or different aspects of a place called *Liv-*

erpool: 'there is a Liverpool in Australia', 'the Liverpool I am talking about is in Australia', 'the Liverpool of the 19th century'. Proper nouns that regularly take an article (e.g. *the Atlantic*; see **4.7.1**) are no exception. In this case the article is, so to speak, part of the name, and there is no distinction between, for example, **Atlantic* and *the Atlantic*. On the other hand, common nouns normally need specification by determiners.

Determiners can be classified into three groups by position: predeterminers, central determiners, and postdeterminers. The majority are central determiners, which do not combine with each other. See Table 5a.

Table 5a: Positional groups of determiners

Predeterminer	Central determiner	Postdeterminer	Head
half	a		pint
half/double	the		cost
all	the	seven	dwarfs
	the	many/few	accidents
both	these		students
	her	first	book
	his	other	friends

5.2 The articles

We can distinguish:

- the **definite article** (e.g. *the car, the cars, the tea*)
- the **indefinite article** (e.g. *a car, an idea*)
- the **zero article** (e.g. *cars, ideas, tea*)

The reason why it makes sense to talk about a zero article (Ø) is that the contrast with the definite and the indefinite article is a signal of the specification of a common noun.

The definite and the indefinite article vary in form (spelling/pronunciation) depending upon the following word:

/ə/	a horse	/ən/	an hour
	a Member of Parliament		an MP
/ðə/	the horse	/ðɪ/	the hour
	the Member of Parliament		the MP

What is relevant is the pronunciation rather than the written form. *University*, which is pronounced with an initial /j/, is preceded by the forms on the left. The forms on the right are used before words that begin with a silent *h*: *heir*, *honest*, *honour(able)*, and *hour*. There is variation with some words beginning with an unstressed *h*: *historic(al)*, *hotel*, *hypothesis*.

5.2.1 The indefinite article

The indefinite article narrows down the reference of the noun phrase to a single member of a class. It is often used to introduce a new entity into the discourse:

1 *A radio motor patrol car* was angle-parked into the kerb when Detectives C and M arrived at the scene. Behind *that* was *a black sedan* that looked like a hearse. C guessed *it* belonged to Homicide.

Later references generally take the form of pronouns (in this case, *that* and *it*) or noun phrases with the definite article (in this case, the writer could have used *the patrol car* and *the sedan*, respectively).

The indefinite article is used in much the same way in English and Norwegian, but note the following differences:

A Subject predicative

English requires an indefinite article with noun phrases in predicative position in sentences like:

2 Kari is *a doctor.*
Kari er *lege.*
3 She is *a Norwegian* (or with an adjective: She is Norwegian).
Hun er *nordmann.*
4 She is *a Catholic.*
Hun er *katolikk.*

Here a person is classified with respect to profession (2), nationality (3), and religion (4). If the reference is to a unique position, the indefinite article is not used. Compare:

5 She is *a member of the board.*
Hun er *medlem av styret.*
6 She is *(the) chairman of the board.*
Hun er *styreformann.*

In (6) it is also possible to use the definite article in English. Note the same type of contrast in noun phrases preceded by *as*:

7 As *a member of the board* I must object to this.
8 As *chairman of the board* I must object to this.

B Direct object
The indefinite article is used more widely in English than in Norwegian in expressions like:

buy a house ('kjøpe hus')
buy a ticket ('kjøpe billett')
get a letter ('få brev')
get a job ('få jobb')
have a family ('ha familie')
have a dog ('ha hund')
have a key ('ha nøkkel')
have a car ('ha bil')
have a party ('ha fest')
have a new address ('ha ny adresse')
take a long time ('ta lang tid')

To generalize, we could say that English requires an indefinite article more consistently with countable nouns. Norwegian can often make do with a bare noun when the focus is more on a type than on a specific entity.

5.2.2 The zero article

The zero article is used to build indefinite noun phrases with uncountables and plural countable nouns:

1 They were drinking *coffee*.
2 P was wearing *a maroon bathrobe* and *brown house slippers*. He seemed to be in his early sixties, a massive man with *a large head* and *enormous hands*.
3 Kari and Ole are *doctors*.
4 They are *Norwegians* (or with an adjective: Norwegian).
5 They are *Catholics*.

Note the co-ordination of the indefinite singular and plural noun phrases in (2). The classifying use in (3) to (5) should be compared with that in (2) to (4) in **5.2.1** above.

5.2.3 The definite article

The definite article combines with all types of common nouns, countable as well as uncountable and singular as well as plural. It specifies that the referent is known to the speaker and the addressee. The knowledge could be based on the preceding text; this is called **anaphoric reference** (backward reference). Consider these examples (adapted from Stephen Pile, *The Book of Heroic Failures*):

1 In 1970 a lion escaped from a circus in Italy. Typically, it found a small boy and started to chase him. Less typically, *the small boy*'s mother turned on *the lion* and badly mauled it. *The animal* suffered severe head and skin wounds, and received treatment for shock.
2 A unique choral competition was held in Wales within the last two years. Only one choir entered *the contest* and then it only managed to come second. *The choir* failed to win first prize, *the judges* said, as a punishment for arriving forty-five minutes late.

The reference of the italicized noun phrases is made clear through the indefinite noun phrases earlier in the texts (cf. **5.2.1**): *a lion, a small boy*; *a unique choral competition, one choir*. The definite noun phrase may repeat the same noun or make use of a synonym: *a lion* vs. *the lion, the animal*; *a competition* vs. *the contest*.

How do we account for *the judges* in example (2)? Clearly, no judges have been introduced earlier in the text. This is a case of **indirect anaphoric reference**. The speaker assumes that the hearer knows that there are judges in connection with choral competitions. These can then be referred to by definite forms without an explicit introduction. Similarly, if a car has been mentioned, it is possible to speak of *the driver, the licence plates, the dashboard*, and so on.

The reference of a noun phrase is often made clear by something following after the article, e.g. a restrictive relative clause (**12.6.3**) or some other modifier of the noun:

3 *The city for which C worked* was divided into five separate and distinct sections, but only *the island of Isola* was referred to as 'the city'.
4 The lady had been killed in *the midtown area*.

This is called **cataphoric reference** (forward reference).

A definite noun phrase is often dependent upon the shared situational context of the speaker and the hearer, as in:

5 There is somebody at *the door*.
6 Why don't you answer *the telephone*?

Situational reference ranges from reliance on the immediate context, as in (5) and (6), to context in a much wider sense: *the sun, the moon, the radio, the papers, the government*, etc.

The reference patterns vary with the type of text. Situational reference is particularly frequent in conversation, which is embedded in a context shared by the speaker and the hearer, who often know each other well and can rely on a great deal of common knowledge. And, should misunderstandings arise, they can be put right in the course of the exchange:

7 A: Where's *the key*?
B: *Which key*?
A: *The key to the front door*.

In writing, on the other hand, reference must generally be established within the text itself, either anaphorically or cataphorically. But stories in fiction frequently open with definite noun phrases:

8 Between the silver ribbon of morning and the green glittering ribbon of sea, *the boat* touched Harwich and let loose a swarm of folk like flies, among whom *the man we must follow* was by no means conspicuous – nor wished to be.

(From the beginning of 'The blue cross' by G. K. Chesterton)

By this device, the reader is brought *in medias res* and is invited to share the fictional world.

5.2.4 Generic reference

Generic reference means reference to a class or a kind. Countable nouns allow three possibilities:

1 *Horses* are intelligent animals.
The horse is an intelligent animal.
A horse is an intelligent animal.

These examples all mean that horses in general are intelligent. The three types cannot be used indiscriminately. The plural indefinite form has the widest applicability. Compare:

2 *Cats* are nice.
The cat is nice.
3 I like *cats*.
I like *the cat*.

While the plural indefinite form is still generic in these examples, the singular definite form refers to a specific cat known to the speaker and the addressee.

Generic reference is common with nominalized adjectives preceded by the definite article: *the rich*, *the supernatural*, etc. See **8.9**.

A Plural definite forms

Plural definite forms of some types of nouns, particularly nationality words, may have generic reference:

4 *(The) Americans* believe in the freedom of the individual.

But compare: *Englishmen* (generic), *the English* (generic), *the Englishmen* (= some particular Englishmen known to the speaker and the addressee).

Note that Norwegian may use plural definite forms more widely with generic reference. Compare:

5 *Teenagers* like dancing and having fun.
Tenåringene liker å danse og ha det moro.
6 *Cars* should be banned from the centre of Oslo.
Bilene burde forbys i sentrum av Oslo.

Whereas the Norwegian versions of (5) and (6) can have both generic and specific reference, 'tenåringer' and 'biler' would be unambiguously generic. However, English requires indefinite forms for generic reference. If not, the reference will be to a particular group of teenagers or cars.

B Generic reference of uncountable nouns

Uncountable nouns require the zero article to express generic reference. Note the difference between English and Norwegian.

7 *Art* is long. *Life* is short.
Kunsten er lang. *Livet* er kort.
8 We must go back to *nature*.
Vi må gå tilbake til *naturen*.
9 What would we do without *electricity*?
Hva skulle vi ha gjort uten *elektrisitet(en)*?

Uncountable nouns with premodification may still be conceived as generic: *computer technology*, *modern art*, *modern American fiction*, *organized crime*.

5.2.5 Some other problematic cases

A Referring to institutions

English uses the zero article with a number of nouns denoting institutions, in particular: *church*, *hospital* (AmE: *the hospital*), *prison*, *school*, *university* (AmE: *the university*).

1 Do you go to *church*?
Går du i *kirken*?
2 She was sent to *hospital*.
Hun ble sendt til *sykehuset*.
3 Don't you like *school*?
Liker du ikke *skolen*?

The zero article is normal when the reference is to the activities associated with these institutions. Compare:

4 *The church* was built in the thirteenth century.
Kirken ble bygd på 1200-tallet.
5 Where's *the school*?
Hvor er *skolen*?

Here the reference is to a particular church/school known to the speaker and the addressee, and the article is used in the normal manner.

B Meals
There is a similar contrast with English words for meals. Compare:

6 *Dinner* is at six.
Det er *middag* klokken seks.
7 *The dinner* was delicious.
Middagen var deilig.

C Time expressions
Nouns for the months and the days of the week normally take the zero article: *on Tuesday*, *in February*, etc. Note that there may be a difference between English and Norwegian with words for holidays and seasons.

8 *Autumn* (AmE: *Fall*) is a beautiful season.
Høsten er en deilig årstid.
9 *Easter* is late this year.
Påsken er sein i år.

But compare: *the autumn of 1996*

5.3 Demonstrative determiners

The demonstrative determiners are like the definite article, but, in addition to signalling that somebody or something is known, they specify the number of the referent and whether the referent is near or distant in relation to the speaker (cf. the adverbs *here* and *there*). Moreover, they are stressed, while the definite article is almost always unstressed. The singular forms combine with both countable and uncountable nouns.

	Singular	Plural
Near	this car this money	these cars
Distant	that car that money	those cars

The reference of noun phrases with demonstrative determiners may be established on the basis of the situation or the preceding or the following text; compare the situational, the anaphoric, and the cataphoric use of the definite article (**5.2.3**).

A Situational reference

Situational reference is natural in conversation. The choice of pronoun reflects the perception of the speaker:

1 Look at *this* map here.
2 Look at *that* man over there.

In examples of the following kind there is a difference in psychological distance: *this wonderful idea* vs. *that crazy idea*. The demonstrative determiners may also indicate location in time (cf. the adverbs *now* and *then*):

3 *This* summer I am going to France.
4 *That* summer I went to Greece.

Compare: *these days* ('nå for tiden'), *in those days* ('da, den gang'), *this evening* ('i kveld'), *that evening* ('den kvelden').

B Anaphoric reference

In writing, the demonstrative determiners typically refer back to the immediately preceding text:

5 They whiled away the time by telling stories. In due course they started acting out *these* stories.
6 I just keep seeing *those* pictures in *that* book. In *this* one picture there was *this* little boy with his hands above his head. And they shot him.

The connection with the original meaning is that *this* and *these* refer to things of more immediate concern. Note the shift in (6) as the narrator narrows the focus of the story (see also **D** below).

C Cataphoric *that/those*

7 She smiled *that* sort of smile that women save for men that have lost their woman.
8 There are *those* of us who don't believe in this.

In (7) the reference is clarified through a following relative clause; in (8), through a following prepositional phrase plus a relative clause.

D Introductory *this/these*

9 There's *this* boy I ride home with on the bus every day ...
10 Last night on my way home I met *these* two young girls ...

These examples illustrate a special conversational use, signalling that the speaker is telling a story. Ordinarily we would expect indefinite noun phrases (*there's a boy ..., I met two girls ...*). The choice of *this/these* gives a feeling of intimacy: it is as if the listener is witnessing the scene.

5.4 Possessive determiners

Corresponding to each of the personal pronouns (see **5.8**), there is a possessive determiner. Possessive determiners specify the head noun by relating it to the speaker or the addressee (*I - my book, we - our book, you - your book*) or to other entities given in the speech situation or introduced in the text (*the man - his book, the girl - her friend, the dog - its food, the children - their toys*). The possessive relationship can be underlined by adding *own*: *my own book, their own toys*, etc.

In spite of the term 'possessive', these determiners do not just express ownership. The meaning varies in much the same way as for the genitive (**5.5.3**). For example, *her book* could mean the book she owns or has written, or even the book she is reading or holding in her hand.

Possessive determiners are used in much the same way in English and Norwegian, with the exception of the special case discussed below.

NB! Note the difference between *its* and *it's*. The possessive determiner lacks an apostrophe: *its name*, *its value*, etc. *It's* is a contraction of *it is* or *it has*: *it's time for tea*, *it's got a blue collar*, etc.

5.4.1 The type *put it in your pocket*

Norwegian regularly uses the definite form of the noun when referring to parts of the body and personal belongings in examples like:

1	Put it in *your pocket.*	Legg det i *lomma.*
2	She broke *her leg.*	Hun brakk *beinet.*
3	*My arm* hurts.	Jeg har vondt i *armen.*
4	Have you brushed *your teeth*?	Har du pusset *tennene*?

English requires a possessive determiner in these cases. However, when the owner is an affected participant, expressed as a direct object or a passive subject, English uses the definite article:

5	He hit me on *the head.*	Han slo meg i *hodet.*
	I was hit on *the head.*	Jeg ble slått i *hodet.*

Note also the definite article in some set expressions: *be armed to the teeth*, *have something on the brain.*

5.5 The genitive

The genitive is a possessive determiner that is based on a noun rather than a pronoun. Compare: *Betty's new dress*, *her new dress*. The genitive is signalled by an inflectional ending (**5.5.1**). Strictly speaking, the ending is added to a noun phrase rather than to an individual noun. This is quite clear in the case of group genitives (**5.5.2**). The genitive may express a range of semantic relationships (**5.5.3**).

The genitive competes with postmodifying *of*-phrases, and the choice is dependent upon a variety of factors (**5.5.4**). In a few special cases, genitives are used in nominal positions, independently of a head noun (**5.5.5**).

5.5.1 The form of the genitive

The genitive is formed in writing by the addition of *'s* to nouns in the singular and plural nouns which do not end in *-s*, and by adding only an apostrophe to plural nouns with the regular *s*-ending: *the girl's mother*, *the two girls' mother*, *the children's mother*. The pronunciation of the genitive ending varies with the preceding sounds in the same way as the plural ending of nouns (**4.4.1**). Examples:

/s/	Kate's bracelet, Dick's hand, the cat's tail
/z/	Tom's bike, Betty's friends, the children's skis
/ɪz/	the horse's mouth, Thomas's book, George's desk

Note the difference between: *the student's* ('studentens') *book*, *the students'* ('studentenes') *books*.

There is some variation in both writing and pronunciation with names ending in -*s*:

Dickens' novels	Dickens's /'dɪkɪnzɪz/ novels
Nicholas' car	Nicholas's /'nɪkələsɪz/ car

The use of an apostrophe only is found particularly with biblical and classical names: *Jesus' teachings*, *Socrates' wife*. With common English names, it is safest to use the spelling '*s* and the pronunciation /ɪz/.

With plural expressions of measure, we find spellings both with and without an apostrophe: *two months(') stay*, *two years(') imprisonment*. It is safest to use the apostrophe. Note that the apostrophe is the rule with singular forms: *a month's stay*, *one year's imprisonment*.

5.5.2 Group genitives

The genitive ending is added to the last word in a noun phrase in examples like: *the Queen of England's speech*, *the Prince of Wales's brother*, *the head of department's office*, *Bob and Jean's five children*, *in a month or two's time*. The group genitive is mostly used with more or less fixed expressions. Where the phrase is complex, there is a preference for *of*-phrases (see **5.5.4**).

5.5.3 Genitive meanings

The genitive may express a wide range of meanings. For example, *Paul's picture* may mean the picture he owns, the picture he has painted, the picture he is holding in his hand, and so on. In spite of the variation, we can identify ownership as the prototypical meaning of the genitive when used with nouns denoting people or other animate beings. Completely different relations are expressed with some other types of nouns.

A Time
last week's Guardian, yesterday's press conference, etc.

B Duration
an hour's stay, a year's membership, a minute's silence, four weeks' holiday, three months' stay, etc.

C Measure
one pound's worth of sugar, two pounds' worth of eggs, five thousand dollars' bail ('kausjon'), etc.

Note also fixed expressions like: *a stone's throw*, *at arm's length*.

D Specifying vs. classifying genitives
Compare the genitive expressions in these examples:

1 *The children's clothes* need washing.
2 We need to buy *children's clothes*.

Example (1) contains a specifying genitive; notice that the genitive can be replaced by the possessive determiner *their*. The genitive specifies what particular clothes we are referring to. In (2), on the other hand, we are talking about a kind of clothes. This is a classifying genitive.

Classifying genitives are typically single-stressed: *'children's clothes* (cf. *the 'children's 'clothes*). They do not allow an intervening adjective: **children's new clothes* (cf. *the children's dirty clothes*). An adjective that precedes the genitive noun modifies the whole noun phrase: *new children's clothes* (cf. *the young children's clothes*). They cannot be paraphrased by an *of*-construction: **clothes of children* (cf. *the clothes of the children*).

We can sum up the features of classifying constructions by saying that they are more like compounds than phrases, and they do in fact generally correspond to compounds in Norwegian. Some more examples are:

beeswax ('bivoks')	a bird's nest ('fuglerede')
crow's-feet ('smilerynker')	a hornet's nest ('vepsebol', usually
a doctor's degree ('doktorgrad')	referring to a troublesome situation)

As with compounds in general (**4.8.1**), the meaning is often idiomatic, and the orthographic form may vary with the individual combination.

5.5.4 The *s*-genitive vs. *of*-phrases

Specifying genitives can often be paraphrased by an *of*-phrase: *the car's owner, the owner of the car*. The choice between the two constructions is dependent upon a range of factors.

A The type of noun

The *s*-genitive is preferred with personal nouns and is also found with collective nouns, geographical nouns, and words for animals: *Laura's car, the government's decision, Norway's economy, the dog's collar*, etc. Other types of nouns appear in expressions of time, duration, and measure (see **5.5.3**), and in some idiomatic phrases: *at my wit's end, in my mind's eye, for goodness' sake*, etc.

Particularly in newspaper texts, we find *s*-genitives much more widely: *the museum's architect, the dollar's weakness*, etc. The *s*-genitive allows a more concise expression than the *of*-construction and is well suited to the needs of journalism. More information can be conveyed in the limited space available.

There are few restrictions on the types of nouns that may be used in *of*-phrases. Note, however, that personal names hardly ever occur in *of*-phrases following a concrete noun: **the car of Laura* (but: *the works of Shakespeare*). All the other examples above, with the exception of the frozen idiomatic phrases, allow an *of*-paraphrase: *the decision of the government, the economy of Norway, the collar of the dog*, etc.

B The parallel between genitive constructions and clauses

The *s*-genitive tends to express semantic relationships associated with subjects; the *of*-construction those connected with objects. This comes out most clearly in examples like:

1 T has painted a portrait of the new minister.
  T's portrait of the new minister
2 The enemy destroyed the city.
  the enemy's destruction of the city

S-genitives are typically shorter and less complex than the postmodifying noun phrases in *of*-constructions. The postmodifying relative clause in (3) makes it impossible to use an *s*-genitive, while (4) allows both constructions.

3 The owner of the car that was stolen has not yet been found.
4 The car's owner / The owner of the car has not yet been found.

Again there is a parallel with clauses: although noun phrases in both subject and object position vary in complexity, subjects tend to be shorter and less complex than objects.

Both *s*-genitives and subjects tend to express information that is given in the context, while *of*-constructions and objects more typically express new information.

5 Tom is the proud owner of a new Ford.
6 The young man stole a new Ford. The car's owner has not yet been found.

The choice of an *of*-construction in (5) and an *s*-genitive in (6) is in agreement with the information principle (**5.14**).

5.5.5 Genitives in nominal position

In special cases, *s*-genitives are used without being followed by a head noun.

A Elliptic genitives

The head noun may be recoverable from the preceding text, as in (1) below:

1 Bob's paper deserves a better grade than John's.
2 Bob's is the better paper.
3 The present government's attitude is stricter than that of any previous administration.

Example (2) illustrates a stylistically marked construction where the head noun is recoverable from the following text. Instead of an elliptic *s*-genitive, (3) has an equivalent *of*-construction (*that of ...*). The latter is used where an ordinary *of*-construction would have been the more natural choice: *stricter than the attitude of any previous administration* vs. ?*stricter than any previous administration's attitude*. Note also that the choice of the *of*-phrase in (3) underlines the contrast, with the contrasting terms in initial and end position of the clause.

B Local genitives

With some types of expressions referring to locations, a head noun cannot be supplied from the surrounding text: *we had lunch at my brother's*, *go down to the grocer's*, *we went to St Paul's*, *I bought it at Heffer's*. The connection with the genitive tends to become weakened with names of companies. Thus, for example, we may find *McDonald's* and *Woolworth's* spelt without an apostrophe.

C The double genitive

The double genitive is a construction which makes it possible to combine a specifying genitive (or a possessive pronoun) and another determiner. Thus:

a friend of Tom's	but not	*a Tom's friend
a friend of mine		*a my friend

The head noun is often preceded by an indefinite article, but we also find the double genitive with plural indefinite noun phrases and with noun phrases preceded by demonstrative determiners:

many friends of Tom's, that crazy idea of Tom's
two friends of mine, these friends of mine

The double genitive should be compared with partitive constructions:

a close/good friend of my sister's
one of my sister's close/good friends

Although *a friend of my sister's* and *one of my sister's friends* would seem to mean the same, the difference comes out when an adjective is inserted. The partitive construction makes it clear that my sister has a number of close/good friends. The double genitive simply picks out a friend of my sister's and says that she is a close/good friend. The difference is even clearer in *she's a great friend of my sister's*, which can hardly be paraphrased as *one of my sister's great friends*.

5.6 Quantifying determiners

Nouns can also be specified for number and amount. The choice of form varies with the type of noun: singular countable, plural countable, or uncountable (see Table 5b). Where the head of the noun phrase is definite, the preposition *of* must generally be inserted: *most girls* vs. *most of the girls*, *some money* vs. *some of her money*, etc. Quantified definite heads imply that we refer to a certain number or amount from a defined totality known to the speaker and the addressee: *most of the girls*. Some problems in the choice of quantifying determiners will be dealt with in the survey of indefinite pronouns (**5.11**).

Table 5b: Quantifying determiners

Singular countable	Plural countable	Uncountable
every/each girl	all (the / of the) girls	all (the / of the) salt
-	most (of the) girls	most (of the) salt
-	more girls	more salt
-	many (of the) girls	much (of the) salt
-	a great many girls	a great deal of salt
-	a lot of / lots of (the) girls	a lot of / lots of salt
-	enough girls	enough salt
-	some (of the) girls	some (of the) salt
-	(a) few (of the) girls	(a) little salt
-	fewer girls	less salt
-	(the fewest girls)	least salt
-	several (of the) girls	-
-	a couple of (the) girls	-
either girl	both (of the) girls	-
one girl	two (of the) girls	-
any girl	any (of the) girls	any (of the) salt

5.7 The role of pronouns

Pronouns replace full noun phrases when the situation or the surrounding text makes it clear what the referent is. This is the role of the personal, reflexive, and reciprocal pronouns (**5.8**), demonstrative pronouns (**5.9**), and possessive pronouns (**5.10**). Two groups of pronouns stand out from the rest: indefinite pronouns (**5.11**), which are used when the speaker cannot or does not want to refer to specific entities, and *wh*-pronouns (**5.13**), which are important devices in building special clause types.

Pronouns normally function on their own as clause elements, but pronoun-headed phrases do occur, particularly with indefinite pronouns: *(there must be) something wrong*, *nothing else*, *everyone who is interested*, etc. See **2.6.2**.

Pronouns greatly simplify the use of language, since they make it unnecessary to specify in detail who the speaker is, who the addressee is, and which other entities are being referred to. It is sufficient that they are identifiable through the speech situation or the surrounding text. The choice between full noun phrase and pronoun is dealt with at the end of this chapter.

5.8 Personal pronouns

The personal pronouns are listed in Table 5c, together with the corresponding possessive and reflexive pronouns. Unlike nouns, the personal pronouns distinguish between a **subject** case (used in subject position) and an **object** case (used in other positions). Note the object form in subject predicative position after *be* (1), after *as* and *than* (2), and in non-integrated noun phrases (3, 4):

1 It's *me/him.*
2 I'm bigger than *him.* / He's smaller than *me.* / He's not as big as *me.*
3 *Me* and my friend Tom, we've been to the movies.
4 A: Who told him?
B: *Me.* / I did.

The object case is normal in these contexts in spoken English. In writing we frequently find subject forms. The case conflict can be avoided by opting for a reflexive pronoun; see **5.8.7A**, example (3).

Table 5c: Personal, possessive, and reflexive pronouns

Person	Personal		Possessive		Reflexive
	Subject	Object	Determiner	Pronoun	
1. singular	I	me	my	mine	myself
plural	we	us	our	ours	ourselves
2. singular	you	you	your	yours	yourself
plural	you	you	your	yours	yourselves
3. singular	he	him	his	his	himself
	she	her	her	hers	herself
	it	it	its	-	itself
plural	they	them	their	theirs	themselves

5.8.1 First and second person pronouns

The first person singular refers to the speaker/writer, and the first person plural to the speaker/writer + other people (including or excluding the addressee). The reference of the first person plural is, in fact, often quite vague. In a personal letter, *we/us* may refer to 'I and my family', 'I and you', 'I and some of my friends', etc. In a political speech, a government minister can exploit the first person plural to good effect, shifting between references to the government, to the party, and to the people. In academic papers, the reference may be to the authors, the author(s) and the readers, or even to a single author. In special contexts, the first person plural may refer to a single speaker only (the royal *we*) or to the addressee only, e.g. in some cases of doctor–patient communication (*How are we feeling today*?).

The reference of the second person is not straightforward either. Present-day English makes no distinction between one or more addressees. There are means of making this explicit, by using forms like *you two*, *you people/guys*, *you all*, etc. There are also dialectal plural forms like *you ones* and *yous*. Generally, however, the reference of *you* must be interpreted in relation to the context.

5.8.2 Third person pronouns

While the first and second person pronouns are interpreted in relation to the speech situation, the reference of the third person pronouns must generally be sought in the preceding text. In other words, there is **anaphoric** reference:

1 C took a small penlight from his coat pocket and flashed *it* over the mailboxes.
2 I saw this car and *he* ran into the fence.
3 A: I don't like *it*.
B: What? What is it you don't like?

The reference of the third person pronouns often requires a good deal of co-operation between the speaker and the addressee, particularly in spontaneous speech. The speaker must make sure that there is enough common knowledge to establish the reference.

In (1) above *it* could theoretically point back to either the penlight or the coat pocket, but only the former interpretation fits the verb. In (2) we interpret the pronoun as referring to the driver of the car; the mechanism is the same as with indirect anaphoric reference of the definite article (**5.2.3**). The reference of *it* is often quite vague, as in (3). In speech the addressee can clear up potential misunderstandings by asking questions. This is, of course, not possible in writing. The good writer pays attention to the use of pronouns and attempts to avoid vagueness of reference.

In special contexts the reference of the third person pronouns is **cataphoric**, i.e. dependent upon the following text:

4 *He* thought of the city as a galaxy. (opening of a novel)
5 *He* shambles on, stained with time and effort, looking like a cashiered Ruritanian general left over from the Crimean War. *He* slumps into an ample chair, and nods off into a fitful doze. *Peter Ustinov* has finally met William Shakespeare. (opening of a review of a theatre performance)

The pronoun in example (4) is used like the definite article in similar contexts (see end of **5.2.3**). Example (5) illustrates a stylistic device that is frequently employed in journalism, presumably to raise the curiosity of the reader.

5.8.3 Pronouns and gender

A Personal vs. impersonal reference

The choice of *he*, *she*, and *it* varies with the type of entity referred to. Though *he* and *she* are normally reserved for people, they may also be applied to animals. The use of *he* and *she* presupposes greater familiarity or a more intimate relationship. The same is true of *he* and *she* vs. *it* with *child* and *baby*. Exceptionally, *he* and *she* are used for inanimate entities, e.g. in connection with personification, where human characteristics are attributed to things or abstract notions. The feminine pronoun was commonly used earlier for countries and ships, but *it* is now the more neutral form. As regards personal vs. impersonal reference, note also the special problems with collective nouns (**4.6.1**).

B In search of gender-neutral expressions

It is a special problem that there is no gender-neutral pronoun in English. Traditionally, *he/him/his* were often chosen with reference to both a male human being and a person in general, as in:

1 The by-laws state that *the chairman* is in charge of the meeting, and everybody present must listen carefully to what *he* has to say.

This use of the masculine pronoun has come in for a great deal of criticism. The same applies to the use of a noun like *chairman* in such cases. Some people choose a gender-neutral noun like *chairperson* instead, but *chair* on its own is increasingly preferred to avoid sexual bias.

There are various more or less clumsy ways of avoiding sexual bias with pronouns: *he or she*, *he/she*, *s/he*, *(s)he*, etc. Frequently the speaker/writer chooses a plural pronoun or determiner, where there is no gender distinction:

2 Everyone said *they* were coming.
3 Nobody remembered to bring *their* textbooks.

In spite of the obvious 'discord', such examples are normal in speech. A number clash can often be avoided by opting for plural nouns as well as pronouns/determiners. Compare:

4 *A doctor* should take good care of *his* patients.
5 *Doctors* should take good care of *their* patients.

5.8.4 Referring to people in general

We, *you*, and *they* can all be used to refer to people in general, corresponding to 'en/man' in Norwegian:

1 In Norway, *we* eat a lot of fish.
2 *You* never know what will happen next.
3 *They* say we'll have a cold winter.

We and *they* retain a tinge of the basic meaning of these pronouns. *You* is an informal way of referring to people in general. A more formal alternative is *one*:

4 *One* cannot have too much of a good thing.

The English passive may also correspond to Norwegian 'en/man':

5 It just isn't done.
Slik gjør man bare ikke.

5.8.5 Special uses of *it*

There are a number of non-referential uses of *it*: *it's raining*, *it's important to act quickly*, *it's this book I want*, etc. See **11.8–11.10**.

5.8.6 Norwegian 'det' and its correspondences in English

English *it* normally corresponds to 'det', both when it is used as a reference pronoun (**5.8.2**) and in the special uses just referred to (**5.8.5**). The problem from a Norwegian point of view is that 'det' has a much wider range of use and may correspond to many other forms than *it*. The points below focus on some fairly regular correspondences.

A *That*

English *it* is unstressed, except in some special expressions (e.g. *that's it*). Norwegian stressed 'det' corresponds to *that* in English.

1 I didn't know that.
Det visste jeg ikke.

B ***So***

English uses *so* rather than *it* with reporting verbs and verbs of opinion:

2 A: Is the book out now?
B: I think so / I believe so / I guess so (AmE) / I am afraid so / I hope so / I expect so / I suppose so / it seems so ('jeg tror det', 'jeg er redd for det', etc.).

Note the negative counterparts: I think not (or: I don't think so) / I believe not (or: I don't believe so) / I guess not (AmE) / I am afraid not / I hope not / I expect not / I suppose not (or: I don't suppose so) / it seems not (or: It doesn't seem so).

Note also expressions of the following kind, with subject–auxiliary inversion (**11.2.1B**): so did I, nor did I ('det gjorde jeg også', 'det gjorde heller ikke jeg').

C Ellipsis

Where Norwegian has 'det' as an object or a predicative, English frequently has ellipsis. 'Det' is very often placed before the verb.

3	A: Do you know the answer?	B: Yes, I do. ('Ja, det gjør jeg.')
4	A: Are you free tonight?	B: No, I'm not. ('Nei, det er jeg ikke.')
5	A: I know the answer.	B: Do you? ('Gjør du det?')

Ellipsis is normal with auxiliary verbs in responses (3, 4) and comment questions (5). The same difference is found with some lexical verbs, e.g.:

6 A: Why didn't you tell me? B: I don't remember.
I forget.
I don't know.

Again, Norwegian often has 'det' in initial position ('det husker jeg ikke', 'det har jeg glemt', 'det vet jeg ikke'). The contrast between the two languages has to do with the different conditions of fronting (**11.3.2**). Unlike Norwegian, English cannot front an unstressed pronoun. In these cases ellipsis is preferred to putting an information-weak pronoun in the place of focus at the end of the sentence.

D ***There***

Norwegian 'det' in presentative constructions corresponds to existential *there* in English. Note, however, that Norwegian presentative constructions must often be rendered in other ways in English (**11.10**).

E *What*

Norwegian 'det (som)' in nominal relative clauses (**12.8.2**) corresponds to *what* in English:

7 What you propose is wrong.
Det (som) du foreslår, er galt.
8 I'll buy what you want.
Jeg kjøper det (som) du vil ha.

5.8.7 Reflexive and reciprocal pronouns

A Reflexive pronouns

The reflexive pronouns (see Table 5c) have three main uses, illustrated in:

1 I cut *myself* with the kitchen knife.
2 I cut the bread *myself*.
3 Tom and *myself* are going to the movies.
This will probably appeal to your friends and *yourself* since ...

The most basic use is shown in (1): the reflexive pronoun marks that the object is co-referent with the subject; the pronoun is usually unstressed. Example (2) illustrates the emphatic use: the reflexive pronoun is stressed and underlines the identity of another noun phrase (cf. the strengthening effect of *own* with the possessive determiners, **5.4**); note that the reflexive pronoun can be left out in (2) without impairing the syntax of the clause. In (3) the reflexive pronoun replaces a personal pronoun. This is a more marginal use often found where there is case variation (see **5.8**).

B Reflexive verbs

There are many verbs in Norwegian which obligatorily contain a reflexive pronoun. Such reflexive verbs are far less common in English (see also **9.7**). Compare:

approach ('nærme seg')
care about ('bry seg om')
change ('forandre seg')
expand ('utvide seg')
feel ('føle seg')
hurry ('skynde seg')
lie down ('legge seg')
marry ('gifte seg')
move ('bevege seg')
open ('åpne seg')
put on ('ta på seg')
sit down ('sette seg')
spread ('spre seg')
turn ('snu seg')

Note that *behave* is normally non-reflexive: *she behaved badly. Behave oneself* means 'oppføre seg ordentlig': *Behave yourself.*

C Reciprocal pronouns

Like the reflexive pronouns, the reciprocal pronouns mark identity between a noun phrase and the subject in the same clause. The difference is that the reciprocal pronouns express a mutual relationship: *X and Y love each other = X loves Y and Y loves X.*

4 They hardly even speak to *each other*.
5 We must all help *one another*.

The two forms are used in much the same way, but *one another* is the more formal alternative.

5.9 Demonstrative pronouns

The relationship between the demonstrative pronouns and the demonstrative determiners is parallel to that between personal pronouns and noun phrases with the definite article. Compare:

the house	it	this/that house	this/that
the houses	they	these/those houses	these/those

Both the personal pronouns and the demonstrative pronouns mark an entity as known. In addition, the demonstrative pronouns specify whether the entity is near or distant in relation to the speaker/writer. The contrast between *this/these* and *that/those* is basically the same as that between the corresponding determiners (**5.3**).

1 Could you give her one of *these*?
2 Where did you buy *those*?
3 What do you mean by *that*?
4 Touch is not a secret sense, and it is limited to objects in physical contact. *This* means that when a foe is identified by touch, it is too late to devise and carry out a strategy.

The reference of *this* and *that* may be quite vague. *That* is typically more informal and is frequent in conversation. *This* is common in academic writing, but it is a good strategy not to overuse it.

5.10 Possessive pronouns

Possessive pronouns are found under the same circumstances as elliptic and double genitives (**5.5.5A**, **C**):

1 My car is better than *yours*.
2 Is she a friend of *yours*?

Note also expressions like *you and yours* ('you and your family/friends') and the use of *yours* in ending a letter:

- *Yours faithfully/sincerely/truly* (formal letters)
- *Yours* (in less formal letters)

The following forms are common in American English: *Sincerely, Sincerely yours*, and *Yours truly*.

5.11 Indefinite pronouns

There is a close relationship between quantifying determiners (**5.6**) and indefinite pronouns. Many of the quantifying determiners can be used as indefinite pronouns if the head noun is recoverable from the preceding text:

1 I've bought some wine. Would you like *some*?
2 They offered me some water, but I didn't want *any*.
3 Some of the guests have arrived, but not very *many*.
4 I invited some friends of mine, but *none* (of them) was/were able to come.

Note that the determiner *no* is replaced by *none* when there is no head noun.

There are four groups of compound indefinite pronouns made up of a determiner and another element:

anybody	everybody	nobody	somebody
anyone	everyone	no one	someone
anything	everything	nothing	something
(anywhere)	(everywhere)	(nowhere)	(somewhere)

The compound indefinite pronouns are used when the reference is very general and no head noun is recoverable from the context. The forms ending in *-body* and *-one* refer to an indefinite person; those in *-thing* have non-personal reference. The *-body* forms are more informal than those ending in *-one*. Each of the four groups has a corresponding place adverb. As the adverbs have a different distribution from the pronouns, they are given within parentheses above.

Some problems in the choice of indefinite pronouns and the corresponding determiners will be taken up in the sections below. The *no*-group is dealt with in connection with negation (**14.2.1B**).

5.11.1 *All, every, each*

These forms have a universal meaning. *All* is used with both countable and uncountable nouns (Table 5b). With countable nouns, *all* focuses on the whole of a group and *every/each* on the individuals.

1 All the students received a prize.
2 Every student received a prize.
3 Each student received a prize.

Note that (1) may mean that the students shared a single prize. The difference between *every* and *each* is slight here. In general, *each* focuses more on the individual member, while *every* has a stronger sense of generality or universality. Since (5) refers to a general state of affairs, *every* is preferable to *each*. Compare:

4 Each teacher / Each of the teachers gave a speech.
5 Every good teacher is also an amateur actor.

Unlike *each*, *every* cannot be used in connection with only two people or things.

Every differs syntactically from *all* and *each* in that it cannot be used alone as a pronoun. The propword *one* (**5.12A**) must be added:

6 They had five copies, but they lost every one /'evri 'wʌn/.
De hadde fem eksemplarer, men de mistet hvert eneste ett.

Every one should be distinguished from the compound indefinite pronoun *everyone* (= *everybody*):

7 Everyone arrived safe and sound.
Alle kom fram i god behold.

5.11.2 *Both, either, neither*

Both is similar to *all*, except that it is used about two persons or things. The contrast between *both* and *either* is similar to the one between *all* and *each* (**5.11.1**). Note the form and meaning of:

either /ˈaɪðə/	BrE,	/ˈiːðər/	AmE	one or the other
neither /ˈnaɪðə/	BrE,	/ˈniːðər/	AmE	not one and not the other

1	Both answers are correct.	Either solution is possible.
2	Both are unacceptable.	Neither of them is acceptable.
3	You can't have it both ways.	You can do it either way.
4	Can you see both of them?	Can you see either of them?

There is no single equivalent to *either* and *neither* in Norwegian: 'begge løsningene' (1), 'ingen av dem' (2), 'på begge måtene' (3), 'noen av dem' (4).

5.11.3 *Much, many, a lot of, lots of*

These forms express a large number or amount. *Much* combines with uncountable nouns, *many* with plural countable nouns, and *a lot of / lots of* with both types (Table 5b). There is a tendency for *much* and *many* to occur in negative and interrogative sentences, and for *a lot of / lots of* to occur in positive declarative sentences. Compare:

1	Has she got many friends?	She has a lot of friends.
2	I don't have much money.	They have lots of money.

A lot of and *lots of* are informal expressions. In formal writing, *much* and *many* are found in positive declarative sentences. They are particularly common in subject position (5, 6).

3 He used to buy many books.
4 She found much of her work boring.
5 Many of the guests were from abroad.
6 Much of the criticism was unfair.

Other expressions for a large number or amount are *a great/good many* and *a great deal (of)*. The former combines with plural countable nouns; the latter with uncountable nouns (Table 5b).

7 A great many changes have taken place.
8 They have a great deal in common.

Though they are more formal, these expressions are similar in meaning and distribution to *a lot of / lots of*.

5.11.4 *Few, a few, little, a little*

These forms express a small number or amount. *Few* and *a few* combine with plural countable nouns; *little* and *a little* with uncountable nouns (Table 5b). *A few* and *a little* are similar in meaning to *some*; *few* and *little* mean *not many* and *not much*, i.e. less than expected. Compare:

1	She has few friends.	She has a few friends.
2	She ate very little.	She managed to eat a little.

5.11.5 *Some* vs. *any*

The determiners *some* and *any* both correspond to Norwegian 'noe(n)'. They combine with both countable and uncountable nouns (Table 5b). The corresponding pronoun forms are given at the beginning of **5.11**. In the text below we will use the capitalized forms SOME and ANY to refer to the groups of *some*-words and *any*-words.

SOME is typically found in **assertive** contexts (asserting the truth of something), and ANY in **non-assertive** contexts (negative, interrogative, and conditional clauses). Compare:

1 She asked for *some* /səm, sm/ money.
2 I must remember to buy *some* /səm, sm/ wine.
3 There is no wine left. I must buy *some* /sʌm/.
4 *Some* /sʌm/ people believe in ghosts.
5 There's *somebody* coming to see me this morning.
6 She didn't ask for *any* money.
7 Did you meet *anybody* on the way here?
8 If you see *anything* suspicious, do let me know.

The determiner *some* is generally unstressed and pronounced with a weak form (1, 2). When *some* is used as a pronoun (3) or when it means 'certain' (4), it is pronounced with a strong form. See further **D** below.

A The meanings of SOME vs. ANY

Some indicates a limited, though unspecified, quantity or number. The compound forms refer to a particular, though unspecified, person (*somebody*, *someone*) or thing (*something*). *Some* and its compounds frequently imply 'existence':

9 There are *some* people who believe in ghosts.
10 I saw *something* nasty in the woodshed.

Any and its compounds mean 'any … at all', or in Norwegian 'noe(n) som helst', i.e. non-limitation. Existence is explicitly denied, or it is in doubt:

11 There aren't *any* people who believe in ghosts.
12 Did you see *anybody* there?

B SOME in non-assertive contexts
When the speaker/writer believes in the existence of something, we may find SOME in non-assertive contexts. Compare:

13a I haven't read *some* of these books. ('visse; en del')
13b I haven't read *any* of these books. ('noen')

14a If you have *some* questions, do not hesitate to ask.
14b If you have *any* questions, do not hesitate to ask.

15a Didn't you receive *some* letters this morning?
15b Did you receive *any* letters this morning?

The speaker assumes that there are some questions in (14a) and that there were some letters in (15a). There is no such assumption in (14b) or (15b). Similarly, when asking a question like *Is something wrong?*, the speaker indicates that he/she has a reason to assume that there is something the matter (e.g. judging by the addressee's behaviour).

SOME is frequently found in interrogative sentences which express suggestions (16, 17), requests (18, 19), and invitations (20, 21):

16 Why don't you say *something*?
Cf. Why didn't you say *anything*? (true question asking for information)
17 Can't we do *something* else?
18 Could *someone* please turn on the light?
Cf. Did *anyone* turn off the light? (true question asking for information)
19 Could you pour me *some* more tea?
20 Won't you have *some* cake?
21 Would you like *some* toast?

The interrogative form suggests an open mind on the part of the speaker; the addressee may accept or refuse. Nevertheless, it is more tactful to assume acceptance, and this is the implication of SOME.

C ANY in assertive contexts

ANY in assertive contexts means 'no matter what/who/which', or in Norwegian 'hvem/hva/hvilken som helst'. It is normally stressed. An unstressed *any* in (24) would imply that the speaker expresses uncertainty with respect to the existence of documents.

22 We welcome *any* new trade links between our two countries.
23 They could read *any* of the books in the library.
24 He would photocopy *any* documents he happened to come across.

Compare the meaning of arbitrariness of ANY vs. the notions of limitation and particularity of SOME:

25 *Some* men believe in *anything*.
26 *Anything* could happen. Cf. *Something* could happen.
27 Tell me *something*! *Anything*!

Note the contrast between the two uses of ANY in negative contexts:

28 Don't tell ˋANYBODY! ('noen som helst')
29 Don't tell ˇANYBODY! ('hvem som helst')

D Stressed *some*

The determiner *some* is stressed when it is contrasted with something else:

30 *Some* people believe in ghosts, *others* don't.

Note also the use of stressed *some* before singular countable nouns in the senses 'en eller annen / et eller annet' (31) and 'litt av en/et, en/et ordentlig, skikkelig …' (32):

31 There must be *some* job he can do.
32 She's *some* pianist!

Finally, note the use of *some* in expressions with numerals: *some three hundred years ago* ('omtrent').

5.12 The pronoun *one*

Apart from being used as a numeral, *one* has two pronominal uses.

A The propword *one*

One may point back to a preceding countable noun in the same sentence, or in a previous sentence:

1 Have you got any books on op art? I would like to borrow *one*.
2 She's bought a new coat instead of her old *one*. ('den gamle')
3 A: Have you got any gold coins?
B: No, I've only got silver *ones*. ('sølvmynter')

The propword *one* is often found after attributive adjectives or nouns. Norwegian uses a nominalized adjective (**8.9.4**) or must occasionally, as in (3), repeat the noun.

The propword *one* also combines with determiners, making the reference more explicit:

4 A: Which of these pictures do you prefer? B: Either (*one*).
Neither (*one*).
This (*one*).
That (*one*).

5 A: Why don't you buy this picture? B: I prefer another (*one*).
I prefer the other (*one*).
Which (*one*)?

The propword is obligatory with the determiner *every* (**5.11.1**).

B Generic *one*

Generic *one* is used with reference to people in general, corresponding to Norwegian 'man/en'. The following forms are available: *one*, *one's*, *oneself*.

6 *One* should not mimic *one's* (AmE: *his*) teachers.
7 *One* can't play well if *one* (AmE: *he*) is too tired.

Generic *one* is more formal than other English expressions for people in general (**5.8.4**). It is also more formal than Norwegian 'man/en'.

5.13 *Wh*-words

The following words are often referred to as *wh*-words:

Pronouns:	who, whom
Pronouns or determiners:	what, which, whose
Adverbs:	how, why
Adverb or subordinating conjunction:	when, where
Subordinating conjunction:	whether

Wh-words are used to build cleft constructions (**11.9**, **12.9.1**), relative clauses (**12.6.1**), and interrogative structures (**14.3.1**): *what I want is a book*, *the book which I want*, *what do you want*, etc. Note the following points:

A *Who* vs. *whom*

The traditional object case form *whom* is becoming increasingly rare, particularly in spoken English, and *who* is commonly found in object position. The only position where *whom* is required is following a preposition:

1 She abandoned her husband, to whom she had been married for twenty years.
2 It is an insult. – To whom?

B *Whose*

While relative *whose* can be used with reference to both persons and things, interrogative *whose* has personal reference only. Compare:

3 He is a man whose word can be trusted.
4 The police checked all vans whose occupants appeared suspicious.
5 Whose book is this? / Whose is this book?

C *Which* vs. *what/who*

While relative *which* always has non-personal reference, interrogative *which* can refer to both persons and things. Interrogative *which* asks for a choice between a limited set of possibilities, often specified in a following *of*-phrase. Compare:

6	What do you want?	Which (of these) do you want?
7	Who did you meet?	Which one did you meet?
8	What colour is the blouse?	Which of these colours do you like best?

5.14 Information structure

The use of pronouns vs. full noun phrases varies with syntactic function and with the type of text. Pronouns are most typically associated with subject position; noun-headed phrases, with positions later in the clause (the subjects are italicized in the passage below):

> When *I* first met the twins, John and Michael, in 1966 in a state hospital, *they* were already well-known. *They* had been on radio and television, and made the subject of detailed scientific and popular reports. *They* had even, *I* suspected, found their way into science fiction, a little 'fictionalized', but essentially as portrayed in the accounts *that* had been published.
>
> *The twins*, *who* were then twenty-six years old, had been in institutions since the age of seven, variously diagnosed as autistic, psychotic or severely retarded.
>
> (From Oliver Sacks, *The Man Who Mistook His Wife for a Hat*)

The subject typically makes reference to something which is known and can be expressed by a pronoun (or a definite noun phrase). New information is generally introduced later in the clause, using noun-headed phrases (usually indefinite in form). The tendency to present information in the order known-to-new may be called the **information principle** (see further **11.1.2**).

The proportion of pronouns vs. nouns varies greatly with the type of text (**16.3.2**). In conversation, pronouns tend to outnumber nouns; in academic prose and news reportage, nouns are about ten times more common than pronouns, reflecting the far more complex subject matter and the tighter packaging of information.

5.15 Anaphoric distance

When a referent has been introduced in a text, it is possible to refer to it later by a variety of means. These are some of the main devices:

- definite article + repeated noun (*the car*)
- demonstrative determiner + repeated noun (*this/that car*)
- definite article + related noun (*the vehicle*)
- demonstrative determiner + related noun (*this/that vehicle*)
- demonstrative pronoun (*this/that*)
- personal pronoun (*it*)

We can rank these devices broadly according to anaphoric distance, i.e. the distance to the form in the text which it points back to (using the example above):

this < it < this vehicle < this car < the vehicle < the car

After introducing a referent, it is most natural to go on with a pronoun. A demonstrative form signals closer distance. As the distance grows and there is a risk of unclear reference, it is more natural to choose a full noun phrase. A repeated noun is the clearest form and tolerates the greatest distance.

5.16 Chains of reference

Within a text we can identify chains of reference, as shown in this example (from Iona & Peter Opie, *Children's Games in Street and Playground*):

'Queenie' is the perpetual delight of little girls aged eight and nine, for it has the great recommendation of combining the mysterious pleasure of guessing with the ball-play to which they are so much addicted. One girl is selected 'Queenie', given the ball, and stands with her back turned to the rest. Without looking behind her, she throws the ball back over her head, and the other girls scramble for it. They then form up in a row, with their hands behind their backs so that the girl in front will not know which of them has the ball; and they let 'Queenie' know they are ready, sometimes addressing her in doggerel verse:

Queenie, Queenie,
Who has the ball?
...

Depending upon the number of referents introduced, we may find interlocking chains using a variety of anaphoric devices.

Terms

determiners:	articles (definite, indefinite, zero) demonstrative determiners possessive determiners quantifying determiners *wh*-determiners	genitive:	classifying specifying group genitive elliptic genitive local genitive double genitive
reference:	anaphoric indirect anaphoric cataphoric situational anaphoric distance chains of reference information principle case (subject, object, genitive) gender	pronouns:	personal reflexive reciprocal demonstrative possessive indefinite *wh*-pronouns generic *one* the propword *one*

Exercises

1 Translate into idiomatic English. (**5.2.1**)

a Naboen min liker å kjøre motorsykkel.
b Hassan er muslim.
c Han skal bygge hytte i Trysil neste sommer.
d Du burde heller ta drosje.
e For første gang er en kvinne blitt valgt til leder av styret.
f Morten skal bli lege.
g Som regel klarer vi oss uten bil når vi har ferie.
h Skriv brev til ham og forklar hvorfor du trakk deg ut.
i Vi hadde til og med bestilt rom på forhånd.
j Motstanderen hans viste seg å være professor i engelsk.

2 What do the italicized noun phrases in the pairs below refer to? (**5.2.1–5.2.4**)

a 1 I am looking for *a Clapton record.*
  2 I am listening to *a Clapton record.*
b 1 It is difficult for *an Englishman* to view the topic dispassionately.
  2 There was *an Englishman* in the group who claimed to be a playwright.
c 1 *The lion* hunts for food.

2 *The lion* is hunting for food.

d 1 *Doubts* were expressed as to the feasibility of this approach.

2 *Doubts* are feelings of uncertainty of opinion.

e 1 *The computer* has revolutionized most aspects of work.

2 He had left *the computer* in the car, and when he came back, the car had been broken into and *the computer* was gone.

f 1 *Snow* fell during the night.

2 They played in *the snow*.

g 1 This isn't beef, it's *lamb*.

2 *The lamb* got caught in the barbed wire.

3 Put in the definite article, the indefinite article, or the zero article in the open spaces in the text below. Give reasons for your choices. Explain any difference in meaning in cases where you think two types of article can be used. (**5.2.1–5.2.4**)

It was a great day when ____ man discovered that ____ speech could be used for ____ narrative. There are those who think that in this respect ____ picture language preceded ____ oral language. ____ man could draw ____ picture on ____ wall of his cave to show in which direction he had gone, or what ____ prey he hoped to catch. I am inclined to think that ____ language has been ____ most important single factor in _____ development of man. Another important development came not long after, at least when we consider ____ history of ____ man in its entirety. That was ____ agriculture. At first ____ agriculture could be practised only in ____ regions where ____ nature fertilized ___ soil after each harvest. ____ agriculture met with violent resistance from ____ pastural nomads, but ____ agricultural way of ____ life prevailed.

4 Translate the following sentences into English. Give the rule which explains the difference between Norwegian and English article usage in such cases. (**5.2.4B**)

a Den menneskelige natur skremmer meg.

b Analfabetismen representerer en stor utfordring.

c Lyset har en utrolig høy hastighet.

d Både ungdommen og alderdommen har sine fordeler.

e Den irske musikken har gitt meg mange gledestunder.

f Dansen betydde alt for ham.

g Tenk deg hvordan livet ville vært hvis ikke bilen hadde vært oppfunnet.

h Det moderne demokratiets vugge stod i det gamle Hellas.

5 Comment on the difference in form and meaning between the two members of each of the pairs below.

a 1 A dog is a man's best friend.
  2 The dog is the man's best friend.
b 1 Did he give you any money?
  2 Did he give you some money?
c 1 They had to pay for some damage they did.
  2 They had to pay for any damage they did.
d 1 Grammar is fascinating.
  2 The grammar is fascinating.
e 1 This people is friendly.
  2 These people are friendly.
f 1 He's just left for school.
  2 He's just left the school.
g 1 Most modern schools have a lot of good computer hardware.
  2 The most modern schools have a lot of good computer hardware.
h 1 Prices are going up all the time.
  2 The prices are going up all the time.
i 1 The David Mall I remember was a totally different person.
  2 I remember David Mall, who was a totally different person.
j 1 Have you got the time?
  2 Have you got *Time*?
k 1 We received little help from them.
  2 We received a little help from them.

6 Put in *it's* or *its* in the open spaces in this text. (**5.4**)

Thank you for the sample you sent us from Birmingham. _____ attracted a lot of attention among our staff. It looks as if _____ specifications meet the very detailed requirements we faxed you after the meeting in Oslo. ____ very likely that we will place an order with you in the near future. We are aware that you have built a new plant outside Birmingham and hope that ____ production capacity will be adequate to meet future demands for your product. We feel that ____ success is guaranteed.

7 What is the difference in meaning between the two members of the pairs below? (**5.3–5.4**)

a 1 I met this ravishing blonde at a party last night.
  2 I met that ravishing blonde at a party last night.
b 1 He put on his shoes.
  2 He put on the shoes.

c 1 She turned her head in the opposite direction.
2 She turned the head in the opposite direction.

8 Put in a demonstrative pronoun or determiner as required by the context. Choose among *this, these, that,* and *those.* Discuss any difference in meaning in cases where you think there is a choice. (**5.3**, **5.9**)

a 'Get rid of them', Nellie said contemptuously. 'You don't want any truck ('ikke noe å gjøre') with _____.'
b ____ were the days my friend, we thought they'd never end.
c ____ days we are happy to receive whatever small contribution we can get.
d I'll see you ____ evening at around ten, then.
e 'You'll not have a hair left on your head one of _____ days, if you go on like _____.'
f Nellie was a damn sight too good for ___ world.
g I hate _____ stupid friends of yours. Why don't you mix with a different lot?
h ____ people have terribly noisy parties which go on all night.

9 Pick out the demonstratives in the sentence below. (**5.3**, **5.9**)

That's that that that is called a demonstrative.

10 What does the use of *that* below tell you about where Richard is, where speaker A is, and where speaker B is? (**5.3**)

A: Open the door, Richard.
Open the door, Richard.
(Pause)
B: Why don't you open that door?

11 Classify the *s*-genitives in the sentences below. Discuss whether the *s*-genitive can or should be replaced by an *of*-construction. (**5.5**)

a You could see that she had Marge's slightly frantic eyes.
b John's has been discussed before.
c Belgium's J-L D and W K, the Dutch prime minister, were also present at the meeting.
d Inflation has soared for reasons outside the National Bank's control.
e Yesterday's decision to ban the group from performing in Japan was surprising.
f He feared her reaction, but even more her family's reaction.
g What's become of that cousin of Bill's?

h So far over a million copies have been sold. The book's appeal can be understood only if we bear in mind how it combines ...
i I got it at Godfrey's in Stonegate.
j Low-level learners make all sorts of strange mistakes, but this type of mistake is common even in advanced learners' English.

12 Rewrite the following text to remove the sexual bias. (**5.8.3**)

An important skill for a teacher is classroom management. She must be able to motivate the learner to achieve his potential and fulfil his aims. She must exercise patience and adopt a positive attitude towards her learners. This means encouraging the slow learner when he has trouble grasping certain points. If the learner who is quick to absorb new material is not given enough challenge, he will rapidly lose interest in the whole process of learning. He may even drop out of the course altogether.

13 Translate into idiomatic English. (**5.8.6**)

a Det er nytt for meg.
b Gentle Star kommer helt sikker til å vinne. – Det tror ikke jeg.
c Stikker du innom i kveld? – Jeg regner med det.
d Tror du pakken kommer fram innen fredag? – Jeg er redd det ikke er mulig.
e Jeg kan ikke forstå dem som reiser til syden midt på sommeren.
f Det som slår meg er at ingen vil ta ansvar for situasjonen.

14 Put in *either, neither, both, each, every, everybody,* or *all* in the sentences below, whichever is most appropriate. Discuss any difference in meaning in cases where you think there is a choice. (**5.11.1–5.11.2**)

a Once _____ two weeks we have a meeting to decide on the programme for the next fortnight.
b You can have ____ cheese or strawberries for dessert, but not ____.
c I can't repeat this ____ time you don't understand it.
d Well, there are more than 20 of us altogether. It doesn't matter. I'm sure ____ will feel welcome at his house.
e _____ had heard anything from Mary.
f I'll give you two _____.
g I am convinced that ____ politician has more personal ambition than ideological vision.

15 Put in a SOME word or an ANY word in the sentences below, whichever is more appropriate. Discuss any difference in meaning in cases where you think both can be used. Also, what degree of stress does the word receive? (**5.11.5**)

a Could you please give me _____ advice on how to fill in this form?
b Has he possibly said ____ that upset her?
c If ____ happens to you while you're away, don't hesitate to call.
d This restaurant will please ____ lover of Italian food.
e He would always stop and chat with _____ friends of his that he happened to meet.
f Why don't you have ____ more tea?
g Is there _____ really good reason why you can't come with us?
h I don't like _____ of his books.
i Don't you feel ____ anticipation now after the contract has been signed?
j He had refused to have ______ to do with the family after that incident.
k You can't prevent ____ from being true to his nature.
l But what if ____ refuses to pay?
m B's statement is not without _____ interest.

16 Correct what is wrong in these Norwegian-produced examples. Explain your corrections.

a Every country in the world have their own history.
b The Norwegian history is a record of kings and wars.
c Some foreigners only think of the Vikings. Others' attention is focused on our fjords and mountains.
d It was Olav Haraldsson who brought the Christianity to Norway.
e It reminds me of something Roosevelt said during the world war 2.
f At that time it was Norwegian's bravery and ability to work with the allied forces that commanded respect.
g In the end, Norway was declared nuclear-free area.
h It can be argued that our economy is to a too large extent based on oil revenues.
i The Olympics were really a fourteen days' long party.
j In addition to sports, Norway is famous for export of salmon.
k My vision of heaven is nothing like neither of these two heavens.
l As children we often heard that we would go to the heaven when we died.
m He works as engineer for the Norwegian company Statoil.
n The most of them couldn't even read or write.

6 Verbs and Verb Phrases

6.1 Introduction

The lexical verb in a clause is crucial, because it determines the syntax of the clause. Noun phrases vary greatly in length. In written English they may be long and short (**4.1.2**); in spoken English they tend to be shorter. Verb phrases, on the other hand, are generally short. Many consist of one or two words. If we include catenatives in the verb phrase, it becomes somewhat longer (**6.4.4**). The finite verb phrases are italicized in the text below.

> Mostly by accident, Britain's recent record on curbing greenhouse-gas emissions, which *contribute* to global warming, *is* one of the best in the world. The collapse of the coal industry and the 'dash for gas' in electricity generation since the mid-1980s *did* wonders for this. Thus Britain *was* one of the few countries on target to spew out no more greenhouse gases in 2000 than it *did* in 1990.

6.1.1 Different verbs – same meaning

The difference between *own* and *belong to* shows how the verbs determine the syntax of (1) and (2), which otherwise express the same content.

1 This house *belongs to* an uncle of mine.
2 An uncle of mine *owns* this house.

6.1.2 Polysemy in verbs

Many verbs have two or more related meanings. If this is the case, they are said to be **polysemous**. *Land* in the sense of 'get' is a transitive verb, but *land* in the sense of 'come to rest/settle (on the ground)' is intransitive. This is illustrated in (1) and (2) below.

1 She landed a nice job with General Accident.
2 The bird landed on the branch.

6.1.3 Same verb – different perspectives on the action

A verb like *close* can be used in many different ways:

1 John *closed* the door. (The clause tells us what John did.)
2 The door *closed* behind him, and there he was, with no key and no possibility of re-entering the house. (The clause tells us that the closing took place of its own accord.)
3 The door *closes* easily. (The clause says that the door has a special property.)
4 The door *was closed* when we arrived at the house. (The clause refers to a state which is the result of an action.)
5 The door *was closed* just as we had managed to push through, and nobody else was allowed in. (The clause tells what happened to the door.)
6 According to the log, the door *was closed* by the night watchman at 1 a.m. (The clause tells us what happened to the door as a result of somebody's action.)

What this little exercise proves is that lexical verbs are flexible and can be used in many different patterns, which convey different perspectives on the action or state denoted by the verb. Admittedly, not all verbs are as flexible as *close*, but it is the principle that deserves attention.

Another example of the great flexibility of verbs is *buy* in (7) and (8). The same sum of money appears as an adverbial of means in (7) and as a subject of the subordinate clause in (8).

The conclusion we must draw is that we should ask not only what verb is used, but also, often more importantly, how the verb is used.

7 I think you can *buy* a nice car for £5,000.
8 I think £5,000 will *buy* you a nice car.

6.2 Double word class membership (noun and verb)

English is different from Norwegian in that very many identical word forms can belong to more than one word class, typically the class of nouns and the class of verbs. The same content can be made thing-like (noun) and action-like (verb). This process is called **conversion.** We take the noun as our point of departure in (1) to (3), but the reverse process is also quite common, i.e. a noun created from a verb (4, 5).

1	The *police* patrolled the area in large numbers.	The area was heavily *policed.*
2	He was the *head* of the group.	He *headed* the group.

3 We went to many *shops* looking for a cheap jacket.	We *shopped* around for a cheap jacket.
4 They *attempted* to solve the problem.	They made an *attempt* to solve the problem.
5 She *walked* around the block.	She went for a *walk* around the block.

A change of class membership is also brought about through the addition of special suffixes added to the word.

6 She was taken to hospital.	She was hospitalized.
7 They were put into classes.	They were classified.
8 The country has a big population.	The country is densely populated.
9 He moans a lot.	He is a moaner.
10 Was John the one who informed you?	Was John your informant?

In some cases the clause changes meaning over and above the change which is related to the change of word class. Such changes may be quite unpredictable and idiomatic, especially if a noun is turned into a multi-word verb (**6.3.3**). Compare:

butter (n.)	*butter somebody up* (v.) ('smigre')
corner (n.)	*to corner somebody* (v.) ('trenge opp i et hjørne')
clock (n.)	*clock in/out* (v.) ('stemple inn/ut')
boss (n.)	*boss somebody about* (v.) ('sjefe over')

6.3 Types of lexical verbs

Lexical verbs can be subclassified on the basis of many different criteria. In this section we will look at subclasses of verbs. In **6.3.1** we distinguish between regular and irregular verbs on the basis of their form, more specifically their endings; in **6.3.2** we consider how verbs can be classified on the basis of the syntactic patterns they occur in. This is also a formal criterion. In **6.3.3** the criterion is whether the verb consists of one or more words. In **6.3.4** we discuss delexical verbs. The formal feature here is that a verb, e.g. *drink*, is rephrased as a delexical verb + noun phrase: *have a drink*. In **6.3.5** we look at verbs whose formal feature is that they have a productive prefix. Finally, in **6.3.6** we give some examples of verb suffixes.

6.3.1 Regular and irregular verbs

The distinction between regular verbs such as *talk, climb, add* and irregular verbs such as *break, go, put* is based on how the two types inflect in the past and the past participle forms. In Table 6a we give all five forms, for the sake of completeness.

Table 6a: The inflection of regular and irregular verbs

Form	Regular verbs	Irregular verbs
Base form	talk, climb, add	break, go, put
-s form	talks, climbs, adds	breaks, goes, puts
Past tense	talked, climbed, added	broke, went, put
Past participle	talked, climbed, added	broken, gone, put
-ing participle	talking, climbing, adding	breaking, going, putting

- The **base form** is used in the infinitive (*to talk, to break*), the present tense (*I talk, they break*), the imperative (**14.4**), and the subjunctive (**7.4.1**).

- The *-s* **form** appears in the third person singular present tense indicative (*she talks, he breaks*). It is therefore a person, tense, and mood marker combined.

- The **past tense** form is used to mark past time (*you talked* (*too much*), *she broke* (*down*)).

- The **past participle** is tenseless, but combines with *have* to build perfective forms (*have talked, had broken*), and with *be* to form the passive voice (*is talked* (*about*), *were broken* (*down*)). The past participle is by nature like an adjective (*the added condition, a broken promise*).

- The *-ing* **participle** is also tenseless, and has very many uses. Most important, it combines with *be* to form the progressive aspect (*are talking* (*nonsense*), *was breaking* (*down*)), and it is used to build *-ing* participle clauses ((*We have a family*) *living in the countryside*). The *-ing* participle can also be used as an adjective (*a charming appearance, the discussion was stimulating*) and as a verbal noun, which we call a gerund (*Smoking can damage your health*).

The irregular verbs must be learnt individually. They are listed in Appendix 1.

6.3.2 Transitivity types

The overwhelming number of English clauses can be shown to conform to one of seven basic clause patterns. This is clause syntax and will be taken up in more detail in Chapter 9. What is important to bear in mind is that it is the sense of the verb which determines the structure of the clause, that is, how many and what types of other clause elements the verb attracts. The term **valency** is used for the number of elements the verb attracts, and **transitivity** for the types of elements it combines with (see **9.4**). Table 6b specifies the main transitivity types.

Table 6b: Transitivity types

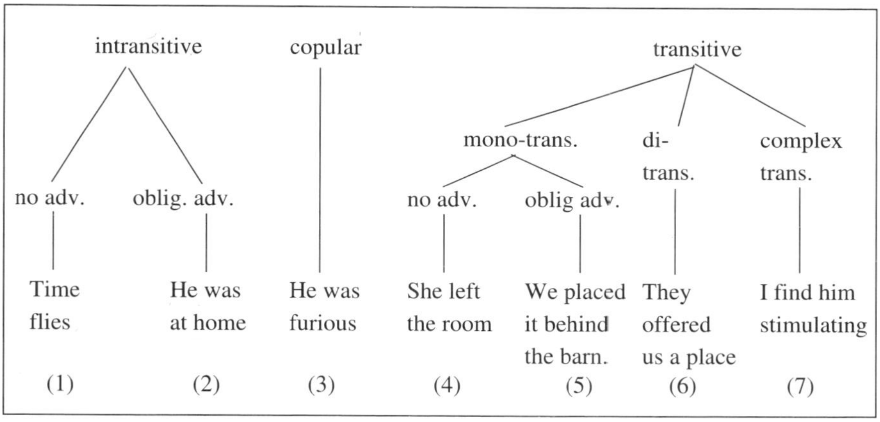

Intransitive verbs do not take objects, though some of them must have an adverbial element. This is particularly the case with the verb *be* in the sense 'exist'. **Copular verbs** are followed by subject predicatives. The corresponding Norwegian terminology is *uselvstendig verb* followed by *subjektspredikativ*. There are three types of transitive verbs. What they have in common is that they all pattern with objects. A **monotransitive verb** may or may not require an adverbial, a **ditransitive verb** takes two objects, and a **complex transitive verb** patterns with an object and an object predicative (Norwegian: *objektspredikativ)*. It should be emphasized that all seven clause patterns accept one or more optional adverbials. It is only in patterns 2 and 5 that an adverbial element is obligatory.

6.3.3 Single-word verbs and multi-word verbs

Verbs like *talk, write, walk, print, live, land, look, mention, continue, contribute, include, encounter* all consist of one word.

1 He *talked* just nonsense.
2 We *print* it twice a year.
3 We *included* a 20% increase in the building costs.
4 The committee *continued* its discussion after lunch.

A Verb plus adverbial
In many cases there is a preposition or an adverbial particle after the verb. The verb may still be felt to constitute a single-word verb phrase because the particle/preposition belongs to a separate sentence element, here an adverbial.

5 He *walked in.*
6 He *walked across* the street.
7 She *talked after* lunch.
8 The plane *landed in* Santa Fe.
9 They *looked into* the house.

B Prepositional verbs
In many combinations there is a preposition that is felt to belong to the verb, i.e. the verb selects the preposition. Such two-word verbs include *apply for, believe in, depend on, laugh at, look into, search for, send for, think of.*

10 I *applied for* a loan.
11 He didn't *laugh at* you.
12 They *looked into* the problem.

These combinations are referred to as **prepositional verbs**. A crucial feature here is that the preposition cannot be separated from the verb and placed after the following noun phrase (**they looked the problem into*). If we accept that the verb phrase consists of a two-word verb, then *a loan, you*, and *the problem* in (10) to (12) must be analysed as direct objects. Many prepositional verbs constitute a single unit of meaning and can be replaced by one verb, e.g. *look into* ('examine/investigate'), *run up (a bill)* ('incur').

C Phrasal verbs
A **phrasal verb** is a two-word verb where the second element is an adverbial particle. Such phrasal verbs can be transitive or intransitive. Note that in contrast to particles functioning as adverbials, the particle in a phrasal verb generally has a non-literal meaning.

13 Something will *crop up.*
14 I don't think this new fashion will *catch on.*
15 They refused to *give in* ('surrender').

Transitive phrasal verbs differ from prepositional verbs in that the particle can be moved after the object, and must be moved if the object is a pronoun (**11.4B**).

16 I'll *bring up* this point / *bring* this point *up* at the next meeting. I'll *bring* it *up* then.
17 Yes, you can *count* me *in.*
18 They decided to *put off* the meeting / *put* the meeting *off* until the next day.

As the literal meaning of the particle is weakened, phrasal verbs often constitute a single unit of meaning. They may be replaced by one verb, e.g. *give in* ('surrender'), *count in* ('include'), *put off* ('postpone'). The single verb alternative tends to be more formal.

D Phrasal–prepositional verbs
Another type of multi-word verb consists of a verb + an adverb + a preposition. As was the case with prepositional and phrasal verbs, their meaning may be idiomatic when the adverb and the preposition have lost their literal meanings. In such cases we cannot arrive at the meaning of the three-word combination by adding together the meanings of the individual elements.

19 Who's going to *see* you *off to* the station?
20 I've got to *catch up on* my reading.
21 This is something I will not *put up with.*
22 They *put* it *down to* carelessness.

E Other multi-word verbs
Some combinations consists of a verb + a noun + preposition, e.g. *take heart from, catch sight of,* and *take care of* below.

23 The company can *take heart from* the latest sales figures.
24 We *caught sight of* the raft 25 miles off the coast.
25 Could you possibly *take care of* it for me?

Other such multi-word combinations include those in:

26 We have to *make do with* what we have. (verb + verb + preposition)
27 *Let go of* the rope! (verb + verb + preposition)
28 We're *running low on* heating oil. (verb + adverb + preposition)
29 What they offered *fell short of* my hopes. (verb + adjective + preposition)

In general such multi-word verbs represent a heterogeneous class with many syntactic and semantic differences. The important point in this connection is that the term **multi-word verb** implies that these combinations are felt to have a unitary meaning. The meaning may be more or less idiomatic, i.e. more or less easy to understand on the basis of the meaning of the individual elements.

English is rich in such idiomatic multi-word verbs, a fact which may discourage a foreign learner who is striving to catch the colloquial flavour of modern English. On the whole, they belong to a more informal style, but very many are fully acceptable in formal writing. Consider finally this example where multi-word verbs are given in italics.

30 I'll *go along with* you as far as the principles are concerned, but I *take issue with* the specifics of the plan. You'll have to *come up with* something that allows us to *phase out* the production of this line of unsuccessful models. The model has been a disaster, and we may even be forced to *close down* our Birmingham plant.

6.3.4 Delexical verbs

Present-day English uses a small number of verbs very frequently in what are called delexical structures. The following five verbs are the most common: *give, have, make, take*, and *do*. In (1) to (6) below they are used with very little meaning. It is the noun in the object function that carries the meaning of the clause. Since the meaning of the verbs is weakened, they are often referred to as **delexical verbs**.

There are a number of points to note about such structures:

- In those cases where there is a full verb that can replace the delexical structure, the verb focuses on the action, and the delexical structure on the completed event (1, 2, 3).
- The noun can be easily modified by an adjective. In (4) *drank quickly* does not have the same meaning as *had a quick drink*.
- The delexical structure often implies a brief event; the alternative with the full verb gives the feeling that the action lasts longer (6).
- In some combinations both *have* and *take* can be used as delexical verbs. *Have* is more common in British English, and *take* in American English (1).

1 I *had/took a look* around the room.	I *looked* around the room.
2 We *had a good cry*.	We *cried* (for a while).
3 Mr B *gave a peculiar response*.	Mr B *responded* in a peculiar way.
4 Everybody *had a quick drink*.	?Everybody *drank* quickly.

5 She *had made great progress.*	She had *progressed enormously.*
6 We *had a chat* about her plans.	We *chatted* about her plans.

Give can be used as a delexical verb with two objects. Examples (7) and (8) are patterned on the normal syntax of *give* sentences: *I gave him a book.*

7 I'll *give it a think* and come back to you.	I'll *think* about it and come back to you.
8 Why don't you *give it a try?*	Why don't you *try?*

Delexical structures are definitely a feature of current idiomatic English.

6.3.5 Prefixed verbs

A verb like *run* is morphologically simple in that it has no prefix; *rerun* and *outrun*, on the other hand, are complex. The prefixed verb denotes an action which often has to be expressed in a more cumbersome way in Norwegian. The prefixes we mention below are normally attached to simple verbs and add the meaning stated in each case.

dis- 'to do the reverse of the action denoted by the simple verb'

disarrange:	The wind had disarranged her hair.
disconnect:	Disconnect the wires from the battery.
discontinue:	We have discontinued our subscription.

It should be noted that, in many verbs beginning with *dis-*, there is no connection with a simple verb (*distort, disturb*), or the meaning is not as straightforward as explained above (*disappoint, dismiss*).

mis- 'to do something wrong, intentionally or unintentionally'

mismanage:	The funds had been mismanaged.
mispronounce:	You mispronounced the second word.
misrepresent:	She accused us of misrepresenting her view.

out- 'to do something better than somebody else'

outrun:	She easily outran her classmates.
outsmart/outfox:	We managed to outfox our competitors.
outnumber:	They are now outnumbered by the Democrats.

over- 'to do something too much'

overreach:	One of these days you'll overreach yourself.
overstep:	It was felt that she had overstepped the limit.
overtax:	The man in the street feels that he is overtaxed.
overwork:	The excuse had been overworked. ('brukt for mye')

re- 'to do something again'

redo:	The last part is not good enough. You'll have to redo it redo it.
reshuffle:	She'll have to reshuffle her ministers.
revitalize:	Certain parts of inner-city Oslo are going to be revitalized.

In many cases *re-* cannot be related to the productive prefix we have given examples of above, e.g. in *regard, react.*

un- 'to do the opposite of what the simple verb means, to reverse the action'; commonly 'løsne, lukke opp, åpne' in Norwegian

unbutton:	He unbuttoned his shirt.
undo:	She undid the clasp of his belt.
unlock:	The door had been left unlocked.
unpack:	We'd better start unpacking.

under- 'not to do something enough'

underachieve:	He's bound to be underachieving no matter what school he goes to.
undersell:	I'm not going to be undersold by anybody!
understaff:	They tend to understaff their hospitals.
underspend:	We have underspent on the office equipment budget.

Most of the prefixed verbs we have exemplified above have past participle forms that can be used as adjectives, as in *He is overworked* ('overarbeidet'), *It became unbuttoned, The door was left unlocked.*

6.3.6 Verb suffixes

In **6.2** we referred to conversion and, very briefly, to suffixes that create verbs from other word classes. The most common and productive verb suffixes in English are listed below. The word class of the base is identified by A (adjective) and N (noun).

-en ('to make A or become A')

hard	harden
soft	soften
wide	widen

-ify ('to make or become A, to make into N')

pure	purify
simple	simplify
solid	solidify
example	exemplify
note	notify

-ise/-ize ('to make A, to put into N')

legal	legalise/legalize
final	finalise/finalize
passive	passivise/passivize
hospital	hospitalise/hospitalize
theory	theorise/theorize

There is a good deal of variation in spelling (see dictionaries). The *-ize* form is typical of American English. In those cases where either can be used, British English accepts both spellings.

6.4 The verb phrase

Two or more verbs may occur together, as in the italicized verb phrases in (1) to (3). We use the term verb when we talk about the clause function of such phrases (**2.8.2**).

1 He *may have heard* about it.
2 She *has been experimenting* with a new type of medicine.
3 We *didn't want* him hanging around the house.

These italicized verb phrases contain the main verbs *hear, experiment*, and *want.* They are the lexical verbs and, as such, also the main verbs in the phrases. However, in addition to the main verbs, verb phrases may also contain many supporting verbs which are crucial for how we understand the actions of hearing, experimenting, and wanting. These important distinctions will be taken up in detail in Chapter 7, but first we will look at the difference between finite and non-finite verb forms.

6.4.1 Finite and non-finite verbs

This distinction, which corresponds to the difference between 'finitt' and 'infinitt' in Norwegian, was introduced already in **2.6.4**. If a simple sentence has a verb phrase consisting of several verbs, the first is always the finite form, unless there is a modal auxiliary (see Table 6d); the others are non-finite (the infinitive, the past participle, and the *-ing* participle). The finite forms appear in italics in the examples below, and the non-finite forms in bold-face italics.

S |--------V-------| |----------dO--------------|
1 She *has* ***been using*** a new type of medicine.

S |-------V---------| |------sP--------|
2 He *must* ***have been*** terribly scared.

S V |-----------dO-----------|
3 She *wanted* ***to leave*** before dinner.

Non-finite verb forms are both verbal and non-verbal in nature. The syntactic analyses provided above show what we mean. In (1) and (2) the verb phrases are *has been using* and *must have been*, respectively. In (3), however, the verb phrase is *wanted*, and *to leave before dinner* functions as a direct object in a non-finite subordinate clause. The verb in this non-finite clause is *to leave*. It is this double-natured property of non-finite forms which allows us to form sentences with non-finite subordinate clauses embedded in quite complex syntactic hierarchies (see Chapter 13). In (4) below the non-finite forms have been italicized. We have clauses at three levels.

4 Tess went down the hill ... and inattentively waited
to take her seat in the van
returning from C to S.

As regards the use of the participle forms as adjectives and nouns, see **2.8.2B** and **6.3.1**.

6.4.2 Main verbs and auxiliary verbs

What we refer to as the main verb in the following is at the same time the lexical verb. It is common to use the term main verb when we think of the head of a verb phrase. The verb phrases in (1, 2, 3) in **6.4** contain both main verbs (*hear, experiment*, and *want*) and auxiliary verbs. The auxiliary verbs have no effect on the meaning of the main verb, but instead tell us how the sender views the process denoted by the main verb, e.g. whether it is completed or still going on, whether it is in the past, present, or future relative to the moment of speaking, etc. Other auxiliaries convey the speaker's view of the state of affairs expressed in the clause.

What we have just said represents a notional way of differentiating between auxiliaries and main verbs. We can also use a formal criterion. A sentence with an auxiliary verb does not need *do*-**insertion** in interrogative, negative, or emphatic affirmative sentences. Compare:

1	He read it out aloud.	*Did* he read it out aloud?
2	He was reading the letter.	*Was* he reading the letter?
3	They have read the report.	*Have* they read the report?
4	They'll read it when it's made available.	*Will* they read it when it's made available?
5	She could be telling the truth.	*Could* she be telling the truth?

It is only in (1) above that *did* is inserted before the subject; in the others, *was, have, will,* and *could* appear before the subject in the interrogative sentence form. They are auxiliaries (but note the exceptions taken up in **C** below). For more examples of *do*-insertion, see **B** below. The role of the auxiliary *do* is further discussed in **11.1.1D**.

A Modal auxiliaries

The modal auxiliaries are *can–could, may–might, must, ought to, shall–should*, and *will–would.* A modal auxiliary can be replaced by another modal auxiliary without affecting the grammaticality of the sentence. Modal auxiliaries have no *-s* form and no non-finite forms (**6.3.1**).

Despite their appearance, pairs like *can–could* rarely indicate a difference in tense between the present and the past. The difference is rather connected with the speaker's attitude towards the addressee. *Could, might, should*, and *would* seem to signal distance. The speaker or writer is concerned not to be too direct, not to impose on the hearer or reader. These historical past tense forms have the communicative effect of toning down the speech act, of making the message sound less imposing or urgent. They are also used in hypothetical situations, i.e. where some action is contingent upon something else. We will use the term **remote** to refer to the forms *could, might, should*, and *would.* This includes their occasional use to refer to past time situations as well as their more common use to signal distance and tentativeness.

Sections **7.10–7.21** give a systematic survey of the modal auxiliaries. Here are some examples:

1 We'*ll* follow you in our car.
2 He *must* have picked up the information from somebody else.

3 'Course there isn't a beast in the forest. How *could* there be? What *would* a beast eat?
4 *Might* I have a few words with you in private?
5 I *would* appreciate it if you *could* send them to the above address.

B Grammatical auxiliaries

In the category of grammatical auxiliaries we include:

- **do** in interrogative, negative, and emphatic affirmative sentences:

6 *Did* you want cream in your coffee, sir?
7 We *did*n't want him hanging around the house.
8 I *do* feel we ought to ask for a second opinion.
9 You *did*n't see him there, *did* you?

- **have** when used to build the perfective forms:

10 *Have* you heard what happened to Bill?
11 Even before he left, he *had* spoken to his senior partner.

- **be** when used to form the progressive aspect (12, 13) and the passive voice (14, 15):

12 Some of Snowball's secret agents *are* lurking among us at this moment!
13 It *was* still raining when I got up this morning.
14 The structure of this savage society *is* built up before our eyes.
15 It *was* announced that an extra potato ration would *be* issued.

C *Be, have,* and *do* as lexical verbs

These three frequent verbs can also be used as lexical verbs:

16 She does the cooking.	Does she do the cooking?
17 She is from Boston.	Is she from Boston?
18 She has a lot of money.	She hasn't (got) any money. (BrE)
	She doesn't have any money.

Lexical *do* requires *do*-insertion (16). Lexical *be*, on the other hand, does not take *do*-support (17); the only exception in Standard English is found in imperatives (see example 6 in **14.4.2**). Lexical *have* sometimes lacks *do*-insertion in British English (18).

D Combinations of grammatical and modal auxiliaries

Modal and grammatical auxiliaries may combine into complex verb phrases. We need to be able to appreciate the exact meaning of combinations such as those in (19, 20). These aspects of meaning will be discussed in Chapter 7.

19 She *may have been* having problems with her boiler ('fyrkjele').
20 *Could* he *have been being* treated for some kind of psychiatric disorder?

6.4.3 Main verbs or auxiliary verbs?

Not all verbs fall nicely into the classes we have set up. In the examples below it is not easy to decide whether the italicized expressions should be called auxiliaries or main verbs.

1 We *need to* clear out the cellar before they arrive.
2 She *was about to* slam the door in my face.
3 I *have got to* finish this chapter by next Sunday.
4 Why do you *keep* reminding me of that incident?
5 We *seem to* lose our way every time we take the shortcut.
6 It *got* pinched as I was having lunch at Betty's.
7 We *happen to* know that they're selling their cottage.

There are a number of formal tests we could have applied here in order to set up a gradience of auxiliary-hood. But what seems to be important is that native speakers intuitively regard *need to clear out, was about to slam, have got to finish, keep reminding, seem to lose, got pinched,* and *happen to know* as unitary verb phrases and consequently also as unitary verbs at the clause level in these sentences.

By contrast, most people will accept that *to leave* is a separate verb in a subordinate clause (as we argued in **6.4.1**) in:

8 She wanted to leave before dinner.

It is instructive, however, that even a relatively clear lexical verb like *want* shows signs of moving towards the class of auxiliaries. For one thing, there is the contracted form *wanna* (cf. *gonna*). Secondly, in British English *want* may be used as an informal auxiliary, e.g. in a situation where somebody gives advice on how to get to a place:

9 You want to take the first road on your right.

What this illustrates is that many of the italicized verbs in (1) to (7) have lost some of their literal lexical meaning and have almost become part of the grammar of English. They may have started on a very slow evolutionary process called **grammaticalization.** Maybe *want* is going the same way. In the following we will look more closely at a few of these types. The category **catenative verbs**, which was introduced in **2.6.3**, includes a number of subcategories which will be taken up in a separate section (**6.4.4**).

A Marginal modal auxiliaries

Verbs like *dare, need, have to*, and *used to* are often referred to as **marginal modals**. The reason is that they can behave either as auxiliaries proper, as explained in **6.4.2**, or as lexical verbs. When they function as lexical verbs, they have non-finite forms and can combine with other modals. Compare:

Positive declarative:	Negative declarative:	Interrogative:
She needs to do it.	She doesn't need to do it.	Does she need to do it?
	She needn't do it.	Need she do it?
He has to leave early.	He doesn't have to leave early.	Does he have to leave early?
	He hasn't (got) to leave early.	Has he (got) to leave early?
She used to like him.	She didn't use(d) to like him.	Did she use(d) to like him?

It is particularly in negative and interrogative contexts in British English that these verbs behave like auxiliaries. This should emerge from the examples above. Since it is always correct to use *do*-insertion with these verbs, i.e. treat them as lexical verbs, which is regularly done in American English, we recommend this usage.

It is also worth mentioning that *have to* is typically expanded to *have got to* in colloquial English, in which case *have* is an indisputable auxiliary. *Used to* ('pleide å') is really only frequent in positive declarative sentences in the past tense. In the present tense we normally use an adverbial (corresponding to Norwegian 'pleier å'): *I usually shop on Fridays.*

B Auxiliary equivalents

To make up for the missing forms of the modal auxiliaries (**6.4.2A**), English uses a number of alternatives which have roughly the same sense: *be able to - can, be willing to - will, be allowed/permitted to - may, be supposed to - ought to, be going to - will, be obliged to / have to - must,* etc. These are called **auxiliary equivalents.** They are handy because the first elements, *be* and *have*, have a full range of forms. In the examples below we have unitary verb phrases.

10 I *was able to swim* across the lake.
11 We *were allowed to rest* for a while between each run.
12 They *were supposed to report* to headquarters at 5.
13 You'*ll have to find* a way out which does not upset your parents.
14 *Are* you *going to open* it or aren't you?

6.4.4 Catenatives

A Aspectual verbs

When we think of a verbal action, it is possible to focus on its beginning, its end, its repetitive nature, its incomplete and ongoing nature, etc., in theory quite independently of the meaning of the lexical verb. A common term for such different ways of conceptualizing an action is **aspect**. English has grammaticalized the particular aspect which tells us that the process is ongoing and incomplete, namely, the **progressive aspect**: *Shut up – I'm talking to you.* Similarly, the aspect which combines completed past action and relevance at the moment of speaking is grammaticalized in the **perfective aspect**: *I have seen him before.* These aspects will be discussed more fully in **7.2** and **7.5–7.6**.

It can be argued that *keep* is an iterative auxiliary expressing repeated action in (1) below, that *start*, *begin,* and even *get* are inchoative auxiliaries expressing the beginning of the process in (2, 3), and that *stop* and *finish* are auxiliaries that express the terminating phase of the process in (4).

1 He *kept reminding* me of this incident.
2 We *started/began walking* at dawn.
3 We'd better *get going.*
4 Have you *stopped accusing* others of things you should have sorted out yourself?

In all the cases our aspectual verbs can be followed by regular noun phrases, as in *kept the book, started the machine / the job, get some money,* and *stopped the fight.* In other words, a syntactic substitution technique provides evidence that our alleged auxiliaries are regular main verbs followed by direct objects. Obviously, so does the *do*-insertion test that we mentioned in **6.4.3**. On the other hand, when the verbs are used as in (1) to (4), the meaning is such that the first verbs behave like aspectual auxiliaries. If we allow this criterion to outweigh syntactic evidence, we will have to treat the italicized sequences in these examples as unitary verb phrases, and as verbs when we analyse the structure of the clause.

B Modalizing expressions

5 He *seems to be enjoying* his new flat.
6 Sarah *appears to be* satisfied with the arrangement.
7 They *are supposed to have left* the victim in the ditch.
8 He *is said to be / assumed to be / believed to be / reputed to* be filthy rich.

Verbs like *seem* and *appear* allow the sender to hedge, i.e. express a guarded attitude, with respect to the truth of the rest of the sentence. In this way they have a communicative function comparable to that of some of the modal auxiliaries proper; compare *he may be enjoying his new flat, he could be filthy rich* with (5) and (8) respectively. A common term for the meaning of constructions used for this purpose, including the hedging expressions above, is **modality**. *Be supposed to* in (12) in **6.4.3** is approximately equivalent to *ought to*; the same form in (7), combined with the perfective *have left*, means roughly *it is said that* ... In the second case, it is used as a modalizing expression.

Going back to our initial question: Should we regard *seem to, appear to, be supposed to*, etc. as main verbs, or should they be classified as auxiliaries? Here again syntax and semantics/pragmatics (i.e. meaning and use) point in different directions. It seems to us that no serious harm is done if we describe the sequences above as containing catenatives with the communicative function we mentioned. On the clause level, (5) thus consists of *He* (S), *seems to be enjoying* (V), and *his new flat* (dO).

C Other uses of *get*

9 It *got broken* when we removed it from the wall.
10 The brochure *got reprinted* last winter.
11 Don't *get caught* with that under your arm.
12 We *got to know* them when we lived in Seattle.

In addition to the aspectual *get* mentioned in **A** above, *get* is used in informal English as an alternative auxiliary in passive sentences which do not have an expressed agent (**11.6.3C**). Whereas the normal passive *the brochure was reprinted last winter* refers to a state which is the result of an action, the *get*-passive seems to focus more on the action leading up to the state. Often the subject referent in such *get*-passives is unfavourably affected by the action, as in (9) and (11).

Get as a catenative should be distinguished from the copular *get* in sentences like *I got sick*. Here *get* is the main verb.

D Other catenatives

13 We *happen to* know that they're selling their cottage.
14 She *tends to* avoid confrontations.

15 I *fail to* see how this relates to us.
16 She has *come to* appreciate the softer sides of his personality.

The four examples above do not exhaust the list of verbs which somehow are in between main verbs and auxiliary verbs and which we have decided to call **catenatives**. While it is clear that most of the expressions in **6.4.4** need *do*-insertion and thus behave like main verbs from a syntactic point of view, they have a semantic or communicative function which resembles that of many regular auxiliaries.

6.4.5 Verb complementation

It seems that the placing of two or more verbs next to each other with nothing in between has, over the centuries, tended to weaken the literal meaning of the first verb and thus 'auxiliarize' it. However, there are innumerable combinations in which the first verb functions as the main verb and what follows is a separate clause element, typically a direct object, whose first constituent is a non-finite verb form. Such non-finite forms are cases of **verb complementation** (see **2.5.1**). They introduce the italicized subordinate clauses in (1) to (6) and will be treated more fully in Chapter 13.

1 I hope *to finish this chapter next week.*
2 Some students chose *to leave the grammar questions unanswered.*
3 We had to remind him *to hand it in early.*
4 Do you mind *baby-sitting for us next week*?
5 I couldn't face *meeting him so soon after the split.*
6 Our doctor suggested *taking a week's holiday in a dry climate.*

6.5 The structure of the unitary verb phrase

In **6.4** we discussed the various elements of meaning that can be said to make up a unitary verb phrase. Table 6c summarizes our discussion. Abbreviations: *aux* = auxiliary, *gram* = grammatical, *mod* = modal, *asp* = aspectual, *pass* = passive, *marg* = marginal, *co-ord* = co-ordination. Note that the table does not specify what combinations are allowed.

Table 6c: The structure of the unitary verb phrase

Aux			Aux equivalent	Catenative				Main verb	
mod		gram		mod	asp	pass	other	co-ord	simple
proper	marg								
									flies
will									follow
		have						heard	
								and	
								seen	
may	have to								leave
		are							added
	used to		be able to						swim
					kept				reminding
				seem to					like
							tend to		forget
						get			pinched
			be allowed to						dry
			be going to						drive
							get to		know
		do							feel
			be supposed to						ring
					get				going
			be to						report
		do					happen to		prefer

While there may some disagreement about whether all the elements in Table 6c should be included in a unitary verb phrase, nobody would deny that the grammatical and the modal auxiliaries proper in the first and third columns belong to a single, unitary verb phrase.

Table 6d below shows the internal structure of combinations of modal auxiliaries, tense, aspect, voice, and main verb. The formal markers of the perfective and progressive aspects and the passive voice include a grammatical auxiliary and a participle form of the main verb. The grammatical auxiliary carries tense; any participle endings are attached to the next verb form on the right. Only tense/modality and main verb have not been put in parentheses. This means that any finite verb phrase must include these elements (exception: imperative and subjunctive forms). Elements that are included in parentheses are structurally optional, but obviously vital from the point of view of meaning. Abbreviations: *pres* = present, *past* = past tense, *perf* = perfective, *progr* = progressive, *pass* = passive, *unm* = unmarked, *rem* = remote (**6.4.2A**).

Table 6d: The structure of the verb phrase with auxiliaries proper

Tense	or Modality	+ (Perf aspect)	+ (Progr aspect)	+ (Pass voice)	+ Main verb
pres past	unm rem	have + -ed	be + -ing	be + -ed	V

Chapter 7 will give a fuller treatment of the use of these verbal categories. In later chapters we will deal with *do*-insertion. Although the grammatical auxiliary *do* does appear in the verb phrase, its occurrence is connected with the overall structure and communicative function of the sentence. See **11.1.1D**, **11.2.1**, **14.2**, **14.2.1**, **14.3**, and **14.4**.

Below follows a set of examples with italicized verbs, with a brief label for each given within parentheses.

1 In most places spring *comes* in March or April. (simple present tense)
2 Mr Wellstone *won* his first Senate race in 1990. (simple past tense)
3 Hello, Willy, *come in*. (imperative)
4 *Can* we *talk* a minute? (unmarked modal + main verb)
5 I *have* never *said* anything to that effect. (present tense + perfective aspect)
6 He informed Salzman why he *had asked* him to come. (past tense + perfective aspect)
7 The Scandinavians *may have brought* with them social-democratic tendencies. (unmarked modal + perfective aspect)
8 Mr B *is trying* to recapture his old Senate seat. (present tense + progressive aspect)
9 I *have been meaning* to tell you for some time. (present tense + perfective aspect + progressive aspect)
10 Parliament *is opened* by the Queen in November. (present tense + passive voice)
11 He *could have been hurt* in that accident. (remote modal + perfective aspect + passive voice)
12 The little boy *was being bullied* by a gang from across the village. (past tense + progressive aspect + passive voice)
13 But I *do feel* embarrassed in such situations. (present tense + *do*-insertion)
14 *Didn't* you *write* to them last week? (past tense + *do*-insertion)

Terms

transitivity types: intransitive, copular, monotransitive, ditransitive, complex transitive

main and auxiliary verb

auxiliary: grammatical, modal

marginal modal auxiliary

multi-word verbs:	prepositional	auxiliary equivalent	
	phrasal		
	phrasal–prepositional	catenative:	aspectual
			modalizing
do-insertion			
finite and non-finite verb		unmarked and remote modal auxiliary	

Exercises

1 Explain how the perspective on the action changes in the sentences below. All have *handle* as the main verb. (**6.1.3**)

a This affair will be handled by one of our agents.
b The new Range Rover handles beautifully.
c Most of the ornaments were handled with great care.
d Eddie handled the situation to everybody's satisfaction.

2 Rewrite the sentences below, starting with the object. The original subject of the first verbs should be left out. Discuss any problems you may encounter. (**6.1.3**)

a They have improved their chances a lot.
b Local people inflect these verbs in many different ways.
c His father drove the car past the supermarket.
d It is easy to drive this Honda.
e We roasted the chicken for quite some time.
f They are showing 'The Prince' at the Odeon this weekend.
g The police gathered the teenagers outside the hall.
h He broke the lock when he tried to force his way into the building.

3 Here is another extract from the parody of Alexander Haig's manner of speaking. (**2.4.3**) Identify words which have been put into unusual word classes and explain what word classes these words normally belong to and which ones they belong to in this example. (**6.2**)

Haig techniqued a new way to vocabulary his thoughts so as to informationally uncertain anybody listening about what he had actually implicationed.

4 Identify all irregular verbs in the following paragraph. Give their *s*-forms, their past tense forms, and their past participle forms. (**6.3.1**)

K.E. was the first native who came to see what I was up to. She was the girl who had stared from the station-master's house at my coat and me, and she was fourteen years old, in her last term at the village school. She was big for her age, blue-eyed and freckled, a knowing-looking girl. In those days I didn't dislike children; in fact, I got on very well with most of them. And I had really great pleasure from the sort I could talk to tongue-in-cheek, who knew this and enjoyed it too – talk for talk's sake like many kids enjoy ice-cream.

5 Identify the grammatical auxiliaries in the following examples. Explain what function they have. For example, in *he was talking to his brother,* the grammatical auxiliary is *was,* and it helps to form the progressive aspect *was talking.* (**6.3.1**)

a I do love you.
b Metaphor and simile are the most widely recognized figures of speech.
c I didn't think it would last that long.
d A surprisingly wide range of industries are doing well.
e What on earth have you been doing?
f We could have reached our production goal if more money had been invested at the right time.
g Is he a friend of yours?
h Having run the marathon 16 times, Mr V should know what he's letting himself in for this time.
i Do be careful!
j He is being so difficult.
k Do you want another cup of tea?

6 All of the following sentences contain an italicized *-ing* form of a verb. Explain what word class the *-ing* participle belongs to in these examples. (**6.3.1**)

a '*Thinking* of Mary, are you?'
b *Stimulating* discussions are rare in those circles.
c *Painting* lost between Fulford and Heslington.
d *Accepting* such ideas means accepting violence.
e *Rocking*-horses are no longer made in Norway.
f I've been *meaning* to talk to him.
g *Applying* rouge to her face, she pondered the consequences of her decision.
h *Supposing* John is willing, we can order the equipment right away.

7 What valency does the italicized main verb in the following sentences have? (**6.3.2**)

a The first sentence *is* the topic sentence.
b Clauses *carry* messages.
c Nobody is *taking* much notice.
d He had *taught* his children to appreciate art.
e You should *wipe* it dry with a piece of cloth.
f Where did you *put* the bottle?
g Nothing sensational *happened* when we were there.
h Today California's economy is *outshining* that of the rest of the country.
i They *told* me to go home and think it over.
j We hope you will *find* this dictionary a genuinely helpful reference book.

8 Identify multi-word verbs in these examples and try to determine what sub-types they belong to. Are there any delexical verbs here? (**6.3.3–6.3.4**)

a The doctor was sent for immediately.
b The plane took off.
c Mr B took off his shoes.
d The gift was wrapped in beautiful paper, but the little child tore it off in a few seconds.
e Students who read this book carefully will sail through their examinations.
f If you leave that early, you'll miss out on the fun.
g You should take advantage of this unique offer.
h When this couple came to have a look at our house, the first thing the man said was, 'We'll get rid of this for a start', pointing to our new living-room wallpaper. 'It'll be a different place altogether when we've done it up.' A bit later I came upon them in one of our bedrooms, giggling and making faces at the wallpaper there. 'We'll have this off too', said the man.

9 Translate the following sentences into English. (**6.3.5**)

a Det er mulig jeg har fått gale opplysninger i denne saken.
b Kona levde 12 år lenger enn mannen.
c Vi bør ikke overdrive betydningen av en slik politisk avgjørelse.
d Det er ingen grunn til å undervurdere en slik motstander.
e Hun løsnet sikkerhetsbeltet med en gang og kom seg ut av bilen i en fart.
f Susan bekreftet enda en gang at hun kunne tenke seg jobben i Paris.

10 Identify the finite verb forms in the following examples. (**6.4.1**)

a Mr Blair has long been unashamedly proud of his patriotism.
b Even his supporters sometimes worry that he aims to bring American-style politics to Britain.
c 'Reasonable people', said George Bernard Shaw, 'adapt themselves to the world. Unreasonable people expect the world to adapt itself to them. Therefore, all progress is made by unreasonable people.'

11 Identify all the non-finite verb forms in the following examples. (**6.4.1**)

a The amount of trade flowing through the Los Angeles customs district has grown by an average of 9 per cent a year since 1987, reaching $170 billion in 1996.
b The clothes-makers established in the inner city have developed a flexible production system that allows them to respond to subtle changes in fashion very quickly.
c Eating, unlike fighting, is a pursuit in which both sexes indulge.
d People with a focused mind have little problem keeping one thought in their head at a time.
e It is amazing to see what extremes people can go to in order to save a few pounds.

12 Identify all the auxiliaries in the italicized verb phrases in the following sentences, and determine whether they belong to the class of grammatical auxiliaries, modal auxiliaries, marginal modal auxiliaries, or auxiliary equivalents. (**6.4.2**, **6.4.3A**,**B**)

a The form *may be bought* at any stationer's.
b He *has revealed* that he has a grudge against women.
c She *must have been going* too fast.
d He *daren't speak* his mind.
e They *mustn't be allowed to leave* the room.
f *Have* you *been able to detect* anything wrong?
g I *was supposed to be* the hostess.
h We *shouldn't be supposed to turn up* every day.

13 Give the structure of the italicized verb phrases in the sentences below, using the distinctions in Table 6c. Determine whether the main verb is a single-word verb or a multi-word verb.

a You *should tell* her.
b We *have to finish* it by noon.

c *We're going to tear* it down next week.
d Why do you *keep coming back* to that painful incident?
e Nobody *can be expected to give up* their right to free speech.
f These reporters *are able to expose* lies.
g I *fail to see* why you can't let him have it.
h We *tend to assume* that immigrants have different values.
i You *don't happen to have* a timetable that I could look at?
j President Reagan's aides *used to become* visibly alarmed at such suggestions.

14 The purpose of this exercise is to help you understand the oppositions in the English verb phrase. The vertical column on the left contains simple one-clause sentences with more or less complex verb phrases. The horizontal row contains the main elements of a verb phrase. Tense is broken down into present and past, modality into unm(arked) and rem(ote) (**6.4.2A**), aspect into perf(ective) and prog(ressive), voice into active and passive. Then there is the main verb. The task is to put a cross in the appropriate column. Since we do not regard the opposition between modal auxiliaries like *can – could* as an opposition in tense, but rather as an opposition between an unmarked modal and a remote modal, any sentence with a modal auxiliary should not be marked for tense. We have done the first one for you. (Table 6d)

	Tense		Modality		Aspect		Voice		Main verb
	present	past	unm	rem	perf	prog	active	passive	
It could have been returned				x	x			x	return
I love you									
He was killed									
I am reading									
It was being restored									
It had been restored									

Have you
heard it?

I may do it

I might do it

I have been
waiting

They have
been fined

They must
have lost

They must
have been
lost

7 Tense, Aspect, and Modality

7.1 Tense

The universal concept of time can be expressed in many different ways in language, e.g. in noun phrases: *the ex-convict, pre-war Europe, my former friend, the then chairman*; and of course in an endless series of different adverbial expressions: *since then, earlier, at that time, during the 80s*. However, it is only when time is expressed systematically in the verbal system of a language that we talk about tense. Tense is a **deictic** category. By that we mean that past, present, and future are all relative to the moment somebody makes an utterance, i.e. relative to the time of coding (speaking or writing). Since coding time obviously varies, what is past, present, and future also varies.

> Today *is* Thursday, yesterday *was* Wednesday, and tomorrow *will see* the start of another long weekend full of possibilities.

As we saw in **6.3.1**, the present tense is marked by the base form of the verb, unless the subject can be replaced by *he/she/it*, in which case we use the *-s* form. The past tense is marked by the past tense ending *-ed* on regular verbs. It is precisely in this sense that the irregular verbs are irregular. The question is whether we can identify a similarly consistent marker for future tense. The answer is no. There are two problems. Even if we are willing to accept that the modals *will/shall,* although not verb endings, are tense markers, we have to acknowledge that these modals are used in many ways beyond that of referring to future situations. Secondly, reference to future time can be expressed in many ways other than by means of *will/shall.* This is why most grammarians talk of just two tenses in English: the **present tense** and the **past tense**. We will deal with the full complexity of future-referring expressions in **7.7**.

7.2 Aspect

In **6.4.4A** we talked about aspect. Here we repeat that the **progressive aspect** and the **perfective aspect** are the two grammaticalized aspects in English. The former allows us to focus on the duration and ongoingness of the action.

1 Snow *is falling* gently on the trees in my garden.
2 When I came in, he *was preparing* a meal.
3 What *have* you *been doing*?

The perfective aspect, when combined with the present tense, allows us to express the notion of a completed past action (with its subsequent resulting state) and the notion of relevance at the moment of coding. Some people refer to the present perfect as the indefinite past, because it does not combine with a definite past time adverbial (6). On the other hand, the present perfect is required with a deictic element like *since* in (7), because *since* implies from then up to now, i.e. the moment of utterance.

4 *Have* you ever *tasted* this new drink, Hooch?
5 John *has been* to England (… so he probably knows something about cricket).
6 Last year I **have heard / heard* the group for the first time.
7 I sent him the report a month ago, and I **did not hear / have* not *heard* from him since.

The two aspects may combine, as shown in (3) above. As regards the combination of the perfective aspect and the past tense, see **7.6.2**.

7.3 Voice

The opposition between the active and the passive voice, although it does show up in the verb phrase, is not a specification of the action, but rather a matter of different perspectives on the same situation (see **6.1.3**). In the active sentence below we state what John did, while in the passive counterpart we are more concerned with what happened to the trees, how the trees were affected. It is significant that some 90 per cent of all passive sentences do not contain an agent phrase, i.e. in our case *by John.* The use of the passive is discussed more fully in **11.6**.

1 (Without asking for permission) John *chopped down* the trees.
2 The trees *were chopped down* (without any permission being granted).

From the point of view of formal structure, the verb phrase in a passive clause normally appears with *be* as the auxiliary and the past participle of the main verb. However, in **6.4.4C** we mentioned the more informal *get*-passive. The passive can combine with many other features in the verb phrase. The list below shows a range of possible combinations. We leave out the *by*-phrases in the passives on the right.

3	He *prepares* the meals in the morning	The meals *are prepared* in the morning.
4	They *are talking* a lot *about* it.	It *is being talked about* a lot.
5	They *were talking* a lot *about* it.	It *was being talked about* a lot.
6	We *have checked* the meter.	The meter *has been checked.*
7	John *has been washing* the dog.	?The dog *has been being washed.*
8	*We'll look into* this later.	This *will be looked into* later.
9	By then I'*ll have finished* it.	It'*ll have been finished* by then.
10	These views are likely *to bar* him from polite circles.	He is likely *to be barred* from polite circles.

The two aspects and voice can be expressed in infinitive forms. An example of the progressive infinitive is *(to) be reading*; an example of the perfective infinitive is *(to) have tried.* There is an example of the passive infinitive in (10) above, *to be barred.*

7.4 Modality and mood

Past and present situations are **factive** in the sense that they are open to objective verification. In a sense they can be shown to be facts. Future situations, as well as hypothetical ones, are **non-factive**. It is precisely in such situations that modern English uses modal expressions of various types.

The modal auxiliaries proper (**6.4.2A**) are used in basically two different ways. When the speaker predicts something about a future situation or can bring about or influence somebody else to bring about a future situation, we talk about **root modality**, as in (1) to (4). If, on the other hand, speakers express their lack of certainty with respect to the truth of past and present situations, they may use the very same modals in a different way. This is **epistemic modality**; compare (5) to (7). All this will be further explained in **7.10–7.20**.

1 There'*ll* be 36 guests at the dinner party tomorrow.
2 I'*ll* give you fiver if you manage to persuade her.
3 *Can* you please leave the room?
4 You *must* talk to your supervisor.
5 There's a noise at the door. It'*ll* be the dog.
6 He *may* have left it with a friend.
7 You *must* be feeling rather tired after this.

7.4.1 Mood

Mood is the traditional term for the **indicative**, **imperative**, and **subjunctive** ('konjunktiv') forms of the verb. The ordinary finite forms (as in *she writes, she wrote*, etc.) are called the indicative. The indicative mood is the unmarked mood, typically used for statements of fact. The imperative is expressed by the base form of the verb (**6.3.1**) and is used for commands and related communicative functions (**14.4**). The subjunctive is used for wishes, recommendations, and the like (**7.4.2**).

7.4.2 The subjunctive ('konjunktiv')

The subjunctive is marginal in present-day English. Like the modal auxiliaries, it is used to express non-facts. One type, the **mandative** subjunctive, occurs in *that*-clauses after verbs, adjectives, and nouns that express recommendations, requests, suggestions, etc. The form of the verb is the base form (**6.3.1**), but the same meaning can be expressed by modal auxiliaries, typically *should*, as shown by the alternatives below. This is an indication of the non-factive status of such *that*-clauses. The mandative subjunctive is more common in American than in British English.

1 They insisted that the prisoner (should) *be* released.
2 It is essential that the company (should) *be* allowed to advance.
3 The demand was that they (should) not *send* troops into the area.

The subjunctive is further used in set phrases such as *suffice it to say, be that as it may, long live the Queen, God bless you* (**14.6**).

Subjunctive forms of the verb *be* are found in subordinate clauses introduced by *if, though, as if,* and *as though.*

4 If I *were* (was) you, I'd resign.
5 He clutched it as if it *were* his most precious possession.
6 It took a great deal of persuading, if the truth *be* told.

The past subjunctive *were* expresses a hypothetical meaning. It is quite common, but can usually be replaced by the ordinary indicative form. The present subjunctive *be*, as in (6), is occasionally found in conditional and concessive clauses.

7.5 Referring to present time

7.5.1 Subjective vs. objective point of view

Unlike Norwegian, English can choose between the simple present tense and the present progressive to refer to present time. In some cases the choice depends on the speaker's subjective perception. In the right-hand column, the events are presented as if they are temporary and incomplete. In the left-hand column, there is no such implication. They are in a sense more neutral, more unmarked, more objective.

1	He *lives* in a small flat.	He'*s living* in a small flat.
2	William, you'*re* first-rate with with our boys.	William, you'*re being* first-rate with our boys.
3	Some of these attacks *seem to backfire.*	Some of these attacks *seem to be backfiring.*
4	Mr W *rebels* against all this.	Mr W *is rebelling* against all this.

7.5.2 Permanent or regularly occurring events

Many situations are such that there is little room for the speaker's subjective perception. The examples in the left-hand column below refer to general and habitual situations or to eternal truths. The progressive aspect would be impossible here. But, the very same verbs may be used in the progressive aspect if we are talking about a temporary, ongoing situation. This is illustrated in the examples on the right.

1	I *get* up every morning at 6 o'clock.	It'*s getting* darker.
2	What *do* you *do* for a living?	What *are* you *doing?*
3	He's a twinkly-eyed sort of fellow who *runs* 100 miles each month.	I don't know who'*s running* for president this time.
4	I always *have* a quick snack before I go to bed.	The noise? Well, we'*re having* a party here.
5	The sun *rises* in the east.	The sun *is rising.*
6	He *speaks* with a Norwegian accent.	Why *are* you suddenly *speaking* so posh?

7.5.3 Contextual clues

Learners of English must pay attention to contextual clues, typically adverbial expressions, which make it clear that one is talking about something habitual, permanent, or unchangeable. In such contexts the progressive is definitely a stranger (see 1, 2, and 3 below). However, adverbials like *always, forever,* etc. may accept the progressive if the sentence refers to something that the speaker feels annoyed about. Example (3) is neutral in tone, while (4) is emotional.

1 Bad students *never* work hard.
2 The Hopis *live* on a reservation in the south-west.
3 I always *have* a snack before I go to bed.
4 You'*re* always *finding* something to criticize.

7.5.4 Stative and dynamic verbs

In some cases a verb must be used in the simple present tense in one sense, but allows the progressive when used in a different sense.

1	I *think* ('synes') this is more than enough for me.	I'*m thinking* of ('vurderer') leaving after lunch.
2	*Do* they *have* ('eie') more than one car?	She'*s having* some problem with grammar.
3	The car *drives* like a Mercedes.	You'*re driving* me mad!
4	I *admire* your courage.	I'*m admiring* these sculptures by Henry Moore.

The verbs are used in a **stative** sense on the left, and in a **dynamic** sense on the right. The dynamic sense means that the verb refers to a voluntary action that can be controlled by the person the subject refers to. Stative verbs denote conditions and properties over which human beings have no control. It is important to bear in mind that quite a few verbs have nothing but a stative sense. Therefore they practically never occur in the progressive aspect.

5 The bottle *contains* (*is containing) a strange mixture.
6 *Do* you *remember* (*are you remembering) what happened to him?
7 It *fits* (*is fitting) the description I saw in the paper.
8 This piece of land *doesn't cost* (*isn't costing) all that much.

Such stative verbs are typically:

- verbs of perception: *see, hear, smell, taste,* etc.
- verbs denoting cognition or emotional states: *know, understand, think, believe hate, love*, etc.
- verbs denoting physical or abstract relationships: *be* (*tall, square, old, possible,* etc.), *remain, own, consist of, suit, resemble, want,* etc.

However, in the immediacy of spoken interaction, even a clearly stative verb may turn up in the progressive.

9 *Are* you *wanting* this scarf, sir?

The progressive is particularly frequent in spoken interaction when people refer to situations that they are right in the middle of.

10 A: Where *are* you *going?*
B: I'*m taking* these over to the finance office. Sam *was asking* for them this morning.

With verbs like *arrive, stop, land, die,* the progressive aspect implies a gradual development towards the end-point of the process (11). Verbs which denote actions of very short duration, so-called momentary verbs, e.g. *knock, tap, jump, flash*, are used in the progressive when the action repeats itself (12).

11 Paul should *be arriving* in the States about now.
12 The lights *were flashing.*

7.5.5 The present tense used about future time

Both the simple present and the present progressive can be used about future time, but whereas the progressive implies a plan for the future that is subject to change, the simple present suggests that the future event is irrevocably fixed or scheduled. This difference is illustrated in (1). Note that a question in the progressive (2) can be a question about what the addressee is intending to drink, i.e. a future drink, and about what he/she is drinking at the moment of speaking.

1 I *leave* Brussels on Monday next. We'*re leaving* early next morning.
2 What *are* you *drinking*?

See further **7.7.3** and **7.7.4**.

7.5.6 Special uses of the simple present

A The instantaneous present

The simple present tense is commonly used to refer to situations of very short duration, or situations which are presented as such, e.g. in running commentaries:

1 Keegan *passes* the ball to Latchford who *shoots*. It's a goal!
2 I *take* two pigeons from the hat, *place* them in this cage and ...
3 Nobody campaigns like Mr Harris. One moment he *waves* his arms before a crowd of students ... the next moment he *drops* to the floor ... then he *bounces* into a day care centre.

B The historic present

The simple present adds a flavour of lively drama to events which belong in the past. It typically occurs in narratives, headlines, and captions:

4 And, you know, the other day I came home and found Peter in bed at 11 o'clock in the morning. He *is* obviously embarrassed and *jumps* up and *starts* to explain why he had been sleeping.
5 Fascist Attacks *Continue*.

C Stage directions and plot summaries

Stage directions for a play are typically written in the present tense (6). Example (7) shows the common use of the present tense in plot summaries.

6 Linda (calling after Willy): Be careful on the stairs dear! The cheese *is* on the middle shelf! (She *turns, goes* over to the bed, *takes* his jacket, and *goes* out of the bedroom.)
7 'Gold oder Rabenschwarz' is the story of two westerners who *move* east in search of adventure. But they *realize* that what divides east and west *involves* more than ... Ms Kellein *explores* this gap.

Summing up our comments on the present tense, we can say it has a common element of meaning: 'valid at the moment of utterance'. Over and above this, it has pragmatic implications; its presentness has the effect of making the event topical, lively, and sometimes even dramatic.

7.5.7 Advice for Norwegians

Norwegians have a tendency to overuse the present progressive. The Norwegian language has not grammaticalized the meaning conveyed by the progressive. Although we have to rely on the total context to tell us whether something is temporarily going on or is regularly the case, it does not mean that we cannot express this opposition explicitly. If the verb in our sentence can be expanded by *holder på å ... / er i ferd med å ... / driver og ...* + verb, then that is a good indication that the progressive is in order in English.

The progressive should be used in cases where there is a clear need to focus on the temporary and incomplete nature of the situation. If not, we ought to use the simple present. Simple forms are called for in the examples below, where the progressive is either wrong or unlikely.

1 *Our children are playing when they are alone.
2 *Many individuals are unable to face reality; they are often joking about life and death.
3 ?The book is describing the relationship between a woman and her unemployed husband.
4 ?*The symbol you see to the left is standing for peace.

7.6 Referring to past time

7.6.1 Simple past or present perfect?

We can refer to an event which is past relative to the moment of speaking in two different ways. If we use a past tense form, as in (1) below, the event is disconnected from the present. In most cases there is some adverbial expression, either explicit or implicit, which anchors the event in the past. The other way is to connect the past event to the moment of speaking, as in (2) below, where the present perfect is used. In both these cases the speaker saw the person some time in the past, but the parenthesized material in (2) shows that the past meeting has relevance at the moment of speaking. That is why the perfective form is preferred.

Norwegian and English allow the same perspectives on such past events, so there is no contrastive problem here.

1 I *saw* him last week.
2 I *have seen* before (so I should be able to recognize him).

The notion of present relevance that we mentioned above can account for some interesting differences in pairs such as those below.

3a *Did* you know Mary for long?
3b *Have* you *known* Mary for long?

4a George Bush *has lived* in the White House.
4b ??John F. Kennedy *has lived* in the White House.

In (3a) Mary is somehow not connected with the moment of speaking; she may be dead, have moved to Australia, etc. Using the present perfective is odd in a sentence about a deceased president (4b), but it is all right in (4a) because George Bush is still among the living.

The simple past form is used about unique events in the past, no matter whether they happened a few minutes or centuries ago (5, 6). It is also used about repeated or prolonged events in the past (6). The past tense removes the action from the moment of speaking, which allows us to exploit this formal feature if we do not want to be too direct or forthright in our interaction with people (7, 8). The past form is also used about hypothetical situations (9).

5 He *was* on the phone a moment ago.
6 In the 9th and 10th centuries there *was* an influx of Scandinavian settlers to the British Isles.
7 I *thought* I could go in your car.
8 *Did* you want to speak to me?
9 I wish I *was/were* rich.

In sentences which refer to one-off past events containing present-time adverbs like *already, yet, just*, etc., Americans readily accept the simple past form, whereas British English speakers prefer the present perfect.

10	*Have* you *eaten* yet? (BrE)	*Did* you *eat* yet? (AmE)
11	Is Bill around?	
	Yes, I'*ve* just *seen* him (BrE)	Yes, I just *saw* him (AmE)

Whereas the lowest common denominator for the meaning of the present tense is 'valid at the moment of utterance', the common denominator for the past tense is 'distant in time or reality'. Like the present tense, the past tense may be used with pragmatic implications, indicating that the speaker is concerned to be polite, not to impose, or to remove his or her utterance from the urgency of the here-and-now situation.

7.6.2 The past perfect

The difference between the present perfect and the past perfect is this: The former links a past event to the present coding time, as in example (2) in **7.6.1**, whereas the latter locates the event in relation to a point of time in the past (1). In (2) below the use of *knew* shows that the point of orientation is in the past (and *now* here actually means 'then'). Before that point she had been ignorant of men's disinterestedness. Notice how the second sentence in James Joyce's 'The Dead' places one past action immediately after another (3).

1 I *had* definitely *closed* the windows when I *left* at 5.30 p.m.
2 She *had* not *known* that men could be so disinterested; now she *knew*.
3 Hardly *had* she *brought* one gentleman into the little pantry behind the office ... than the wheezy hall-door bell *clanged* again.

The past perfect is used in much the same way in Norwegian and English.

7.6.3 A visual representation of the perfective aspect

The essential feature of the perfective aspect is that it connects an event with a point of orientation which follows the time of that event. As shown in Figure 7a, the point of orientation may be in the past, present, or future.

before past	past	before present	present	before future	future
——→	x	——→	x	——→	x
I had seen her before she left	I saw her when she left	I have seen her before	I see her regularly	I will have seen her by next Friday	I'll see her next Friday

Figure 7a: Tense and time reference

7.6.4 Past tense and progressive aspect combined

The progressive aspect easily combines with the past tense and perfective aspect, provided the lexical verb is dynamic. The simple past is preferred when we want to present a past situation as a complete whole (1, 2). A series of consecutive events is typically reported in the simple past tense. This is very common in narratives (3). The past progressive, on the other hand, allows us to focus on the incomplete and ongoing nature of the action. In (4, 5) the progressive is used in its typical **framing function**. By that we mean that a durative action 'frames' or surrounds a momentary event.

1 I *drove* down to Brighton after lunch.
2 She *dismissed* the past – *trod* upon it and *put* it out, as one treads on a coal that is ...
3 The porter *led* them along a corridor and *opened* a door. Then he *set* his unstable candle down on the toilet-table and *asked* at what hour ...
4 I *was driving* down to Brighton yesterday when I *tuned* in to BBC and heard ...
5 When Geoff *was approaching* them, John *moved* away from the door.

7.6.5 *-ing* participles after perception verbs

After verbs like *see, hear, watch, observe* there is a difference between the base form and the *-ing* form which parallels that between the simple past and the past progressive. Strictly speaking, *making* in (1) is not a progressive form since there is no auxiliary, but the meaning is that of an ongoing, incomplete action.

1 He saw his wife *making* her way towards him through the waltzing couples.
2 I saw him *make* it to the top.

It takes time to manoeuvre across a floor through waltzing couples. The *-ing* form captures precisely that fact. However, in (2) the point is not the prolonged process but rather the result, the accomplished feat. That is why the simple form is used. In other words, if an action lasts long or is perceived to last long, the speaker has good reason to select the *-ing* form.

7.6.6 Combinations of perfective and progressive aspects

When the progressive combines with the present perfect, the effect is that the event is presented as if lasting up to the moment of speaking. The situation may be incomplete and continue beyond that point of orientation (1), but may also have been brought to an end so recently that effects of the event are still visible, as in (2). In (3), which has been included to allow a comparison with (1), the point is that the same verb without the progressive aspect implies a completed cooking job. The focus is on the dish which resulted from it and the experience the speaker now possesses.

1 I'*ve been trying* to get through to him, but his line is busy all the time.
2 A: What on earth *have* you *been doing*? You look awful!
B: I'*ve been washing* the dog.
3 I'*ve tried* one of her recipes but the result was a disaster. It could be me being a bad cook.

We see the same distinction if the tensed verb is in the past:

4 While he had been full of memories of their secret life together, she *had been comparing* him in her mind with another.
5 I *have compared* the two books, but find it difficult to say which is the better one.

7.7 Referring to future events

Perhaps a good way of introducing this section is to invite Norwegians to think a little about the situation in their own language. Below we use three different verb forms to refer to the same future event. Do they mean exactly the same thing? If not, how do they differ?

1 Jeg reiser til England neste uke.
2 Jeg skal reise til England neste uke.
3 Jeg kommer til å reise til England neste uke.

What is important is that the simple present with reference to future time is very common in Norwegian, but rare in English. The form with 'skal' is also common in Norwegian, whereas *shall* in English is rare. 'Kommer til å' appropriately translates more than one English form. So contrastive problems may arise.

English has even more ways of referring to future events than Norwegian. In many contexts two or more can be used with very little difference in implication, but there are other contexts which call for one particular form. These are some of the essential parameters:

- To what extent is the future event definite or certain at the moment of speaking?
- To what extent is it pre-planned?
- To what extent is it fixed and irrevocable?
- To what extent has the speaker been in on the decision-making?

We will now examine these in more detail with reference to the most frequent future-referring expressions in English.

7.7.1 *Will/shall/'ll* + base form of lexical verb

The *will/'ll* future is the most common and neutral way of referring to future events. In spoken English *'ll* is the normal form (1, 2, 3). In declarative sentences *shall* is restricted to first person subjects in rather formal English (4), but it is frequent in interrogative sentences which typically count as suggestions (5). *Shall* is more common in British than in American English.

There is some degree of uncertainty attached to future events. A weakly stressed and contracted *will* captures this uncertainty and makes it into a prediction. However, in many cases with personal subjects, *will/'ll* may convey the subject's willingness to do something in the future as well as the speaker's prediction of a future event (6). We can, in other words, talk about a modal *will* and a temporal *will*. The stronger the stress on *will*, the stronger its modal function.

1 Sorry to keep you waiting. I*'ll* be with you in a minute.
2 And when you feel better, come back, and we*'ll see* if we can work something out.
3 If only 48% turn out this year, it *will be* higher than the 1992 turnout.
4 We *shall take* up this point later in the book.
5 *Shall* we *go* for a walk?
6 I*'ll help* you sort it out after lunch.

7.7.2 *Be going to* + base form of lexical verb

Going to + verb (*gonna* + verb in colloquial English) is a very common future-referring expression. The tensed verb is in the present, which means that there is some present fact or circumstance upon which we can base our statement about the future. In (1) it is a present premeditated intention; in (2, 3) it is a present certainty that a future event will take place. Notice that the alternative in (1), *I'll buy*, implies a spontaneous expression of willingness rather than a premeditated decision. In (4) *be going to* is used in a question. With *are you* the question is about the addressee's intention, but with *am I* the speaker asks for the listener's advice on what to say.

1 A: We're out of milk.
B: I*'ll buy* some this afternoon / I*'m going to buy* some this afternoon.
2 The way he's driving he*'s gonna have* an accident one of these days.
3 With all these different opinions *it's going to be* difficult to reach an agreement.
4 What *am* I / *are* you *going to tell* them?

It is easy to understand how 'present intention', which is part of the meaning of *be going to*, can be used to express strong or weak determination. The neutral *will* feels tame in (5).

5 I'*m gonna* / I'*ll smash* his face in if he doesn't pay what he owes me.

7.7.3 The present progressive

The present progressive is often used about future events if they are anchored in a present arrangement or plan that the subject has made. The event is most often in the near future, typically shown in an adverbial expression, as in (1) to (4). It is the idea of arrangement which distinguishes this form from the *going to* future, which, as we saw, suggests intention on the part of the speaker. This subtle difference can perhaps be appreciated if we compare (2) and *We're going to have a few friends over this Friday and wondered if you would like to come.*

1 I'*m going* over there this afternoon, so I'll ask them.
2 We'*re having* a few friends over this Friday and wondered if you would like to come.
3 He'*s arriving* in Manchester tomorrow morning, and I've promised to be at the airport.
4 W *is starting* on his whistle-stop tour of five states early Monday morning.

As regards references to a plan or arrangement for a future event in the past, see **7.7.7B**.

7.7.4 The simple present tense

Unlike Norwegian, English only rarely uses the simple present tense with future reference. The simple present in English chiefly refers to events that are fixed in the present, and it gives them an appearance of unchangeable definiteness. Such sentences most often contain a time adverbial which anchors the event in the future, relative to the time of speaking/writing. Note that if we replace *next Wednesday* by, say, *on October 5th*, sentence (3) may be a statement about a regularly occurring event, i.e. the use dealt with in **7.5.2**. It is the use of the deictic *next* which places *Wednesday* in the future relative to the moment of speaking.

1 (Our itinerary says that) we *arrive* in Athens next Friday at 4 a.m.
2 The country *goes* to the polls on November 3rd.
3 Week 0 *starts* next Wednesday.

The simple present tense is regularly used with future reference in subordinate clauses of time (4) and condition (5). This also applies to sentences where there is an expression of contingency (6).

4 When you *meet* him tomorrow, try not to get upset. He can be pretty arrogant.
5 If she *comes* back here after I have left, would you tell her to call me?
6 Suppose we *try* to sort out this before we go.

The simple present tense is also found in informal questions like (7), which should be compared with the less informal forms in (8).

7 How *do* we *get* to see them when they come?
8 How *will* you / *are* you *going* to take care of them once they are on your doorstep?

7.7.5 *Shall/will/'ll* + progressive forms

This construction is used in two different ways. With durative verbs the focus tends to be on ongoing, incomplete situations located at a specific point in the future, most commonly defined by a time adverbial (1). The other common use, typically involving a verb which is not durative, is to refer to a future event which has been planned at the moment of speaking (2). In (2) the future event is seen as something that is going to happen as a matter of course. It de-emphasizes the speaker's will and intention, and thus makes him/her less likely to be challenged on personal motives. This effect is particularly noticeable in questions. Example (3) avoids being personal by suggesting that the action will happen in due course. In (4) a verb like *need*, which is normally not used in the progressive, is quite acceptable. B's response shows that he/she regards A's question as a request to borrow the car.

1 Millions of people *will be watching* the opening ceremony next Monday.
2 I*'ll be moving* into Oslo some time next year.
3 I trust you *will be settling* this overspending soon.
4 A: *Will* you *be needing* your car this afternoon?
B: No, you can borrow it if you want to.

7.7.6 *Be to* + base form of verb

The *be to* + base form of verb is used to signal planned or arranged decisions. With a personal subject the implication is that somebody other than the subject referent has made the decision (2). A non-personal subject allows the interpretation of an official plan or a requirement for a future event (3, 4). Example (4) is a case of 'headlinese', where the tensed verb has been omitted.

1 The committee *is to draft* a plan of action by April.
2 We *are to see* the real estate man at 10 tomorrow.
3 The road *is to be closed* after midnight tomorrow.
4 British Gas *to adopt* stricter internal controls.

7.7.7 Problems for Norwegians

A Past from a future point of orientation

Examples (1) and (2) below show that Norwegian can use the present perfect to refer to events which are in the past relative to a moment of orientation in the future (*in a week's time* and *by the time you receive this letter*). Some Norwegians use 'vil vi ha truffet' and 'vil du ha glemt', but the simpler form above is very common. It is impossible in English.

1	Når du mottar dette brevet, har vi sikkert allerede truffet hverandre.	By the time you receive this letter, I'm sure we*'ll* already *have met.*
2	Om en uke har du glemt alt sammen.	In a week's time, you *will have forgotten* everything.

B Future from a past point of orientation

When reference is made to a plan or arrangement for a future event in the past, Norwegian regularly uses 'skulle'. *Should* is impossible in English, as it invariably points forward from the moment of speaking. Provided they are marked for past tense in the auxiliary, the *going to* form (**7.7.2**), the *be to* form (**7.7.6**), and the *supposed to* construction are all possible, with different shades of meaning. Note also the use of *would* with reference to future in the past (**7.20**).

3	Vi skulle møte dem foran Sentralstasjonen, men de kom ikke.	We *were to meet / were going to meet /were supposed to meet* them in front of the Central Station, but they did not turn up.
4	Skulle ikke du ringe ham i går?	*Weren't you going to / weren't you supposed to call* him yesterday?

7.8 Verb forms in conditional contexts

Conditional contexts are among the non-factive situations we touched on in **7.4**. In (1) below we have an **open condition**. This means that the subject *you* may or may not sell the house. The conditional clause predictably has the simple present tense (**7.7.4**), and the main clause has the *will*-future.

Example (2) illustrates a **hypothetical condition**. In this case the speaker wants to be tentative in his/her suggestion and chooses the past tense form *sold*, which, as we said in **7.6.1**, removes it from the immediacy of the here-and-now sphere. The main clause must have the auxiliary *would*.

The third example contains a **counter-factive conditional**. The subject referent did not sell the house; hence the condition is contrary to fact. In such cases English must have *would have* + main verb in the main clause, while the conditional clause has the past perfect, as in Norwegian. The Norwegian translation shows that we can use the past perfect 'hadde fått', but this form is definitely incorrect in English.

1 If you sell your house now, it'*ll* probably *fetch* a nice price.
2 If you sold your house now, it *would* probably *fetch* a nice price.

3 If you had sold your house then, it *would have fetched* a nice price.	Hvis du hadde solgt huset da, hadde du fått en god pris.

Unless as a negative conditional can be used to express open conditions (4), but *if not* is required in counter-factive conditionals (5).

4 I'*ll* report you to the manager, unless you withdraw that statement.
5 We *would have had* to leave our equipment if we hadn't been airlifted from the glacier.

In all these conditional contexts the main clause contains the auxiliaries *will* or *would*.

We have now established two common uses of *will*: one is to make neutral predictions about future events; the other is to refer to future events in open conditions. The *if*-clause in (8), which tells us what the speaker bases his/her certainty on, makes the use of *will* very close to an epistemic modal. Main clauses with *will* and, even more strongly, with *would* are coloured by some kind of uncertainty or contingency. This is noticeable even if none is expressed (9, 10, 11). The parenthesized words are added for clarification.

6 They'*ll find* a solution next week.
7 They'*ll find* a solution if they keep at it the way they have started.
8 They'*ll find* a solution, if I'm not terribly mistaken.
9 It's a lovely book. It'*ll make* a beautiful film (if somebody decides to film it).
10 That wall-hanging *will/would look* wonderful in your dining room (i.e. if you hang it there).
11 I'*d be* very *grateful* to you, sir (if you could find time to look at the manuscript).

The long and short of this is that the many uses of *will/would* not only overlap but have in common the non-factive contingency which can be exploited when language users do not want to be too direct or categorical.

7.9 Verb forms in indirect speech

Verb forms in indirect speech are adjusted to the reporting situation.

1 The policeman asked, 'Where are you going with that suitcase?'
2 The policeman asked me where I was going with the suitcase.
3 Later the officer exclaimed, 'But I was here when it all happened.'
4 The officer exclaimed that he had been there when it all happened.
5 She said, 'I can do it.'
6 She said that she could do it.

The examples illustrate the regular **back-shift** in tense that takes place when the reporting verb has past time reference. Present tense in direct speech is shifted to past tense in indirect speech (1, 2), and the past tense is shifted to the past perfect (3, 4). Other deictic forms are also changed: *you* (1) becomes *I* (2), *that* (1) becomes *the* (2), *I* (3) becomes *he* (4), *here* (3) becomes *there* (4), *I* (5) becomes *she* (6). Modal auxiliaries are also back-shifted: *can* (5) to *could* (6), *may* to *might*, *shall* to *should*, *will* to *would*.

Back-shift may not take place. In (8) *has* suggests that the time of speaking is probably still before lunch, and *had* that it is after. If the statement in direct speech is considered valid by the one who reports it, no back-shift takes place. Back-shift shows that the statement is reported from the original speaker's perspective (10).

7 He said, 'I have to leave before lunch.'
8 He said he has/had to leave before lunch.
9 Everybody agreed, 'English is a demanding subject.'
10 Everybody agreed that English is/was a demanding subject.

For more comments on indirect speech, see further **16.9.2–16.9.3**.

7.10 The main uses of modal auxiliaries

The modal auxiliaries *can, could, may, might, must, ought to, shall, should, will*, and *would* are very flexible and can express many shades of meaning. In **7.4** we referred to a basic difference between root modality and epistemic modality. However, while it is true that all modals, except *shall,* can be used in both a root sense and an epistemic sense, we would be up against a problem if we assumed that every single occurrence of any modal can be assigned to either one or the other category.

In face-to-face interaction modalized utterances often assume a pragmatic function over and above the mere function of expressing a statement. In the dynamics of such interaction, which can be pretty delicate on the personal level, people are concerned to tread carefully, not to impose or offend, not to sound too nosy in their queries or too categorical when expressing opinions. It is precisely in such contexts that the modal auxiliaries (and for that matter many other modal expressions) are very useful. The historical past tense forms *could, might, should*, and *would* make the utterance sound even more detached from the moment of speaking than the forms *can, may, shall,* and *will.*

In the following we give a survey of the most common meanings of the modal auxiliaries proper, and then add at the very end a summary of the points that Norwegian learners must be aware of. The survey does not contain any examples of back-shifted *could, might, should,* or *would* in indirect speech.

7.11 *Can*

Whereas *can* is virtually impossible as an epistemic modal, the negative *cannot/can't* is common in an epistemic sense. Examples (3) to (14) are normally considered root uses.

A Epistemic (the speaker thinks it is not possible that X is the case)

1 He *can't* have realized what he was letting himself in for.

2 There *cannot* be any doubt about this.

B Root uses

- **ability**

3 Watch little Sophie – she *can* juggle three balls.

4 I *can't* do it. I'm too old.

- **permission**

5 You *can* keep it until Wednesday.

6 *Can* I have a look at it?

- **possibility/willingness**

7 We *can* drop you off outside the station.
8 He wants to propose a deal to JR before CP, the opposition leader, *can* get to him.

- **inherent quality in the subject referent**

9 Young boys *can* be real bullies.
10 Going abroad *can* give you a new perspective on your native culture.

Pragmatically, *can* is often used to convey the speaker's request: either a request for action (11) or a request for information (12). It is also frequent in suggestions (13). *Can't* expresses a rebuke or a suggestion, as the case may be (14).

11 *Can* you put it in my pigeon-hole when you've read it?
12 *Can* you tell me, please, when you first noticed the lump?
13 He *can* step in for you when you're away.
14 *Can't* you turn down that music?

7.12 *Could*

Could is used in much the same way as *can*, but it conveys a stronger sense of tact or tentativeness. In some of its root uses, *could* refers to past time.

A Epistemic (the speaker thinks it is possible that X is the case; less certain than *can*)
1 It *could* be a fake.
2 *Could* she really be thinking of quitting?
3 I *could* have been more direct with her, I guess.

B Root uses
- **past ability**

4 At that time he *couldn't* even talk properly.
5 We *could* carry the stuff half-way up, but then had to get some help.

- **permission**

6 Before the new programme was put into operation, students *could* choose whether to write in English or Norwegian.

7 *Could* I borrow your computer tomorrow?

• **possibility/willingness**

8 I *could* help you if you wish.

Could is often preferred in requests, as it is considered more polite than *can* (see also 7 above):

9 *Could* you possibly take this to the printer? (request)
10 *Could* we leave this for the next board meeting? (suggestion)

7.13 *May*

A Epistemic (the speaker thinks it is possible that X is the case)
1 John *may* have lost his way.
2 We *may* have overlooked a few things.
3 You *may* be reading too much into this.

B Root uses
• **permission**

4 Only members of the club *may* enter the bar after 6 p.m.
5 *May* we ask you to refrain from smoking?
6 You *may* leave now, Jones.
7 *May* I come in?

In expressions of permission, *may* is polite and formal. The speaker is in a position of authority (6). *May* is also used in speaking to a person in authority (7). *Can* is more frequent and relaxed; compare examples (5) and (6) in **7.11**.

• **possibility** (it is possible for X to ...)

8 I *may* be able to finish it before I go home today.
9 The problem *may* be solved in several ways.

• **wish**

10 *May* God give you peace!

7.14 *Might*

A Epistemic (the speaker thinks it is possible that X is the case; less certain than *may*)

1 This approach *might* be too time-consuming.

2 They *might* have drowned if it hadn't been for the heroic effort of the coast guard.

B Root uses

- **hypothetical**

3 This system also increases the number of Labour votes, an advantage to which Mr B *might* not be entirely indifferent if he ...

- **tentative request or opinion**

4 *Might* I trouble you for your ticket, sir?

5 You *might* want to run through this again and see if you can detect any mistakes.

7.15 *Must*

A Epistemic (the speaker concludes that X is the case)

1 It *must* have been some crank that called us this morning.

2 You *must* be Dr Wallis.

3 That dress *must* have cost a fortune.

Note that *mustn't* is generally not used epistemically. The closest negative counterpart of epistemic *must* is *can't* (**7.11A**).

B Root uses

- **obligation or prohibition** (i.e. obligation not to do something)

4 You *must* go and see a doctor.

5 Each guest *must* use an approved sleeping bag.

6 Blankets *must* not be removed from the rooms.

7 I *must* confess that I don't like living in these parts.

8 You *must* be very diplomatic.

Example (7) literally conveys a self-imposed obligation, but *must* is used here to make a guarded statement. Example (8) is ambiguous between a) an obligation for proper behaviour at some future point in time and b) the speaker's conclusion about a successfully accomplished task. *Must not* expresses a prohibition in (6) and should be compared with *don't have to* and *don't need to*, which express lack of necessity in a sentence like *You don't have to / need to tell me if you don't want to.*

Note that the epistemic *must* in (3) may very well function pragmatically as a concealed request for information. The speaker draws a conclusion, but also expresses uncertainty, which he/she asks the hearer to remove.

7.16 *Ought to*

A Epistemic (the speaker thinks that X is the case)

1 It *ought to* be possible to lift it through the window.

2 Events down under (i.e. in Australia and New Zealand) *ought to* calm down supporters of proportional representation in Britain.

B Root

- **obligation/advice**

3 He *ought to* sort out his registration before it is too late.

4 *Oughtn't* you stop smoking?

The obligation sense in (3) is weaker than if *must* had been used. *To* is sometimes dropped in negative and interrogative sentences, but *should* is the more common choice (**7.18**).

7.17 *Shall*

We have already remarked that *shall* does not have an epistemic meaning. It can be used as a neutral future marker with first person subjects (**7.7.1**). A negated *shan't* occurs in British English. It may have a neutral tone or a tone of defiance. *Will/'ll* are much more common as neutral future markers. Otherwise *shall* is used only in restricted contexts in present-day English.

Root uses

- **neutral future** (first person subject, formal)

1 I *shall* return to this in my lecture tomorrow.

2 What kind of government the Kiwis will end up with, we *shall* see.
3 I *shan't* have anything to do with him from now on.

- **speaker's definite determination** (second or third person subject)

4 You *shall* regret this bitterly.
5 They *shall* be judged only by God.

- **suggestions** (first person interrogative)

6 *Shall* we say tomorrow, then?

- **legal use**

7 All payments *shall* be made by the end of the month.
8 Thou *shalt* / You *shall* not steal.

7.18 *Should*

A Epistemic (the speaker thinks it can be expected that X is the case)
1 He *should* be back by now.
2 The West *should* have learnt the lesson from Somalia.

B Root uses
- **obligation or what is advisable**

3 A: I can't be bothered about this.
B: Well, you *should.*
4 Nobody *should* accept bribes.
5 Bikes *should* be locked.
6 You *should* have told him the first time around.

The obligation is weaker than with *must* (**7.15**). Note the related use of *should* as a subjunctive-equivalent (**7.4.2**).

- **distancing *should***

7 It's amazing that he *should* feel so strongly about it.

In (7) it is the very idea, not the fact, that surprises the speaker. Distancing *should* occurs in nominal *that*-clauses.

- **hypothetical *should***

8 If you *should* / *Should* you see him, tell him I want a word with him.

- **tentative *should*** (often reduced to *'d* in spoken English)

9 I *should* see a doctor, if I were you.
10 I *should* have thought you'd have been too busy to discuss this now.
11 I'*d* be much obliged, sir.

In (9) to (11) *should* can be replaced by *would.* In either case there is a hypothetical ring to such sentences, but it is only in (9) that this is made explicit in the *if*-clause (cf. **7.8**). Note the difference between (6), which pragmatically may count as a reproach for not having done something, and (10), which is a very tentative, roundabout way of expressing an opinion. In both cases *should* + perfective aspect is used.

7.19 *Will*

We have touched on *will* earlier (**7.7.1** and **7.8**). Here we briefly mention these uses and add some more.

A Epistemic (the speaker states with confidence that X is the case)
1 There's a noise at the door. It'*ll* be the dog.
2 It'*ll* be clear to you when you see the report.

B Root uses

- **neutral future marker**

3 There'*ll* be more to come.
4 I'm not sure what *will* happen next.

- **habitual activity**

5 Often when I ask him for a favour, he'*ll* just sit there for a while without answering. It is most annoying. I guess it's his way of saying no.

- **property of non-personal subjects**

6 Pigs *will* eat anything.
7 Dishwashers *won't* wash everything clean.

- **volition**

8 *Will* you post this for me, please?
9 You*'ll* arrange something for the weekend then, *won't* you?
10 She *will* use WordPerfect even if everybody else uses a different program.
11 You *will* go straight back to camp!

Pragmatically, (8) and (9) are requests for action. Example (11) functions as an order from somebody in authority. The non-contracted form in (10) shows that when *will* receives stress, it implies insistence.

7.20 *Would*

We have already directly or indirectly touched on some uses of *would* (**7.8**).

A Epistemic (the speaker states with confidence that X is the case; more tentative than *will*)
1 A car at that price *would* be a Jaguar or a Mercedes.

B Root uses
- **past habitual activity**

2 Every time the door bell rang, Ola Billig *would* come out from the back room.

- **past volition**

3 In those days she *wouldn't* even consider moving to that part of town.

- **hypothetical**

4 That *would* mean cheating destiny.
5 *Would* I enjoy teaching in the USA? I didn't know. It was all too hypothetical.

- **tentative opinion or advice**

6 I *would* suggest admitting a few too many, and then see if anybody drops out later.

- **polite offers and requests for action or information**

7 *Would* you mind closing the window?
8 *Would* you like another piece of Christmas cake?

- **future in the past**

9 Later in his life he *would* develop a remarkable social conscience.

In (9) the speaker or writer says something about the development of the person referred to in the subject. This remarkable social conscience manifested itself in the past relative to the moment of speaking, but in the future relative to the time of the story. That is why it is called 'future in the past'. An alternative form is *he was to develop ... Should,* corresponding to Norwegian 'skulle', is not possible here. As regards future in the past, see further **7.7.7B**.

7.21 Main points to note for Norwegian learners

Norwegian modal auxiliaries can be inflected in much the same way as lexical verbs, i.e. they have infinitive and participle forms as well as regular past tense forms. English modals, as we have seen, are different. They have no non-finite forms, and the forms that look like past tense forms (*could, might, should, would*) usually do not refer to past time. From this it follows that Norwegian past tense and non-finite forms must regularly be rendered by English modal auxiliary equivalents (**6.4.3B**).

A The use of auxiliary equivalents to replace missing forms of the English modals

It is particularly important not to use *should* in English to refer to plans in the past (1). English *should* invariably points forward from the moment of speaking, unless, of course, it combines with the perfective aspect: *I should have told him.*

1	Jeg *skulle* reise dagen etter.	I *was supposed to / was going to leave / was leaving* the following day.
2	Vi *måtte* vente på ham en hel time.	We *had to* wait one full hour for him.
3	Bendik *kunne* svømme da han var to.	Bendik *was able to* (*could*) swim when he was two.
4	Jeg har *kunnet* svømme i to år.	I have *been able to* swim for two years.

5	Vi *fikk lov til* å spise i klasserommet.	We *were allowed to* eat in the classroom.
6	Jeg *ville* finne ut hva han mente.	I *wanted to* find out what he meant.
7	Det gjelder å *ville* det.	It is a question of *wanting to* do it.

Examples (6) and (7) show that *ville* can mean 'ønske' in Norwegian. *Want to* is therefore a good translation, although it is not really an auxiliary equivalent.

B The restricted use of the simple present tense in English to refer to future events

Norwegian frequently uses the simple present tense about future events. English rarely does. Instead, we can choose between quite a few future-referring expressions (**7.7**).

8	Vi *snakker* om det i morgen.	We*'ll* talk about it tomorrow.
9	Neste år *er* det fire år siden han kom til Norge.	Next year it*'ll* be four years since he came to Norway.

C Past-in-the-future constructions

Norwegian can use the present perfect to refer to 'past in the future' (**7.7.7A**). English must use a form with *will.*

10	Neste desember *har* vi *bodd* her i 12 år.	Next December we *will have lived* here for 12 years.

D The Norwegian tendency to drop 'ha' when modals and perfective aspect combine

When a Norwegian modal combines with the perfective aspect, the grammatical auxiliary 'ha' is often dropped. This omission is unacceptable in English.

11	Jeg *skulle (ha) fortalt* ham det før.	I *should have told* him before.
12	Tore *kunne sagt opp* før, men bestemte seg for å gjøre det nå.	Tore *could have resigned* earlier, but decided to do it now.

E Counter-factive conditionals

Counter-factive conditionals regularly drop the modal in the main clause in Norwegian. This tendency must not be transferred into English.

13	Hvis jeg hadde kjørt fortere, *hadde* jeg sikkert *blitt tatt* for råkjøring.	If I had gone faster, I'm sure I *would have been caught* speeding.

14 Hvis du ikke hadde vært så utålmodig, *hadde* du kanskje *klart* det.	If you hadn't been so impatient, you *would* probably *have made* it.

F Common errors

Take care not to overuse:

- the present progressive (**7.5.7**)
- *shall*, which is far more restricted in use than Norwegian 'skal' (**7.7**, **7.17**).
- do not use *should* with reference to 'future in the past' (**7.7.7B**, **7.21A**).

Terms

tense:	present past	mood:	indicative imperative subjunctive
aspect:	perfective progressive	conditional contexts:	open condition hypothetical condition counter-factive condition
voice:	active passive		
modality:	epistemic root		future-referring expressions stative and dynamic verbs direct and indirect speech

Exercises

1 What are the arguments for saying that English has two tenses, the present tense and the past tense, and not three, the present, the past, and the future tense? (**7.1**)

2 What aspects are expressed in the italicized verb phrases in the examples below? (**7.2**)

a No ticket-holder *has come* forward to claim the prize.
b The noise *was spreading* from the yard across the entire estate.
c Who'*s been telling* lies about my sister?
d The city *was being abandoned* to the pigeons.
e I *hadn't heard* of it before you mentioned it the other day.
f Why, the computer world *is asking*, did Microsoft announce on 6 August that it would invest $150 million in struggling Apple Computer?

g They *keep reminding* him of his pledge not to use such pictures.
h We'd better *get moving* before it's too late.

3 Identify passive verb phrases in the following extract. (**7.3**)

So, if governments should continue to enlist business people, what can be done to avoid a repeat of past embarrassments? The already strict rules on conflicts of interest are being tightened in the wake of this painful affair to ensure that ministers do not take decisions on matters where they have a direct interest. If, say, BP had launched a takeover bid for a rival, Lord S would have been barred from taking part in deciding whether to refer it to this new commission as long as he held shares in the firm. But indirect conflicts of interest just have to be lived with.

4 Choose the simple present or the present progressive of the italicized verbs in these sentences, whichever is the more appropriate. Make necessary changes in word order. Explain what you go by when you make your choice. If you feel that both forms can be used, explain any difference in meaning. (**7.5**)

a They occasionally *ask* me to dinner.
b 'What you *talk* about?' she said in an angry tone.
c The country *continue* inland for ninety miles or so until you *cross* the maritime plain and the mountains *break* into view.
d A:What *do* the man for a living?
B: He *run* a publishing firm.
A: It *do* well?
B: Oh yes, the reading public *get* bigger and bigger, you know. The firm *sell* about two hundred thousand paperbacks every year.
e Whenever I *drive* through Oslo, I *get* irritated at the slow traffic.
f It *rain* a good deal at this time of the year. As you can see it *rain* now.
g She always *lose* her gloves and *send* me looking for them.
h In the foreground you *see* Mary, who *watch* a group of ostriches. They *move* peacefully about between a herd of antelopes which *graze* in the long grass. In the background the mountains *rise* to the sky, their peaks hidden in dark clouds.
i On the western slopes of the United States, south of Puget Sound, warm, gentle rain *fall* almost constantly. On these mountain slopes, giant Douglas firs *grow* as they *grow* nowhere else in the world. Pine and fir and other evergreen trees *cover* the western side of the Cascade Mountains.

5 The italicized verbs / verb + adjective combinations in the next set of examples can be used as stative verbs and dynamic verbs. Choose a present tense form, simple or progressive, whichever is appropriate in the context. Explain the meaning of the verb in each case. (**7.5.4**)

a What you *think* of?
b What you *mean* I am wrong about him? His face *read* like an open book.
c These chairs *stack* easily.
d John *read* The Grapes of Wrath these days.
e You *think* we should offer him the job?
f We *have* a farewell party next Friday. *Care* to come along?
g I *have* my own copy, so I *not need* to borrow his.
h Don't take any notice of her. She just *be obstinate*.
i I *love* apple pie and whipped cream.
j You *feel* the party is a success? – Yes, of course, look at them; they all *love* every moment of it.
k We *consider* him fully qualified for this position.
l The family *consider* selling their house and *move* somewhere closer to the city centre.
m Her husband *care* for her parents this week, while she's away at a conference.

6 Correct any wrong or unlikely present tense forms in the sentences below. (**7.5**)

a When I was a child, I learnt about foreign countries and how people are living in those countries.
b Most of the things we use every day are coming from oil.
c Throughout the whole of New England, there is also a widely developed tourist industry which entices vacationers to the region's forests, mountains, and sea.
d More and more people become aware of the need to recycle tins, bottles, and paper.
e This cliché – 'Norway, the land of the Vikings' – is obviously true as long as it is only stating a historical fact.
f The greatest part of America's heavy industry depends on three resources.
g The committee is consisting of world famous experts in fields such as chemistry and physics.

7 What is the difference in meaning between the two sentences below? What does this contrast tell you about the difference between the simple present tense and the simple past tense? (**7.5**, **7.6.1**)

a Mary plays a good game of tennis.
b Mary played a good game of tennis.

8 Choose the appropriate past tense form, the simple past tense or the past progressive, of the italicized verbs in the sentences below. Explain your choice with reference to the wider context. Discuss any difference in meaning in sentences which accept both forms. (**7.6.4**)

a You forget: I didn't stop your father's horrible book. I merely *manage* to get certain passages changed or omitted.
b I *ring* you about seven o'clock, but nobody answered the phone. – Well, you see I *cut* the grass then so I couldn't hear it.
c Just then I happened to look out of the window. A car *overtake* a lorry and I knew it was going to crash.
d While my wife did the shopping, I *look* after the baby.
e We *cross* the lake in our little rowing-boat when suddenly there *be* a flash of lightning.
f The drive *give* him a distinct feeling of power. When he *reach* the house, he *park* in front of the main entrance. Caroline and Fred were pleased to see him. They *find* him quietly dignified. They *settle* him into a chair, *press* a whisky on him and *start* the business of proffering condolences.
g For a short while he *manage* his father's shipping firm, but then *start* his own business soon afterwards.
h I could see from your face that he *be rude* to you.
i We crossed the river at dusk. Soon we *tramp* across the plain.
j The scene was quite remarkable. The huge ferry *glide* through the narrow strait, lots of small boats *follow* in her wake. The lights on the other side *shine* like stars against the dark hill. Suddenly Ann *whisper* in my ear ...

9 Choose an appropriate verb phrase for the italicized verbs in the passage below. In those cases where you think more than one form can be used, you should explain possible differences in meaning. (**7.5–7.6**)

'Boxer!' *cry* Clover in a terrible voice. 'Boxer, get out! Get out quickly! They *take* you to your death!'

All the animals *take* up the cry of 'Get out, Boxer, get out!' But the van already *gather* speed and *draw* away from them. It was uncertain whether Boxer *understand* what Clover *say*. But a moment later his face *disappear* from the window and there was the sound of a tremendous drumming of hoofs inside the van. He *try* to kick his way out. The time *be* when a few kicks from Boxer's hoofs would have smashed the van to matchwood. But alas! His strength *leave* him, and in a few moments the sound of drumming hoofs *grow* fainter and *die* away. All the animals, except the two stupid brutes that *draw* the van, realized what *happen.*

(From George Orwell, *Animal Farm*)

10 In the sentences below you should choose either a perfective or non-perfective progressive form of the italicized verbs, whichever is the more appropriate. Make any changes in word order that are required. Identify clues in the sentences that you go by when you make your choices. (**7.6.6**)

a The Norwegian government *put* pressure on the British government for a long time to reduce their emissions of sulphur dioxide into the atmosphere.
b I do not think I ever *see* her so angry before.
c This regulation *be* in force since 1980.
d The Unionists in Northern Ireland *demand* this for decades.
e His breath smelt of alcohol. He must *drink.*
f Union membership *fall* sharply in recent years.
g We *know* for a long time that they support the extreme right.
h As we speak, hundreds of passengers *wait* at the station for more than an hour.
i How long you *work* for Telenor?

11 Try to explain why the progressive is not acceptable in (a) but all right in (b). (**7.6.6**)

a She has been writing most of our Christmas cards, but she still has a few more to do.
b She has been writing Christmas cards all evening.

12 William Carlos Williams's short poem 'This is Just to Say' is given below. What effect would it have if *have eaten* in line 1 were replaced by *ate*? Also, why would a non-progressive *saved* sound odd in stanza 2?

This is Just to Say

I have eaten
the plums
that were in
the icebox

and which
you were probably
saving
for breakfast

Forgive me
they were delicious
so sweet
and so cold

13 The poem below is Robert Frost's 'The Gift Outright'. The first line contains two past tense forms, *was* and *were*. Do they have the same time reference in the past? What time does *now* (line 7) refer to? The same line has two forms of *possessed*. Which is a verb at the clause level? How would you describe the other form? What time reference do *was* and *would become* have in line 16?

The Gift Outright

The land was ours before we were the land's.
She was our land more than a hundred years
Before we were her people. She was ours
In Massachusetts, In Virginia,
But we were England's, still colonials,
Possessing what we were still unpossessed by,
Possessed by what we now no more possessed.
Something we were withholding made us weak
Until we found out that it was ourselves
We were withholding from our land of living,
And forthwith found salvation in surrender.
Such as we were we gave ourselves outright
(The deed of gift was many deeds of war)
To the land vaguely realizing westward,
But still unstoried, artless, unenhanced,
Such as she was, such as she would become.

14 Comment on the difference in form and meaning between the members of each pair below. (**7.5–7.7**)

a 1 She went to visit him in his new house.
  2 She was going to visit him in his new house.
b 1 The patient died.
  2 The patient was dying.

c 1 When they came back from their fishing trip, I was making tea.
  2 When they came back from their fishing trip, I made tea.
d 1 I wonder if you could help us.
  2 I was wondering if you could help us.
e 1 Did you stay at the Royal York Hotel?
  2 Have you stayed at the Royal York hotel?
f 1 I have cleared out the shed.
  2 I have been clearing out the shed.
g 1 They were terribly offended.
  2 They were being terribly offensive.

15 In the paragraph below, most of the verb phrases have been replaced by their corresponding base forms, printed in capital letters. Complete the text, choosing verb phrases which incorporate suitable combinations of tense, aspect, voice, and modality. In each case explain your choice. (**7.5–7.7**)

It was mid-afternoon on Thursday 21 September, and Philippa (1) SIT in the basket chair at the open window of her room. She and her mother just (2) RETURN from a visit to Brompton Oratory to see the Mazzula Marbles and there (3) BE an hour before they (4) NEED to set out for work. Her mother (5) SAY that she (6) MAKE the tea. From the kitchen Philippa (7) HEAR small noises which (8) BE extraordinarily pleasurable. The voices which (9) DRIFT in through her own window (10) SEEM far-away shouts of joy from another world. It (11) BE a hot oppressive day with the threat of thunder, but in the last half-hour the sky (12) LIGHTEN and now the room (13) FILL with the strong mellow light which (14) COME before the dusk.

16 Each of the sentences below refers to a future time event. Choose an appropriate form of the italicized verbs and justify your choice with reference to the wider context. If you think more than one form is possible, discuss any difference in meaning. (**7.7**)

a According to the timetable my train *leave* Newcastle at 7.34 tomorrow morning and *arrive* in York at 8.41. I'd better take a taxi from home.
b I trust you *clear* this debt as soon as possible.
c When asked about the new release, the Prime Minister said he *buy* the CD.
d It looks as if we *get* some snow this afternoon, but according to the weather report it *clear up* later so we *be able* to drive over to Rufforth as planned.
e Have you decided what you *do* about the leak?

f In the Premier League Tottenham *take* on Chelsea tomorrow. Kick-off time *be* 4 p.m.
g Mr Blair is hoping that there *be* enough agreement between employers and unions to make legislation irrelevant.
h Is that the telephone? – Yeah, I *get* it.
i We *plan* to re-do the kitchen next week, so we *not be able* to do any cooking. It *give* us a chance to lose a few pounds.

17 Translate the following sentences into English. On the basis of your correct translations, what rule can you give which captures the essential difference between English and Norwegian? (**7.7.7**) What special rule applies when translating the time clause in (g)? (**7.7.4**)

a Neste fredag har vi sikkert hørt noe fra ham.
b Om 10 år er det nesten like mange 70-åringer som 20-åringer.
c Vi kjøper nok en ny leilighet til våren hvis ikke prisene stiger for mye.
d Vi kommer til Katmandu tidlig i april og noen dager senere er vi på plass i leiren vår.
e Han har sikkert ombestemt seg i morgen.
f Reiser du videre dagen etter?
g Når du kommer tilbake neste år, har du sikkert opplevd mer på ett år enn jeg har opplevd de siste ti årene.

18 Translate the following sentences into English. Give a rule which captures the essential difference between English and Norwegian. (**7.21E**)

a Hvis du ikke hadde vært så fordømt sta, hadde du fått billetter til konserten.
b Jeg er ganske overbevist om at dette hadde skjedd selv om du hadde fortalt henne det på forhånd.
c Tenk i dag hadde faren min vært 100 år.
d Turen hadde ikke blitt avlyst hvis det ikke hadde regnet så mye.
e Jeg hadde gjort det på en annen måte hvis jeg hadde vært deg.

19 Translate into idiomatic English. (**7.7.7**)

a Vil du høre den nye CD'n til Lillebjørn?
b Kunne du komme tilbake i morgen?
c Burde ikke du kjøre ham hjem etter festen?
d Skulle ikke du kjøre ham hjem etter festen i går?
e Jeg skal treffe ham i morgen.
f Vi måtte skifte clutch ifjor.

g Vi skulle skrive under kontrakten dagen etter.
h Jeg kunne skimte båten i det fjerne.

20 Stanzas 7 and 8 from Sylvia Plath's 'Daddy' are given below. What does the italicized modal mean? What effect would it have on the poem if the modal was dropped and the lines read *I think I am a Jew* and *I am a bit of a Jew*?

An engine, and engine
Chuffing me off like a Jew.
A Jew to Dachau, Auschwitz, Belsen
I began to talk like a Jew.
I think I *may* well be a Jew.

The snows of the Tyrol, the clear beer of Vienna
Are not very pure or true.
With my gypsy ancestress and my weird luck
And my Taroc pack and my Taroc pack
I *may* be a bit of a Jew.

21 Explain the exact meaning of the italicized modals in this extract from Kingsley Amis, *One Fat Englishman.* (**7.10**)

Then, there's Helen. Of course the whole thing is very wrong and I *shouldn't* be asking you to let me commit a sin, but *won't* you let me arrange something? If you only *would,* I *could* get it all cleared up: I*'ll* take her away and marry her, or else I*'ll* stop seeing her. Either way I *shan't* be going on like this, which I agree is very bad. I'm only asking for this one chance. You *must* know how much I want it, for Christ's sake.

22 Translate these sentences into English. (**7.7.7B**)

a Du kjører som du skulle ha drukket.
b Hva skal dette bety?
c Dagen etter skulle vi gå fra Bessheim til Gjendesheim, men været stoppet oss.
d Skal du smake?
e Han skal sannelig få høre hva jeg mener om det.
f Uka før skulle vi egentlig male huset, men så ble Ola syk.

23 Translate the following sentences into English and explain how they differ in meaning. (**7.8**)

a Hvis du kjører fortere, så kommer vi fram tidsnok.

b Hvis du kjørte fortere, så kom vi fram tidsnok.
c Hvis du hadde kjørt fortere, hadde vi kommet fram i tide.

24 The following Norwegian sentences contain combinations of two or more modal auxiliaries, which some people might find awkward. Such combinations are virtually impossible in English. How would you translate them? (**7.21**)

a Dette kurset ville ha kunnet blitt gitt hvert annet semester hvis interessen hadde vært stor nok.
b Dette kurset vil kunne gis hvert annet semester hvis interessen er stor nok.
c Det måtte kunne være mulig å bygge en garasje der.
d Skulle du kunne tenke deg å holde en kort innledning på møtet?
e Hvis du spurte ham, tror du du kunne få lov til å gå litt før?
f Vi ville ha måttet solgt bilen for å ha hatt råd til en ny hytte.
g Vi hadde måttet selge bilen for å få råd til en ny hytte.
h Jeg synes de burde kunne akseptere denne prisen.
i Jeg synes de burde kunnet akseptere denne prisen.

25 Comment on the difference in form and meaning between the two members of each pair below.

a 1 You mustn't tell Virginia, of course.
  2 You don't have to tell Virginia, of course.
b 1 We needn't have worried about money.
  2 We didn't need to worry about money.
c 1 She'll be contacting you in Newcastle.
  2 She's to contact you in Newcastle.
d 1 Since Brussels have accepted the application, we can start planning for next year.
  2 Since Brussels accepted the application, we have been planning for next year.
e 1 John's been discussed already.
  2 John's has been discussed already.
f 1 I could take him home.
  2 I was able to take him home.
g 1 He would have had a profound influence on European thinking.
  2 He would have a profound influence on European thinking.
h 1 You should have left him alone.
  2 You should leave him alone.
i 1 When that happened, he would get into his car and go for a drive just to calm down.
  2 When that happened, he got into his car and went for a drive just to calm down.

8 Adjectives and Adverbs

8.1 The form and meaning of adjectives

Sample text

Dora felt *restless* and *dejected*. In spite of *certain* moments of satisfaction, when the warmth of the weather and the beauty of the scene lifted her above her anxieties, she had not been *able* to settle down at Imber. She still felt *nervous* and *shy* and as if she were acting a part. It was not that she disliked anyone, though she did find Michael and James, especially James, a bit *alarming*. Everyone was *nice* to her, she had an *easy* time, she didn't even have to get up at what James called 'shriekers', which she discovered to mean crack, or shriek, of dawn.

(From Iris Murdoch, *The Bell*)

The italicized words in the text above are all adjectives. Adjectives typically modify nouns, either as part of a noun phrase or following a copular verb. Most adjectives can be said to be descriptive in that they denote a quality or a property of something (e.g. *restless, dejected, able, easy* in the text above). Other adjectives limit the reference of a noun (e.g. *certain* in *certain moments*). Yet others (not represented in the example text) emphasize a part of the meaning of the noun (e.g. *complete, utter* in *a complete stranger* and *utter stupidity*).

There is no morphological feature which is unique to adjectives. The following endings are frequently found with adjectives, but many of them can be associated with other word classes as well.

-able	countable	*-ish*	outlandish
-al	philosophical	*-ive*	addictive
-ed	confused	*-less*	pointless
-esque	picturesque	*-like*	lifelike
-ful	helpful	*-ly*	lovely
-ible	irresistible	*-ous*	jealous
-ic	electric	*-some*	tiresome
-ical	critical	*-worthy*	noteworthy
-ing	interesting	*-y*	sunny

Some adjective endings are productive; i.e. they are used for forming new adjectives with stems from other word classes.

- *-able* can be added to a verb, such as *drink*, to form an adjective, *drinkable*, indicating the property that it is possible to drink something.
- *-ful* and *-less* can be added to a noun to indicate that something has or lacks a certain property, e.g. *purposeful, meaningless.*
- *-like* can be added to a noun to indicate that something resembles something else, e.g. *ghostlike.*
- *-ish* added to a noun also indicates that something has some of the same qualities as the referent of that noun, e.g. *foolish, bookish. -ish* added to an adjective tends to make the meaning of the adjective approximate: *reddish* is 'nearly red', *smallish* is 'relatively small'. Adjectives composed in this manner are associated with an informal style.

8.2 Adjective comparison

Adjectives can be compared in two ways in English. One is by means of the inflectional endings *-er* (in the comparative) and *-est* (in the superlative), and the other by means of the modifiers *more* and *most*. The way in which an adjective is compared is largely dependent upon its length, as shown in Table 8a.

Table 8a: Comparison of adjectives

	Positive	**Comparative**	**Superlative**
One syllable	big fun	bigger more fun	biggest most fun
Two syllables	happy careful	happier more careful	happiest most careful
Three or more syllables	interesting	more interesting	most interesting

Most monosyllabic adjectives take the inflectional ending, with a few exceptions which are compared with *more* and *most*. Note particularly *fun, real, right, wrong* and participles functioning as adjectives, such as *known, torn, soaked.*

In the case of adjectives of two syllables, the tendency is for adjectives ending in *-y, -ow, -er, -le,* and *-ure* (for example, *early, narrow, sober, subtle, mature*) to take the inflectional endings, and for other adjectives to be compared by means of *more* and *most*. Many adjectives of two syllables may occur with one or the other type of comparison, such as *obscure, quiet.*

Adjectives of three syllables which begin with the negative prefix *un-* can be compared by means of inflectional endings, depending on the usual inflection of the part following the prefix. Thus we find *unhappier*, but *more unselfish.*

Some adjectives and quantifying determiners (**5.6**) have irregular comparative and superlative forms:

good - better - best
well ('frisk') - *better - best*
bad - worse - worst
many ('mange') - *more - most*
much ('mye') - *more - most*
little ('lite') - *less - least*

Old and *far* can be compared in two different ways, with a slight difference in meaning:

old - older - oldest (the most common, general meaning of *old*)
old - elder - eldest (used about the age of family members, e.g. *their eldest son*)
far - further/farther - furthest/farthest (*Further - furthest* is most common. *Farther - farthest* is used only about physical distance, e.g. *They were moving towards the farthest north.*)
Little (describing size) cannot be compared. Instead *smaller - smallest* can be used.

Comparative forms are often accompanied by a phrase or clause introduced by *than*, which denotes what the subject referent is being compared with.

1 He is taller than me.
2 They can be more difficult than most other people.

Note that, unlike Norwegian, English does not normally use the superlative form in comparisons of two items, particularly not in more formal styles. Instead the comparative form is used. In informal speech, the superlative form may be heard, even in comparisons of two things. However, as this is considered incorrect by many, the comparative form is to be recommended.

3 I was considering whether to go by train or by air, and decided that the train would be *more convenient*. (Cf. Norwegian: Jeg vurderte om jeg skulle ta tog eller fly, og bestemte meg for at toget ville være *mest praktisk*.)

In the same way as we use *more* and *most* to express a higher degree of the quality in question, we use *less* and *least* to express a lower degree of that quality. Note that *less* and *least* are used also with adjectives of one or two syllables, since there are no morphological forms to express a lower degree.

4 I find his latest novel less interesting than his previous one.
5 It is less hot than usual this month.
6 Jennifer was the least self-conscious woman I had ever met.

The superlative is nearly always accompanied by the definite article or a possessive determiner.

7 Anna was the cleverest girl in our school.
8 This is my latest acquisition.

In speech and informal writing the determiner is sometimes omitted. However, this cannot be done in a noun phrase which is postmodified by a prepositional phrase denoting the items that are being compared.

9 This watch was cheapest.
10 This watch was the cheapest of them all. (Cf. Norwegian: Denne klokka var billigst / den billigste av dem alle sammen.)

8.3 Complementation of the adjective – adjective phrases

Adjectives can combine with other words, or with other phrases and clauses, to form **adjective phrases**. Adverbs which precede the adjective are called **modifiers**, while phrases and clauses that follow the adjective are called **complements of the adjective**. Adjective phrases are composed in the following ways (see also **2.6.5**):

A Adverb + adjective / adjective + adverb

an *extremely narrow* road
a *rather clumsy* person
It's *good enough* for us.

B Adjective + prepositional phrase

I'm *hopeless at golf.*
I'm *interested in sports.*
Paul is *fond of dancing.*
She felt *sorry for herself.*

C Adjective + nominal subordinate clause, *-ing* participle clause, or infinitive clause

I'm *afraid (that) he's away.*
The president has never been *sure which direction he wanted to go in on this issue.*
They were *busy doing other things.*
They were *quick to spot the mistake.*

D Compared adjectives (8.2)

They were *quicker than anyone else.*
Anthony is the *most clumsy* person *I have met.*
They were *no less impressed than I was.*
Henry is *nearly as tall as his brother.*

A nominal subordinate clause or a non-finite clause that complements an adjective is never preceded by a preposition. Since Norwegian and English differ in this regard, Norwegian learners should pay attention to constructions with adjectives such as *afraid* and *sure*, which can combine with either a prepositional phrase or a subordinate clause. See also **12.8.2**.

1	I'm afraid of dogs.	Jeg er redd for hunder.
2	I'm afraid (that) I can't help you.	Jeg er redd for at jeg ikke kan hjelpe deg.
3	I'm afraid to go out in the dark.	Jeg er redd for å gå ut i mørket.

Adjective phrases serve the same syntactic functions as adjectives.

8.4 Types of adjectives

8.4.1 Qualitative adjectives

This group of adjectives can be divided into two. On the one hand, we have **descriptive** adjectives, which typically denote such qualities as shape, size, and age. They give a relatively objective description of the referent of the head noun. Examples are *round, square, small, over-sized, ancient, new.*

On the other hand we have **evaluative** adjectives, which typically imply an evaluation by the speaker/writer. Thus they give a more subjective description of the referent of the head noun. Examples are *beautiful, comfortable, elaborate, glamorous, resentful, worrisome.*

Not all qualitative adjectives fit neatly into one of these groups, and some adjectives may belong to both types, depending on their use. One example of this is *great*, which can denote size and extent (*great danger*), or a positive quality (*a great singer*). The important point is whether the adjective denotes a relatively objective or a relatively subjective quality. In the former case, it counts as descriptive; in the latter, as evaluative.

8.4.2 Colour adjectives

On the basis of meaning, this group of adjectives could well be looked upon as a subtype of descriptive adjectives. They simply denote the colour that something has, e.g. *a blue sweater*. However, when colour adjectives occur in a series of premodifiers in a noun phrase, they behave differently from other descriptive adjectives; see **8.8**.

8.4.3 Participles

This group of adjectives differs from the two groups described above in that it is distinguished on the basis of form rather than meaning. It consists of participles (present and past) which are used as adjectives. As such, they are usually qualitative adjectives at the same time. The reason why they are mentioned here as a separate group has to do with their position as premodifiers in a noun phrase; see **8.8**.

Present participles, or *-ing* participles, tend to denote an effect that the referent of the noun phrase has on something else. This is particularly true of participles of transitive verbs. *Alarming news* makes you alarmed, and a *reassuring smile* makes you feel reassured. Participles of intransitive verbs, on the other hand, tend to denote a state or a process, as in *rising numbers* and *shining silver.*

When past participles of transitive verbs are used as adjectives, they usually have a passive meaning. *Worn shoes* have been worn by somebody, and *a written statement* has an author. However, participles of intransitive verbs tend to have an active meaning, as in *a retired officer* or *a fallen angel*.

Some adjectives look like participles in that they end in *-ed* or resemble the participle form of an irregular verb, such as *well-known, unimpressed,* and *homemade*, but the fact that there are no corresponding infinitive forms (**to well-know, *to unimpress, *to homemake*) suggests that these are not regular participles. Many participles can, however, be combined with a prefix, particularly the negative *un-*, to form an adjective. Examples are *unborn, unchanged, unemployed, unknown, unprepared.*

Furthermore, many adjectives which end in *-ed* or *-en*, and thus look like participles, are derived from nouns. Examples are *blue-eyed, disadvantaged, middle-aged, talented, brazen, wooden.* This is a reminder that *-ed* and *-en* are adjectival suffixes which may be added to a noun as well as serve as markers of the past participle.

Finally, participles may form phrases of a slightly different type than other adjectives, as shown in (1) and (2). (Note that participles also occur in the more common type of adjective phrases, as described in **8.3**.) These participle phrases are clause-like in their structure; compare *That feature is now rapidly disappearing* and *The bedroom had been carefully decorated.* In premodifier position it is still clear that the function of these phrases is adjectival. See further **13.5–13.6** on participle clauses.

1 Two years ago the paddle-steamer preservation society was formed to preserve in running order an example of that once so familiar but *now rapidly disappearing* feature of our seaside towns, the faithful old paddle-steamer.
2 It looked alien in the *carefully decorated* pastel bedroom.

8.4.4 Emphasizing adjectives

Some adjectives emphasize the speaker's or writer's feelings about the referent of the head noun. Examples are *absolute, complete, perfect, utter,* in *a complete/perfect idiot, absolute/utter confusion.* Other examples, which more explicitly convey the speaker's feeling, are such words as *bloody, blasted, blinking.*

Note the contrast between *perfect* and *bloody* used as emphasizing adjectives in (1) and (2), and as qualitative adjectives in (3) and (4). When they are used as qualitative adjectives, these adjectives have a distinct meaning of their own, but as emphasizers they simply convey the speaker's or writer's attitude.

1 What he said made perfect sense under the circumstances.

2 He's been saying the same bloody thing over and over again.
3 It was obviously going to be a perfect day for swimming.
4 The conflict developed into a bloody war.

8.4.5 Limiters

Some adjectives are rather like determiners. In a noun phrase, they are placed immediately after the determiner. These adjectives restrict the reference of the noun to a particular specimen or group. Some examples are *certain, chief, exact, following, former, last, main, next, only, other, particular, past, previous, same, such, very*.

1 Certain rooms are open to the public.
2 They had been there often in the past few years.
3 You're the very man I wanted to talk to!

The limiters *certain* and *such* occur only with indefinite noun phrases. Note that the indefinite article is always placed after *such*.

4 I have never known anyone with such a grasp of European history. ('et slikt grep på europeisk historie')
5 They warned her not to do such a thing.

In contrast to the Norwegian 'samme', the English *same* cannot occur without an accompanying determiner.

6 They continued in the same way as before.	De fortsatte på samme måte som før.
7 Debbie was the same age as me.	Debbie var på samme alder som meg.

Note that some of these words also have a nominal use.

8 All their food tasted the same.	All maten deres smakte det samme.
9 Who's next?	Hvem er nestemann?

8.4.6 Origin, style, material

An adjective can describe where something or somebody comes from or belongs (e.g. *Irish, urban*), what style it is (e.g. *Victorian, modern*), or what it is made of (e.g. *woollen*). These adjectives are often derived from nouns, and tend to have a classifying function (**8.6**).

1 She tried to explain the system to confused *foreign* visitors.
2 Along this street are some beautiful *Georgian* houses.
3 I remember having to sit for hours on a hard *wooden* chair.

8.5 Gradability

Most qualitative adjectives are **gradable**. This means that we can specify the degree to which a thing or person has the quality denoted by the adjective. Somebody or something can be more or less interesting, negative, sad, etc. Gradable adjectives meet at least one of the following two criteria:

- they can be compared for degree (cf. **8.2**)

happy - happier - happiest
good - better - best
unfortunate - more unfortunate - most unfortunate

- they can co-occur with intensifying adverbs such as *very, rather, quite*, etc.

very happy - moderately happy
unusually good - terribly good
rather unfortunate - extremely unfortunate

Certain adjectives have absolute meanings, and so they are not normally gradable. One example is *dead*. Nothing can really be more or less dead; it is either dead or alive (exception: the expression *more dead than alive*). Another example is *faultless*. 'More faultless' does not make sense, since the word in itself implies perfection, and 'less faultless' would be a contradiction in terms. However, we find the expression *more perfect* in (1), which then must carry a special meaning.

1 We, the people of the United States, in order to form *a more perfect union*, establish justice, insure domestic tranquility, provide for the common defense, promote the general welfare and secure the blessings of liberty to ourselves and our posterity, do ordain and establish this Constitution of the United States of America.

(Preamble to the Constitution of the United States)

Adjectives that denote origin, style, or material are not normally gradable. If these adjectives are found with intensifiers, for example *very American*, the meaning of the adjective has been changed slightly to mean 'typical of America', rather than 'from America'.

2 It's goodbye to Britain from Hollywood superstar Dustin Hoffman, but we may be seeing him again soon *in that most British of all parts* – Captain Hook in a film version of Peter Pan.

8.6 Syntactic functions of adjectives

An adjective is typically found either as a premodifier of a noun in a noun phrase or as a subject predicative after a copular verb. The position in front of a noun is called **attributive**, and the position after a copular verb is called **predicative**.

8.6.1 Attributive vs. predicative adjectives

Most adjectives can be used both attributively and predicatively without any difference in meaning.

a *happy* man	The man is *happy*.
a *good/correct* answer	The answer is *good/correct.*
a *perfect* solution	The solution is *perfect.*

The position of an adjective may, however, have an effect on its communicative role. In (1) below, *extremely good* is not likely to be disputed by an interlocutor, while in (2) it might very well be. We may conclude that an adjective in attributive position seems to point to an inherent property of the head noun (truthfully or not), while an adjective in predicative position forms part of an assertion which may be disputed.

1 I read an extremely good novel by Minette Walters.
2 Minette Walters's latest novel is extremely good.

8.6.2 Attributive-only

Many adjectives are only used attributively. This is true of the adjectives belonging to the groups of limiters and emphasizing adjectives, and those that have a classifying function (**8.7**).

the main/chief argument	* The argument is main/chief.
That's an outright lie!	* Your lie is outright.
civil engineering/disobedience	* The engineering/ disobedience is civil.

8.6.3 Predicative-only

Some adjectives are used only in predicative position. This is true of most adjectives beginning in the prefix *a-* (e.g. *awake, ablaze*). Note also the adjectives *ill, unwell,* and *well* ('healthy'), which are used only predicatively.

* an asleep/afraid student	The student is asleep/afraid.
* my ill/well father	My father is ill/well.

Adjectives followed by complements (**8.3**) tend to be predicative. Only in very special contexts, for instance in advertising language, can we find complemented adjectives in attributive position. The effect of this usage is that the adjective phrase seems to denote an inherent quality of the product, while the corresponding expression with the predicative adjective phrase is more likely to state a fact concerning the product. Note the use of hyphens when such adjective phrases are used attributively.

1 These new *easy-to-use* sewing machines are on offer this week.
2 These new sewing machines are *easy to use*.

8.6.4 Other functions of adjectives

A Postmodifier in noun phrases

Adjectives sometimes function as postmodifiers in a noun phrase. This generally happens when the head of the noun phrase is an indefinite pronoun or a noun with a very general meaning, or when the head is preceded by a modifier such as *only, first,* or *best.*

1 Is there anything *funny*?
2 I'm interested in things *Irish*.
3 Mr Smith is the only man *present/alive* who understands this problem.
4 This is the *best possible* way / the best way *possible*.

We may also find adjectives and adjective phrases as postmodifiers in indefinite noun phrases, particularly when the adjective (phrase) denotes a temporary quality.

5 We'll look for a person *brave enough to do it*.
6 This was of great interest to people *eager for a quick cure*.
7 Are there any *available* seats / any seats *available*?

The meaning of some adjectives depends on whether the adjective is placed before or after the noun.

8 I'll talk to the parents *concerned*. (= the relevant parents)
9 I'll talk to the *concerned* parents. (= those who are worried)
10 Nobody *present* knew the name of the *present* manager.
11 I finally found the person *responsible*, who really turned out to be a *responsible* person.

In (10) the postposed *present* means 'who was there', while the preposed *present* means 'current'; compare Norwegian 'nærværende' vs. 'nåværende'. In (11) *the person responsible* denotes the person who was responsible for a particular arrangement, while the preposed *responsible* attributes a quality to the person.

Note also that some idiomatic expressions have postposed adjectives, such as *Asia Minor, heir apparent, secretary general, court martial, F sharp, B flat, C minor, E major*.

B Object predicative

An adjective phrase placed after the direct object of a clause can have the syntactic function of an object predicative, if it describes the referent of the object, and at the same time has a strong link with the verb phrase (see **9.3.5B**).

12 Sheila found her job *quite fulfilling*.
13 The drought in the area has made food *scarce*.

C Free predicative

Sometimes the adjective need not be placed next to the noun it modifies, or it is separated from it by means of a comma. Such adjectives may be seen as verbless clauses (reduced relative clauses), and analysed as free predicatives (**9.8.3**). They may resemble manner adverbs (**10.6**), but it is clear that they describe the referent of a noun in the sentence, usually the subject.

14 *Bewildered*, she turned to the others for help.
15 He was lying there *unconscious*.
16 This dessert is best served *chilled*.
17 I remembered his eyes, *tearful and pleading*. (= his eyes were tearful and pleading)

8.7 Classifying and specifying modifiers

If we compare the relationship between the adjective and the noun in expressions such as *personal style* and *personal computer* or *a red house* and *a red herring*, we see that in the second member of each pair the adjective and the noun form a very close unit in a way that resembles the relationship between the two parts of a compound noun (such as *flower pot*). While *personal* is simply descriptive of *style*, it singles out a type of computer. A *red herring* does not describe the colour of any fish, but denotes something that takes the attention away from the focus of a discussion.

The modifiers in *personal style* and *red house* are **specifying** in that they are descriptive of the head noun. The modifiers in *personal computer* and *red herring*, on the other hand, are **classifying** in that they either single out a certain type of something, or go together with the noun to form an idiom, with a meaning which cannot be predicted from the usual meanings of the adjective and the noun. Here are some further examples of specifying and classifying modifiers. Note that the nouns modified by a classifying adjective often correspond to a compound noun in Norwegian.

Table 8b: Specifying and classifying adjectives

Specifying	**Classifying**
a comprehensive programme	a comprehensive school
a drunken husband	drunk(en) driving ('promillekjøring')
fine clothes	fine arts ('kunst og kultur')
a single thing	a single parent ('eneforsørger')
blue eyes	a black eye ('blått øye')
a civil answer	a civil engineer ('bygningsingeniør')

Other types of premodifiers can also be divided into specifying and classifying, such as genitive expressions (*his doctor's advice* vs. *his doctor's degree*) or uninflected nouns (*a top score* vs. *a top hat*); see **5.5.3D** and **8.10.1A**.

8.8 The order of premodifiers in a noun phrase

When there is a series of premodifiers in a noun phrase, the modifiers generally follow a certain order. Informally, we can say that the adjectives that most objectively characterize the noun referent are placed closest to the head of the noun phrase.

When we consider the different types of adjectives described above, as well as some nouns which can function as premodifiers, the order is as follows:

i) limiters (e.g. *certain, same, main, entire*)
ii) emphasizing adjectives (e.g. *absolute, blasted*)
iii) qualitative adjectives:
  a) evaluative (e.g. *beautiful, priceless, doubtful, horrible, revolting*)
  b) descriptive (e.g. *huge, tiny, round, uneven, old, young*)
iv) colour adjectives and participles (e.g. *red, yellow, stolen, missing, beloved*)

v) origin, style, material (e.g. *Irish, 18th century, modern, woollen*)
vi) classifying modifiers:
  a) adjectives derived from nouns (e.g. *literary, medical, social*)
  b) uninflected nouns (as in *phone number, fir tree, road sign, V-neck sweater, school bus, grammar lecture*)
  c) classifying genitives (as in *doctor's degree, Parkinson's disease, teachers' centre*)

1 I've got the *same gorgeous, big, red garden* chairs as you have. (limiter + evaluative + descriptive + colour + classifying)

An adjective that denotes a temporary quality is usually placed before one that denotes a permanent quality of the noun referent.

2 Everyone looked for the *missing white sports* car. (the participle *missing* denotes a temporary state; the colour *white* denotes a permanent quality)

Note that the meaning of an adjective may depend on its position, e.g. in *a proper English name* vs. *an English proper name*. In the former case, *proper* is a qualitative adjective meaning something like 'genuine', while in the latter case *proper* functions as a classifying modifier, forming an idiomatic expression with *name*.

8.9 Nominalized adjectives

Under special circumstances an adjective can function as the head of a noun phrase. There are, however, quite a few restrictions on nominalized adjectives in English. They tend to denote either a group of people or an abstract concept.

8.9.1 Groups of people

An important subcategory here consists of some nationality adjectives ending in *-ish* and *-ch*: *the British, the English, the Dutch, the French, the Irish.*

1 That terrible battlefield, which *the French* call Neerwinden and *the English* call Landen ...

Another subcategory consists of adjectives which characterize a group of people, such as *the elderly, the young, the poor.*

2 The church runs a shelter for *the homeless*. ('for de hjemløse')

3 Give me your *tired*, your *poor*,
Your huddled masses yearning to breathe free,
The wretched refuse of your teeming shore,
Send these, the *homeless*, *tempest-tossed* to me:
I lift my lamp beside the golden door.
(Poem etched into the base of the Statue of Liberty)

It should be noted that the nominalized adjectives in this category have a plural meaning, even if they are not accompanied by the plural suffix *-s*. Thus they can never refer to only one person, and they cannot be preceded by the indefinite article or the numeral *one*. In talking about just one person, we use an adjective plus a noun (*an elderly woman, a homeless person*).

In the case of nationality adjectives there are fixed compounds, such as *an English(wo)man, a French(wo)man*. Note also that many nationality adjectives have corresponding nouns, so that corresponding to the adjectives *Swedish* and *Danish* we have the nouns *Swede* and *Dane*, which are regular, countable nouns (see the list of nationality words in Appendix 2).

8.9.2 Abstract, uncountable nouns

Certain adjectives with an abstract meaning can be nominalized. They then become uncountable nouns, typically with generic reference (**5.2.4B**).

1 Peter is fascinated by *the supernatural.*
2 They went on into *the unknown.*

Superlative adjectives can also be nominalized, and thus become uncountable nouns.

3 *The worst* is still ahead of us.
4 *The latest* is that they've found the stolen car.

8.9.3 Nominalized adjectives with countable use

Some nominalized adjectives which refer to people behave as regular, countable nouns. They can occur in the singular, and they take a plural *-s*. Examples are *an American, a criminal, an intellectual*. These are exceptions to the general rule for nominalized adjectives, and are best looked upon as full nouns.

Other adjectives used as regular nouns include *a medical, a facial, an oral*, which must be seen as abbreviations of complex noun phrases ('a medical examination', 'facial treatment', 'an oral examination').

8.9.4 Some contrastive observations

There are fewer restrictions on nominalized adjectives in Norwegian than in English. Normally, English requires a noun after the adjective, unless the adjective refers to a group of people or an abstract concept. It is common to use nouns with a rather general meaning in this position, such as *thing, person*, or the prop-word *one* (**5.12A**).

1	*Det rare* er at ...	*The funny thing* is that ...
2	*Det samme* skjedde igjen.	*The same thing* happened again.
3	Det er *det eneste* som hjelper.	It's *the only thing* that helps.
4	Jeg foretrekker *den gule*.	I prefer *the yellow one*.
5	Han var *den rette* til oppgaven.	He was *the right person* for the job.
6	*En hjemløs* vil ha vansker med å finne arbeid.	*A homeless person* will have trouble finding work.

8.10 Adjectives and other word classes

8.10.1 Adjective or noun?

A Nouns as premodifiers

Premodification in a noun phrase is typically an adjectival function. Still, we may see other word classes in this position. Consider the following noun phrases:

a long list	a hit list
the nearest station	the train station

Even if the premodifiers in the right-hand column have a syntactic function similar to that of an adjective, it is best to see them as nouns with a premodifying function. We may note that premodification by means of an uninflected noun is often classifying. Such combinations of noun + noun may be fixed enough to count as compound nouns. See **4.8.1**.

B Adjectives and nouns with identical form

When adjectives and nouns have the same form, as is the case with *criminal, classic, green, Indian*, it is the syntactic environment of the word that indicates which word class it belongs to. If the word is a modifier of a noun, it is an adjective. If it is the head of a noun phrase (i.e. accompanied by determiners and/or modifiers), or the complement of a preposition, it is a noun, as in (1) and (2). Furthermore, if the word in question has a nominal function, such as subject or object, it can be classified as a noun, even if there are no determiners or modifiers, as in (4) and (5).

1 They met on the village green. (head of noun phrase = noun)
2 Ms Manser was dressed in green. (complement of preposition = noun)
3 Ms Manser was wearing a green suit. (modifier of noun = adjective)
4 Ms Manser was wearing green. (direct object = noun)
5 Green is my favourite colour. (subject = noun)

Sometimes there is not much difference in meaning between an adjective and a noun in predicative position, as in (6) and (7).

6 I am Norwegian. (adjective)
7 I am a Norwegian. (noun)

8.10.2 Adjective or verb?

A The past participle

Many past participle forms can function as adjectives and modify nouns, as in (1) below. In addition, they can of course have a verbal function. An adjectival past participle following the verb *to be* can look very similar to a passive verb construction with *be* + a past participle. The easiest way to distinguish them is to see whether it is possible to insert a modifier that normally combines only with adjectives (such as the intensifying adverb *very*) in front of the participle. Adjectival participles can also occur with copular verbs other than *be*, so if it is possible to replace *be* by for example, *look* or *seem*, we have an adjective phrase, as in (4). Furthermore, we can check if there is an agentive phrase with *by* following the participle, or whether it is possible to insert one. When a *by*-agent is possible, we have a passive verb phrase, as in (3) and (6).

1 They had to squat in *condemned* buildings. (adjective)
2 This name is (well) *known* (to everyone). (adjective)
3 This name is *known* by every schoolchild. (verb)
4 Pamela looked very *bored.* (adjective)
5 Pamela was *bored* with television. (adjective)
6 Pamela was *bored* by the film. (= the film bored her; verb)

B The *-ing* participle

An *-ing* participle following the verb *to be* can be either a predicative adjective or part of a verb phrase in the progressive. Here, too, the tests of inserting *very* or replacing *be* by another copular verb can be used to single out the adjectives. Thus we find that the participles in (7) and (9) function as adjectives, while those in (8) and (10) are main verbs in finite verb phrases in the progressive.

7 It was a trying experience for us. (= The experience was trying.)
8 We were trying to do something.
9 She is (very) calculating.
10 She is calculating the costs.

	S |------V------| |--dO--|	S V |--------sP--------|
11	They are annoying people.	They are annoying people.

Sentence (11) is simply ambiguous out of context. Its meaning can be either 'they are doing something to annoy other people', which is the SVdO interpretation, or 'these people are a nuisance', which is the SVsP interpretation.

8.11 Discontinuous adjective phrases

So far we have looked at adjective phrases in which the complement follows the head immediately. This need not, however, be the case.

1 Alison owns a *larger* stamp collection *than anyone else I know.*
2 ... the *most stunning* scenery *imaginable.*
3 Neil Armstrong was the *first* man *to set foot on the moon.*

In (1) to (3) the adjective phrase is split in two by the noun that it modifies. This is typically the case when a premodifying adjective is compared and complemented, as in (1) and (2), since the adjective phrase then becomes too long to be placed in front of a noun (see **11.1.3**: the end weight principle). Furthermore, adjective phrases composed of words such as *first, last, only,* etc., complemented by a clause, are often split by the head of the noun phrase, as in (3). Similarly, adjective phrases premodified by *so, such,* or *too* and complemented by a clause are often split, as in (4), (5), and (6).

4 The children were *too excited* by the play *to sit still in their seats.*
5 The children were *so excited* by the play *that they could not sit still in their seats.*
6 This was *such a gradual* development *that it escaped most people's notice.*

8.12 The form and meaning of adverbs

Sample text

> *Sometimes* she missed breakfast and scrounged a bite *later* on from the larder. She did nothing all day *quite agreeably*, without anyone looking *askance*. *Even* Mrs Mark seemed to have forgotten about her, and was *quite* surprised when Dora offered to help with this or that. Her only regular duty, besides doing her room, was washing *up*, and she could do this *quite serenely* in a dream. What nagged her *however* was a certain new sense of her inferiority; that, and the prospect of going *home* with Paul when all this, unnerving as it was, was *over*.
>
> (From Iris Murdoch, *The Bell*)

As we can see from the italicized words in the text above, adverbs are a highly heterogeneous word class, and it is difficult to identify any one common characteristic of all adverbs.

One class of adverbs is very similar to adjectives. These are the ones that typically end in *-ly*. They are descriptive in meaning, often describing the manner in which something is done, and most of them are gradable (**8.5**). Examples from the text above are *agreeably* and *serenely*.

Other adverbs have meanings which are associated with degree, time, place, or reason (*quite, sometimes, later, home*). Two small, but important, groups are **negative adverbs** (e.g. *not, never, hardly, barely*) and **focusing adverbs** (e.g. *only, even, particularly, nearly*). Finally, we have **linking adverbs** such as *however, therefore, so*, whose meaning and function are related to conjunctions.

Descriptive adverbs are typically formed by adding the suffix *-ly* to a qualitative adjective, such as *nice - nicely*. Note, however, that not all adjectives can be turned into adverbs in this way. A few other adverb-forming suffixes can also be found, particularly in informal English, such as *-ways* (*sideways*), *-wise* (*clockwise, weather-wise*), and *-fashion* (*parrot-fashion*).

8.13 Adverb comparison

Most adverbs of the descriptive type can be compared in the same way as adjectives (see **8.2**). A higher degree is usually expressed by means of *more* and *most*. However, the inflectional endings *-er* and *-est* are used for adverbs of one syllable, plus the disyllabic adverb *early*.

Table 8c: Comparison of adverbs

	Positive	**Comparative**	**Superlative**
One syllable	fast	faster	fastest
Two or more syllables	slowly terribly	more slowly more terribly	most slowly most terribly

1 Vivian arrived very late – in fact, latest of the whole party.
2 They came down the hill even more slowly than they had gone up it.
3 Christians in the West must take this initiative much more seriously, and at the same time prepare themselves more effectively to take advantage of the opportunities it affords.

Some adverbs have irregular comparative and superlative forms:

badly - worse - worst
far - further/farther - furthest/farthest
little - less - least
much - more - most
well - better - best

In informal English *slowly* often has the forms *slower* and *slowest* in the comparative and the superlative.

A lower degree is expressed by means of *less* and *least*:

fast - less fast - least fast
politely - less politely - least politely

4 Jerry answered less impolitely than I had feared.

The same degree is expressed by means of *as ... as*:

5 Tom could ski as fast as Tina. ('like fort som')
6 He thought he could write music as brilliantly as Mozart. ('like strålende som')

8.14 Adverb phrases

Like adjectives, adverbs can combine with other words to form phrases. Modifiers in front of adverbs are either intensifying or focusing adverbs, as in *quite agreeably, relatively easy, only here/there, just now.* Some other types of adverb phrases are shown below.

A Adverbs with adverbial postmodifiers
well *enough*
very well *indeed*
somewhere *else*

B Compared adverbs
They finished the job *much earlier than I had expected.*
This department has contributed *more significantly than anyone else* to the development of the company.

C Adverbs modified by *too* or *so* + complement
You are going *too fast for me.*
She told the story *so vividly that everybody cried.*

Adverb phrases which contain clauses or long prepositional phrases can often be discontinuous, as shown in (1) and (2).

1 Elisabeth Schwarzkopf sang *so magnificently* Saturday night at Hunter College *that it seems a pity to have to register any complaints.*
2 Two of the best pitchers in baseball, Roger Clemens and Randy Johnson, have thrown the ball *harder and more effectively* so far this early season *than at any time in their careers.*

8.15 Syntactic functions of adverbs

8.15.1 Descriptive and degree adverbs

A descriptive or a degree adverb can function either as a modifier in an adjective or adverb phrase, or as a modifier of a verb phrase or of a whole sentence, in which case it functions syntactically as an adverbial.

A Modifier of adjective
1 Their comments were *unusually* sarcastic.
2 She was *quite* surprised when Dora offered to help with this or that.

B Modifier of adverb
3 George got on *extremely* well with his girlfriend's family.
4 She did nothing all day *quite* agreeably.
5 They did not take it seriously *enough.*

C Adverbial (see further Chapter 10)
6 He cried *bitterly*. (manner adjunct)
7 My brother admires the Beatles *tremendously*. (degree adjunct)
8 The train arrived *early*. (time adjunct)
9 *Fortunately*, I was there early enough to catch it. (disjunct)
10 *Similarly*, rivers entering the ocean may sometimes continue as underflows. (conjunct)

8.15.2 Focusing adverbs

The semantic function of focusing adverbs is to draw the attention to some other element in the sentence. Usually these adverbs are placed immediately before the element they highlight. Both syntactically and semantically, they seem to be very closely linked to the highlighted elements, but they may still be analysed as adverbials.

1 *Even* Mrs Mark seemed to have forgotten about her.
2 That carpet has *just* the right colour.
3 The marketplace is very lively, *especially* on Saturdays.
4 It hurts *only* when I laugh.

8.15.3 Negative and restrictive adverbs

A sentence can be made negative by means of the negator *not* or the negative and restrictive adverbs *never, barely, hardly, rarely, scarcely, seldom*. *Not* is a negative adverb in itself, though it is often analysed as part of the verb phrase, as it combines very closely with auxiliaries, particularly in contracted forms. However, the other negative adverbs are analysed as adverbials on the clause level. Note that only *not* and *never* make a sentence totally negative, while the others merely approach a negative meaning: 'almost not', or 'almost never'.

1 This has *never* been a question of political orientation.
2 He *seldom* took a bath.

8.15.4 Adverbial particles

Some short adverbs, such as *up, down, in*, which we may call **adverbial particles**, can have a variety of functions. Naturally they can function as adverbials, in which case they tend to have a literal meaning, as in (1) and (2). Such particles can also enter into a construction with a verb to form a transitive verb phrase, as in (3) and (4). The particle typically has a non-literal meaning in such constructions, and is usually analysed as part of the verb phrase (see **6.3.3C–D**).

1 Come in!
2 They looked up into the sky.
3 I had to fill in (AmE: out) a lot of forms.
4 They looked up all the new words.

8.15.5 Other adverbs

Adverbs that say something about time, place, reason, or manner tend to function as adverbials in a clause; see further Chapter 10.

1 The Queen was *here yesterday*.
2 This is something you have to do *alone*.
3 *Often* they stay up *late* watching the telly, and *consequently* they get more run down *physically*.

Some adverbs, particularly place adverbs, can postmodify the nearest preceding noun, as in (4) and (5).

4 Have a look in this jug *here*.
5 The article by your political correspondent, Mr Ian Waller, drawing attention to the concern over MPs' sponsored trips *abroad*, raises an issue that has been avoided for years.

8.16 Adjective or adverb?

8.16.1 Syntax

The distinction between adjectives and adverbs is a well-known area of difficulty for learners of English. Since Norwegian does not have such a clear distinction between adjectival and adverbial forms as English, it is often necessary to consider the position and the syntactic function of the adjective/adverb. The general rule is that adjectives modify nouns, while adverbs modify verbs, adjectives, and other adverbs. In this section we discuss some areas where the application of this general rule does not seem to be quite straightforward.

A Copular verbs

When the verb of the clause is *to be* or another copular verb (such as *become, get, seem*), an adjective always follows.

1 I was speechless.
2 They were careful with their money.

It may be difficult to determine what constitutes a copular verb. Some verbs clearly have both copular and non-copular uses. The verb *appear* is an example.

3 They appeared *quickly*. (= They showed up quickly.)
4 They appeared *quick*. (= They seemed to be quick.)

It is important to note that it is the meaning of the verb which determines whether it should be treated as a copular verb or not. When it serves as a link between the subject and a clause element which describes the subject referent, it is a copular verb. A useful rule of thumb is that if you can replace the verb by some form of *be* or *become* without altering the meaning dramatically, you can safely assume that the verb has a copular function.

B Perception verbs

Whenever a perception verb (*to feel, taste, smell, sound,* and *look*) is followed by a word which describes the subject referent, that word is an adjective (and functions as a subject predicative on the clause level).

5 Hillary's cough sounded *bad*. (not badly)
6 This medicine tastes *awful*. (not awfully)

Perception verbs can be used in two different ways as regards adverb and adjective use. The important thing to note is whether the description given in the adjective/adverb should apply to the subject or to the verb in the sentence.

7 The soup smells delicious. (*delicious* describes the soup)
8 The dog smells carefully. (*carefully* describes the way in which the dog is sniffing around)
9 The cook smelt the delicious soup carefully. (*delicious* is a premodifier of *soup* and thus an adjective which is part of the direct object; *carefully* describes the way in which the action was carried out, and functions as an adverbial)
10 Peter looked uncomfortable. (*uncomfortable* describes *Peter*)
11 Peter looked uncomfortably for the exit. (*uncomfortably* describes the way in which Peter looked for the exit)

C Object predicative

An object predicative describes the referent of the direct object (a noun phrase) and is thus an adjective. In (12) *clear* describes the windscreen after it was wiped, not the manner in which it was done. Likewise, in (13) *open* describes the door after it was pushed.

12 I had to wipe the windscreen *clear*.
13 They pushed the door *open*.

D Adjective phrases

An adjective may be modified by an adverb. However, it is also possible to have two (or more) adjectives in front of a noun phrase. Thus if a noun is preceded by an adverb and an adjective, the adverb modifies the adjective, as in (14). If a noun is preceded by two adjectives, both adjectives modify the noun, as in (15). In the latter case, the adjectives tend to be separated by a comma, though this is not always the case.

14 They asked me some *terribly difficult* questions.
15 They asked me some *terrible, difficult* questions.

8.16.2 Word class membership

In a few cases the same word form can function either as an adjective or as an adverb. Compare the adjectival use in the left-hand column and the adverbial use in the right-hand column below.

It was *early/late* afternoon.	They arrived *early/late*.
Liz is *pretty*.	Liz is *pretty* smart.
He was feeling *well* (= healthy).	He was doing *well*.

Other words that can be either adjectives or adverbs are *fast, hard, long, short, high, deep, close*. With the exception of *pretty*, which means 'relatively' rather than 'beautiful' when it functions as an adverb, these words express approximately the same meaning whether they are used as adjectives or adverbs. The main difference between the adjectival and the adverbial use is thus their syntactic function, i.e. what sort of words they modify.

Some of these adverbs have related adverbs ending in *-ly* (e.g. *hard - hardly*). However, the members of such pairs are by no means synonymous. Thus, *Our secretaries work hard* means that they work a lot, while *Our secretaries hardly work* means that they work very little. The adverb *high* is used to denote a position (in contrast to *low*), but *highly* is used as a degree adverb (*He praised the picture highly*) and as an intensifier (*This is a highly sensitive problem*). *Close/closely* and *deep/deeply* behave in a similar fashion. Generally, the adverb without the *-ly* ending tends to have a more concrete meaning, as shown in the list below.

close	*live close to the river*	closely	*look closely at something; closely related*
deep	*it lies very deep*	deeply	*be deeply in love; deeply impressed*
fine	*it went fine*	finely	*adjust something finely; finely cut*
hard	*they tried hard*	hardly	*they hardly tried; it is hardly true*
high	*fly high*	highly	*value highly; highly confidential*
late	*arrive late*	lately	*I haven't seen her lately*
near	*to draw/come near(er)*	nearly	*he nearly fainted*
short	*he cut his hair short*	shortly	*the train will arrive shortly*

Note that the *-ly* ending is not only found with adverbs; many adjectives end in *-ly* as well, such as *daily, early, elderly, friendly, kingly, likely, lively, lovely, masterly, monthly, pearly, poorly (*'skral'*), sickly (*'sykelig'*), stately, yearly.* These words cannot form adverbs by means of the *-ly* suffix. With the exceptions of *daily, early, monthly, weekly, yearly*, they cannot function as adverbs with approximately the same meaning as the adjective, though some adjectives ending in *-ly* have homonymous adverbs which are derived from other adjectives, such as *poorly* (from the adjective *poor*) and *sickly* (from the adjective *sick*).

8.17 Indeterminate uses

In a few cases, adverbs with and without *-ly* are used more or less interchangeably. You can talk loud or loudly, or buy something cheap or cheaply. *Drive slow* may be seen on road signs and in instructions, but is not normally used in other contexts (? *I drove my car slow into the garage*).

Direct is frequently used as an adverb, but only about movement in space. *Directly* is also used with this meaning, but in addition it can be used to express time (meaning 'very soon') and as a modifier, as in *directly after lunch, directly below us*. Only *direct* is possible in connection with means of transportation.

1 You can go from here to Leeds *direct*, without changing trains.
2 They were looking *directly* at me.
3 The money goes *direct/directly* to the developing countries.

Particularly in colloquial American English we often hear adverbial usage without the *-ly* ending.

4 That was *real* good.
5 You'd better come *quick*.
6 He is breathing *normal* again.

This is not considered correct in Standard English, and should be avoided, particularly in writing.

8.18 Creative adverbial modification

We sometimes see unusual combinations of adverb + adjective where the semantic role of the adverb goes beyond that of an intensifier. Consider the following examples.

1 There was a time when teachers were *shockingly underpaid.*
2 His style of attack is *savagely whole-hearted* ...
3 Humphrey just kept on walking between the metals, *blissfully unaware* of the iron monster behind him ...

Such adverbial modifiers seem to convey the speaker's view of the situation, in much the same way as a disjunct adverbial does (**10.7**).

8.19 Properties of adjective classes: summary

Table 8d sums up some of the properties of the adjective classes outlined in **8.4**. The pluses and minuses indicate whether or not members of an adjective class typically have a certain property. Note that the table points to general tendencies, and that there may be exceptions within each class. +/- means that some adjectives in the class typically have this property, while others do not.

Table 8d: Properties of adjective classes

Type of adjective	Gradable	Attributive	Predicative	Form *-ly* adverbs
Descriptive	+	+	+	+/-
Evaluative	+	+	+	+
Colour	+	+	+	-
Participles	+/-	+	+	+/-
Emphasizing	-	+	-	-
Limiters	-	+	-	-
Origin	-	+	+/-	-
Style	-	+	+/-	-
Material	-	+	+/-	-

Terms

types of adjectives:
- qualitative
- descriptive
- evaluative
- colour
- participles
- emphasizing
- limiters
- origin, style, material

adjective functions:
- attributive
- predicative
- classifying
- specifying
- postmodifier
- object predicative
- free predicative

nominalized adjectives
adjective complementation
gradability

comparison:
- positive
- comparative
- superlative

types of adverbs:
- descriptive
- focusing
- negative
- particles
- time, place, etc.

adverb functions:
- modifier
- adverbial

Exercises

1 Adjective form: Underline the words in the 'Jabberwocky' poem, by Lewis Carroll, that you would take to be adjectives. Give reasons why you think they are adjectives. (**8.1**)

'Twas brillig, and the slithy toves
Did gyre and gimble in the wabe:
All mimsy were the borogroves,
And the mome raths outgrabe.

2 Complementation of adjectives: Use the notes given in parentheses to complement the adjective in each of the sentences below. (**8.3**)
Example: She is fond … (She likes dogs.) – She is fond of dogs.

a I feel sorry … (I pity his wife.)
b Susan is good … (She can paint.)
c He is not afraid … (He may show his feelings.)
d She seems quite unwilling … (She won't listen to anybody.)
e They seemed totally incapable … (They can't change their ways.)
f They were only glad … (They willingly helped us.)
g We are all really sorry … (This shouldn't have happened.)
h The politician was not quite sure … (The politician did not quite know the answer.)
i The government is concerned … (The spread of drug-addiction is disturbing.)
j We were all concerned … (We thought there might be too few of us.)
k Smokers are conscious … (Smokers know about the danger to their health.)
l He suddenly became conscious … (He suddenly realized that he had said too much.)

3 Pick out the adjectives in the following text and state which category they belong to, and whether they are gradable or non-gradable. (**8.4–8.5**).

In January there came bitterly hard weather. The earth was like iron, and nothing could be done in the fields. Many meetings were held in the big barn, and the pigs occupied themselves in planning out the work of the coming season. It had come to be accepted that the pigs, who were manifestly cleverer than the other animals, should decide all questions of farm policy, though their decisions had to be ratified by a majority vote. This arrangement would have worked well enough if it had not been for the disputes between Snowball and Napoleon. These two disagreed at every point where disagreement was possible. If one of them suggested sowing a bigger acreage with barley, the other was certain to demand a bigger acreage of oats, and if one of them said that such and such a field was just right for cabbages, the other would declare that it was useless for anything except roots.

(From George Orwell, *Animal Farm*)

Is other an adjective here
How is possible an adjective

4 Pick out the adjective phrases in the text in exercise 3. Identify the head of the adjective phrase, and state the types of phrases/clauses that complement the adjective. (**8.3**)

5 Adjective or verb? Determine whether the italicized participle forms are used as adjectives or as parts of verb phrases. Give reasons for your answers. (**8.4.3**, **8.10.2**)

a They were *drawn* into the quarrel.
b Her brows were usually *drawn* together defiantly.
c Her eyes were *closed*, but the tears were *glistening* on her cheeks.
d All the shops in the village were *closed* at eight o'clock that night.
e He was *moving* like a ballet dancer.
f He was *moving* in the ballet performance.
g Things that are sweet and fat are more *filling*.
h The concert hall was gradually *filling* up.

6 Attributive and predicative adjectives: Which of the adjectives in the following sets of adjective + noun can be only a premodifier of the noun, and which ones can be only a subject predicative? In case both constructions are possible, is there any difference in meaning? (**8.6.1**)

a black – dress
b white – tie
c unwell – boss
d alive – dinosaur
e certain – colleague
f concerned – families

7 Move the adjective in the following noun phrases to predicative position wherever possible. Account for any difference in meaning between the two versions. Give a reason if you think predicative position of the adjective is impossible. (**8.6.1–8.6.3**)
Example: a superb cook – The cook is superb.

a a delicious dessert
b the atomic bomb
c outdoor activities
d the yellow line
e pink elephants
f a talented musician
g a conscientious objector
h English grammar

8 Turn these clauses with predicative adjectives into noun phrases with premodifiers wherever possible. Account for any difference in meaning between the two versions. Give a reason if you think premodification is impossible. (**8.6.1–8.6.3**)
Example: The habit is nasty. – A nasty habit.

a The man was sorry.
b The doctor is responsible.
c These weapons are heavy.
d The two women are alike.
e The workers are skilled.
f This action is legal.
g Their jeans are blue.
h The country is free.

9 Explain the linguistic ambiguities in the following jokes. (**8.7**, **8.8**)

A: It's the royal garden party on Wednesday.
B: Oh, have you been invited?
A: No, but my garden has.

A: Is he a personal secretary?
B: A bit.

10 Translate the following sentences into English. (**8.9**)

a Sekretæren vår er den rette til å svare på det.
b Den gamle ristet på hodet.
c I dette området bor det bare hvite.
d Her er vi mest interessert i det spesielle ved samekulturen.
e Det rare er at ingen har tenkt på det før.
f Mor Teresa arbeidet blant de fattigste i Calcutta.
g Måtte den beste vinne!

11 Rewrite the following sentences, turning the italicized adjective into an adverb where possible, and otherwise using it as part of an adverbial expression. Your paraphrase must contain the verb given in parentheses after each sentence. (**8.12**)
Example: Martha has a beautiful singing voice. (sing) – Martha sings beautifully.

a Stephen has a *charming* smile. (smile)
b Ronnie is a *busy* writer. (write)
c Margaret was *friendly* towards the woman. (treat)
d Fred was the *last* person to arrive. (arrive)
e These women have a *hard* life. (live)
f I had no *negative* thoughts about my father. (think)
g They began to hold *monthly* meetings. (meet)

12 Identify all the adverbs in the text below and state the syntactic function of each (modifier or adverbial). (**8.15**)

At last, feeling this to be in some way a substitute for the words she was unable to find, she began to sing 'Beasts of England'. The other animals sitting round her took it up, and they sang it three times over – very tunefully, but slowly and mournfully, in a way they had never sung it before.

They had just finished singing it for the third time when Squealer, attended by two dogs, approached them with the air of having something important to say. He announced that, by a special decree of Comrade Napoleon, 'Beasts of England' had been abolished. From now onwards it was forbidden to sing it.

(From George Orwell, *Animal Farm*)

13 State whether the italicized words are used as adjectives or adverbs, and give reasons for your answers. (**8.16**)

a The train was approaching *fast*.
b Paul is an *only* child.
c She looked *well* after her first baby.
d Things are *pretty* much the same around here.
e Gina was feeling *down*.
f He tilted his *homely* face towards the dry bed of the river.
g *Late* September finds Quebec's colours at their peak.
i The farmer must get up *early* and, at times, work *late* at night.
j The people up there talk *funny*.

14 Adjective or adverb? Cross out the unacceptable alternatives in the sentences below. In case both alternatives are acceptable, explain any difference in meaning and/or style. (**8.16, 8.17**)

a That course sounds interesting/interestingly.
b I shall deal with those present/presently.
c The patient listened silent/silently to what the nurse said.
d Sarah felt good/well.

e You have to drive real/really slow/slowly.
f The actors in this series are natural/naturally beauties.
g It will give me real/really pleasure to do this.
h Things turned out wonderful/wonderfully well.
i The buffet looks delicious/deliciously.
j You should serve this dish hot/hotly.
k She wore such beautiful/beautifully ironed muslin dresses in those days.
l My hands would ache terrible/terribly if I went near a fire.
m The cat curled up comfortable/comfortably in our best armchair.
n There are obvious/obviously flaws in the system.
o He saw the grey landscape through the gentle/gently falling snow.

15 Comment on the difference in form and meaning between the members of the following sentence pairs.

a 1 Surprisingly, they found the old man at home.
  2 They were surprised to find the old man at home.
b 1 We can make that job easy.
  2 We can do that job easily.
c 1 You were not honest with yourself then.
  2 You were honestly not yourself then.
d 1 Sandy looked at her mother with intensely bright eyes.
  2 Sandy looked at her mother with intense, bright eyes.
e 1 He looked at me hopefully.
  2 He looked hopeful to me.
f 1 The answer was a definite 'yes'.
  2 The answer was definitely yes.

9 The Simple Sentence

9.1 The notions of 'clause' and 'sentence'

A sentence is in many ways a practical way of organizing written language in suitable chunks. It can be described as a structure which extends from an initial capital letter up to a final full stop, question mark, or exclamation mark. As mentioned in **2.9**, a sentence can contain one or more clauses. Clauses are divided into two major categories: main clauses and subordinate clauses. Of these, only main clauses are capable of forming independent, complete sentences. A main clause must contain a subject (apart from imperatives) and a finite verb, while a subordinate clause can be finite or non-finite. Whereas it is difficult to give a good linguistic definition of a sentence (the length and complexity of a sentence may vary widely), the clause can be defined as a string of elements that are syntactically connected with each other.

9.2 The building blocks of the clause

When we interpret the meaning of a clause, we automatically take into account the syntactic relations between words and phrases. If we compare the sentences *The dog bit the man* and *The man bit the dog*, we know that they mean two completely different things, because the position of the noun phrases in relation to the verb tells us who bit whom. In English, at least, the fact that a noun phrase is placed before the verb indicates that there is a certain relationship between the noun phrase and the verb, typically one of 'doer' and 'action'. We can describe such relationships in terms of **syntactic functions**. Stating the syntactic function of a word or a phrase is stating its role in the build-up of the clause. We use the term **clause element** or **clause constituent** to denote a word, phrase, or clause that fulfils a syntactic function in a clause or a sentence. Constituents in a simple sentence will be realized as words and phrases. If a constituent is realized as a clause, this makes the sentence complex. Complex sentences are dealt with in Chapters 12 and 13.

9.3 Constituents in clause patterns

The major elements which may enter into a clause pattern are the following:

Subject: *Dora* bought a book.
Verb: Dora *bought* a book.
Direct object: Dora bought *a book*.
Indirect object: Dora bought *me* a book.
Subject predicative: The book is *exciting*.
Object predicative: Dora found the book *exciting*.
Adverbial: Dora finished the book *last night*.

Constituents are distinguished primarily on the basis of their syntactic relations to the verb. Nevertheless, it is possible to identify some semantic properties that tend to go together with certain syntactic functions. It should be noted that the sections below do not list the whole gamut of semantic roles that can be expressed by each type of constituent, but mention some of the most typical ones. The semantic roles of adverbials are described in detail in Chapter 10, and have therefore been omitted in this chapter.

9.3.1 The verb (V)

The verb phrase may be simple or complex, and it may express a range of different meanings. All the examples given in the paragraph above have simple verb phrases. An example of a highly complex verb phrase is given in (1). The verb phrase may also contain a multi-word verb (**6.3.3**), and thus include an adverb, preposition, or some other particle. An example is given in (2).

1 They *may have been being cheated*.
2 I *typed up* my essay, *printed* it *out*, and *handed* it *in*.

As for meaning, the verb can express both **stative** and **dynamic** situations (**7.5.4**). Briefly, dynamic verbs are those that denote activity, process, movement, etc. Some typical examples are *work, laugh, change, run*. Stative verbs, on the other hand, denote stable, unchanging situations which do not involve any action on the part of the subject referent. Examples are *be, have, belong, contain*.

9.3.2 The subject (S)

The referent of the subject of a sentence is typically somebody who performs an action, or an **agent**:

1 *Jack* mowed the lawn.
2 *The police* blocked the road.

A similar type of subject referent is what we call **instrumental**, as illustrated in (3). The difference between an agent and an instrumental subject is that the referent of an agent subject actively and (typically) intentionally performs an action. An instrumental subject cannot be associated with intention or positive action.

3 *The snow* blocked the road.

Furthermore, the subject can refer to something or somebody that is **affected** by an action, as in (4). It is not by coincidence that we have chosen a passive sentence, as passives typically have affected subjects.

4 *The road* was blocked.

Finally, in sentences describing a state of affairs, the subject referent may be something or somebody that is **characterized**, as in (5) and (6). The subject referents here do not take part in any action.

5 *Peter* is a school teacher.
6 *The river* is difficult to cross.

The function of subject is a **nominal** one, which means that subjects are realized by a noun (phrase) or a pronoun. In complex sentences, the subject can also be realized by a finite or non-finite subordinate clause (see Chapters 12 and 13).

9.3.3 The direct object (dO)

The referent of a direct object is typically **affected** by the action. This is very clear in (1), though the degree of affectedness need not be as dramatic as that, as shown in (2).

1 They destroyed *a trading house* and pillaged *the goods*.
2 Dora bought *a book*.

Alternatively, the direct object may denote a referent which is a result of the action. We may call this type of object **resultative**, or **effected**. In (3), for instance, the book comes into existence as a result of Dora's writing.

3 Dora wrote *a book*.

Occasionally the action is denoted by the verb and the direct object in conjunction. The verb then typically does not carry a lot of independent meaning, while the object denotes an activity or an action. We may call such objects **eventive** (see also **6.3.4**).

4 Dora took *a walk*.
5 We all had *a good laugh*.

Like the subject, the object is a nominal constituent, which can be realized by a noun, a noun phrase, or a pronoun. In complex sentences, the subject can also be realized by a finite or non-finite subordinate clause (see Chapters 12 and 13).

9.3.4 The indirect object (iO)

The referent of an indirect object is typically somebody who benefits from the action, i.e. a **recipient** of something, as shown in (1). It is often possible to describe the same semantic relationship by means of a prepositional phrase with *to* or *for* (*I gave the present to Anne*). The recipient role can be less obvious, as in (2), where we can still say that the action is directed towards the referent of the indirect object.

1 I gave *her/Anne* a present.
2 They asked *me* a lot of questions.

An indirect object is a nominal constituent, typically realized by a noun (phrase) or a pronoun. It precedes the direct object, though paraphrases with *to* or *for* are placed after the direct object.

9.3.5 Subject and object predicative (sP, oP)

Both subject and object predicatives are typically used to denote properties of a nominal referent. For this reason we may identify their semantic role as **attributive**.

1 Felix was *very happy*. (sP)
2 The news made Felix *very happy*. (oP)
3 This is *the greatest pair of jeans I've ever had*. (sP)

Predicatives are usually either adjectival, as in (1) or (2), or nominal, as in (3). However, in some cases a prepositional phrase may function as a predicative rather than as an adverbial. This is the case in (4) and (5). The prepositional phrases are often locative phrases which are used in a metaphorical sense, as in (4), or idiomatic expressions, as in (5). Such prepositional phrases often have an adjectival flavour, in that they can be gradable (note the use of *completely*) and that it is often possible to use a verb other than *be*, such as *feel* or *seem*, which would not have been possible in front of a prepositional phrase functioning as a place adverbial.

4 She is completely *at home* in politics.
5 They all seemed *in favour of the change*.

9.3.6 Obligatory adverbial (A)

Adverbials may be either optional or obligatory. In the latter case they are needed in order to make the sentence grammatical, and form part of the basic clause pattern. As examples (1) to (3) show, these adverbials can express a whole range of meanings. See further **9.5.2C** and **10.2**.

1 Peter and Margaret are *on holiday*.
2 How do you get *to the train station*?
3 This year, owner-occupied houses have been selling *at very good prices*.

9.4 The central role of the verb

In terms of syntax, the verb is commonly seen as the most important element in the clause. One practical example of this is the way people usually go about analysing a sentence (e.g. *Jenny was whistling a tune.*): they identify the verb first (*was whistling*), and then find the subject by asking '*who was whistling?*', and the object by asking '*what was Jenny whistling?*'.

The centrality of the verb is also shown by the fact that the verb phrase determines what other syntactic elements the clause can contain. We call this property of the verb **valency** (**6.3.2**). This term has been borrowed from chemistry, where 'valency' is defined as 'a property of atoms or groups, equal to the number of atoms of hydrogen that the atom or group could combine with or displace in forming compounds' (*Collins English Dictionary*). In grammar, it denotes a property of the verb which indicates the number of constituents this verb must combine with in order to form a grammatical clause. Hence, a verb with a valency of one, such as *walk*, needs to combine with only one other constituent (namely, a subject) in order to form a simple sentence. A verb with a valency of two, such as *steal* or *become*, needs two constituents in order to form a simple sentence, and a verb with a valency of three, such as *put*, needs three. No English verb has a valency of more than three.

In this chapter, we shall use the terms **one-place verb**, **two-place verb**, and **three-place verb** to denote verbs with a valency of one, two, and three, respectively. Examples of all three types are given in (1) to (3). Note that valency covers *obligatory* constituents only. In addition to the elements that are required by the verb, the clause may contain any number of optional elements, typically adverbials (**10.2**).

1 The train stopped. (SV pattern; one-place verb)
2 Calvin has a treehouse. (SVdO pattern; two-place verb)
3 The sight of the garden took him back into the past. (SVdOA pattern; three-place verb)

Related to the concept of valency is that of **transitivity**. The transitivity of a verb depends on whether or not this verb requires a direct object to complete the sentence. A transitive verb requires an object. The opposite is intransitive. Examples:

4 It is raining. (intransitive)
5 These people live in caves. (intransitive)
6 I bought a new carpet. (transitive)

9.5 Clause patterns – basic structures

Working from the valency of the verb, we can distinguish seven basic clause patterns in English. These clause patterns show the ways in which the different constituent types can be combined in a clause, disregarding optional constituents. As already pointed out, optional constituents are typically adverbials, which may be added to any clause, but we also find free predicatives (**9.8.3**), vocatives, and inserts (**9.8.4**). Whereas a clause can contain only one obligatory constituent of each type (i.e. one subject, one direct object, etc.), there may in theory be any number of optional constituents. Note that the basic clause patterns do not necessarily say anything about the order of the constituents. They may occur in a different order, for example in interrogative sentences.

9.5.1 One-place verb

Some verbs are able to form a complete sentence with only a subject. The resulting clause pattern is SV. These verbs are intransitive. Note that optional adverbials can be added to the SV pattern, as in (2).

1 The baby was crying.
2 The baby has been crying all night.

A sentence which occurs in the passive voice often has the SV pattern, e.g. (3), although the verb is transitive when it occurs in an active construction. (Cf. the corresponding active sentence *We have received your letter.*) The distinction between the active and the passive voice thus also affects the transitivity of the verb phrase.

3 Your letter has been received.

9.5.2 Two-place verb

A two-place verb attracts one of three different kinds of constituent: a direct object, a subject predicative, or an adverbial. Verbs that require a direct object in order to form a complete sentence are **monotransitive** verbs. Those that require a subject predicative are called **copular** verbs, while there is no particular label for those that require an adverbial (except that they are a category of intransitive verbs).

A SVdO (monotransitive verb)

When the verb is transitive, an object follows it. As noted in **9.3.3**, the referent of an object is usually affected or effected by the action denoted by the verb. Transitive verbs may be either stative, as in (1), or dynamic, as in (2) and (3).

1 Mary had a little lamb.
2 They have eaten all the strawberries.
3 You could have hurt yourself.

B SVsP (copular verb)

The most important copular verbs are *be* and *become*. Other verbs can also have a copular function, if their meaning is similar to *be* or *become*. For a discussion of copular verbs, see **8.16.1A**.

Copular verbs link together the subject and a subject predicative. The subject predicative can give a characterization of the subject referent. This is the **ascriptive** type of SVsP pattern, and it is shown in (4) to (6). The ascriptive type is also found in passive versions of sentences with object predicatives (**9.5.3B**), as in (7), where *chairman of the board* is a subject predicative.

4 You should be more careful.
5 The receptionist seemed tired.
6 She may become famous.
7 Arthur was elected chairman of the board.

In other cases there seems to be full identity between the referent of the subject and that of the subject predicative. The verb phrase could have been replaced by an equals sign (=). This is the **equative** type of SVsP pattern.

8 Margaret is my mother's name.
9 All you need is love.

In an equative construction it is generally possible to reverse the order of the subject and the subject predicative. Thus (8) and (9) can be rendered as (10) and (11), which mean the same, except for a difference in focus. We still analyse the constituent before the verb as the subject, however, and the one after the verb as the subject predicative.

10 My mother's name is Margaret.
11 Love is all you need.

C SVA (intransitive verb – obligatory adverbial)
Certain verbs require an adverbial specification. These are normally verbs that denote movement, or verbs that imply a location of some kind. It is thus mainly place adverbials that are obligatory in this way, but as (14) and (15) show, other types of adverbial can also occur in the SVA pattern. You can easily test whether or not the adverbial is obligatory by trying to remove it.

12 This road goes to Oxford. (*This road goes.)
13 The students live off campus. (*The students live.)
14 This car handles beautifully. (*This car handles.)
15 The meeting lasted two hours. (*The meeting lasted.)

Note that *to be* has an intransitive use, in which case it requires an adverbial, and not a subject predicative, to complete the sentence.

16 The students are in the library.
17 This letter is for you.

9.5.3 Three-place verb

Three-place verbs are also of three different kinds. They all combine with a direct object and, in addition, with an indirect object, an object predicative, or an obligatory adverbial.

A SViOdO (ditransitive verb)
Verbs that combine with a direct and an indirect object are referred to as

ditransitive, which means that they take two objects. The indirect object is placed before the direct object. Examples are given in (1) to (3).

1 Ruth gave her son a present.
2 I can show you my notes.
3 I paid her the full amount.

The indirect object can often be paraphrased by means of a prepositional phrase with *to* or *for*. Thus (3) can be rendered as *I paid the full amount to her*. Such a prepositional phrase is analysed as an oblique object; see **9.8.2**.

B SVdOoP (complex transitive)
A complex transitive verb requires the direct object to be followed by an object predicative. Object predicatives are related to the object in the same way as a subject predicative is related to the subject in an ascriptive SVsP pattern, i.e. they attribute a quality or an identity to the referent of the direct object. Complex transitive verbs often have to do with change, naming, or electing, as in (4) to (7), or with perception or judgement, as in (8) and (9).

4 The jokes made everybody uneasy.
5 They named their son Frederick.
6 They painted the town red.
7 You're driving me crazy.
8 They found the joke tasteless.
9 He left the question unanswered.

Object predicatives may resemble postmodifiers, because they typically follow a noun phrase and modify it. However, an object predicative may be obligatory in the clause, while a postmodifier never is. Furthermore, if the direct object is replaced by a pronoun, a postmodifier will be included in the reference of the pronoun, while an object predicative will remain unchanged, as in *They found it tasteless* (cf. example 8).

C SVdOA (transitive verb – obligatory adverbial)
A small group of verbs require an adverbial in addition to the direct object. The obligatory adverbials in such sentences are usually place adverbials, as shown in (10) to (12). For a discussion of obligatory vs. optional adverbials, see **10.2**.

10 I keep my car outside the house.
11 She stuck her hand in her pocket.
12 You should put the flowers in a vase.

9.6 Verbs which occur in more than one pattern

It should be noted that many verbs can occur in more than one clause pattern. *Make* is an extreme example; it can occur in five different constructions, as shown in (1) to (5). Often the meaning of the verb varies with the pattern in which it occurs. In the examples below, we see that *make* means 'produce', 'become', 'go', 'cook', and 'cause to become'.

1 Liz made a lovely decoration. (SVdO)
2 Liz made a good teacher. (SVsP)
3 Liz made for the exit. (SVA)
4 Liz made him breakfast. (SViOdO)
5 Liz made him famous. (SVdOoP)

Occasionally, the fact that a verb can occur in more than one pattern produces ambiguous sentences, as in (6) and (7).

6 Ken found her a brilliant author. (SViOdO or SVdOoP)
7 Ken saw her home. (SVdOA or SVdO)

Example (6) means either that Ken considered the woman in question to be a brilliant author or that he found a brilliant author for her. In (7) reference is made either to what Ken saw (the determiner *her* is part of the direct object) or to where he accompanied the woman (the pronoun *her* by itself is the direct object).

A Verbs used transitively or intransitively with the same subject

Sometimes the same verb may occur with or without an object without much difference of meaning, as in (8) to (11). The only differences there might possibly be between (8) and (9) and between (10) and (11) are that there is more focus on the verb in (8) and (10), and that the presence of an object in (9) and (11) limits the possible reference of the verb.

8 Jim was reading.
9 Jim was reading the evening paper.
10 Jane had eaten.
11 Jane had eaten a bag of crisps.

Some verbs seem to presuppose an object even when they occur without one, such as *wash* in (12). The implied object here is Max himself, and it could not have been anything else. In (13), however, we see that it is possible to specify a different object as well. Examples of other verbs that behave in the same way are *adapt, adjust, dress, hide, move, shave*. (The intransitive use of these verbs generally corresponds to reflexive verbs in Norwegian: 'tilpasse seg', 'kle på seg', etc.; see further **9.7**.)

12 Max washed twice a week.
13 Max washed his car twice a week.

Other verbs as well may presuppose a certain object when they are used intransitively. Typical examples are *drink* (with the presupposed object 'alcohol'), *smoke* (with the presupposed object 'tobacco'), and *drive* (with the presupposed object 'a car'). Of course, it is always possible to specify some other object, as shown in (15) and (16).

14 How did you get here? – I drove.
15 No, thanks, I don't drink, but I would love a cup of tea.
16 Can I drink this water?

B Verbs used transitively or intransitively with a different subject
With certain verbs the affected participant may occur either as an object in a transitive pattern or as a subject in an intransitive construction, as in (17) and (18). The difference in meaning is similar to that between a sentence in the active voice and the short passive (**11.6.1**).

17 I broke the teapot. (transitive: SVdO)
18 The teapot broke. (intransitive: SV)

Other verbs which pattern in the same way are *open, close, boil, bake, turn.* Often such verbs require some sort of adverbial complementation when they are used intransitively; these include *handle, sell, wash.* Examples (19) and (20) further illustrate such intransitive uses of transitive verbs.

19 I boiled the potatoes. / The potatoes boiled for an hour.
20 This material doesn't wash very well.

9.7 Some contrastive points

Not all English verbs combine with the same type of constituents as the corresponding Norwegian verbs. Learners should make a note of the verbs *tell*, *assure*, and *inform*, which require an indirect object in English (but not in Norwegian) when the direct object is a subordinate clause.

1 Han fortalte at han skulle på ferie.
He told/informed us/them (etc.) that he was going on holiday.

It was mentioned in the previous section that verbs that combine with a reflexive pronoun in Norwegian often correspond to intransitive verbs in English, as is further illustrated in (2) and (3). See also **5.8.7B**.

2	Vi må skynde oss.	We must hurry.
3	Han kom seg ikke ut av huset.	He couldn't get out of the house.
4	Hun bet seg i fingeren.	She bit her finger.
5	Ta av deg skoene.	Take off your shoes.

Examples (4) and (5) illustrate another use of the reflexive pronoun in Norwegian which is unmatched in English. But note that English expresses a similar meaning by means of the possessive determiner in the object noun phrase (cf. **5.4.1**).

9.8 Clause patterns – special structures

In the sentences we have looked at so far, the clause elements have corresponded well to the basic clause patterns. But once we start looking at sentences as they occur in natural discourse, we find that they may not fit the patterns quite so easily. In this section we shall take a look at some variations of the basic clause patterns.

9.8.1 Anticipatory subject or object (aS/aO)

In some sentences we find that the subject or the object has a 'double' realization, as in (1).

1 There is a fly in my soup.

There occupies the normal position of a subject, while *a fly* meets the semantic criteria for a subject. In such sentences we analyse *there* as the **anticipatory subject** and *a fly* as the (notional) subject. What an anticipatory subject does is fill in for the notional subject, so that we expect, or anticipate, the notional subject, which is presented later in the sentence.

The words that can function as anticipatory subjects in English are *it* and *there*. See further **11.7–11.8** for details on their use. *It* can function both as an anticipatory subject and as an anticipatory object when the notional subject or object is realized as a subordinate clause, as in (2) and (3).

```
  aS V  sP |------------S---------------------|
2 It is sad that you have to leave so early.
```

S V aO oP |-----------dO-------------------|
3 They found it sad that we had to leave so early.

9.8.2 Oblique object

The term 'oblique object' covers a type of constituent which shares many of the semantic characteristics of a direct or indirect object, but where there is a less direct formal tie to the verb. Oblique objects also share some of the features of adverbials, particularly as regards their realization as prepositional phrases.

A Variations on indirect object

We mentioned in **9.5.3** that indirect objects can usually be paraphrased by means of a prepositional phrase introduced by *to* or *for*. Obviously, there is not much difference in meaning between (1) and (2). However, we would like to reserve the term 'indirect object' for a nominal constituent which (normally) precedes a direct object.

S V |-----iO---| |-------dO-------|
1 I sent my friend a birthday card.

S V |------dO-------| |-----oO-----|
2 I sent a birthday card to my friend.

Sentences with an oblique object may not always have an obvious counterpart with an indirect object. This is the case in (3) and (4), where the oblique objects have been italicized. In (4) the prepositional phrase is introduced by *from*, and the meaning is the opposite of that of 'recipient', which is otherwise typical of the indirect object (**9.3.4**).

3 Could you post a letter *for me*?
4 Pike had stolen mules *from Harris* during the Santa Fe expedition.

B Phrasal and prepositional verbs

In the examples so far in this chapter, the sentences have contained simple verbs. As shown in **6.3.3**, the verb may also include an adverbial particle (phrasal verbs) or a preposition (prepositional verbs). With both phrasal and prepositional verbs, the verb and the particle/preposition go together to create a meaning which is not predictable from the meanings of the individual words that make up the phrase. Most commonly, the preposition or the particle has a non-literal meaning. In (5) we see a phrasal verb which is followed by a direct object. As is often the case with phrasal and prepositional verbs, the verb group can be paraphrased by a simple verb without a particle, as in (6). By contrast, in (7) *up* has a literal meaning, and introduces a prepositional phrase which functions as an adverbial. Note also that in (5) there is a tight bond between the verb and the particle *up*, whereas in (7) one may replace the preposition by, for instance, *down* or *across* without changing the meaning of the verb.

S |---V--| |-----dO----|
5 They gave up the project.
6 They abandoned the project.
7 They live up the road. (SVA)

Constructions with prepositional verbs, as in (8) below, are in a way intermediate between phrasal verbs and the type illustrated in (7). As with the two parts of phrasal verbs, there is a bond between the verb and the preposition. The preposition cannot be replaced without changing the meaning of the verb. Phrasal and prepositional verbs differ, however, in that the former allow the particle to be placed after the direct object (*They gave it up*), while such reordering is not possible with prepositional verbs (**He waited it on*).

8 He waited on our table.

With prepositional verbs there is quite a close connection between the preposition and the following noun phrase, much as between a preposition and its complement in a prepositional phrase. Thus it is possible to see the noun phrase following a prepositional verb, such as *the table* in (8), as the complement of the preposition rather than the direct object of the verb. A noun phrase following a prepositional verb may be referred to as an oblique object to make it clear that it is less directly tied to the verb than an ordinary direct object.

Some prepositional verbs occur with both a direct and an oblique object, and may even allow the same noun phrase to occur in both functions. In (9) *the rescue team* functions as a direct object, and *with a gold medal* as an oblique object. In (10) *a gold medal* functions as the direct object, and *to the rescue team* as an oblique object.

9 The president presented the rescue team with a gold medal.
10 The president presented a gold medal to the rescue team.

Further examples of prepositional verbs with both direct and oblique objects are given in (11) to (13). In each case the direct object is underlined, and the oblique object italicized. The preposition is analysed as part of the verb phrase.

11 My lawyer convinced <u>the jury</u> of *my innocence*.

12 The chairman thanked the people of Northern Ireland for *their support.*
13 It looks very ghostlike, and reminds me a little of *Holyrood Chapel.*

9.8.3 Free predicatives

In (1) *afraid of seeing a doctor* is a verbless clause, and as such it represents a way of condensing language. An expanded version of the sentence might be *Dorothy was afraid of seeing the doctor, so she begged painkillers from her sisters.* Here we see that *afraid of seeing a doctor* functions as a subject predicative. In (1), however, it cannot have that function, since there is no copular verb to link it to the subject. Still the italicized phrase clearly describes *Dorothy*. We call such a constituent a **free predicative**. It is 'free' because it is not linked to the subject by means of a copular verb, and because it is to some extent mobile in the sentence, as we can see in (2).

1 *Afraid of seeing a doctor*, Dorothy begged painkillers from her sisters.
2 Dorothy, *afraid of seeing a doctor*, begged painkillers from her sisters.

Free predicatives modify the subject of the sentence. This is true even if the free predicative is placed relatively far from the subject, as in (3).

3 He left the room hastily, satisfied that the alarm was now set.

9.8.4 Vocatives and inserts

Some sentence elements are quite peripheral to the clause structure, and are never obligatory. One such element is the **vocative**, which is typically realized as a name or a noun phrase that refers to the addressee of an utterance, such as *son* in (1) and *Carol* in (2). They are typically used to attract the attention of the addressee.

1 What's your name, *son*?
2 *Carol*, I really must tell you about that awful woman.

Inserts (**2.4.1**) are another class of words which are not integrated in the clause structure. They convey a primarily emotive or interpersonal meaning, such as *well, oh, ouch, oh dear, hooray, drat. Yes* and *no* are also usually included among inserts. Like vocatives, inserts are always optional, and are not closely integrated in the clause structure. Examples are given in (3) and (4).

3 *Well*, I don't really mind being a scriptwriter.
4 *Oh god*, I was so scared!

Vocatives and inserts often occur together, as both may be effective attention-getters. In syntactic analysis we can use the abbreviations 'Voc' and 'Ins', respectively (as regards 'v', see **9.8.6** below).

Ins Voc v S V |--------dO---------|
5 *Hey, Liam*, have you got any more of these?

9.8.5 Connectors

A clause is often introduced by a conjunction. This happens particularly in complex and compound sentences (see **12.2**). In syntactic analysis we may use the term **connector** (abbreviated 'c') for the function of the conjunction. The analysis will be as shown in (1) and (2).

1 c S A V iO |------dO------|
But I never promised you a rose garden.

2 |--------S--------| V |---sP--| |------------------A---------------------------|
c S A V |--------dO------| oP
The electric bill was so high because we always had the electric fire on.

9.8.6 Discontinuous clause elements

When the verb phrase is complex, it is possible to put an adverbial between the auxiliary and the main verb (**10.9.1B**). We still regard the verb phrase as one constituent, however. The analysis will be as shown in (1), with a lower-case 'v' used for auxiliaries which are separated from the main verb.

S v A V |-----------sP--------------|
1 I have always been fond of English grammar.

In interrogative sentences, the verb phrase is usually split because an auxiliary precedes the subject, as in (2) and (3).

2 *Does* anybody *recognize* the woman in the picture?
3 What *would* you *have done* about it?

Constituents that are realized as long phrases may also be discontinuous. For example, a postmodifier may be separated from its head noun by some other constituent, as in (4) and (5).

4 The time has come for one of their members to lead the country.

5 Both Muskie and Snowcroft have shown a willingness in the past to challenge the man who appointed them.

In (4) the subject is *the time for one of their members to lead the country*. However, since the postmodifier makes the subject so long, it has been placed after the verb phrase, though it is still a part of the subject. In (5) the direct object (*a willingness to challenge the man who appointed them*) has been made discontinuous by the insertion of the adverbial *in the past*.

6 Of the textbooks available, none treats these concepts in enough detail.

In (6) the sentence starts with the postmodifier of the subject noun phrase (*none of the textbooks available*). When we reconstruct the noun phrase in this way, we see that the *of*-phrase is part of the subject. Speakers or writers may choose this word order to connect the sentence to the preceding text. As regards discontinuous structures, see further **11.5**.

9.9 Delimiting constituents: postmodifier vs. adverbial

It is sometimes difficult to determine the length of a constituent, i.e. how many words and phrases should be included in it. The simplest way of going about this is to try to replace the constituent with one single word, usually a pronoun for the nominal constituents, and an adverb for adverbials. Examples (1) to (3) illustrate the problem.

1 I know the bloke with the beard in the corner over there.
2 We stationed the bloke with the beard in the corner over there.
3 He photographed the bloke with the beard in the corner over there.

In (1) we could say *I know him*, but hardly *I know him in the corner over there*. Thus we can safely include these prepositional phrases in the direct object, as postmodifiers of *bloke*. In (2), however, *we stationed him* seems incomplete, since *station* is a verb which takes the SVdOA pattern. *We stationed him in the corner over there* is definitely better, and we analyse *in the corner over there* as an adverbial.

Example (3) presents a different problem because it is ambiguous. *In the corner over there* can either describe the place in which the photographer took the picture, in which case it is an adverbial, or it can specify which person was being photographed, in which case it is a postmodifier and part of the direct object.

9.10 Concord between the subject and the verb

We mentioned above that the minimum requirement of a simple sentence (except imperatives) is that it must contain a subject and a verb. There is a tight bond between the subject and the verb. Formally, this is shown in that there has to be **grammatical concord** between the two; i.e. the subject and the verb have to agree in person and number. For most verbs in English, it is only the third person singular of the present tense that has a special form, namely, one that ends in *-(e)s* (*I leave - he leaves*). The exceptions are *be*, which has three present tense forms (*am, are, is*) as well as two past tense forms (*was, were*), and the modal auxiliaries, which have only one form (*I must leave - he must leave*). Note also that the ordinary concord rules do not apply to subjunctive verb forms (**7.4.2**).

In most cases it is relatively straightforward to decide the person and number of the subject. The simplest way is to see if any of the third person pronouns *he, she*, and *it* can be used. However, there are cases which may be a bit more complicated, and which we discuss below.

9.10.1 Existential *there*

In sentences with existential *there*, *there* functions as an anticipatory subject, and the notional subject is placed after the verb. The verb generally agrees in number and person with the notional subject.

1 There *was* an old apple tree in their garden.
2 There *were* many old apple trees in their garden.

In colloquial English, *there's* is often used regardless of the number and person of the notional subject, as witnessed by (4). *There's* can then be regarded as a frozen formula, which functions as a signal that something is going to be presented. Interestingly, (4) is acceptable only with the contracted form of *there* + *is*. Note that standard written English always requires a plural verb with a plural subject in *there*-constructions.

3 There's a car outside.	(cf. There is a car outside.)
4 There's three cars outside. (informal)	(cf. *There is three cars outside.)

When the notional subject is a co-ordinated noun phrase, the verb tends to agree with the noun phrase that immediately follows it. Thus a singular verb is used in (5), and a plural one in (6), even if the subjects are logically the same. See further **9.10.2**.

5 There *is* a book and two articles that I still haven't read.

6 There *are* two articles and a book that I still haven't read.

Finally, when the notional subject is a non-finite clause, as in (7), the verb takes the singular form (see further **9.10.9**).

7 For those people there *was* no going back.

9.10.2 Co-ordinated noun phrase as subject

Subjects that are realized as co-ordinated noun phrases may present a problem as regards concord. When the subject consists of two singular noun phrases co-ordinated by means of *and*, the verb is generally in the plural, as in (1) and (2). In (3) the singular form of the verb indicates that 'his brother' is also 'his best friend', i.e. we are talking about just one person.

1 Mr and Mrs Smith *are* coming to dinner.
2 His brother and best friend *were* there.
3 His brother and best friend *was* there.

Co-ordination with *or* is different. Consider (4). Here the verb takes the singular form because only one person is coming. In (5) and (6) the problem is that the co-ordinated noun phrases differ in number. As a rule, the verb agrees with the nearest noun phrase; thus we get a singular verb in (5) after *my brother*, and a plural verb in (6), after *my sisters*.

4 (Either) John or Mary *is* coming.
5 Either my sisters or my brother *is* coming.
6 Either my brother or my sisters *are* coming.

Neither – nor can behave either like *and* or like *or*. In (7), where both noun phrases are singular, standard written English uses a singular verb, since 'neither John nor Mary' is equal to 'nobody'. But in informal English, a plural verb is often used.

7 Neither John nor Mary *knows* (informal: *know*) the answer.
8 Neither the students nor the teachers *know* the answer.

Further, English has some expressions that resemble co-ordinating conjunctions in meaning, notably *as well as* and *(along/together) with*. However, as regards syntax, they are different from the conjunctions, as can be seen in (9) to (14). The verb agrees with the first noun phrase, and the second noun phrase (introduced by *as well as, (along/together) with, like*, or *unlike*) is treated as a parenthetical remark.

9 John as well as Mary *knows* the answer.
10 Ted, like most of his friends, *is* a womanizer.
11 Peter, as well as myself, *is* coming.
12 (Along) with her friend Sarah, she *was* a leading member of the society.
13 That, together with the address of the hotel in Bath, *was* lost in the chaos.

9.10.3 Indefinite pronouns and determiners

Indefinite pronouns are syntactically third person singular. This is important to remember for Norwegians, who often seem to associate plural meaning with pronouns such as *everybody, everyone, anybody*. Note the contrast with *all*, which combines with a plural verb when it refers to people, as in (4) and (5), and with a singular verb when it refers generically to 'everything', as in (6).

1 Everybody *has* arrived; let's start.
2 Usually everything *is* very informal.
3 Nobody *has* ever been here before.
4 All the students *have* been given an assignment.
5 All *are* present.
6 All *is* well that ends well.

Noun phrases with the determiners *each* and *every* are singular. Again this is something that should be noted specifically by Norwegian learners, since Norwegian often expresses the same kind of meaning by means of a plural noun phrase (cf. the Norwegian translation of example 7: *Alle studentene har fått en oppgave.*).

7 Each student *has* been given an assignment.
8 Every man *is* speaking for his own country.

9.10.4 Uncountable nouns

When the subject is realized as an uncountable noun, the verb agrees with the form of the noun. Thus in most cases the verb will be singular, as in (1) and (2).

1 All the coffee *is* gone.
2 The population *is* living in poverty.

9.10.5 Collective nouns

When the subject is realized as a collective noun (**4.6**), American English always uses a singular verb. In British English, however, there are two possibilities. If a collective noun, such as *family*, is used to denote the family as a unit, the verb will be in the singular, as in (1). We then have the **unit** reading of the noun. But if the reference is to the individual members of the family, the verb will be in the plural, as in (2). This is the **distributive** reading of the noun.

1 Our family *has* been traced back to the 15th century.
2 My family *are* (all) perfectly normal.

With names of sports teams, a distributive meaning, and thus a plural verb, has become quite common in British English, as shown in (4).

3 Liverpool *is* leading 1–0.
4 Liverpool *are* attacking again. (AmE: *is* attacking)

Some verbs seem to favour a distributive reading of the noun, such as *disagree*, since obviously it takes at least two parties to produce a disagreement. On the other hand, a verb such as *consist of* favours a unit reading.

5 The committee *disagree* on almost every point. (AmE: *disagrees*)
6 The committee *consists* of six members.

9.10.6 Plural-only nouns

Some nouns look singular in form but have plural meaning. These are *cattle, clergy, people, police,* and *staff* (**4.4.5B**). They are different from collective nouns in that they always combine with the plural form of verbs; i.e. a 'unit reading' is not possible.

1 The police *are* coming.
2 People *are* demanding changes.

Note that *people* has a different meaning in which it behaves like an ordinary, countable noun, namely, that of 'race' or 'nation'.

3 He looked in the eyes of a new people that *was* to supplant his own.

Other plural-only nouns, which end in *-s* but have no corresponding singular noun (**4.4.5C**), also combine with plural verbs, as in (4) and (5).

4 These waters *are* dangerous.
5 Physical surroundings *are* only part of a total environment.

Note that singular nouns ending in *-s* (see **4.4.5D**) combine with singular verb forms, as in (6).

6 Gymnastics *uses* every part of the body and *requires* a great deal of character as well.

9.10.7 Nominalized adjectives

Nominalized adjectives (**8.9**) that refer to groups of people behave grammatically in the same way as *cattle, clergy, people, police,* and *staff*, i.e. they have a plural meaning and combine with plural verbs. As illustrated by (3), this group includes nationality adjectives.

1 The extremely old *need* a great deal of attention.
2 The young in spirit *enjoy* life.
3 The British *have* control over the bridge.

Nominalized adjectives that refer generically to an abstract entity combine with singular verbs, as shown in (4) and (5).

4 The supernatural *has* never appealed to me.
5 The best *is* yet to come.

9.10.8 Equative SVsP-pattern

In sentences with an equative SVsP pattern (**9.5.2B**), the subject and the subject predicative sometimes differ in number. Normally, the verb agrees with the subject, as in (1), but it also happens that the verb agrees with the predicative. This occurs particularly when the subject has a rather general meaning, as in (2). If the subject is very clearly marked for number and person, the verb must agree with the subject, as in (3).

1	What I want is two volunteers.	(cf. Two volunteers are what I want.)
2	All I ask for *is/are* these three books.	(cf. These three books are all I ask for.)
3	Who is it? – It's the neighbours.	

9.10.9 Clausal subject

When the subject is realized as a clause, the verb takes singular form. Subordinate clauses that can function as subjects are finite nominal clauses, as in (1) and (2), as well as *-ing* participle clauses and infinitive clauses, as in (3) and (4).

1 How many countries you have been to *is* totally irrelevant. (= it is ...)
2 That so many people objected to the regulations *was* new to the minister. (= it was ...)
3 Seeing my in-laws for the first time *was* a trying experience. (= it was ...)
4 To make a good technical sketch *does* not require any artistic talent. (= it does not ...)

9.10.10 Quantifier expressions with *of*

In noun phrases involving a quantifier with *of*, either the singular or the plural form of the verb may be used. As a general rule, if the quantifier can be replaced by *many*, the plural is used. We see examples of this in (1) and (2). Here *people* and *children* respectively can be regarded as the head of the subject noun phrase. In (3), on the other hand, it is the number, not the children, that is growing, so the verb agrees with *number*.

1 A lot of people *are* so peculiar that they don't like cats. (= they are ...)
2 A number of children *are* growing up in poverty. (= they are ...)
3 The number of poor children *is* growing. (= it is ...)

After expressions with *neither/none of* + a plural noun, it is common to use a plural verb form. However, usage varies here, and it may be noted that traditional grammars have insisted on the singular.

4 Neither of the films *were/was* very interesting.
5 None of these books *have/has* been translated into Norwegian.

In expressions with fractions or percentages, the verb tends to agree with the noun that is quantified. Thus in (6) there is a singular verb because *food* is uncountable. In (7) both the singular and the plural can be used because *population* is in the singular, though *ninety-five* speaks in favour of the plural. Example (9) has a plural verb due to the noun phrase *people in the village*, plus the fact that the subject predicative is a plural noun phrase. However, in expressions such as these, usage is uncertain, even among native speakers.

6 Two-thirds of most food *is* water.
7 Ninety-five per cent of the population *is/are* black.

8 One per cent of the population *is* black.
9 One per cent of the people in the village *are* children.

9.10.11 Concord in relative clauses

In relative clauses the subject is often represented by a relative pronoun (**12.6.2**). The verb then agrees with the number and person of the **antecedent** of the relative clause. Thus in (1) a plural verb must be used because the antecedent is *books*, and in (2) a singular verb follows from the singular *an idealist.*

1 These are all the books that *are* available on the subject.
2 He's an idealist who energetically *promotes* a healthier environment.
3 He is one of those environmentalists who *want* (*wants*?) to close down all industry.

In (3) the plural verb form is the one that correctly agrees with the antecedent. However, the singular is often found in such sentences with the word *one* in the antecedent.

4 They provided me with a map and a phrase book, which *were* very helpful.
5 They provided me with a map and a phrase book, which *was* very helpful.

In sentential relative clauses (**12.6.4**) the verb is in the singular, since the antecedent is the whole main clause. Thus *was* is used in (5), in contrast to the plural form in (4), where the antecedent is *a map and a phrase book.*

9.10.12 Notional concord

The term **notional concord** means that the verb may agree with the *meaning* rather than the *form* of the subject noun phrase. For example, in (1) below, 'fish and chips' is the name of a dish, and thus treated as singular rather than plural. Similarly, in (2), the concept of 'law and order' is seen as one rather than two entities. Example (3) is perhaps a bit different; here 'love' and 'devotion' are seen as two sides of the same coin, and thus treated as singular. A plural verb would also be possible.

1 Fish and chips *is* my favourite food.
2 Law and order *has* now been re-established.
3 Her love and devotion *makes* (*make*) him very happy.

Other cases where the verb agrees with the meaning rather than the form of the subject are the following:

A Titles

4 'The Dead' *is* a short story.

5 *The New York Times has* a picture of the President on its front page.

B Names of countries and organizations

6 The United States often *sees* itself as a world policeman.

7 The United Nations *has* its headquarters in New York.

C Amounts and measurements

8 Twenty years *is* a long time. (= the period is long)

9 Three hundred pounds *is* missing from club funds. (= the sum is missing)

D Fact expressions

10 Reduced prices *means* a lower income for the retailer. (The fact that prices have been reduced means a lower income ...)

9.10.13 Proximity concord

We saw in **9.10.2** (about co-ordinated subject noun phrases) that, in some cases, the verb agrees with the nearest noun phrase rather than the whole subject. This is what is meant by **proximity concord**. It is particularly conspicuous in cases of false co-ordination (**9.10.2**). In (1) the 'correct' usage is certainly the singular form of the verb, since the head of the subject phrase is *nobody*. However, sentences such as these often occur with a plural verb. It should be noted that the plural may be regarded as sloppy or wrong, at least in written English.

1 Nobody except her parents really *knows* (*know*) her.

There are also some cases of long noun phrases where even native speakers produce concord mistakes, in that they let the verb agree with the nearest noun phrase rather than the head of the subject noun phrases. Examples such as (2) may occur, but must be regarded as slips.

2 *Electronic equipment, such as cellular phones and computers, *have* become cheaper.

Terms

sentence
clause

transitivity types: intransitive
monotransitive
ditransitive

			complex transitive
			copular: ascriptive
			equative
clause elements:	subject	semantic roles:	agent
	verb		instrument
	direct object		characterized
	indirect object		affected
	subject predicative		effected
	object predicative		recipient
	adverbial		attributive
	anticipatory subject/ object	concord:	grammatical
	oblique object		notional
	free predicative		proximity
	vocative		
	insert		
	connector		
valency			

Exercises

1 Give a syntactic analysis of the following sentences. (**9.3**)

a RH Form has chairs for all types of people.
b I lost my wallet somewhere in London.
c The class remained silent and very tense.
d She kept her eyes closed for quite a while.
e That tray had just been prepared for me by the cook.
f Miss Honey stood there helpless before this great red-necked giant.
g Who would want to go to university at the age of 15, for heaven's sake?
h A devoutly religious man, Souter is an evangelical Christian.
i There was a high hedge of hazel on either side of the path.
j Therefore, a research group at the Johns Hopkins Hospital in Baltimore recently compared bedside presentation with presentations in a conference room.
k She had always regarded her purely as a teacher, a person who turned up out of nowhere and taught at school and then went away again.

2 Account for the different uses and meanings of the italicized verbs, considering the way in which they pattern with other clause elements. (**9.5– 9.6**)

a 1 We must *keep* the river clean.
2 This fence *keeps* the sheep out.
3 He always *keeps* his word.
4 I *keep* telling him how to behave.

b 1 We will *call* a meeting in early September.
  2 They *call* themselves environmentalists.
  3 The film was *called* 'Sunday in Greenwich Village'.
  4 The meeting was *called* off.

c 1 She *stayed* financially dependent on her parents.
  2 Perhaps it is better to *stay* at home.
  3 They *stayed* for a long time.

d 1 She might have *tasted* the coffee if it had still been hot.
  2 Tonight his drink *tasted* like cod-liver oil.
  3 It was icy cold and *tasted* delicious.

e 1 The bus *turned* right along Inverness Road.
  2 The nation is *turning* conservative.
  3 Rather than go bankrupt, Mercer *turned* his firm over to a bank.
  4 She *turned* and walked towards the lift.
  5 He had *turned* his ankle slightly.
  6 Peter *turned* off the TV.

3 Explain the syntactic and semantic ambiguity of the following sentences. (**9.6**)

a She found him an excellent cook.
b They are amusing children.
c We photographed the man in the corner over there.
d Enraged cow injures farmer with axe.
e The stolen painting was found by a tree.
f They gave her cat food.

4 Comment on the difference in form and meaning between the members of the following sentence pairs.

a 1 The man turned red.
  2 The man turned left.
b 1 Greg sounded a trumpet.
  2 Greg sounded a fool.
c 1 I placed the vase on the shelf.
  2 I liked the vase on the shelf.
d 1 They found the boy a nuisance.
  2 They found the boy a nurse.
e 1 He couldn't work the cassette player.
  2 He couldn't work the following Tuesday.

f 1 Jill ran up a hill.
  2 Jill ran up a bill.
g 1 He's driving me mad.
  2 He's driving my car.
h 1 The door was closed by midnight.
  2 The door was closed by Joe.
i 1 You should call her Rachel.
  2 You should call her, Rachel.

5 Translate the following sentences into English. (**9.7**)

a Roger tok på seg pyjamasen og gikk og la seg.
b Han fortalte at han var søvnig.
c Hun smakte ikke en gang på maten.
d Catherine ønsker seg et piano til bursdagen sin.
e Tom ligner på bestefaren sin.
f Gamle tante Ellen klarer seg fint selv.

6 Identify cases of discontinuous clause elements in the following sentences and state the syntactic function of each. In what way has the phrase been split up? (**9.8.6**)

a Guiteau had many reproductions made of his mugshot.
b I had never really thought about it.
c There will be a strong desire among the leaders present to show their solidarity.
d This is a bigger problem in India than it is here.
e Of the handful of painters that Austria has produced in the 20th century, only one, Oskar Kokoschka, is widely known in the United States.

7 Select the appropriate present tense form of the verb given in parentheses. Give reasons for your choices. (**9.10**)

a The news _________ (BE) good.
b His clothes _________ (BE) expensive.
c Knowledge of the matters _________ (BE) needed.
d His family _________ (BE) old.
e The committee _________ (DISAGREE) on the matter.
f The homeless _________ (HAVE) nowhere to go.
g The police _________ (BE) coming.
h People _________ (BELIEVE) anything.
i Two hundred dollars _________ (BE) needed to cover the expenses.
j What you see here _________ (BE) the crown jewels.

k *The Times* _________ (HAVE) changed.
l Times _________ (HAVE) changed.
m 'The Dead' _________ (BE) a short story by James Joyce.
n There _________ (BE) a boy and a girl in the picture.
o There _________ (BE) a lot of things to do.
p Neither Mr nor Mrs Blake _________ (HAVE) signed the contract.
q The teacher as well as the children _________ (BE) unhappy about the timetable.

8 Select the appropriate present tense form of the verb given in SMALL CAPITALS. Give reasons for your choices. (**9.10**)

More usually, solving crime (1) BE incidental to the private investigator's major task, which (2) BE to establish a defence for a client facing criminal charges. Occasionally, private eyes (3) BE employed to uncover crime, but it (4) BE almost always white collar crime or employee theft, where confidentiality (5) BE an issue or where the police (6) DO not have the resources or the incentives to dig deep and find out what (7) BE going on inside a company.

The other area where private eyes (8) OPERATE against criminals (9) BE in the growth area of fraud. Usually, insurance companies (10) BE the victims, and they (11) CALL on PIs to protect their interests and establish a case against the defrauders. Janette Estrella often (12) WORK cases like this on behalf of automobile insurance companies.

There (13) BE a lot of different types of auto insurance fraud, but one of the most common (14) BE something called ghost passengers, in which the claimant (15) ARRANGE for a friend to deliberately rear-end his car. He then (16) MAKE a claim, saying that several people were in the car and suffered injuries.

(From Val McDermid, *An Unsuitable Job for a Woman*)

9 Cross out any inappropriate alternatives in the sentences below. Explain your choices. If both alternatives are possible, account for any difference in meaning and/or style. (**9.10**)

a Your trousers is/are dirty!
b A war of words has/have broken out between academics and industrial leaders.
c All the new technology has/have made production easier.
d What they need is/are sympathy and love.
e The crossroads is/are right ahead of us now.
f Nobody has/have suggested that the ethical effects of the art was/were irrelevant.

g Is/are there anyone here who has/have sold their house recently?
h Twelve per cent of the country's population is/are illiterate.
i The uneducated has/have a lot of trouble finding work.
j All the money has/have been refunded.
k This pair of shoes was/were not made for walking.
l The general public does/do not know where to go for help.
m Enormous amounts of money is/are being spent on administration.
n Provoking responses has/have not really brought us any further.
o Lots of locally produced cheese was/were served there.
p Where one or the other of the effects of an action is/are uncertain, this has/have to be taken into account.

10 Write sentences in the present tense with the following phrases as subjects. In each case, state your reason for choosing the singular or the plural form of the verb. (**9.10**)

a sixty miles
b gin and tonic
c gin and whisky
d both the author and the readers
e either the author or the publisher
f the mentally ill
g growing plants
h improved housing conditions

11 Comment on the difference in form and meaning between the members of the following sentence pairs. (**9.10**)

a 1 The TV series is endless.
  2 The TV series are endless.
b 1 The nursing staff was against the change.
  2 The nursing staff were against the change.
c 1 A number of accidents have escaped media attention.
  2 The number of accidents has escaped media attention.
d 1 French was difficult.
  2 The French were difficult.
e 1 Flying planes are dangerous.
  2 Flying planes is dangerous.

10 Adverbials

10.1 Introduction

The adverbial has been shown to be the most frequently occurring clause element after the subject and the verb. It is also the only type of clause element which can occur more than once in the same clause. But in spite of the familiarity of the phenomenon, it is hard to come up with a good definition of the term **adverbial**. Rather than trying to explain at this point exactly what an adverbial is, let us look at the following text, in which all the sentences contain at least one adverbial. These adverbials have been italicized. Adverbials which belong to a subordinate clause have been listed below the text.

> Dallas Sherman of Cincinnati divorced his wife, Irene, *after she intentionally wrecked two of the family cars during arguments with him*. They were reconciled, *however*, and remarried. *Unhappily*, they were divorced *again after another little contretemps in which Irene shot Dallas twice in the chest and once in the hand*. She was placed *on probation* and he recovered. *While they were trying to effect another reconciliation* another family fracas erupted and poor Dallas was shot *yet again*. He recovered and succeeded *in his reconciliation*. The Shermans were married *for the third time in 1977*.
>
> (From Bill Bryson, *Bizarre World*)

intentionally	*in the chest*
during arguments with him	*once*
twice	*in the hand*

10.2 Adverbials – circumstantials in the sentence

When we study the adverbials occurring in the text in **10.1**, it is not easy to see what they have in common. Perhaps for this reason, the term **adverbial** tends to be negatively defined. It is *not* the verb phrase, and it is *not* one of the elements that denote participants in the action, in the same way as a subject or an object. Rather, an adverbial tends to denote some aspect of the *circumstances* of the action expressed by the verb phrase. It can denote the time or the place where the action took place; it can describe the way in which the action was carried out; it can denote the condition for the action taking place; it can express a relationship of cause and effect, or give the speaker's view of the whole situation, among other things (see further **10.6**).

Adverbials enter into some of the basic clause patterns (**9.5**), but they can also occur in clauses where they are not required by the verb. Adverbials can thus be obligatory, as in (1) to (3), or optional, as in (4) and (5).

1 She was placed *on probation.*
2 He lives *in an expensive Knightsbridge flat.*
3 Keep this *to yourself.*
4 She *intentionally* wrecked two of the family cars.
5 *Unhappily*, they were divorced *again after another little contretemps.*

It can sometimes be hard to draw the line between obligatory and optional adverbials. Sometimes an adverbial which is optional from a purely grammatical point of view may express the most important part of the sentence from the point of view of meaning. In (6) we see an example of this. Obviously, *at three o'clock* is the whole point of B's utterance. Still, *He leaves work* constitutes a grammatically well-formed sentence, which would work well in a different context. Thus the adverbial is optional.

6 A: When do you expect him back?
B: He leaves work *at three o'clock.*
7 I keep a diary.
8 I keep my diary under lock and key.

In (7) and (8) we see two different meanings of *keep*. The first is 'write regularly', and the second 'have (in a certain place)'. With the second meaning, *keep* is naturally followed by an adverbial. This adverbial is obligatory, since leaving it out would change the meaning of the verb. In (6), by contrast, the meaning of the verb is not dependent on the absence or presence of the adverbial.

10.3 Adverbs vs. adverbials

In Chapter 8 we studied the form and function of adverbs and adverb phrases. Obviously, the terms adverb and adverbial are related. This does not mean, however, that they are synonymous. The most important difference is that **adverb** denotes a word class, while **adverbial** denotes a syntactic function. The syntactic function of adverbial can be realized by adverbs, but also in other ways (see **10.4**). Conversely, adverbs do not always function as adverbials, but may have other functions, such as modifier in an adjective phrase (**8.15**).

10.4 The realization of adverbials

As you can see from the text quoted at the beginning of this chapter, adverbials can have a range of different realizations. Here are some further examples.

1 **Adverb**: Our adviser feels certain that the bill has been *incorrectly* made out.
2 **Adverb phrase**: His words tumbled out *as involuntarily as Mrs Clarke's did.*
3 **Prepositional phrase**: You're putting words *into my mouth.*
4 **Noun phrase**: The manager wants to see the accounts *this Friday.*
5 **Finite subordinate clause**: People will kill each other for a parking space in New York *because they think, 'If I don't get this one, I may never get a space.'*
6 **Non-finite subordinate clause**: *Looking around,* I reflected that only the telephone belonged to the present century.
7 **Verbless clause**: *Back in her car,* she pencilled in a rough timetable for the following morning.

Studies of large quantities of text show that the most frequent realization of adverbials is the prepositional phrase. It is, however, clearly impossible to define adverbials on the basis of form. It is rather on the basis of meaning that an adverbial can be recognized.

10.5 Classes of adverbials – adjuncts, disjuncts, conjuncts

We can divide adverbials into three main types: adjuncts, disjuncts, and conjuncts. These three classes are based on considerations of the meaning and the syntactic functions of adverbials.

If a clause is negated by means of *not* (with *do*-insertion where required), the adverbial may or may not be affected by the negation. In (2) the adverbial *in this building* is affected by the negation; the doctor's surgery is somewhere else. However, the adverbial *fortunately* is not affected; the speaker is still presenting a fact as fortunate, only this fact is the opposite of that in (1).

1 *Fortunately,* the doctor's surgery is located *in this building.*
2 *Fortunately,* the doctor's surgery is not located *in this building.*
3 It is *in this building* that the doctor's surgery is located.
4 *It is *fortunately* that the doctor's surgery is located in this building.

Furthermore, (3) and (4) show that the two adverbials in (1) differ in that only one of them can be the focus of a cleft construction (**11.9**). Those adverbials that can be affected by clause negation and that can be the focus of a cleft construction can be said to be closer to the 'core' of the clause. These are adjuncts. We have already seen that adverbials can be obligatory or optional (**10.2**). It is only adjuncts that can be obligatory, while disjuncts and conjuncts are always optional.

In speech, we can often hear that conjuncts and disjuncts are separated from the rest of the clause by means of tone unit boundaries, as in (5) and (6), while adjuncts have a greater tendency to occur in the same tone unit as the verb of the clause in which it occurs.

5 | but F˅ORTUNATELY | they both issued exactly the same ˋORDERS |
6 | I do not THˋINK | HOW˅EVER | that the Labour Party could keep their other wing under CONTRˋOL |

In writing, such tone unit boundaries are often represented by commas. However, none of these 'tests' are sufficient to distinguish between adjuncts, disjuncts, and conjuncts, so it is necessary to take a closer look at the meaning conveyed by these classes of adverbials.

10.6 The meanings of adjuncts

Adjuncts can be said to express the where, when, how, and why of the sentence. In other words, they denote such relations as time, place, manner, reason, purpose, condition, agent, and instrument. Examples (1) to (14) illustrate the kinds of meaning that can be expressed by adjuncts. Note that the list is in principle open-ended. Some adverbials may seem to be on the borderline between two of the groups mentioned here, while others may not seem to fit into any of them. This simply illustrates the great diversity of meaning that can be expressed by means of adjuncts.

1 **Time**: *When I read the book*, it elicited an emotional reaction in me.
2 **Place**: The family lived comfortably *in a succession of pleasant New Jersey towns.*
3 **Manner**: The family lived *comfortably* in a succession of pleasant New Jersey towns.
4 **Instrument**: A thug struck a cab driver in the face *with a pistol* last night.
5 **Means**: It would be financed *by boosting the social security payroll tax.*
6 **Agent**: Doctor bills would still be paid *by the patient.*
7 **Degree**: I hate the book *so much that I choose not to finish it.*
8 **Reason**: I have to hire a stenographer *because I can't spell straight.*
9 **Purpose**: Some dentists offer headphones *to distract from their drilling.*
10 **Condition**: I know the expedition is liable to fall through *if you don't come.*
11 **Concession**: There were lights glinting in the city, too, *even though it was now dark enough for a few stars to become visible.*
12 **Focusing**: Player was *almost* in tears.
13 **Viewpoint**: *Politically*, Einstein was a socialist.
14 **Respect**: Our hypothesis does not conflict *with the results of our experiment.*

Some of these groups of adjuncts can in turn express a range of different meanings, some of which are presented below.

- **Time adjuncts** can express either definite time (*yesterday, in 1997*), indefinite time (*the other day, some time*), duration (*for a week, during the holidays*), or frequency (*often, occasionally, never*).

- **Place adjuncts** include references to distances (*he ran 10 miles*) and to directions (*from Bergen, to Los Angeles, westwards*).

- **Focusing adjuncts** usually serve to highlight an element in the clause. They can also serve to limit the reference of the element they highlight. They are typically realized by focusing adverbs such as *only, nearly, practically* (see **8.12** and **8.15.2**).

- **Viewpoint adjuncts** are close to disjuncts in meaning. They can usually be paraphrased 'from a ... point of view', and express the angle from which an event is described.

- **Adjuncts of respect** specify circumstances of the action which may sometimes be approaching the meaning of manner adjuncts (*she's helping him with the accounts*), and sometimes that of a place adjunct, though respect adjuncts are somewhat more abstract (*I'm working on my essay*). Further examples are given in (15) and (16).

15 They were talking *about team spirit and that sort of thing*.
16 They wanted to restore the classic tradition *to life*.

10.7 The meanings and functions of disjuncts

The common denominator of disjuncts is that they are evaluative. They convey the speaker's comment on some aspect of the message. Some disjuncts, of the type *probably, certainly, allegedly, I suppose/think* (as comment clauses; cf. **12.9.3**), express the speaker's degree of certainty that whatever the clause expresses is true. By using such disjuncts, speakers avoid having to take responsibility for the truth of what they are saying. (Note that even disjuncts such as *certainly* or *no doubt* make a statement less accurate than the corresponding statements without a disjunct.) This is roughly the same meaning and communicative function that can be expressed by epistemic modal auxiliaries (**7.4**). For this reason, they are sometimes referred to as **modal disjuncts**. Other disjuncts, such as *of course, naturally, fortunately, as a matter of fact, (quite) unexpectedly, in my opinion,* give the speaker's comment on how he/she views the fact expressed by the clause. These may be called **fact-evaluating** disjuncts. Yet others, such as *frankly, honestly, briefly, to tell you the truth, to put it mildly*, allow speakers to comment on the way in which they are expressing themselves, and may be called **style-evaluating**. In the examples below, (1) and (2) contain modal disjuncts. Examples (3) and (4) illustrate fact-evaluating disjuncts, which show us the speaker's opinion. The disjunct in (5) is close to this, though it also includes an evaluation of the subject referent. Examples (6) and (7) contain style-evaluating disjuncts, by which the speaker gives information about how the message is presented.

1 He is right, *probably*.
2 The book is *certainly* in the library.
3 *Fortunately*, I managed to get there in time.
4 *To my great disappointment* there was no food left.
5 *Wisely*, he withdrew from the whole thing.
6 *Frankly*, my dear, I don't give it a damn.
7 *In other words*, you told him to get out.

Sometimes the same word or phrase may function either as an adjunct or as a disjunct. The interpretation usually depends on intonation, punctuation, or the position of the adverbial in the sentence (see further **10.9.1**).

8 They were looking at us *strangely*. (manner adjunct; They were looking at us in a strange manner.)

9 *Strangely (enough)*, they were looking at us. (disjunct; I find it strange that they were looking at us.)

Sentential relative clauses (**12.6.4**) express a comment on the content of the main clause, and thus function as disjuncts, as in (10) to (12).

10 Gwen is leaving, *which is sad.*
11 Alexandra, her father often said to himself, was like her grandfather – *which was his way of saying that she was intelligent.*
12 'We shall never surrender and even if, *which I do not for the moment believe*, this island or a large part of it were subjugated and starving, then our empire beyond the seas, armed and guarded by the British Fleet, will carry on the struggle until in God's good time the New World with all its power and might, sets forth to the liberation and rescue of the Old.'
(Winston Churchill)

Comment clauses, such as *you know, I mean, I suppose, I think, you see,* function as disjuncts in sentences such as (13) to (15). Comment clauses occur frequently in speech, as they often address the listener or refer to the speech situation in other ways. The emphasis is not on what anyone knows, thinks, or supposes. The meaning of a comment clause is clearly subordinate to the rest of the message. Besides, the verbs in comment clauses do not normally vary for tense, which shows them to be more or less fixed expressions. This use is clearly different from the use of the same subjects and verbs in main clauses with a following direct object, as in (16) and (17).

13 | you ˊKNOW | this bloody university will be the ˋDEATH of me | (*you knew, this bloody university would be the death of me)
14 | because HˋART | as you KNˋOW | is a man who ·knows ˋEVERYTHING | I mean – he's certainly not the usual woolly-minded PROFˋESSOR | who doesn't even know where his FˋILING system is | (*... I meant – he was certainly not ...)
15 | I've only seen her ˋONCE | since I HˋEARD this news I think |
16 | I think it's a GˋOOD PˏICTURE |
17 | and as soon as it starts to go DˋOWN | you know you've PˏASSED it | and you twiddle it slightly BˋACK again |

10.8 The meaning of conjuncts

As the term **conjunct** suggests, the function of conjuncts is similar to that of conjunctions, in that they connect sentences and ideas. Conjuncts are thus text-structuring elements. They can express a wide range of meanings. Some examples are given in (1) to (5) below.

1 From his play, the child learns that a piece of string may be made shorter by cutting a piece off, or a stick made shorter by breaking it. *Likewise* he learns that sticks and ropes may be joined to other sticks and ropes and so made longer.
2 Girls are generally more comfortable curling up with a book. *However*, there are still a lot of keen boy readers about.
3 Claude didn't want to go, didn't want to accept favours – *nevertheless* he went.
4 Her latest novel is extremely entertaining, and *consequently* has sold more than 50,000 copies.
5 Even the most careful cook lets the milk boil over sometimes. *So* it is most important that the top should be easy to clean.

We see that conjuncts can express similarity or contrast with something that has been mentioned before, as in (1) to (3). Furthermore, they can express a logical connection between two clauses, such as cause–effect, as in (4) and (5).

Other conjuncts do not so clearly refer back to the preceding context, but they are still text-structuring elements. They may perhaps be viewed as signposts that speakers can use to inform hearers how far they have come in the text.

6 And, *secondly*, I think people will get tired of this.
7 *Finally* there is a principle which may overlook both the immorality and the harmful outcome of pornography.
8 *To begin with*, the all-powerful Los Angeles Times does not publish a transcript of these press conferences. *Next*, because of the time differential, the conferences come on the networks during the middle of the day.

Some conjuncts may have the same form as adjuncts. To interpret their function, we have to consider the context. Intonation and punctuation, as well as the position of the adverbial, may also be of help. Thus we see that *still* means two different things in (9) and (10). In (11) *finally* is a time adjunct, in contrast to its use as a conjunct in (7).

9 I'm not sure the plan is realistic. *Still,* I think it's very interesting. (conjunct, expressing a contrast)
10 I've been giving a lot of thought to the plan. I *still* think it's very interesting. (adjunct, expressing time)
11 Taylor knew that winter had *finally* come.

10.9 The placement of adverbials

10.9.1 Adverbial positions

An English sentence has many 'slots' into which an adverbial can fit. We choose to describe the position of adverbials in relation to other elements in the same clause.

A Initial

The slot before the subject is referred to as **initial position**. In sentences with inversion, initial position is the slot before the finite verb. However, an adverbial in initial position can be preceded by a conjunction, as in (3). If there are two adverbials before the subject, as in (4), both are said to be in initial position.

1 *Unhappily*, they were divorced again.
2 *While they were trying to effect another reconciliation* another family fracas erupted and poor Dallas was shot yet again.
3 I have to be in Swansea by three, *and if I don't leave very soon,* I won't make it.
4 *Anyway, as I told you,* he has brown eyes.

B Medial

Roughly speaking, **medial position** covers any slot between the subject and the last obligatory element in a clause. More accurately, medial position denotes the following slots: (i) between the subject and the verb, as in (5); (ii) between an auxiliary and the main verb, as in (6) and (7); (iii) between the main verb and an object or a predicative, as in (8) and (9).

5 Things *suddenly* changed for the better.
6 His father has *probably* left the country by now.
7 I would *never* have told that to anybody.
8 The police officer described *in detail* how they had found the body.
9 At 80, she is *still* an activist.

C End

As the term suggests, **end position** denotes the slot after all the obligatory elements in a clause. An obligatory adverbial is also said to be in end position if it follows the other obligatory clause elements, as in (10). Quite frequently there may be two or more adverbials occurring together in this slot, as in (12). We do not, however, distinguish between such adverbials as regards placement; all occur in end position.

10 She was placed *on probation.*
11 Dallas was shot *yet again.*
12 Rose sat *awkwardly in the armchair for what seemed like an eternity.*

10.9.2 Typical positions of adjuncts

For most types of adjuncts, end position is the most common one. Obligatory adjuncts are nearly always placed in end position. Likewise, adverbials which seem to be central to the action expressed by the verb phrase are generally placed in end position, as shown in (1). Adverbials which modify the whole sentence, on the other hand, can be placed either in initial position or in end position, as in (2) and (3).

1 The fabulous French brasserie has its roots *in the beer cellars of Germany.*
2 My wife was away making a film *earlier this year.*
3 *Earlier this year* my wife was away making a film.

Manner and degree adjuncts, particularly those that are realized by adverbs ending in *-ly*, are often placed in medial position, though end position is usually an alternative.

4 A fine 18th-century cottage has been *subtly* converted into a showroom.
5 The dish was *extravagantly* presented.
6 The living room could *easily* be turned into two rooms.
7 The Blauels had to finance the next step *privately.*

A small class of time adverbs are usually placed in medial position. These are mainly frequency adverbs, such as *always, never, often, usually, sometimes, hardly.* They are placed in the position after the first auxiliary in sentences with a complex verb phrase, as in (8), and after the verb in sentences where the verb is a simple form of *be*, as in (9). (This is also the position of the negator *not.*)

8 The schoolmaster was *already fast* disappearing.
9 Peter is *never/usually/always* well prepared for class.

Focusing adverbials, such as *only, almost, nearly, practically,* are generally placed before the element they highlight. However, this rule can be broken, and it often is, particularly in speech, where intonation will indicate which element is focused on, as in (13). In writing, however, one does best to put the focusing adjunct immediately before the focused element in order to avoid ambiguity.

10 It was *nearly* dinner-time when he reached Dijon.
11 But that is *simply* untrue.
12 He insulted *virtually* everyone.
13 | I've only seen her `ONCE | since I H`EARD this news I think | (Cf. I've seen her only once ...)

In colloquial speech we often find expressions such as *sort of* and *like*, which function as a mixture between a focusing adverbial and a modal disjunct in that they make the meaning of the following element less absolute and clear-cut.

14 Here, I mean I've seen, *like*, ten-year-old girls in there, but really pretty ten-year-old girls, you know what I mean, blue eyes and blonde hair from them flats.
15 I've never really been, *like*, single single cos I'm always *sort of like*, not actually going out with somebody but I'm always, I've always got someone who *sort of* fancies me or I'm flirting with.

10.9.3 Typical positions of disjuncts

Disjuncts may be placed in any of the three positions described above. However, there are some strong tendencies associated with the different types of disjuncts. Initial position is widely used for all types of disjuncts, particularly those that are style-evaluating, as in (1), or fact-evaluating, as in (2).

1 *To be honest*, I don't feel grown-up at all.
2 *Predictably*, the Duracell rabbits beat their instruments long after their zinc-acid-equipped rivals had fallen silent.

Modal disjuncts realized as adverbs are regularly found in medial position, as shown in (3) and (4). But initial position is also an option, particularly for the adverbs *perhaps* and *maybe*, as illustrated by (5).

3 But there's *probably* less storage space now.
4 That is something that you cannot *possibly* expect me to discuss.
5 *Perhaps* Esther knows about it, but *perhaps* she doesn't even know for sure.

In clauses where the verb phrase is complex, there is a slight difference between British and American English as regards medial position for disjuncts. Whereas British English prefers to have the adverbial after the (first) auxiliary, as in (6), American English allows the adverbial to be placed between the subject and the (first) auxiliary, as in (7). However, disjuncts can be found in both these positions in both British and American English.

6 Last year, we would *probably* have given him £350 for a comparable machine.
7 Last year, we *probably* would have given him $700 for a comparable machine.

Disjuncts do not often occur in end position, but when they do, they normally occur after all other elements in the clause, as illustrated in (8).

8 But they've stopped making that dish now, *sadly*.

10.9.4 Typical positions of conjuncts

The most common position for conjuncts is initial. This is natural, since conjuncts usually act as a link between the sentence in which they occur and the preceding context. An initial conjunct is usually followed by a comma in writing, and by a tone unit boundary in speech.

1 *Besides*, it would cost more, and you couldn't live so cheaply up there.
2 | BES`IDES | training will be `INTERESTING |

Conjuncts may also occur in medial position (generally after the first auxiliary if the verb phrase is complex). In that case, they are normally enclosed by commas in writing, and frequently by tone unit boundaries in speech. As with the other types of adverbials, it is chiefly conjuncts that are realized by an adverb that can occur in medial position.

3 There is, *however*, one curious discrepancy in this broad and flattering picture.
4 | there might HOW,EVER | be certain groups at special R`ISK |

Finally, end position is also sometimes used for conjuncts, as is shown in (5).

5 'If it isn't a secret', he said, 'I'd like to know how you ever got into the British army, *anyway*.'

10.9.5 The order of adverbials in the same slot

Quite frequently we find examples of two or more adverbials occupying the same slot. This happens particularly in end position, as in (1) and (2), and in initial position, as in (3).

1 Gertrude ran *across the beach into the surf.*
2 He was *there recently on the proceeds from his musical comedy tunes.*
3 *In a cheap, residential section of The Bronx one day last week,* 75 concealed agents, city detectives, and state troopers watched a man come out of a small stucco house.

It is a general principle that adverbials realized as subordinate clauses are put after other adverbials. Apart from this, the relative order of adverbials depends on the slot in which they are placed.

In initial position, we generally see the order conjunct – disjunct – adjunct (in the rare case of having all three types consecutively). An example such as (4) is at least theoretically possible.

4 Anyway, fortunately, next week it'll be back to normal again.

In end position we generally see the order adjunct – conjunct – disjunct (though conjuncts do not often occur in end position if there are other adverbials there). An example such as (5) is possible, but awkward.

5 We'll all be back to normal next week, however, fortunately.

As regards adjuncts, those that are obligatory are usually placed before those that are optional, as in (6). The obligatory adjunct has been italicized.

6 We'll all be *back to normal* next week.

Furthermore, it is common for adjuncts to appear in the following order (though it is hardly likely that all these types of adjuncts would occur in the same sentence):

respect	agent manner instrument means	place	time	reason purpose condition concession

7 The efficiency with which animals convert grains and forages to meat has risen *steadily in the United States since the 1930s.* (manner – place – time)
8 The division could not work *on the line until then because of the large amount of acid sewage from jewellery plants in the area.* (respect – time – reason)

9 The mood could change *dramatically overnight if such a view was expressed by a government minister*. (manner – time – condition)
10 Shea was named *by Mayor Wagner three years ago to head a committee that included James A. Farley, Bernard Gimbel, and Clint Blume*. (agent – time – purpose)

As regards information structure (**11.1.2**), those adverbials that express new or important information are generally placed last, where they will receive nuclear accent, as shown in (11).

11 | and I will get back into London half past F\OUR |

In principle, there is no limit as to how many adverbials can belong to the same clause. Note, however, that speakers tend to avoid overly long clusters of adverbials. If there are more than three adverbials in a clause, at least one of them tends to be moved away from end position into initial or medial position.

10.9.6 Some contrastive observations

There are some differences between Norwegian and English as regards the placement of adverbials. These differences are chiefly associated with initial position and medial position.

In both Norwegian and English an adverbial can occupy initial position. However, for most types of adverbials, initial position is more common in Norwegian than in English.

1 På den tiden arbeidet jeg i et aksjemeglerfirma.
I was working for a stockbroker at the time.
2 Der hadde hun også stått en gang.
She, too, had once stood there.

On the other hand, Norwegian grammar requires the verb to be the second clause element, which means that it is more difficult to place two adverbials in initial position in Norwegian. A Norwegian translation of (3) and (4) would probably move one of the adverbials to medial or end position.

3 Besides, in Frankfurt, Enid was thought very pretty.
4 From the time we entered the concert hall, however, she was a trifle less passive.

Note, incidentally, that in contrast to Norwegian, English does not normally have inversion of the subject and the finite verb in clauses with an adverbial in initial position (**11.2**).

Another adverbial position in which Norwegian and English differ is medial. First of all, the time adverbs such as *never, always, sometimes* (which take the same position as *not*; see **10.9.2**) are placed in the same position in English regardless of whether the clause is a subordinate or a main clause. This is different from Norwegian, as illustrated by examples (5) and (6).

5 Mary har *aldri/ofte* vært i Kanada.
Mary has *never/often* been to Canada.
6 Mary sa at hun *aldri/ofte* hadde vært i Kanada.
Mary said that she had *never/often* been to Canada.

Secondly, medial position is used for most types of adverbials in Norwegian, in contrast to English, where we generally find only very short adverbials, mainly disjuncts, conjuncts, and frequency adjuncts in medial position. Norwegian learners should thus be aware that adverbials realized as phrases or clauses should be placed either in initial or in end position in English. Examples (7) and (8) illustrate this difference.

7 Regjeringen har *gjennom flere år* arbeidet for å øke tilgangen på personell til helsesektoren.
Over many years the government has been striving to increase the availability of staff in the health sector.
8 Byrådet kom *i brev til Miljøverndepartementet* med en uttalelse om alternativ 2.
The city council issued a statement about alternative 2 *in a letter to the Ministry of the Environment.*

Conjuncts and disjuncts are very often placed in medial position in Norwegian; see (9) and (10). As we saw in **10.9.3** and **10.9.4**, the most common position for these adverbials in English is initial (though medial is possible, too).

9 Vi har *heldigvis* betalt den regningen allerede.
Fortunately, we have paid that bill already.
10 Tidsrommet var *imidlertid* preget av industrialisering og urbanisering.
However, this period was characterized by industrialization and urbanization.

Note that Norwegian and English differ as regards the placement of adverbials in medial position in declarative sentences with a simple verb phrase. Norwegian always has the finite verb in second position because of the verb second constraint (**11.2**). An adverbial in medial position must thus come after the finite verb. In English, however, the second position may well be filled by a short adverbial; compare (11). When the verb phrase is complex, the adverbial is generally placed after the finite auxiliary in both Norwegian and English, as in (12).

11	We *often* go to the theatre.	Vi går *ofte* i teater.
12	I have *already* met them.	Jeg har *allerede* truffet dem.

10.10 Adverbials and types of text

As we stated at the beginning of this chapter, adverbials are extremely frequent in all types of text. However, the nature of the text will influence the kinds of adverbials that occur there. For example, a text which is concerned with concrete events, typically a narrative, tends to contain a lot of references to time and place.

1 In a little house in a little old village in Japan lived a little old man and his little old wife. One morning when the old woman slid open the screens which form the sides of the Japanese houses, she saw on the doorstep a poor little sparrow. She took him up gently and fed him. Then she held him in the bright morning sunshine until the cold dew was dried from his wings. Afterward, she let him go, so that he might fly home to his nest, but he stayed with her to thank her with his songs.

Each morning, when the pink on the mountaintops told that the sun was near, the sparrow perched on the roof of the house and sang out his joy. The old man and woman thanked the sparrow for this, for they liked to be up early and at work. But near them lived a cross old woman who did not like to be awakened so early. At last she became so angry that she caught the sparrow and cut his tongue. Then the poor little sparrow flew away to his home. But he never could sing again.

(From 'The tongue-cut sparrow', Japanese folk tale)

Modal disjuncts, like modal auxiliaries, contribute to making the text tentative. Thus they come in handy when the speaker wants to be indirect and non-assertive, or to avoid making claims about the truth of the statement; see (2), from a news report, and (3), from a fictional text. Incidentally, news reporters often use disjuncts such as *apparently* and *allegedly* when they report crimes which have not yet been tried in court, because otherwise they might be accused of branding a suspect as guilty before he or she has been convicted.

2 The explosion sent the hood of the car flying over the roof of the house. The left front wheel landed 100 feet away. Police laboratory technicians said the explosive device, containing either TNT or nitroglycerin, was *apparently* placed under the left front wheel. It was first believed the bomb was rigged to the car's starter. Gladden had been the target of threatening telephone calls in recent months and *reportedly* received one last night.

3 Liz Peabody, *he thought*, might spend some time grieving for her lost lover, but he doubted that she would launch an investigation. He judged her to be a woman of some pride, though not much sense. Still she would *probably* have sense enough not to call in the local sheriff to find her boyfriend who, *apparently*, had run away.

A text which is argumentative can be expected to contain adjuncts of reason, purpose, and condition, along with fact-evaluating disjuncts, and conjuncts which mark contrasts and logical relations. The following text is an example of this.

4 What has gone wrong? Nothing and everything. Nothing in that, *since our electoral system is dominated by big parties,* there is not much that a new, small party – especially one associated with a sole non-politician such as Sir James – can do. *Even the SDP, with its leadership of four well-known political professionals, and army of defectors from one of the two big parties*, could achieve little in the end. *To avoid the same fate*, there is nothing much the Referendum Party could have done.

But everything has *also* gone wrong. The Referendum Party's private polls apparently showed that Sir James was not very popular, *though in this bland age, that might be a sad reflection on the voters rather than Sir James*. The party *therefore* kept his face and name off its posters. *As a result*, voters fail to connect the posters with him, and *therefore* with anything or anyone in particular, save a fringe party. And at general elections, the British do not vote for fringe parties.

Note

Some spoken examples in this chapter have been taken from the London–Lund Corpus. The examples are reproduced here using a simplified transcription.

Terms

adverb		disjuncts:	modal
adverbial:	adjunct		fact-evaluating
	disjunct		style-evaluating
	conjunct		
		positions:	initial
optional and obligatory adverbials			medial
			end

Exercises

1 Do the adverbs in these sentences function as adverbials or modifiers? If they are modifiers, what do they modify? (**10.2**, **10.3**)

a The highlight of the evening, however, came after the speeches.
b The hotels had improved only slightly since their honeymoon.
c She seemed quite oblivious to the route I was taking.
d 'What?' I said a little too loudly.
e The loss of those accounts was fully explained in the report.
f As you well know, I never drink before dinner.
g I ran upstairs with the paper.

2 Determine whether the adverbials in the following sentences are optional or obligatory. State their realization (adverb, prepositional phrase, etc.), and whether they are adjuncts, disjuncts, or conjuncts. (**10.4**, **10.5**)

a Despite this, women are buying them as well.
b I actually couldn't understand a word of his speech because of his accent.
c He had only comparatively recently emerged from the US Army.
d She usually gets our names wrong.
e He had been out of the house for over a year.
f Where I came from, there were no fields at all.
g They even go there in the winter, you know.
h Generally, thirty years ago, companies were a lot smaller.
i He behaved exactly as I had told him to.
j I probably wouldn't be able to live with myself if I had to lie and twist the truth.

3 Identify the adverbials in the following text and determine whether they are adjuncts, disjuncts, or conjuncts. Remember that adverbial clauses may in turn contain adverbials. (**10.5–10.8**)

In fact, the very name of the Woodstock Festival was a misnomer. The garden of Mitchell's song – a dairy farm owned by a man named Max Yasgur – was actually 60 miles from the town of Woodstock, close to a village named Bethel. The organisers expected 50,000 people. Some 400,000 turned up. The site was officially designated a national disaster area. Lavatories overflowed. There were three deaths, two births, four miscarriages. *The New York Times* described it as 'outrageous'. And yet, miraculously, the mood was beatific, harmonious. And some great myth was born. Woodstock. It meant innocence, idealism, good vibes, man. Or, that hippie nonsense. Some people talked of it for years afterwards, as if it were the only moment they had truly been alive. To others, it would come to mark a nadir in human absurdity. Either way, it began an industry that grew like topsy.

(From Mick Brown, *American Heartbeat*)

4 A number of adverbials have been extracted from the text below and printed in SMALL CAPITALS after the sentence to which they belong. Place each of the expressions in an appropriate position in its sentence. Classify each expression in terms of adjunct, disjunct, or conjunct. (**10.5**, **10.9**)

a Sandy thought this might be an attempt to keep the Brodie set together at the expense of the glimpsed individuality of its members. (NEWLY)
b She turned and said. (IN HER NEW MANNER OF SUDDEN IRRITABILITY), (ON HIM)
c 'We'd look like one big Miss Brodie.' (PROBABLY)
d He laughed and looked at her. (AS IF FOR THE FIRST TIME), (MORE CLOSELY), (IN A DELIGHTED WAY)
e She looked back. (WITH THE NEAR-BLACKMAILING INSOLENCE OF HER KNOWLEDGE), (JUST AS CLOSELY), (THROUGH HER LITTLE EYES)
f He kissed her. (LONG AND WETLY), (YET)
g He said. (IN HIS VERY HOARSE VOICE)
h 'That'll teach you to look at an artist.' (LIKE THAT)

5 Use the conjuncts given below to complete the following text. State the meaning relationship expressed by the conjunct in each case. Each word should be used only once. (**10.8**)

after all, furthermore, incidentally, therefore

Felix was the exception. He had retained his hat and his horn, and, whatever fun might still be going, he was ready to join it. That, _____, might give you some idea of what Felix was like. _____, he hadn't happened upon us in that second-floor hall without warning.

The ME's boys had finished their on-the-spot examination and the body had been removed for autopsy. The meat wagon, _____, was not out in front of the house any more, but the cluster of squad cars was still there and there was a cop on the door downstairs to screen any comings and goings. There was, _____, the crowd of curious onlookers gathered in the street and a couple more cops to hold them at a decent distance.

6 Comment on the difference in form and meaning between the members of the following sentence pairs.

a 1 From Paris Chris wrote postcards to all his friends.
  2 Chris wrote postcards to all his friends from Paris.
b 1 Still, she may be able to do it.
  2 She may still be able to do it.
c 1 Tomorrow we'll arrange with head office to send the forms to Brussels.
  2 We'll arrange with head office to send the forms to Brussels tomorrow.
d 1 We asked them nicely to behave.
  2 We asked them to behave nicely.
e 1 Well, the doctor treated me in the end.
  2 The doctor treated me well in the end.
f 1 We took the signs literally.
  2 We read literally all the signs.
g 1 I mentioned it to him briefly yesterday.
  2 Briefly, I mentioned it to him yesterday.
h 1 Annie will need to finish this job one day.
  2 Annie will need one day to finish this job.

11 Word Order and Related Matters

11.1 The uses of word order

When we speak about word order, we are normally concerned with **constituent order**, i.e. the order of the elements of the clause. Word order is one of the principal means of signalling syntactic structure in English (see **11.1.1**). Within the limits set by grammar, and sometimes overruling purely grammatical principles, word order is also used for other purposes: to mark given vs. new information (**11.1.2**), to produce a desired distribution of weight (**11.1.3**), and to achieve special stylistic effects (see **11.1.4**).

English word order is primarily determined by grammatical principles (except in the case of optional adverbials; see Chapter 10).

11.1.1 Word order as a grammar signal

Word order marks syntactic structure in three main ways.

A Clause elements

The core elements of the clause (subject, verb, objects, predicatives, obligatory adverbials) are typically placed in the following order in relation to each other:

- the subject before the verb;
- the verb before the other core elements of the clause;
- the indirect object before the direct object;
- the direct object before object predicatives and obligatory adverbials.

For examples, see the presentation of the basic clause patterns in Chapter 9.

B Clause type

Word order is also used as a signal of special clause types:

- Interrogative sentences have subject–auxiliary inversion (**11.2.1A**).
- Some conditional clauses are marked by subject–auxiliary inversion (**11.2.4B**).
- *Wh*-interrogative clauses, exclamatory clauses, and relative clauses have the *wh*-element in front position irrespective of its function within the clause (**11.3.1**).

C The proximity principle

Phrases which realize a clause element are not normally broken up. If a sequence of words can be moved as a unit, it is indeed a sign that it is a phrase. Compare the passive and active versions of this example:

1 *This book* will be published by *Scandinavian University Press.*
2 *Scandinavian University Press* will publish *this book.*

There are, however, a number of exceptions to the proximity principle (see **11.5**). In particular, verb phrases are often split by adverbials (note the placement of *often* and *obligatorily* in this sentence), and they are obligatorily split in interrogative sentences (see the text below).

Sample text

In this passage, we have marked the clause elements, both in main clauses and in subordinate clauses. The clause elements are identified by brackets with a label which identifies the function of the element. The order is in agreement with our three grammatical principles, except that verb phrases are split in the interrogative sentences.

> [Chance]$_S$ [turned on]$_V$ [the TV]$_{dO}$. [He]$_S$ [wondered]$_V$ [whether [a person]$_S$ [changed]$_V$ [before or after [appearing]$_V$ [on the screen]$_A$]$_A$]$_{dO}$. [Would]$_v$ [he]$_S$ [be changed]$_V$ [forever]$_A$ or [only]$_A$ [during the time of his appearance]$_A$? [What part of himself]$_{dO}$ [would]$_v$ [he]$_S$ [leave]$_V$ [behind]$_A$ [when [he]$_S$ [finished]$_V$ [the program]$_{dO}$]$_A$?
>
> (From Jerzy Kosinski, *Being There*)

D The role of the auxiliary *do*

The uses of the auxiliary *do* in English may seem multifarious (see **6.4.2B**), yet there is unity in diversity. The auxiliary *do* gives the English clause a regular structure:

- Emphatic affirmation in declarative sentences is expressed in the same position, by stressing an auxiliary preceding the main verb (see **14.2**).
- The negative particle *not* is regularly attached to an auxiliary preceding the main verb (see **14.2.1A**).
- Interrogative sentences regularly have an auxiliary preceding the subject (with the exception taken up in **14.3.1**). Through the insertion of *do*, we get a compromise between inversion and SV-order. The main verb is allowed to keep its place adjacent to its complements.

The *do*-insertion in declarative sentences with subject–auxiliary inversion (**11.2.1B**) can be accounted for in the same way as interrogative sentences. The main verb is allowed to keep its place next to its complements. On the other hand, the auxiliary *do* is not inserted in the case of subject–verb inversion (**11.2.2**), which is found only with intransitive verbs (where there are thus no complements that may be separated from the main verb).

The use of the auxiliary *do* in English can thus be interpreted as a reflection of the dominance of grammatical principles in determining English word order. The main anomaly is that *be* is treated as an auxiliary in all its uses and does not combine with *do* when it is used as a lexical verb (except in imperatives; see **14.4.2**).

11.1.2 The information principle

There is a general tendency to present information within the sentence in the order **given to new**. Information which has been introduced in the preceding text or is retrievable from the context is typically presented early in the clause, and new information is characteristically introduced at the end. This is often referred to as the principle of **end focus**. In our grammar we speak instead of the **information principle**.

The information principle and the grammatical principles frequently work in unison. The subject is very often a pronoun or a definite noun phrase (see also **5.14**):

1 Mrs O'C was somewhat deaf, but otherwise in good health. *She* lived in an old people's home. One night, in January 1979, *she* dreamt vividly, nostalgically, of her childhood in Ireland.

This is the opening of a story. The first sentence, which introduces Mrs O'C, contains new information only. In the second sentence *she* (subject, given information) is chosen as the starting-point, and the third sentence continues with the same subject (placed after an initial time adverbial). The elements presenting new information are placed at the end.

The order of the elements of the clause sometimes follows the information principle rather than the regular grammatical order:

2 *The road* is carried on sets of four concrete columns that march along its 13 miles every 50 ft. *Linking the columns to form the base of the roadway* is a steel deck. *On top of this* is concrete, each section meeting within a fraction of an inch on top of the columns. *Into this gap* is placed a T-shaped buried point. *It* is a composite that looks like rubber and allows the road to expand and contract in different weather conditions. *On top* is the rough asphalt surface.

(From *The Sunday Times*)

Note how consistently this passage is arranged in accordance with the information principle. Each sentence opens with given information, from the subject in the first sentence (*The road*, referring to something already given) to the initial adverbial in the last sentence (*on top*, i.e. *on top of this*). New information is consistently placed at the end, leading to subject–verb inversion in four of the sentences in the passage.

An arrangement in accordance with the information principle gives coherence to the text and at the same time simplifies the task of the speaker and the hearer, in providing a starting-point for speaking and interpretation, and preparing for new information to come. To a large extent, we can use the information principle to explain deviations from the normal order of clause elements, e.g. the subject–verb inversion in (2) above, and to account for the choice of special grammatical structures such as the passive (**11.6**) and clauses with existential *there* (**11.7**).

11.1.3 The principle of end weight

There is a tendency to place relatively long and heavy elements towards the end of the sentence. Since such elements typically carry a high information load, this principle of **end weight** generally pulls in the same direction as the information principle. Frequently there is complete agreement between grammar, weight, and information structure:

1 She lived in an old people's home.

This sentence (taken from example 1 in **11.1.2**) has the regular subject–verb order, and it moves from given to new information, and from light to heavier elements.

As in the case of the information principle, we can use the principle of end weight to account for the choice of special structures, such as extraposition (**11.8**), and to explain deviations from the normal order of clause elements, e.g. postponement (**11.4**):

2 He discussed with Newsweek's Jane Friedman last week his views on the CIA and his plans for a new book.

In (2) the long direct object (*his views ... book*) is postponed to the end, following the two adverbials. A short noun phrase as direct object would have had to follow immediately after the verb (*He discussed them / his plans with* ...). A special advantage of postponing the heavy noun phrase in (2) is that this order prevents a misinterpretation of the sentence. Compare:

3 He discussed his views on the CIA and his plans for a new book with Newsweek's Jane Friedman last week.

Here it is not clear whether the *with*-phrase is an adverbial (in which case the meaning is the same as in the original version) or a postmodifier (referring to a book to be written jointly with Jane Friedman).

11.1.4 Stylistic effect

Departures from the normal grammatical word order are sometimes chosen to achieve some stylistic effect, such as **contrast** or **double focus**. A contrast may be created by putting an element in an unusual position, e.g. by fronting an object:

1 You need me as a respectable front. *That* I can do. But you also want me to risk my reputation.

The contrast is signalled here both by the fronted object and by the conjunction *but* in the following sentence. Both the beginning and the end – the two most prominent positions in the clause – may be exploited to achieve a kind of double focus, as in:

2 Something had to give. And *give* it *did.*

By splitting the verb phrase in this way, the speaker/writer places special focus both on the lexical verb and on the fact that the event actually occurred.

11.2 Inversion

Centuries ago English was predominantly a verb-second language (like present-day Norwegian and the other Scandinavian languages). The verb was generally placed in second position in the clause, whether it was preceded by the subject or some other clause element, in the latter case causing inversion of the subject and the verb.

In present-day English the subject generally stays before the verb – with the exception of interrogative sentences – regardless of whether there is some other preverbal element or not. Nevertheless, inversion does occur also outside interrogative sentences. There are two main types: subject–auxiliary inversion (**11.2.1**) and subject–verb inversion (**11.2.2**). The two types may also be referred to as partial inversion and full inversion, respectively. Both are triggered by some element other than the subject which is placed in clause-initial position. Yet the uses of the two types are quite different.

11.2.1 Subject–auxiliary inversion

A Interrogative sentences

In interrogative sentences the subject is obligatorily preceded by an auxiliary (except where the subject is a *wh*-word). If there is no other auxiliary, *do* is inserted. Note that the verb *be* behaves like an auxiliary in all its uses, and that the lexical verb *have* sometimes behaves like an auxiliary in British English.

1 *Is it* really true? It's true, *isn't it*? (copular *be*)
2 Where *are you* going? (progressive auxiliary *be*)
3 *Have* you (got) any money? (lexical *have*)
4 Who *did she* see? (*who* as direct object)
5 *Who saw* her? (*who* as subject)

There is no inversion in (5), where the *wh*-word is the subject.

B Declarative sentences

Subject–auxiliary inversion is also found in declarative sentences opening with a negative or restrictive element, such as *never*, *hardly*, *scarcely*, *rarely*, *seldom*, *only*, *under no circumstances* (the elements triggering inversion are italicized in the examples below):

6 *Never* had I seen such a terrible sight.
7 *Under no circumstances* must you reveal the secret.
8 *Only in the first act* did tension sag.

Note that the auxiliary *do* must be inserted in (8). For inversion to occur, the negation must affect the whole sentence. Thus there is no inversion in examples like:

9 *Not many minutes later* the plane landed in Paris.

10 *Not surprisingly*, they won the match.
11 *Only yesterday* I saw her.

In (9) and (10) the main body of the sentence expresses a positive statement. In (11) *only* means 'as late as' and does not have its ordinary restrictive meaning.

Opening elements containing the degree adverb *so* followed by an adjective or adverb also cause inversion:

12 *So unhappy* was he that he burst into tears.
13 *So graciously* did she dance that everyone watched her with admiration.

Declarative sentences with subject–auxiliary inversion are usually stylistically marked and are characteristic of a literary or rhetorical style. The exception is the inversion after the linking words *neither*, *nor*, and *so*, which is common in colloquial English:

14 Ole doesn't like spaghetti. *Nor/neither* does \`KARI.
15 Ole hates spaghetti. *So* does \`KARI.
16 A: Ole hates spaghetti.
   B: *So* he \`DOES.

In (14) and (15) the sentences opening with *nor/neither* and *so* express a comparison. The main focus is on the subject. In (16), on the other hand, the main focus is on the verb. Speaker B agrees with the statement of the previous speaker.

All uses of subject–auxiliary inversion in declarative sentences carry a kind of **double focus**: normal end focus and focus on the initial element triggering the inversion. There is an emphatic effect (cf. **11.1.4**). Test the difference by choosing a paraphrase without inversion in the examples above.

11.2.2 Subject–verb inversion

Subject–verb inversion occurs most typically under the following circumstances:

- The sentence opens with an adverbial, often a locative expression giving the background or setting of a situation (e.g. *here*, *there*). The initial element often expresses given information and has a connective function in the text.
- There is an intransitive lexical verb, often denoting position or motion (e.g *be*, *stand*, *sit*, *lie*, *run*, *jump*).
- The subject is normally heavier than the verb (and is never an unstressed pronoun) and often introduces new information.

In other words, structures with subject–verb inversion conform to the information principle and the principle of end weight. Examples (the triggering element is italicized; see also example 2 in **11.1.2**):

1 *Here* comes the winner of the game. (Cf. Here she comes.)
2 A cordon of police officers was formed on each side of the exit. *Behind the cordon* was a line of pickets.
3 *On one of the walls* hung a row of family portraits.
4 *Then* came the turning point of the match.

But *not*:

5 *Here comes she.
*Now had that moment arrived.
*In the shop bought Jean a record.

Note also subject–verb inversion after adverbial particles denoting direction:

6 *Out* darted a ˋRABBIT. (Cf. Out it ˋDARTED.)
7 *Up* flew the BALˋLOON. (Cf. Up it ˋFLEW.)

The structure in (6) and (7) has a dramatic effect. Note how the focus shifts depending upon the order of the subject and the verb. This type of structure is used in dramatic narration, particularly in fiction, to draw attention to a sudden change or event.

Subject–verb inversion is further found after fronted subject predicatives (see **11.3.2B**).

11.2.3 Inversion in reporting clauses

Reporting clauses following, or in the middle of, direct speech may have inversion provided that:

- the subject is a full noun phrase (not a pronoun) and
- there is a simple lexical verb (without an auxiliary).

Examples:

1 'I don't understand', said Ford / Ford said. (but only: he said)
2 'This film', remarked the critic / the critic remarked, 'is the best I have ever seen.' (but only: he remarked)

A reporting clause preceding direct speech normally has subject–verb order, though inversion does occur, particularly in journalese.

3 Says commander Mervyn McCord: 'There has grown up a regimental tradition ...'

11.2.4 Inversion in subordinate clauses

A Indirect questions

The form of an indirect question sometimes reflects the order of the corresponding direct question, though pronouns and verb forms are changed as compared with direct speech:

1 She asked whether she could do anything.
2 She asked *could she* do anything. (Cf. Can I do anything?)
3 ... that was what brought them every two minutes to the banisters to ask Lily *had Gabriel or Freddy* come. (Cf. Has Gabriel or Freddy come?)

The pattern illustrated in (1) is the normal one; the one in (2) and (3) is characteristic of free indirect speech (**16.9.3**).

B Conditional clauses

Conditional clauses are sometimes marked by inversion rather than by a conjunction:

4 *Should anyone* phone, tell them I am not at home.
5 *Had I* known, I would have come earlier.

Such inversion is restricted in English to clauses opening with *had*, *should*, and *were*. Norwegian allows a much wider range of verbs. Compare:

6 *If you can* prove it, I'd be very grateful.
Kan du bevise det, vil jeg være takknemlig.
7 *If she went* straight down the street now, she would meet Jan.
Gikk hun rett nedover gaten nå, ville hun møte Jan.

In examples like (6) and (7), English uses an ordinary conditional clause.

C Comparative clauses

Comparative clauses introduced by *as* and *than* sometimes have inversion:

8 His new book is not as well written as (was) his last one.

9 Present-day English uses inversion less often than (did) Old English.

Note that the subject is heavier and more informative than the verb (which can often be omitted). Subject–verb order is also possible here: *as his last one was, as Old English did.*

11.2.5 Other special cases of inversion

Inversion is found in a small number of more or less set expressions:

1 Far be it from me to ...
Suffice it to say that ...
Be that as it may ... } (formal)
So help me God.
So be it.
2 Enter the King. (stage direction)

Note the subjunctive verb forms. Such expressions are restricted in use in present-day English.

Inversion is normal in wishes and maledictions opening with *may*, and in imperative sentences with an expressed subject:

4 May it not be true!
5 May an anti-hygiene group declare your house a shrine! (from the comic strip *BC*, 'The Curse Exchange')
6 Don't you ever mention this to anyone!

11.3 Fronting

By fronting in this context we understand clause-initial placement of objects, predicatives, and other core elements which are normally found in postverbal position. As regards optional adverbials, see Chapter 10.

11.3.1 *Wh*-clauses

Fronting is completely normal in clauses introduced by *wh*-words, whether these are relative clauses (1), indirect questions (2), *wh*-questions (3), or exclamations (4).

1 At the party I met a boy *whom* I had known at school. (Cf. I knew him at school.)

2 I know *what* you want. (Cf. I want this.)
3 *What* do you want? (Cf. I want this.)
4 *What a lovely day* we had yesterday! (Cf. We had a lovely day yesterday.)
5 *Such a dear boy* he is! (Cf. What a dear boy he is!)
6 *Fine brother* I've got, don't you think? (Cf. What a fine brother I've got!)

As the last two examples show, fronting in exclamations extends beyond sentences opening with a *wh*-word. Note the ironic effect in (6).

A Deeply embedded *wh*-elements

The fronted *wh*-element may belong to a finite (7) or non-finite (8) subordinate clause:

7 This is something *which* I thought I would never see.
8 *Who* did you say you were going to meet?

In (7) *which* is the object of *see*, and in (8) *who* is the object of *meet*. Note the difference between English and Norwegian in examples of the following kind:

9 He bought a book whose author I don't know.
Han kjøpte en bok *som* jeg ikke vet hvem (som) har skrevet.
10 Who did she ask you to invite?
Hvem spurte hun deg om hun skulle invitere?

To convey Norwegian examples of this kind (with a so-called *setningsknute*), we must choose a simpler structure.

B Stranded prepositions

When a *wh*-word is fronted, a preposition is often 'stranded' at the end of the clause:

11 ?*Of whom* are you afraid?
Who are you afraid *of*?
12 *To whom* did you give the letter? (formal)
Who did you give the letter *to*?
13 *In which place* was the murder committed?
?Which place was the murder committed *in*?
14 The book *to which* you refer is out of print. (formal)
The book (which/that) you refer *to* is out of print.
15 Moreland sat brooding for a full minute, *during which* I made each of us a new drink.
*... which I made each of us a new drink *during*.

The choice of structure is partly dependent upon the function of the prepositional phrase and partly upon style. Where the prepositional phrase functions as an adverbial, the preposition tends to precede the *wh*-element (13, 15). Preposition stranding is normal where the preposition is closely tied to a preceding word (e.g. *afraid* in 11, *refer* in 14). It is also the more informal option.

11.3.2 Fronting in main clauses of declarative sentences

In main clauses of declarative sentences, fronting is an infrequent option in English compared with Norwegian (except for optional adverbials; see Chapter 10). This is easy to understand if we consider the overall pattern of English vs. Norwegian word order. Compare these patterns:

English:	SVdO	Norwegian:	SVdO
	dOSV		dOVS
Examples:	I like this.		Jeg liker dette.
	This I like.		Dette liker jeg.

As the subject has to stay before the verb in English, the opening of a clause with a fronted object becomes heavier than in Norwegian. In Norwegian, which is a verb-second language (see the beginning of **11.2**), the verb keeps its central position, and the structure is more balanced.

The difference in frequency is correlated with a typical difference in effect. In Norwegian, elements are characteristically placed in initial position for the purposes of cohesion, i.e. the sentences open with given information in accordance with the information principle. Fronting in English, on the other hand, often carries some special effect above and beyond facilitating cohesion.

A Fronting of objects and deeply embedded noun phrases

Fronting of non-subject noun phrases is far less common in English than in Norwegian. Compare:

1 (Where does he come from?) I don't know.
Det vet jeg ikke.

2 I didn't know (*that*).
Det visste jeg ikke.

3 But I guess you don't need to tell me *that*.
Men *det* trenger du ikke fortelle meg.

4 One cannot escape *the facts*.
Kjensgjerningene kommer vi ikke forbi.

5 *This* is none of your business.
Dette har du ikke noe med.
6 *The name of the firm he was looking for* was not immediately visible.
Det firmanavnet han lette etter, fant han ikke med en gang.

There are several ways of translating Norwegian sentences with fronted objects. A fronted 'det', which is very common in Norwegian, often has no counterpart in English (1, 2), or it may be rendered by a postverbal pronoun (2, 3). A full noun phrase may be placed after the verb (4), or the translator may find a structure which preserves the same order as in the source language (5, 6).

Where fronting does occur in English, it typically signals contrast or double focus:

7 She could claim the room for her own now. *This*, however, she had no desire to do.
8 He was allowed one pint of beer; *the potato crisps* he had to buy himself.
9 You don't believe that Christ personally heard somebody's prayer, do you? – No, *that* I don't. (Cf. No, I don't (believe that).)
10 *What has happened here*, I never thought I would ever live to see. (Cf. I never thought I would ever live to see what has happened here.)

We find a clear contrast in (7), underlined by the conjunct *however*, and in (8), where we could easily insert the conjunction *but*. The effect in (9) is one of double focus; both the object pronoun and the negated verb are made prominent. There is a similar effect in (10). Note how the effect is lost if we change the order.

At the same time as there is a special effect, the fronting is also in agreement with the information principle. Note the markers of given information in the examples: the demonstrative pronouns in (7) and (9), the definite noun phrase in (8), and the adverb *here* in (10). If we choose the normal grammatical order, we also reduce the marking of cohesion.

B Fronting of predicatives

Subject predicatives in initial position often contain a reference to the preceding text, frequently in the form of a comparative expression (11, 12):

11 It is a pleasant occasion. It is pleasant, for instance, to see ... *No less pleasant* is the general air of slightly astonished efficiency ... *Most pleasant of all* is the enthusiasm.
12 *Just as disturbing* is the likely effect of the ever-warming greenhouse on the Arctic region.

13 *Present at the meeting* were the Prime Minister, the Secretary of State, and three members of Congress.

Because of the subject–verb inversion, we have a balanced distribution of the clause elements, and we lack the special focus associated with object fronting. The fronting clearly marks cohesion and is in agreement with the information principle, with end focus on the subject.

Fronting of predicatives may, however, also be used for contrast and double focus:

14 Most people still tend to feel that sport should be untainted by politics, and so did many at the table tennis tournament. But *political it was*, and not simply because ...
15 The Galbraith show is always entertaining; it's sometimes provocative and occasionally inventive, too, but *a lesson in economics it is not*.

Here we have personal pronouns as subjects, and there is no inversion. The contrast is underlined by the conjunction *but*. There is a double focus: on the fronted predicative and on the clause-final element (*was* in 14, *not* in 15).

If the normal order is chosen in examples like (14) and (15), the special effect is lost in writing, though it could easily be expressed in speech (cf. Chapter 16). The same effect can be retained with the normal grammatical order, both in speech and in writing, if we insert the adverb *really*: *it really was political; but it really isn't a lesson in economics*.

C Fronting of postmodifiers

Postmodifiers in noun phrases can be fronted in examples like (see also **9.8.6**):

16 There were 30 participants. *Of these* 15 were men, and 15 women. (Or: Fifteen of them ...)
17 There were 30 participants, *of whom* 15 were men, and 15 women. (Or: 15 of whom ...)

The fronting in (16) conforms to the information principle; in (17) it is conditioned by the *wh*-element. In both cases there is an alternative order without fronting.

11.4 Postponement

Fronting and inversion both affect the beginning of the sentence. There is far less variation after the verb. Deviations from the normal grammatical order are generally in agreement with the information principle and/or the principle of end weight.

A The direct object and the object predicative
A complex object may be placed after the object predicative:

1 He proved wrong all those who had predicted that he could not win the election. (Cf. He proved them wrong.)

Note that this order eases the interpretation of the structure (see **11.1.3**). If the object predicative is placed in its normal position, the overall structure is not revealed until the reader reaches the last word of the sentence.

B The direct object of phrasal verbs
A personal pronoun is obligatorily placed before the particle (2) of phrasal verbs (**6.3.3C**). A short noun-headed phrase may precede or follow the particle (3, 4). When the object is realized by a very long noun phrase, it is normally placed at the end of the clause (5).

2 She *took* it *off*.
3 She *took off* her hat.
4 She *took* her hat *off*.
5 Yesterday I *called up* a friend I hadn't seen for ten years.

The order in (5) eases the interpretation of the structure in much the same way as the pattern in (1) above.

C The direct and the indirect object
Many ditransitive verbs allow two alternative patterns, one with an indirect plus a direct object, the other with a direct object plus a prepositional phrase. The alternative with a preposition is what we referred to as an oblique object in **9.8.2A**.

6 She gave me a new book on biology.
7 She gave it to her best friend.
8 She gave it to me. (Also: She gave it me, BrE; She gave me it, AmE)

The pattern in (6) is preferred where the direct object is longer and more informative than the indirect object. The prepositional pattern tends to be chosen in examples like (7) and (8).

D Postponement of postmodifiers
A relative clause does not always follow immediately after its antecedent (see e.g. example 6 in **12.6.2**). Other postmodifiers may also be split off from a complex noun phrase (see also **9.8.6**):

9 A fascinating account is given in the book *of the author's adventures during his travels in South America.*

Note how front-heavy the sentence becomes if the postmodifier is placed immediately after the head noun. Alternative ways of ordering the information, without postponement, would be to choose *the book* or *the author* as subject (*The book gives a fascinating account of ..., The author gives a fascinating account of his adventures ...*).

11.5 Discontinuous structures

In spite of the proximity principle (**11.1.1C**), discontinuous structures do occur. Verb phrases are regularly split in connection with subject–auxiliary inversion (**11.2.1**); adverbials may be placed between auxiliary and main verb (**10.9.1B**). Separation of the two parts of phrasal verbs is also a common occurrence (**11.4B**).

Other phrase types are much more rarely split up. It is possible to front and postpone postmodifiers of noun phrases under special circumstances (**11.3.2C**, **11.4D**). Complex adjective phrases may also be split (**8.11**). A type of discontinuous structure which has come in for criticism from prescriptive grammarians is the **split infinitive**, where an adverbial is placed between the infinitive marker *to* and its infinitive (see **13.4.2**).

11.6 The passive

The passive provides a systematic means of selecting a participant other than the agent as the starting-point for the message, without departing from the ordinary subject–verb order. As the term suggests, the subject is passive and typically denotes an affected participant, i.e. the role usually expressed by the direct object (cf. **9.3.2**, **9.3.3**).

Most clauses with an active transitive verb have passive counterparts:

1 The hunter shot the moose. (SVdO)
The moose was shot (by the hunter). (SV(A))
2 The board will offer Ann a new job. (SViOdO)
Ann will be offered a new job (by the board). (SVdO(A))
A new job will be offered (to) Ann (by the board). (SViO(A))
3 The teacher put the books on the desk. (SVdOA)
The books were put on the desk (by the teacher). (SVA(A))
4 The security guard found the door open. (SVdOoP)
The door was found open (by the security guard). (SVsP(A))

Note the following structural differences between the active and passive versions:

- The direct object in the active clause corresponds to the subject in the passive version. Where there is both a direct and an indirect object, there are two passive counterparts (2). The version where the indirect object has become the subject is the more common one.
- The main verb in the active clause is replaced by a passive verb phrase, with the auxiliary *be* (in the same tense as the active verb) + the past participle of the main verb.
- The subject in the active clause corresponds to a *by*-phrase with agent adverbial function in the passive version, or it is left out.

Compare:	The hunter	shot	the moose.
	The moose	was shot	by the hunter.

There are two main types of passives, the agentless **short passive (11.6.1)** and the **long passive (11.6.2)**, with an expressed agent. The choice of these is not random, but is intimately connected with the context of use.

11.6.1 The short passive

The great majority of passives, about 90 per cent, do not contain an agent phrase. The main reason why the short passive is chosen is exactly that it is not possible or desirable to specify an agent:

1 The rest of the apartment was in a state of disorder as violent as what they had found in the kitchen. Cushions *had been removed* from the sofa and *slashed* open, the stuffing *pulled out* and *thrown* onto the floor. The sofa and all the upholstered chairs in the room *had been overturned* ... It seemed evident, if not obvious, that someone had been looking for something. (from a description of a crime scene)
2 Alterations *were being made* to the Physics Laboratory.
3 His bedroom *could* only *be approached* by way of a large bathroom.

Though the agent is unexpressed, the situation referred to is presented as involving an agent. In (1) the agent is obviously unknown; note the indefinite pronoun *someone* in the last sentence. In (2) it is irrelevant who was in charge of the alterations. Example (3) is a statement about the accessibility of the bedroom; the *by*-phrase here expresses the means of reaching the bedroom, and it is immaterial who the agent is.

Note the tactful avoidance of the agent in (4) and the indication of agency through an adverb in (5):

4 Enough has been said here of this matter. (= by the author/chair)
5 Their ideas are not universally accepted. (= by everybody)

The passive can easily be abused, as it makes it possible to leave out critical information:

6 I am told that Senator X has accepted bribes.
7 Senator X has been accused of accepting bribes.
8 The information cannot be revealed yet.

In (6) and (7) there is no indication of who is responsible for the information. The accusation in (7) could just as well derive from a personal enemy as from an investigating body. In (8) it is not clear who is withholding the information.

11.6.2 The long passive

The long passive is generally chosen in accordance with the information principle and the principle of end weight. The subject is typically short and expresses given information; the agent phrase is heavy and introduces new information:

1 This prediction is made by leaders of Britain's welfare charities.
2 When he retired in 1974, his place was taken by Sir Kenneth Berrill, a Cambridge economist who ...
3 The caverns were discovered by a cowboy who saw a huge cloud of bats come out of a hole in the ground.
4 The Prime Minister stepped off the plane and was immediately surrounded by journalists.

Note the long agent phrases in (1) to (3) and the signals of given information in the subject noun phrases: the demonstrative determiner in (1), the possessive determiner in (2), and the definite article in (3). In (4) the agent phrase is short, but the choice of the passive is in agreement with the information principle and is a convenient means of continuing with the same subject.

11.6.3 Some complications

There is not a passive version available for every clause with a direct object.

A The verb

Certain transitive verbs are excluded from passive constructions, particularly *have*, *lack*, and *resemble* (as well as *fit*, *suit*, and *become*):

1 She has a new flat.
2 He lacks courage.
3 Peter resembles Paul.

Non-passive verbs are typically stative and do not involve a genuinely affected participant. In dynamic senses *have* can be used in the passive:

4 Eggs can be had in the shop on the corner. (= obtained)
5 She is not easily had. (= made a fool of)

B Phrasal and prepositional verbs

The passive is available with many complex verbs:

6 The conference has been put off until next year.
7 The old woman is cared for by a nurse.

The passive is freely used with transitive phrasal verbs, as in (6). With prepositional verbs, the passive construction is more likely if there is a clearly affected subject, as in (7). Occasionally, a passive version is even found in cases where the active counterpart would have an intransitive verb plus an adverbial, as in (8). Note that there is a notion of affectedness here as well (= *this bed has not been used*).

8 This bed has never been slept in.
Cf. Nobody has ever slept in this bed.

C *Get*-passives

Though *be* is the regular passive auxiliary, we also find passives with *get* in colloquial English (see also **6.4.4C**):

9 They got invited to the party.
10 She got mugged in the middle of Oslo.

Get is normally restricted to short passives. Unlike *be*-passives, which may be either stative or dynamic (**11.6.4A**), *get*-passives are always dynamic.

D The object

The passive is excluded with certain types of direct object: deverbal nouns (11), cognate objects which refer to an action indicated by the verb (12), reflexive and reciprocal pronouns (13, 14), and infinitives without a subject of their own (15).

11 She needs a good wash.
12 They live a peaceful life.
13 He cut himself. / He cut his hand.
14 They love each other. / They hate each other's guts.
15 They hope/expect/promise/want etc. to leave.

E Negation and quantifiers

Sentences containing negative expressions and quantifiers often do not have straightforward active and passive counterparts.

16 People have not done anything.
   *Anything has not been done.
17 Nothing is considered to be beautiful by all peoples everywhere. Every revered object is considered ugly by someone, somewhere.
   *All peoples everywhere consider nothing to be beautiful. Someone, somewhere, considers every revered object to be ugly.

In (16) a passive counterpart would have to take the form *Nothing has been done*. To express (17) in active form, one would have to say something like:

18 There is nothing which all peoples everywhere consider to be beautiful. For every revered object, there is someone, somewhere, who considers it to be ugly.

11.6.4 Differences between English and Norwegian

While passives in English are formed with the auxiliary *be*, Norwegian (like the other Scandinavian languages) has both an inflectional *s*-passive and a passive formed by auxiliary plus verb. Compare: *is made* vs. 'lages', 'er/blir laget'. The three differences taken up below may cause problems for Norwegian learners of English.

A Stative passives

Many English *be* + past participle constructions express a stative, rather than a dynamic, relationship. Compare:

1 The door was closed by the security guard. (= 'ble lukket') dynamic?

2 The door was closed when we arrived. (= 'var lukket')

The dynamic passive focuses on the action expressed by the verb; the stative passive, on the resultant state.

Stative passives are best analysed as SVsP constructions (**9.3.5**). A great many stative *-ed* forms refer to a state of mind, especially an emotional state: *alarmed, amazed, amused, astonished, bored*, etc. They are typically used with personal subjects and are often followed by prepositional phrases: *alarmed at, bored with*, etc.

Stative passives are more common with action verbs in Norwegian than in English and must often be rendered by an English dynamic form (with a change of tense):

3 The picture *was taken* in Oslo.
Bildet *er tatt* i Oslo.
4 The ship *was built* in Gothenburg.
Fartøyet *er bygd* i Göteborg.
5 The letter *has been sent* already.
Brevet *er* allerede *sendt*.
6 You have heard that your employer *has been murdered*?
De har hørt at Deres arbeidsgiver *er myrdet*?
7 The former reading room *has* now *been rebuilt* into offices.
Den tidligere lesesalen *er* nå *bygd om* til kontorer.

As these examples show, there is a greater tendency in Norwegian than in English to focus on the resultant state of actions.

B Complex passives

The passive is freely used with *that*-clauses in extraposition (**11.8**):

8 It is hoped that compulsory primary education will cover all children in the 6 to 11 age-group.
9 It was agreed that they should pick me up after the performance.

English allows an embedded noun phrase to be 'raised' to subject position in the superordinate clause in examples like:

10 People expect her to arrive tomorrow.
She is expected to arrive tomorrow.
11 Everybody believes her to be honest.
She is believed to be honest.

Note also *be said to, be supposed to, be rumoured to, be reputed to,* which have no straightforward active counterparts.

Norwegian double passive constructions of the following kind do not have exact English equivalents:

12 It is proposed that the measures should take effect from the autumn.
Tiltakene *foreslås iverksatt* fra høsten av.
13 An attempt is being made to break down the leader's resistance.
Lederens motstand *forsøkes brutt ned.*

Typical verbs in such Norwegian constructions are 'anta', 'melde', 'vente', 'forsøke', 'ønske', 'kreve', 'foreslå'.

C Norwegian 'det'-passives

Unlike English, Norwegian allows passives with intransitive verbs. The dummy subject 'det' replaces an agentive subject:

14 Lørdag møttes drosjeeierne fra hele distriktet. *Det ble pratet* om alt fra kjøring av jenter med brukne ben til fremtidens drosje. Mellom munnfuller med stek *ble det sunget og diskutert.*

In English we must resort to an active construction or to a clause with existential *there*: *they talked about, there was singing and discussion.*

The dummy subject 'det' may also replace agentive subjects of transitive verbs:

15 Horrible rumours about him were being spread about.
Det ble satt ut de verste rykter om ham.
16 Four new pumps were provided.
Det ble skaffet til veie fire nye pumper.

English uses an ordinary passive construction with a full noun phrase in subject position, except in expressions of the type *it is expected/said/rumoured that ...*, with anticipatory *it* and a clausal subject in extraposition (**11.8**).

11.7 Existential *there*

Existential *there* is a formal device used to predicate the existence or occurrence of something. It differs from the locative adverb *there* in the following respects:

- phonologically, it is normally reduced to /ðə(r)/;

- the original locative meaning is lost;
- syntactically it functions as a grammatical subject rather than as an adverbial.

Most typically, a clause with existential *there* has the following structure:

there	+	*be*	+	indefinite NP	(+ place adverbial)
aS		V		S	A

Existential *there* serves as an anticipatory subject. The indefinite noun phrase is often called the notional subject. We use *aS* for the anticipatory subject and a capital *S* for the **notional subject**. The place adverbial is optional and is placed within parentheses.

Examples (1) and (2) both contain two instances of existential *there* and one example of locative *there*:

1 *There*'s somebody *there* (e.g. at the door), isn't *there*?
2 *There* are two cars *there* (e.g. in the garage), aren't *there*?
3 *There's* apples in the kitchen if you want one.

Locative *there* is normally placed in final position, like place adverbials in general. Existential *there* takes the same position as other subjects. The notional subject determines concord with the verb (1, 2). In colloquial English there is a strong tendency, however, to use the form *there's*, irrespective of the number of the notional subject (3); see **9.10.1**.

11.7.1 Discourse function

The main function of existential clauses is to present new entities into the discourse. As existential *there* serves to delay and prepare the ground for new information (expressed in the notional subject), its use is in agreement with the information principle (**11.1.2**). The fairy-tale opening is well known:

1 Once upon a time there were three bears ... They all went for a walk down the woods ...

As in this example, the sentence with existential *there* often serves as a springboard in telling a story. At other times, it is used to describe a scene:

2 Breakfast was the best meal of the day in our hotel, and it was all laid out on a huge table in the middle of the dining-room from which you helped yourself. There were maybe fifty dishes to choose from on that table. There were large jugs of milk, which all Norwegian children drink at every

> meal. There were plates of cold beef, veal, ham, and pork. There was cold boiled mackerel submerged in aspic. There were ...
>
> (From Roald Dahl, *Boy: Tales of a Childhood*)

Constructions of this kind are usually called **presentative constructions** (*presenteringskonstruksjoner*).

11.7.2 Some complications

A The verb

Although *be* is by far the most frequent verb in existential clauses, we also find other verbs denoting existence or appearance, e.g. *be*, *exist*, *live*, *sit*, *stand*, *come*, *go*, *remain*, *appear*, *emerge*, *begin*, *develop*, *occur*. Note, however, that the range of verbs is much smaller than in Norwegian 'det'-constructions (**11.10B**).

1 Once upon a time there lived a king who had three sons.
2 There appeared/emerged a strange, three-headed monster.

The existential verb may be preceded by hedging expressions of different kinds, as in (3) and (4):

3 There seems to be a mistake here.
4 There is likely to be a rush at the office.
5 There's no milk in the fridge.

By using the hedging expressions *seem* and *be likely to*, the speaker avoids making a categorical statement, but (3) and (4) clearly have the features of existential clauses: *there*, *be*, indefinite noun phrase, place adverbial. Needless to say, the speaker can also make a negative assertion (5).

B The notional subject

The notional subject is often followed by a postmodifying clause, frequently an *-ing* participle clause:

6 There's a man waiting at the door.
7 There was a plan worked out by a firm of consultants in Leeds.
8 There are three things (which) I want to do.

Although the notional subject is typically an indefinite noun phrase, we also find definite notional subjects:

9 There's the family next door; we mustn't forget to invite them.
10 This evening there were matters more grave to brood upon than Roy's showing off for his uncle. There was the uncle himself, whose secret had finally been revealed; there was Ellie, who knew the secret; there was Mrs Sowerby, who did not; and there was herself.
11 There was this Peruvian pilot a million years ago, a young lieutenant colonel who ... (opening of chapter in a novel)

A speaker may use a definite notional subject to remind the addressee (or himself/herself) of the existence of some known person or entity (9). Definite noun phrases in existential clauses occur quite often when there is a series of elements to be introduced (10). Example (11) illustrates a type commonly found in telling a story in conversation. The noun phrase is formally definite, but *this* means much the same as the indefinite article. The role of the demonstrative determiner is to create a feeling of familiarity (see also **5.3.D**).

C The place adverbial

A statement of existence or coming into existence typically, but not necessarily, combines with a place adverbial (normally in end position; see the examples above). Initial position suggests that the place has already been brought into the discourse. Compare:

12 There is a telephone in the kitchen.
13 In the kitchen there is a telephone.

The first answers the question *Where can I find a telephone?*; the second, *What's in the kitchen?* Place adverbials may be missing because the place is irrelevant or implicit:

14 There are no unicorns (in the world).
15 There's no bus (to Oslo).
16 There remains one more unsolved problem (here).

D Modal constructions

Existential clauses of the following kind have a modal meaning:

17 There's no knowing where this will end. (= it's not possible to know ...)

11.8 Dummy *it*

It is used as a dummy subject anticipating a following finite or non-finite clause in examples like:

1 It is obvious that we have made a mistake.
Cf. That we have made a mistake is obvious.
2 It is illegal to drive over 70 mph.
Cf. To drive over 70 mph is illegal.
3 It is no use telling him that.
Cf. Telling him that is no use.

It in these constructions is generally referred to as an **anticipatory subject**. The clause is said to be in **extraposition**. A clause with anticipatory *it* often has the following structure:

it	+	*be*	+	adjective	+	finite nom. clause
		seem		indefinite NP		infinitive clause
						-ing clause
aS		V		sP		S

The use of the anticipatory subject is in accordance with the information principle (**11.1.2**) and the principle of end weight (**11.1.3**). Variants without extraposition are possible (see above), except in examples like:

4 It seems that they can't stand it any longer.
*That they can't stand it any longer seems.
5 It is believed that they went down with the ship immediately after the collision.
*That they went down with the ship immediately after the collision is believed.

The verb phrases here are not informative enough to appear in final position, unless we add some expansion: *seems obvious, is widely believed.*

It can also anticipate a clausal object. In such cases there is no alternative to extraposition.

6 He owes it to her to apologize for his behaviour.
7 They found it odd that nobody had inquired into the matter.

Again the use is in agreement with the information principle and the principle of end weight.

Dummy *it* is also found as an empty subject in clauses about weather, time, temperature, and distance:

8 It is raining/sunny/cloudy.
9 It is ten o'clock.
10 It's a long way to Tipperary.

Empty *it* is inserted where there are no participants to fill the obligatory subject slot.

11.9 Clefting

Clefting is a syntactic focusing device by which a clause is broken up into two parts, each with its own verb. There are two main types: ***it*-clefts** (2) and ***wh*-clefts** (3). The focused elements are italicized in the examples below.

1 I want a book. (SVdO)
2 It's *a book* I want. (SVsP)
3 What I want is *a book*. (SVsP)

It is obviously possible to highlight *a book* in (1) by phonological means. In (2) and (3) the syntactic structures make it quite clear that the speaker/writer wants a book and nothing else (and in speech there is in fact a double marking of focus, as *a book* attracts the nuclear tone). The rest of the statement is downgraded into a subordinate clause, in (2) within the sP, and in (3) within the S.

It-clefts consist of (i) the pronoun *it*; (ii) a form of the verb *be*, optionally accompanied by the negator *not* or an adverb like *only*; (iii) the focused element; and (iv) a relative-like subordinate clause introduced by *that*, *who/which*, or zero. The focused element is usually a noun phrase (2), a prepositional phrase (4), or an adverb phrase (5).

4 It was *from Francis* that she first heard the news.
5 It is *tomorrow* we are going to have a picnic.

The *it*-cleft is typically contrastive: it was from Francis and nobody else, it is tomorrow and no other day.

Wh-clefts consist of (i) a clause introduced by a *wh*-word, usually *what*; (ii) a form of the verb *be*; and (iii) the focused element. The focused element is usually a noun phrase (3) or a finite or non-finite nominal clause (6, 7).

6 What you're saying in effect is *that the pipeline is the sole means of life-support in those parts.*
7 What I want you to do is *come right up the road to Hangman's Turn.*

The *wh*-cleft provides a means of preparing the addressee for new information, without making it explicitly contrastive. The *wh*-clause typically contains given information. The focused element is placed where the most important information usually goes, i.e. at the end (**11.1.2**).

11.9.1 A comparison of *it*-clefts and *wh*-clefts

It-clefts and *wh*-clefts are not equivalent as focusing devices. Only *it*-clefts can focus on a prepositional phrase and an adverb phrase; only *wh*-clefts can focus on a nominal clause. The focused element in *it*-clefts is characteristically short, and the subordinate clause may be very long; the opposite is true of *wh*-clefts (see the examples above). With both types of cleft, special advantage is taken of the final position, which can accommodate long and complex constituents. There are also important differences in discourse function:

- *Wh*-clefts are especially common in conversation. The *wh*-clause contains given information, either information which is retrievable from the preceding text or information which the speaker can assume to be in the hearer's consciousness. The association between *wh*-clefts and conversation probably has to do with the low information content that we typically find in the *wh*-clause. A speaker may use a *wh*-clause to summarize something that has just been said or as a springboard in starting a new utterance: *what I think ... / what I want to say ... / what we need ... / what this means is that ...*
- *It*-clefts commonly occur in both speech and writing. There are two main types, each with a distinct distribution of information. Compare:

1 Who broke the window? – It was Tom (who did it).
2 The word photography was first used in 1839, and it was in that year, too, that Louis J. M. Daguerre revealed to the French Academy that an image formed on a silvered metal plate covered with a thin film of silver iodide could be developed in the presence of mercury vapor.

In (1) the new information is expressed in the element following *be*, and the subordinate clause can be left out altogether; in (2) the focused element is anaphoric, and the new information is expressed in the subordinate clauses. Since it is included in a subordinate clause, the new information is marked as known, as something which is not at issue. It has been pointed out that such clefts are characteristic of written texts where the writer does not wish to take personal responsibility for the truth or originality of the statement.

11.9.2 Clefting in English vs. Norwegian

English and Norwegian have similar types of cleft constructions, which nevertheless have somewhat different conditions of use. Clefts are used more frequently in Norwegian than in English, particularly in interrogative sentences:

1 What's happened?
Hva er det som er hendt?
2 Who painted that picture?
Hvem er det som har malt dette bildet?

Ordinary Norwegian clefts correspond to so-called **reversed *wh*-clefts** in English, which most often consist of a demonstrative pronoun + *be* + a *wh*-clause:

3 That's what I said.
Det var jo det jeg sa.
4 That wasn't what I asked.
Det var ikke det jeg spurte om.
5 That's why we sent for you.
Det var derfor vi ba deg komme.
6 Is this where you live?
Er det her du bor?
7 That's how it all began.
Det var slik det hele begynte.

Reversed *wh*-clefts of this kind are very common in English, particularly in conversation. They contain little new information. Their main purpose seems to be to underline or sum up what has been said or written in the preceding text.

11.10 Learning problems

A *It* vs. *there*

As the dummy subjects *it* and *there* both correspond to 'det' in Norwegian, learners frequently confuse the two (most often overusing *it*). The uses of *it* and *there* are summarized in Table 11a.

Table 11a: Meanings and uses of it *and* there

Form	Meaning	Examples
Locative *there*	The form is an adverb denoting position or direction.	Are you comfortable there? I want to go there on holiday.

Form	Meaning	Examples
Existential *there*	The form acts as a dummy subject in clauses of existence and appearance.	There are two patients in the waiting room. There occurred a revolution in public taste.
Referential *it*	The personal pronoun *it* refers to something mentioned earlier.	She bought a book and gave it to her sister.
Anticipatory *it*	The form fills in for a subordinate clause later in the sentence.	It's good to see you. It's no use telling him that. It seems that we have made a mistake.
Empty *it*	The form acts as the subject in clauses about weather, temperature, time, distance.	It's raining. It's half past nine. It's two miles from here.
Cleft *it*	The form is used as the subject in cleft constructions that focus on a particular element.	It was Paul who won the race. It was a race Paul won. It was yesterday Paul won the race.

B English renderings of Norwegian presentative constructions

Norwegian uses presentative constructions with a wide range of verbs (both passive and active), and English often requires a different kind of structure. Table 11b summarizes the main ways of rendering Norwegian presentative constructions in English. Which type is chosen in any one case is dependent upon the demands of the particular context.

Table 11b: English renderings of Norwegian presentative constructions

Structure	Examples
Existential *there*	Det er litt flesk i kjøleskapet. There is some bacon in the fridge.
Existential *there* with a change of verb	Det står tre sykler i garasjen. There are three bikes in the garage.
Existential *there* in combination with a postmodifier	Det meldte seg flere frivillige senere på dagen. There were more volunteers signing up later in the day.

Structure	Examples
The noun phrase to be presented is made the subject in English.	Det ble skaffet til veie fire nye pumper. Four new pumps were provided.
A personal or indefinite pronoun is inserted as subject.	Det må tas et initiativ for å løse denne saken. Somebody must take the initiative to resolve this matter. Det var snøstorm i går. We had a blizzard yesterday.
The complement of a prepositional phrase is made the subject in English.	Det manglet dørhåndtak i noen av rommene. Some of the rooms did not have door knobs.

Terms

word order as a grammar signal
information principle
principle of end weight
contrast, double focus

subject–auxiliary inversion
subject–verb inversion
fronting
postponement

long and short passives
stative and dynamic passives

presentative construction
existential *there*
notional subject
anticipatory subject/object

dummy *it*
referential *it*
empty *it*
extraposition

clefting: *it*-cleft
wh-cleft
reversed *wh*-cleft

Exercises

1 Discuss how the information principle is evident in the following passage. **(11.1.2)**

The drift was thickly overgrown, a dark tunnel out of whose bushy sides the tendrils of brambles and briar roses caught at his clothes. One of these whipped back at him and as he caught at it a thorn drove into the fleshy pad of his finger. That thorn had been there, festering, for months.

2 Rewrite the following sentences so as to make them agree better with the principle of end weight. (**11.1.3**)

a That I didn't know my mother may be odd.
b The rate at which the American people are using up the world's supply of irreplaceable fossil fuels and their refusal to admit that the supply is limited is the real problem.
c The value of trying to identify the problem and to provide the tools necessary is not questioned.
d A young, ambitious journalist from one of the local newspapers wrote the article.
e A whale's tooth in the shape of a galleon carved by a local artist was what they had bought in Norway.
f They gave the four-year-old girl who lives next door to my parents a new dress.
g A couple of times when she thought she had got the better of me, Amanda laughed.
h The vicar of St Peter's, who was there as a character witness to prove what a pillar of the community Menzies was, was the first witness.
i A letter which made me realize it might be necessary to follow every word of the trial was sent to me.
j To find a job that is well paid and fulfilling at the same time is difficult.
k Einstein's theories have made a whole range of important technological developments possible.

3 Change the word order of the following sentences, starting with the sentence element that has been italicized. If inversion is required, state whether it is subject–verb inversion or subject–auxiliary inversion. (**11.2**)

a I will *never* make that mistake again.
b I will never make *that mistake* again.
c Crime *rarely* pays so well as Mr Jones seems to think.
d The nation has *scarcely ever* suffered such a recession.
e He spoke *so monotonously* that everyone left.
f He did not listen to *some of the speakers*.
g He *not only* protested: he also refused to pay his taxes.
h Peter continued *nevertheless*.
i Your sister is *in the next room*.
j They followed him *wherever he went*.
k A little brown rabbit sat *under a bush*.
l The children are playing *outside*.
m They went *away*.
n The servant went *away*.

o I despise *his character.*
p I'm not fond of *his face* either.
q Willy Ferguson is *coming into the picture.*
r All their savings were *hidden in their mattress.*

4 Analyse the following sentences and identify the type of word order variation each sentence exemplifies. (**11.2–11.9**)

a 'Mind your own business', said my brother.
b It was in this fashion that her mother lived on inside her.
c Only in the floodlit world of network television could a simple career move cause such shock waves.
d Also of great importance are the number and kinds of fish in the tank.
e Not a seat could be found in the cathedral that day.
f What was common was for families to rent or own a summer house in the mountains or by the seaside.
g On the edge of the grass, where a strip of flower border separated it from the paved drive, lay a rubber ball dented with toothmarks.
h It was quite clear to me that we simply didn't have anything in common any more.
i The door opened, and in marched the minister himself.
j So far had he walked that his shoes were completely worn out.

5 Correct any word order mistake in the following sentences. Give reasons for your corrections. (**11.2–11.5**)

a 'Is that really true?' asked she.
b And to top it all I am often sentimental on purpose.
c In the Pyrenees did he often go hiking for weeks at a time.
d Through the SBA's Management Counseling Program is practical, personalized advice on sound management principles available upon request.
e The gates were opened, and out rode the Prince.
f This museum have I not very often visited.
g Nevertheless, it will seem funny to have to send for a mechanic to improve conversation.
h 'Everything went real smooth', the sheriff said.
i Not until long after the war did they get a hint of the reason.

6 Comment on the difference in form and meaning between the members of the following sentence pairs. (**11.2–11.5**)

a 1 Once he did not offer to help.
  2 Not once did he offer to help.
b 1 So hostile did these factions become that civil war broke out.
  2 So these factions became hostile and civil war broke out.
c 1 Only when she heard Tony's voice she remembered Anne would be late.
  2 Only when she heard Tony's voice did she remember Anne would be late.

7 Rewrite the following sentences in the passive voice. Comment on any difficulty you encounter, as well as on any difference in meaning between the active and the passive versions. (**11.6**)

a Nobody knows what comes next.
b Would you allow me to live here for a while?
c He tipped off the police.
d You'll get the money on one condition.
e The chef put him in a corner of the kitchen.
f Tom has never known his father.
g The customer handed the book back to the clerk.
h He could face anything.
i She has lost her job.
j He had not found many things to be sentimental about.

8 Rewrite the following sentences in the active voice. Comment on any difficulty you encounter, as well as on any difference in meaning between the active and the passive versions. (**11.6**)

a A man was seen leaving her flat.
b Otto was asked by one of his relatives to look after a woman who was crossing on the same boat.
c I fear your time has been wasted.
d I shall need to have these carpets looked at by an expert.
e The question can be put to the defendant.
f These warnings must not be treated lightly.
g This new song has never been performed before.

9 Identify the passive constructions in the texts below (from the Brown Corpus). Are they long or short passives? Suggest reasons why the passive may have been used. Note that sample (b) represents non-standard English. (**11.6**)

a The research team was concerned that responses from firms in the state of Washington might not be typical of those throughout the country, or that the results might be different when no phone or personal follow-up was made. Accordingly, another test of the questionnaire was made. The revised draft was mailed in July, 1960, to 100 firms throughout the United States. Fifty of the 100 firms were selected on a random basis from 3,500 names submitted by member companies of the Aerospace Industries Association (AIA list) and fifty were selected in a similar manner from a list of 1,500 names compiled by the research team from the Thomas Register (TR list). The method of compiling the AIA and TR lists will be described later.

b The cowboy's humorous name for a cow givin' milk was a 'milk pitcher'. Cows givin' no milk were knowed as 'strippers'. The terminology of the range, in speakin' of 'dry stock' and 'wet stock', was confusin' to the tenderfoot. The most common reference to 'wet stock' was with the meanin' that such animals had been smuggled across the Rio Grande after bein' stolen from their rightful owners. The term soon became used and applied to all stolen animals.

c I keep thinking of a young woman I knew during the Occupation in Austria. She was from Prague. She had been picked up by the Russians, questioned in connection with some pamphlets, sentenced to life imprisonment for espionage. She escaped, crawled through the usual mine fields, under barbed wire, was shot at, swam a river, and we finally picked her up in Linz. She showed us what had happened to her.

10 *It* or *there*? Cross out the inappropriate alternative. If both can be used, account for the difference in meaning between the two alternatives. (**11.7–11.10**)

a It/there is time to prepare a decent meal.
b I think it/there is a very good book.
c It/there was a thoroughly good time.
d I feel it/there is too much now to confess.
e It/there is a lot that we don't know about.
f It/there was October, and the weather was getting worse.
g It meant it/there was always work for her to do.
h In all these families it/there was a musical heritage.
i It was/there were eighteen miles to the nearest town.
j In any event, it/there doesn't appear to have been anything terrible in his background.
k It/there was a semi-detached house with a nice garden.
l I knew it/there was virtually the end of his career.

m I remember it/there was an Australian lady living upstairs with her daughter.
n Then it/there was the living room.
o At the boarding school it/there was very difficult to meet girls.

11 Is the word *there* existential or locative in the sentences below? Give reasons for your answer. (**11.7**)

a Is there going to be TV or not?
b There wouldn't be enough room for everybody at the dining-room table.
c In the middle of Central Park, there he was.
d There was a memorial there with an angel.
e There is an easier way through the woods.
f The fact that he was there will not be apparent.
g There stands this monk in a habit with a tonsure, and he says, …

12 Identify the types of *it*-construction used in the sentences below. (**11.8–11.10**)

a Don't do this. Your father won't like it.
b It is when you are young that you need that kind of attention.
c If a picture went missing, it was my job to find it.
d We liked to play outside if it wasn't raining too hard.
e Believe it or not, I passed the grammar exam.
f She hid it from me that she had actually run over the neighbours' poodle.
g I found it very difficult to move around.
h Their father didn't think it was a good idea.
i I went to school in the village, and it was pretty far to walk.

13 Comment on the difference in form and meaning between the members of the following sentence pairs. (**11.7–11.10**)

a 1 It is difficult to be absolutely honest.
  2 It is difficult, to be absolutely honest.
b 1 It was a small, black table model.
  2 There was a small, black table model.
c 1 You wouldn't eat it if you had a choice.
  2 You wouldn't eat there if you had a choice.
d 1 I love this ice-cream. It has cream in it.
  2 I love this ice-cream. There is cream in it.
e 1 She thought it was very important to be firm.
  2 She thought it was very important to the firm.

12 Clause Combinations: Finite Clauses

12.1 Introduction

Up to this point in the book we have mainly been concerned with the structure of simple sentences, i.e. sentences which consist of only one clause. In this and the following chapter we will expand the analysis to include **compound** and **complex sentences**, i.e. sentences which consist of two or more clauses. Whether a sentence is simple or compound/complex (see **12.2**) is most easily seen by considering the number of verb phrases in it. While simple sentences contain only one verb phrase, complex and compound sentences contain at least two, usually with accompanying subjects. In the following text most of the sentences are either compound or complex. All the finite verb phrases have been italicized.

> When I *try* to write about Flora I *keep* wandering off into the villainy of men. The point *is* that pretty young women *are* expendable. Nobody *likes* them, except the men who *are* currently *involved* with them. Their mothers *envy* them, their plainer siblings *resent* them, their teachers *dislike* them. They *have* a hard time growing up and a hard time when grown. A pretty girl driving a Mini *will be driven* off the road by lorry drivers as a matter of course. What'*s* she *doing* on the road? Driving *is* <u>work</u>, not entertainment. Professors *refuse* to give them degrees, in case they'*re accused* of prejudice. Their husbands *don't trust* them. Everyone *knows* what a pretty girl *is* <u>for</u>, that'*s* the trouble. If Flora *had been* plainer, Bernard *might have married* her and not *treated* her like a skivvy and a slave.
>
> (From Fay Weldon, *The Heart of the Country*)

12.2 Co-ordination and subordination

Co-ordination and **subordination** denote two principal ways in which clauses can be combined in sentences. In the case of co-ordination, two (or more) clauses on the same level are joined together, usually by means of one of the co-ordinating conjunctions: *and, but, or, nor.* As an example, the main clauses in (1) can be combined as in (2).

1 The night-shift was finally over. I drove home. It was rather late. John still hadn't left the house.
2 The night-shift was finally over, and I drove home. It was rather late, but John still hadn't left the house.

Even when main clauses are combined in this way, they are syntactically independent of each other, and have equal status in the sentence. This is shown in the analysis in that they are analysed on the same level, just like two clauses which happen to be placed next to one another. We call such sentences **compound sentences**.

```
S V  |----A----|  c   S   A |----V----| |----dO---|
It was rather late, but John still hadn't left the house.
```

The sentences in (2) can be combined in a different way, by means of subordination, as shown in (3). The resulting sentences are **complex**. Clauses that are combined in complex sentences differ in status, in the sense that one of them, the **matrix clause**, is perceived as the most important part (see **2.9**). Any other clauses have a function which is subordinate to this clause. The clauses are thus related hierarchically to each other, as shown in the analysis below.

3 When the night-shift was finally over, I drove home. Although it was rather late, John still hadn't left the house.

```
|-----------------A-----------------------| S  V    A
  c  |-------S--------| V    A   A
When the night-shift was finally over, I drove home.
```

There are two important things to note here. One is that *When the night-shift was finally over* and *Although it was rather late* cannot function independently as complete sentences. The other is that each has a function with respect to the rest of the sentence. Syntactically this function happens to be adverbial in both cases. Semantically it is that of specifying a time in the former, and that of expressing concession in the latter. (See further **10.6** ff. on semantic types of adverbials.)

Complex clauses are thus main clauses which contain one or more subordinate clauses. We say that a subordinate clause is **embedded** in the clause in which it has a syntactic function. In most of the examples discussed in this chapter, the subordinate clauses are embedded in main clauses. But they may also be embedded in other subordinate clauses; see **12.10**. It is therefore useful to have the term **superordinate clause** (in contrast to subordinate) for any clause which contains an embedded clause. Furthermore, we may refer to the superordinate clause minus the subordinate clause as the **matrix clause**. In (3) the matrix clause is thus *I drove home*.

Note that subordinate clauses may also be co-ordinated, as in (4). In this case both subordinate clauses function as postmodifiers of the same noun phrase.

4 We are particularly proud of this collection, which is extremely large, and which includes some very rare items.

12.3 Some further remarks on co-ordination

When two co-ordinated clauses have the same logical subject, the subject is usually not expressed in the second clause, as illustrated by (1).

1 He turned the key and opened the door.

Furthermore, auxiliaries can be omitted from the second clause in a compound sentence, in order to avoid superfluous repetition. This is shown in (2), where *Bernard might have* is simply understood in the second clause.

2 Bernard might have married her and not treated her like a skivvy and a slave.

Compound sentences are sometimes formed without the use of conjunctions. The text in **12.1** has an example of three main clauses put together in one sentence, separated only by means of commas. We still recognize the structure of a compound sentence, where each of the clauses is capable of forming an independent, complete sentence.

3 Their mothers envy them, their plainer siblings resent them, their teachers dislike them.

A more common structure of three co-ordinated clauses would be one in which the final clause is prefaced by a conjunction, as in (4).

4 We can ask her now, we can wait till tomorrow, or we can just forget about it.

Nor differs somewhat from the other conjunctions. For one thing, it can occur together with other co-ordinating conjunctions, namely, *and* (5) or *but*, though the conjunct *neither* is far more common in these combinations. Secondly, *nor* often connects sentences as well as main clauses within a sentence, as in (6). In these respects, *nor* is similar to a conjunct adverbial (**10.8**). However, the other co-ordinators, especially *but*, are also found as sentence openers, in spite of prescriptive reactions against this usage (see also **15.3.2** and **15.3.3**).

5 Such reforms do not yield results overnight, and nor (usually: and neither) do they seem likely to happen overnight.
6 If they're right, I needn't worry. Nor need any of us here.

The four co-ordinating conjunctions are alike in that they may form part of a complex conjunction: *both ... and ...*, *not only ... but ...*, *either ... or ...*, *neither nor ...* (7).

7 Neither had he remained discreetly silent nor had he made any attempt to explain in public the reasons for his resignation.

The complex conjunctions stress the meaning of addition, alternative, or contrast. At the same time, they also single out each of the co-ordinated elements.

12.4 Types of subordinate clauses – an overview

There are many types of subordinate clauses. The categories are based partly on the form of the subordinate clause, and partly on its meaning and syntactic function. Unlike main clauses, subordinate clauses are usually introduced by a subordinator, i.e. a subordinating conjunction (**12.7.1**), a relative pronoun/adverb (**12.6.2**), or an interrogative pronoun/adverb (**12.8.4**). Also in contrast to main clauses, subordinate clauses need not contain a finite verb (cf. *driving* in line 6 of the text in **12.1**); thus we talk about finite and non-finite subordinate clauses. The finer distinctions as regards finite subordinate clauses are based on syntactic and semantic functions. Figure 12a gives an overview of the different groups which will be more thoroughly described below (while non-finite clauses are the topic of Chapter 13).

In connection with subordinators, we may note that subordinating conjunctions serve merely as connectors, while relative pronouns and interrogative pronouns/adverbs have other syntactic functions (usually subject, object, or adverbial).

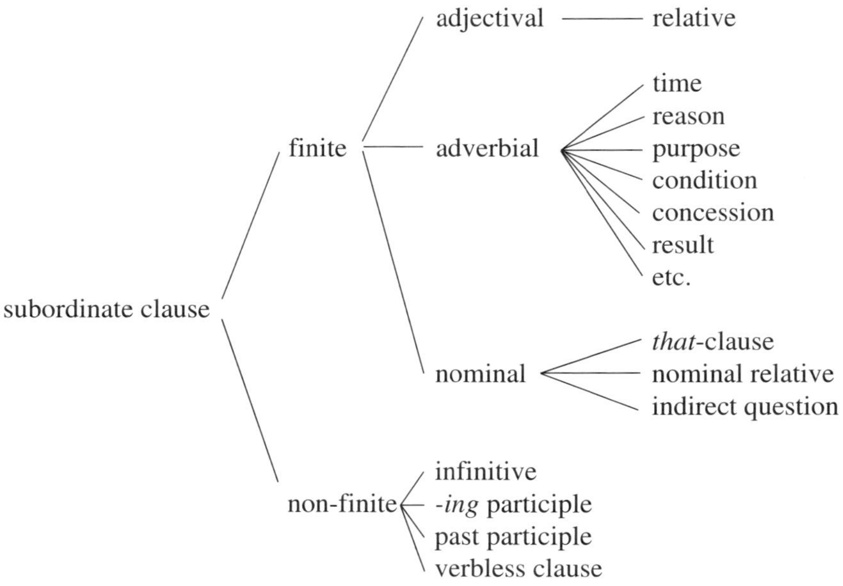

Figure 12a: Types of subordinate clauses

12.5 Syntactic functions of finite subordinate clauses

As shown in Figure 12a, the functions of subordinate clauses can be adjectival, adverbial, or nominal. This means that they can have the adjectival function of modifier in a noun phrase, the adverbial functions of specifying time, place, manner, reason, etc., or any of the syntactic functions associated with noun phrases (subject, direct/indirect object, subject/object predicative, complement of preposition). Examples (1) and (2) illustrate adjectival clauses, (3) to (5) adverbial ones, and (6) to (11) nominal ones.

1 John has an uncle *who lives in America.*
2 Nobody likes them, except the men *who are currently involved with them.*
3 *When I try to write about Flora* I keep wandering off into the villainy of men.
4 Professors refuse to give them degrees, *in case they're accused of prejudice.*
5 *If Flora had been plainer*, Bernard might have married her.
6 It is a pity *that it is raining*. (S)
7 Everyone knows *what a pretty girl is for*. (dO)

8 He offered *whoever was interested* a guided tour around his estate. (iO)
9 The point is *that pretty young women are expendable*. (sP)
10 They have made him *what he is today*. (oP)
11 We were arguing about *what we were going to do next*. (complement of preposition)

12.6 Adjectival clauses

Subordinate clauses are said to have an adjectival function when they modify nouns, since noun modification is also a typical function of adjectives. Finite subordinate clauses with an adjectival function are called **relative clauses**.

12.6.1 Relative clauses

The most common syntactic function of a relative clause is that of modifying a noun, more precisely as a postmodifier. Examples (1) and (2) show how clauses can be combined by making one of them a relative clause.

1 There is a house in New Orleans. They call it 'The Rising Sun'.
2 There is a house in New Orleans which they call 'The Rising Sun'.

In (2), which is a complex sentence, we see that the direct object *it* of the second sentence in (1) has been replaced by *which* in (2). *Which they call 'The Rising Sun'* gives further information about *a house in New Orleans*. *House* is the head of the noun phrase, as well as the **antecedent** of the relative clause, i.e. the noun that the relative clause refers back to.

12.6.2 Relative pronouns

Relative clauses are introduced by one of the relative pronouns: *who, whom, which, that, whose,* or *Ø* (zero). By contrast, Norwegian has only two relative pronouns: 'som' and *Ø*. The relative pronoun refers back to the antecedent of the relative clause. In the relative clause, the relative pronoun represents the antecedent and has the same syntactic function as a full noun phrase would have in its place, as shown in (1) and (2).

```
          S    V  |------------dO----------|
                            S  V |---sP---|
1   Andrew has a sister who is a doctor.

    |---------S-------| V |---sP---|
2   Andrew's sister is a doctor.
```

The choice of relative pronoun depends on the syntactic function of the pronoun in the relative clause as well as on the nature of its antecedent. An important distinction is whether the antecedent refers to a person or not. The factors determining the choice have been summarized in Table 12a at the end of this section.

Who is used when the antecedent of the relative clause refers to a person (or a pet animal associated with personality), and when the pronoun has subject function in the relative clause, as in (3). It is also common to use *who* with an object function, particularly in spoken and informal written English, as in (4). Furthermore, *who* can be used as a complement of a preposition, if the preposition is 'stranded' at the end of the relative clause, rather than before the pronoun, as in (5). Learners are advised to use *whom* in formal written English in examples like (4) and (5), though *who* will do fine in ordinary speech.

3 He was separated from the one person in life who ever meant anything to him.
4 There were all these friends like Albert and Amelia, who(m) you've met.
5 Everyone who(m) I spoke to was just sent back.

Whom is the traditional object form of the relative pronoun with a personal antecedent. In present-day English it is increasingly being replaced by *who*. However, in formal written English *whom* is used when the relative pronoun has an object function in the subordinate clause, e.g. in (6). The object form is obligatory after a preposition, as in (7).

6 Someone was sitting at one of the tables whom she recognized.
7 According to the census, there were 31 million women workers, of whom 25 million were in agriculture.

Whose differs from *who* and *whom* in that it is used with both personal (8) and non-personal (9) antecedents, and in that it functions as a determiner in the relative clause rather than replacing a whole noun phrase. A *whose*-clause denotes a possessive relationship between the antecedent and the noun following *whose*. In written English *whose* may be discarded in favour of *of which* with non-personal antecedents, as in (10).

8 William Beveridge was a British economist whose *Report on Social Insurance and Allied Services* formed the basis of social-security legislation in Britain.
9 Blanched peanuts, as prepared for making peanut butter or for eating as nuts, are roasted seeds whose seed-coats have been rubbed off.

10 These voters view the political process as a secret conspiracy, the object of which is to plunder them. (Cf. ... whose object is to plunder them.)

Which is used with non-personal antecedents, and can function as the subject, object, or complement of a preposition in the subordinate clause; compare (11), (12), and (13), respectively.

11 Colonies which were given dominion status usually had a majority of white settlers.
12 It only does harm to talk to troops about new and desirable equipment which others may have but which you cannot give them.
13 It was plain from the new animation with which he spoke that he was feeling there had been a great improvement.

That and *Ø* are used with both personal and non-personal antecedents, but chiefly in restrictive relative clauses (see **12.6.3**). *That* is used with both subject and object function, but not as a complement of a preposition. Zero-relatives are used only where an expressed relative pronoun would have functioned as an object, or where there is a stranded preposition at the end of the relative clause. (Some dialects of English allow *Ø* in subject position, but in Standard English this usage should be avoided.)

14 She is the sort of student that usually does very well in the exam.
15 This is the house (that) Jack built.
16 I got a postcard from someone I used to work with.

Table 12a: The use of relative pronouns: a summary

	Antecedent	**Syntactic function in relative clause**
who	personal	subject, object
whom	personal	object, complement of preposition
whose	personal non-personal	determiner (expressing a possessive relationship)
which	non-personal	subject, object, complement of preposition
that	personal non-personal	subject, object
Ø	personal non-personal	object

12.6.3 Restrictive and non-restrictive relative clauses

Relative clauses, as well as other postmodifiers, can serve two principal functions. One is to specify the reference of the head of the noun phrase. The other is to add extra information about the head of the noun phrase. We call the former type **restrictive** and the latter **non-restrictive**. Some examples will make this clearer.

1 There is a house in New Orleans which they call 'The Rising Sun'.
2 At the end of the driveway you can see their house, which they call 'The Rising Sun'.

In (1) the relative clause is restrictive. It points out that, of many houses in New Orleans, there is one called 'The Rising Sun', and this is the one we are interested in. In (2), by contrast, there is only one house in question, so the relative clause is not needed in order to identify that house. Rather, it informs us of the name of the house as a kind of afterthought. This is, by the way, what underlies the corresponding Norwegian terms for these types of clauses. *Nødvendige relativsetninger* (restrictive relative clauses) are needed in order to identify the reference of the antecedent, while *unødvendige relativsetninger* (non-restrictive relative clauses) are not needed for this (but are, of course, useful for other purposes).

In writing one can usually see the difference between restrictive and non-restrictive relative clauses simply by looking at punctuation. A restrictive relative clause is never preceded by a comma, while a non-restrictive relative clause is regularly preceded and followed by commas. This reflects a tendency in speech to have a tone unit boundary before a non-restrictive clause, but never before a restrictive one. In speech, therefore, (1) and (2) may be represented as (1a) and (2a).

1a | There is a house in New Orleans which they call 'The Rising ˋSUN' |
2a | At the end of the driveway you can see their ˏHOUSE | which they call 'The Rising ˋSUN' |

When the antecedent of the relative clause is a plural noun phrase, a restrictive relative clause serves to restrict the group. Thus in (3) the children who arrived later did not get any sweets, while in (4) all the children arrived first, and they were all given sweets.

3 The children who arrived first were given a bag of sweets each.
4 The children, who arrived first, were given a bag of sweets each.

When the antecedent of a relative clause is an indefinite pronoun (**5.11**), the relative clause is always restrictive. This is because the reference of an indefinite pronoun is by definition vague. The postmodifying clause serves to narrow down its reference.

5 Anyone who has watched children develop a taste for literature will understand what I mean.

On the other hand, if the antecedent is a proper noun, the relative clause is regularly non-restrictive. A proper noun is in itself usually sufficient to identify a referent, so a following relative clause can only add extra information about this referent. Thus the restrictive relative clause in (6) singles out the American uncle from a possible set of uncles, while the non-restrictive one in (7) gives us the extra information about John that he lives in America.

6 John has a rich uncle who lives in America.
7 John, who lives in America, has a rich uncle.

It should be noted that whereas *wh*-pronouns can be used in restrictive and non-restrictive clauses alike, it is only restrictive relative clauses that normally allow *that* and *Ø* as subordinators. *That* and *Ø* are often regarded as less formal alternatives, particularly with personal antecedents.

8 I mistrusted bake shops that called themselves 'Sanitary Bake Shops'.
9 These have never gone out of style in Scandinavian homes and now seem to be reappearing here and there in shops which specialize in handicrafts.

12.6.4 Sentential relative clauses

Relative clauses introduced by *which* can sometimes refer back to all of the preceding (matrix) clause instead of the nearest preceding noun phrase. This is clear in (1), where the relative clause does not give a description of John's uncle, but rather comments on the fact that John inherited his fortune.

1 John inherited a fortune from his uncle, which he truly appreciated.

We call this type of relative clause **sentential** because it has the preceding clause as its antecedent. It conveys the speaker's/writer's comment on a situation or a fact, and can thus be analysed as a disjunct adverbial. Note that this is the only type of relative clause that does not function as a postmodifier in a noun phrase (except for nominal relative clauses; cf. **12.8.3**). We may note a certain similarity in meaning with co-ordinated clauses; compare *John inherited a fortune from his uncle, and he truly appreciated it.*

Sentential relative clauses may be seen as non-restrictive, in that they convey new information, and are not needed to identify the reference of the antecedent. The verb in a sentential relative clause is always in the singular. In (2) and (3) the form of the verb reveals that the relative clause in (2) is a postmodifier of *poems* (the poems are interesting), while in (3) it conveys the speaker's opinion of the fact that somebody has written all these poems (the speaker finds this interesting). Example (4) is ambiguous, since the verb must be in the singular when the antecedent of the relative pronoun is singular. The context will usually indicate which interpretation is intended.

2 He has written all these poems, which are interesting.
3 He has written all these poems, which is interesting.
4 He has written this poem, which is interesting.

12.6.5 Relative clauses with other subordinators

Where, when, and *why* can function as subordinators in relative clauses in addition to the more common relative pronouns discussed above. We still recognize the function that relative clauses have, namely, that of postmodifying a noun. It is often possible to substitute a preposition + *which* for any of these words when they introduce relative clauses.

1 Then he thought of a time when Clayton's horse had fallen lame in the Gap. (… a time at which …)
2 There are many places where we can use their vigour and new ideas. (… in which …)
3 Really there is no reason why this fine exercise should not find its way into your leg programme at all times. (… for which …)

12.6.6 Other English counterparts of Norwegian 'som'-clauses

The Norwegian word 'som' has an adverbial use in comparative clauses, where the subordinate clause introduced by 'som' is part of a modifier in an adjective or adverb phrase. The English counterpart of this 'som' is *as*.

1 Jeg løper like fort som du gjør.
I run as fast as you do.

A further adverbial use of 'som' is in manner clauses, also introduced by *as* in corresponding English clauses.

2 Jeg lurer på hvorfor de handler som de gjør.
I wonder why they act as they do.

Finally, a structure resembling a relative clause may combine with an adverb such as *now* rather than a nominal antecedent. Thus in sentences such as (3) the *that*-clause has an adverbial, rather than an adjectival, function.

3 Now that she had gone there was no longer any need for all that dieting and exercising. ('Nå som hun hadde dratt ...')

12.7 Adverbial clauses

Adverbial subordinate clauses most commonly function as adverbials in superordinate clauses. They generally function as adjuncts, and can express the whole range of adverbial meanings discussed in **10.6**.

1 *When everybody has finished*, we'll go home. (adjunct of time)
2 Mary refused to go to the zoo *because she is allergic to animals*. (adjunct of reason)
3 This is what you have to do *if you want to succeed*. (adjunct of condition)

In addition, an adverbial clause can function as a postmodifier in a noun phrase, as in (4).

4 The last few days *before we go on a holiday* are always chaotic.

12.7.1 Subordinating conjunctions

Finite adverbial clauses are usually introduced by a subordinating conjunction which indicates the semantic function of the whole clause. Table 12b gives a survey of the most common of these conjunctions.

Table 12b: Subordinating conjunctions introducing finite adverbial clauses

Meaning of adverbial clause	**Conjunctions used**
Time	after, as, before, once, since, till, until, when, while
Place	where, wherever
Reason	as, because, since
Result	so, so that
Purpose	so that, in order that
Condition	if, unless, as long as
Concession and contrast	although, even if, even though, though, while, whereas
Manner and comparison	as, like, the way, as if, than

Some of the conjunctions listed in Table 12b may have various meanings and are therefore listed more than once. This is true of *as* (time, reason, manner/comparison), *since* (time, reason), and *while* (time, concession/contrast).

Conjunctions may be expanded and modified without losing their function as subordinating conjunctions. In (1) *after* is modified by *24 hours*.

1 The disclosure came 24 hours after the government had ordered the investigation.

Furthermore, an adverbial clause may be introduced by an expression which is synonymous with a subordinating conjunction. In (2), for example, we have a time clause beginning with *the minute* instead of a conjunction such as *once*.

2 The minute he was capable of real thought, he was also capable of communicating that thought.

Conditional clauses sometimes occur without a conjunction. In these cases the conditional clause begins with an auxiliary, as in (3). See further **11.2.4B**.

3 Had I waited a day longer to speak, I would have been too late. (Cf. If I had waited ...)

12.7.2 The position of adverbial clauses

Adverbial clauses are most commonly placed at the end of a sentence, as in (1), but they also commonly occur at the beginning, as in (2).

1 Mark will stay *because he feels somewhat responsible*.
2 *If the door is blocked up by smokers*, it's a real problem.

However, in contrast to Norwegian, English does not normally allow adverbial clauses in the middle of a main clause (**10.9.6**).

3 Den sviktende ressurstilgangen kan dersom situasjonen vedvarer føre til et vesentlig dårligere studietilbud.
Diminishing revenues can lead to a significantly less adequate academic offer if the situation continues.

The choice between initial and end position for a subordinate clause often has to do with information structure (**11.1.2**). Generally, if the subordinate clause expresses given information, it is placed in initial position, while subordinate clauses expressing new information are placed in end position. The cohesion of a text is a related matter. A subordinate clause which has a topic similar to that of the preceding sentence(s) will usually be placed in initial position, as shown in (4), while one that introduces a topic which is developed in the next sentence will be placed in end position.

4 The other type of direct users are managers, accountants, doctors, librarians, and other professional groups who interact with a computer system in a less constrained way and know how to use particular software packages. *Because these users are not computer experts*, they depend upon products being intelligible and easy to operate.

Though there are no absolute rules for the placement of adverbial clauses, some types seem to have preferred positions. Concessive clauses and conditional clauses introduced by *if* have a slight preference for initial position. (But note that *unless*-clauses tend to be placed in end position.) *Because*-clauses are most often placed in end position (but cf. example 4), as well as clauses expressing result, while clauses introduced by *as* or *since* are frequently found in both initial and end position. Furthermore, clauses of manner and comparison are most commonly found in end position. Note that a comparative clause must follow the adjective or the adverb that it is a complement of, as in (5); see **8.3**.

5 In general, Mr Loesser has done a *more consistent* job as lyricist *than he has as composer.*

12.7.3 Sentences with embedded conditional clauses

There is a difference in verb forms in sentences with embedded conditional clauses in Norwegian and English. This is illustrated by (1) to (3). See also **7.8** and **7.21E**.

1 If you drop this, it will explode.
Hvis du slipper denne, eksploderer den.
2 If you dropped this, it would explode.
Hvis du slapp denne, eksploderte den.
3 If you had dropped this, it would have exploded.
Hvis du hadde sluppet denne, hadde den eksplodert.

While it is possible to use the same tense in the matrix clause and the conditional clause in Norwegian, English has the following pattern:

- present tense in subordinate clause → *will*-future in matrix clause (1)
- past tense in subordinate clause → *would* + infinitive (first conditional) in matrix clause (2)

- past perfect in subclause → *would* + perfective aspect (second conditional) in matrix clause (3)

Examples (1), (2), and (3) also clearly express different meanings. Example (1), with the present tense in the conditional clause, expresses a real, or open, condition; i.e. there is a real possibility that something will explode. In (2) we have a more hypothetical situation. Here it is not very likely that the person is going to drop the device with a subsequent explosion. In (3) the condition is rejected. There is no longer any possibility of dropping or exploding anything, as the sentence describes a situation in the past. The same pattern can also be used to describe something that is contrary to fact, so that again the condition in the subordinate clause is rejected, and the situation denoted by the matrix clause is not going to take place, as in (4). Furthermore, the example illustrates the possibility of using another modal in the place of *would*.

4 If Flora had been plainer, Bernard might have married her.

12.8 Nominal clauses

There are three types of nominal subordinate clauses: *that*-clauses, nominal relative clauses, and indirect questions. They have the same syntactic properties, but differ in form and in the meaning they express.

12.8.1 *That*-clauses

That-clauses are introduced by the subordinating conjunction *that* or Ø (zero). They are quite parallel to Norwegian *at-setninger* which are introduced by 'at' or Ø.

1 Mary thinks (that) nobody likes her. (Mary tror (at) ingen liker henne.)
2 That he was drunk was obvious.
3 It is funny that you should think so.

The *that*-clause in (1) functions as a direct object. It is in this object position that we most frequently find zero *that*-clauses. The conjunction must be kept when the *that*-clause functions as the subject, as in (2), and is usually also kept when the subject is in extraposition (**11.8**) after the anticipatory *it*, as in (3).

A *that*-clause can also function as part of a clause element, as in (4) and (5). In (4), its function is **appositional**, because the subject noun phrase consists of two equal parts: *the idea* and *that the earth is flat*. The *that*-clause explains the content of the noun *idea*. (This type of noun phrase is called an apposition; see **4.10**.) In (5), the *that*-clause is a complement of the adjective *sure*.

4 The idea that the earth is flat sounds quaint today.
5 She was sure (that) she had seen him before.

In Norwegian a clause introduced by 'at' can readily function as the complement of a preposition, as in a translation of (5): *Hun var sikker på at hun hadde sett ham før.* In English the combination of preposition + *that* must be avoided; i.e. the preposition is omitted. Further illustration is given in (6) and (7). The syntactic functions of these *that*-clauses are complement of the adjective and apposition, respectively.

6 Hun var lei for at hun hadde glemt fødselsdagen hans. (Cf. Hun var lei for det.)
She was sorry that she had forgotten his birthday. (Cf. She was sorry about it.)
7 Bobbie kom hjem med nyheten om at John hadde fått jobben.
Bobbie came home with the news that John had got the job.

Note that where Norwegian would use a preposition plus 'at', English frequently uses an *-ing* participle clause following a preposition, as in (8) and (9). Other corresponding English expressions include *the fact that*, as in (10). Some more examples are given in (11) and (12).

8 De hadde regnet med at de skulle treffe ham i byen.
They had counted on meeting him in town.
9 Å snakke om at Pappa skulle dø var synd.
To speak of Papa dying was a sin.
10 Konflikten kommer av at lærere vanligvis lønnes etter ansiennitet.
The rub arises from the fact that teachers are usually paid on the basis of time served.
11 Jeg unnskyldte meg med at jeg hadde dårlig tid.
I excused myself by saying that I was in a hurry.
12 Han ventet på at moren skulle komme tilbake.
He was waiting for his mother to return.

There is one exception to the rule about avoiding prepositions in front of a *that*-clause, namely, the expression *in that* (meaning 'in the sense that'), as in (13).

13 These trials were properly termed 'political cases' in that the trials themselves were political acts producing political consequences.

12.8.2 Nominal relative clauses

Nominal relative clauses are introduced by a *wh*-pronoun: *what(ever), who(ever), whichever*, etc. They differ from adjectival relative clauses in that they do not have an antecedent. The *wh*-word introducing the nominal relative clause can be seen as the antecedent and a relative pronoun fused into one word, as in (1) to (3).

1 She usually gets *what she wants*. (… that which she wants.)
2 *Whatever he touches* turns to gold. (Everything that he touches …)
3 He smiles at *whoever he meets*. (… everybody whom he meets.)

The grammatically closest parallel in Norwegian to English nominal relative clauses with a subordinator ending in *-ever* is a construction with 'hva/hvem/hvor … enn'. However, it is more common to express this kind of meaning by means of a pronoun plus an adjectival relative clause; compare the translations of (1) to (3) given below. Other nominal relatives are often translated into Norwegian as 'det/den/de (som), alt (som)'.

1a Hun får vanligvis det (som) hun vil ha.
2a Alt (det som) han tar på, blir til gull.
3a Han smiler til alle (som) han møter / hvem han enn møter.

Note the difference in meaning between (4) and (5). The former refers to something specific which the addressee wants, while the latter refers non-specifically to anything the addressee might possibly want.

4 You can find what you want in that shop. (Du kan finne det du vil ha i den butikken.)
5 You can find whatever you want in that shop. (Du kan finne alt du vil ha i den butikken.)

12.8.3 Indirect questions

Indirect questions are introduced by an interrogative pronoun or adverb (*who, which, where, when, why, how*) or the conjunction *if* or *whether*. Formally, these clauses resemble *wh*-questions, but they do not have the same communicative function (**14.3.1**). However, semantically an indirect question often conveys an underlying (reported) question, as illustrated in (1).

1 She wondered if she should enquire after the baby. (Should I enquire after the baby?)

While *if* and *whether* echo *yes/no*-questions, the others echo *wh*-questions (**14.3.1**). Thus in (2) one can easily imagine the question 'Who has been at work?', and in (3), 'What shall we do next?' Note, however, that the question underlying the subordinate clause need not always be obvious, as in (4).

2 She tried to figure out who had been at work.
3 We didn't know what we should do next.
4 She knew immediately who had been at work.

In Norwegian, 'som' can occur together with the subordinator in an indirect question, as in the translation of (4): 'Hun visste med en gang hvem som hadde vært på ferde.' Note that this 'som' has no counterpart in English.

12.8.4 Nominal relatives vs. indirect questions

Formally, nominal relatives and indirect questions may be practically identical. Both types are introduced by a *wh*-word, and both have nominal functions. The two types are distinguished on the basis of meaning. As mentioned in **12.8.3**, indirect questions imply that there is an underlying question; a piece of information, represented by the *wh*-word, is missing from the clause. This is not the case in nominal relative clauses. Examples (1) and (2) will make this clearer. While (1) contains an indirect question, and we can imagine the speaker asking himself a question, (2) does not echo any such question; it simply assumes that she meant something.

1 I was wondering what she meant.
2 That was exactly what she meant.

Translating the examples into Norwegian may also bring out the difference. The indirect question will be introduced by an interrogative pronoun or adverb in Norwegian as well, while the nominal relative will usually have 'det (som)' or 'alt som'. (Cf. 'Jeg lurte på hva hun mente.' vs. 'Det var akkurat det hun mente.')

12.9 Other constructions involving subordination

12.9.1 Cleft sentences

Cleft sentences (**11.9**) are focusing devices which involve at least one subordinate clause. *It*-clefts, illustrated in (1) to (3), contain a *that*-clause which resembles a restrictive relative clause. In (2) we can even use *who* instead of *that*, which further indicates the similarity to relative clauses. Still, since the subordinate clause does not do the usual job of a restrictive relative clause, namely, to identify the reference of its antecedent, it is better to classify it simply as part of an *it*-cleft structure. The subordinate clause follows immediately after the focused element. The focused element is italicized in the examples below.

1 It was *'Jane Eyre'* that Jack and Jill were reading last night.
2 It was *Jack and Jill* that/who were reading 'Jane Eyre' last night.
3 It was *last night* that Jack and Jill were reading 'Jane Eyre'.

Wh-clefts contain a nominal relative clause in either subject position, as in (4) and (5), or predicative position, as in (6).

4 What Jack and Jill were reading last night was *'Jane Eyre'*.
5 What Jack and Jill were doing last night was *reading 'Jane Eyre'*.
6 *'Jane Eyre'* was what Jack and Jill were reading last night.

12.9.2 Indirect speech

Sentences with indirect speech consist of a main clause with an embedded nominal subordinate clause which is either a *that*-clause or an indirect question. The subordinate clause can be analysed as a direct object. It contains the reported speech, and is placed after a matrix clause containing a subject and a 'speaking' verb (e.g. *ask, claim, say,* or *tell*). See further **7.9** and **16.9.2**.

1 An old man told me that he had been kicked in the head by a fractious mule when he was a boy.
2 I asked her whether she had ever heard any of Wagner's operas.

12.9.3 Comment clauses

Comment clauses represent a way of combining clauses which is on the borderline between subordination and co-ordination. Comment clauses do not usually involve the use of conjunctions. Examples are given in (1) and (2).

1 You're right, I suppose.
2 It is rather difficult to make real lace, you know / you see.

Comment clauses tend to be relatively fixed expressions, such as *I suppose, I think, I mean, you know, you see*. They usually contain a reference to either the speaker or the hearer, and function as some kind of comment on the rest of the sentence (whether this is the speaker's opinion, whether the hearer is supposed to know this, etc.). Further, it is typical of comment clauses that they are thrown in as parenthetical remarks. They are usually not accented, unless they occur in a separate tone unit. These last two points strongly suggest that comment clauses should be seen as subordinate. We suggested in **10.7** that these clauses should be analysed as disjunct adverbials.

A structure such as (2) is of course similar to a structure with a nominal *that*-clause functioning as a direct object, as shown in (3).

3 The film shows you how real lace is made, and you see that it is rather difficult.

However, when *see* functions as the verb of a matrix clause, it is likely to be given more weight, both in intonation, where it is likely to be accented, and as regards meaning. Furthermore, a comment clause can to some extent be moved about in the sentence, while the similar-looking matrix clause must stay in front of the *that*-clause.

12.10 Complex embedding

The complexity of sentences frequently goes beyond that of embedding a subordinate clause in a main clause. Thus we may see subordinate clauses containing other subordinate clauses, as in (1), where a *that*-clause contains an adverbial clause. Example (2) has an even more complex structure. In the overall clause pattern, the *why*-clause is part of the notional subject, and the *unless*-clause is an adverbial. Within this adverbial clause we find another adverbial clause (*when ... Irish*), which in turn contains a nominal clause (*how ... Irish*).

1 It was obvious that, even if he did not believe her, he wanted to.
2 There is no reason why most theatregoers should not have a pretty good time at 'Donnybrook', unless they are permanently in the mood of Enright when he sings about how easily he could hate the lovable Irish.

Theoretically there may be any number of steps in such a hierarchy of embedding. In practice, however, there is of course a limit to how complex a sentence can be before it becomes too difficult to understand.

12.11 Clause combination and style

It is often said that co-ordination is typical of speech and subordination is typical of writing. Though there is a great deal of truth in this, the statement needs some modification. After all, we need not search long in order to find subordination in speech and co-ordination in writing. However, studies have shown that sentences are longer on average in (formal) writing than in (informal) speech, and long sentences are typically an effect of subordination.

Long sentences with a lot of subordination may (but need not) be relatively difficult to understand for a reader/hearer because of their very complex syntax. For example, it is often noted that politicians use long and difficult sentences in order to evade an issue. Co-ordinated main clauses do not of course enter into such complex relationships, and are thus easier to decode. Furthermore, complex sentences often require careful planning and editing. This goes some way towards explaining why they do not occur so much in informal speech situations, where there is little time for such preparation.

It should be noted that subordination may be a more economical way of combining clauses than co-ordination, which often entails repetition. Subordination also leaves more room for variation, since there are so many possibilities of combining clauses in a hierarchy. Both of these qualities speak in favour of using subordination in writing, where both economy of space and a varied style are valued qualities.

Compare finally (1) and (2), which illustrate informal speech and formal writing, respectively.

1 She was a poor old thing after all. And mother went wild with me. She thought this was terrible, and that I couldn't see her point of view at all. And of course I did see her point of view. But I didn't want her to ring her up and say anything awful to her, because she's nice and kind and mild. So this went on for weeks and I thought I'd better ring my mother up and pretend I've never said it. I'd just ring up and ask how she's getting on and so on. And so I rang up. And my sister answered the phone. And she really gave me a terrible harangue.

(From the London–Lund Corpus)

2 Although Faulkner was the heir in his own family to this tradition, he did not have Stark Young's inclination to romanticize and sentimentalize the planter society. The myth of the Southern plantation has had only a tangential relation with actuality, as Francis Pendleton Gaines showed forty years ago, and I suspect it has had a far narrower acceptance as something real than has generally been supposed. Faulkner has found it useful, but he has employed it with his habitual independence of mind and skeptical outlook. Without saying or seeming to say that in portraying the Sartoris and the Compson families Faulkner's chief concern is social criticism, we can say nevertheless that through those families he dramatizes his comment on the planter dynasties as they have existed since the decades before the Civil War. It may be that in this comment he has broken from the conventional pattern more violently than in any other regard, for the treatment in his books is far removed from even the genial irony of Ellen Glasgow, who

was the only important novelist before him to challenge the conventional picture of planter society.

(From the Brown Corpus)

Terms

sentence:	simple	co-ordination	
	compound	subordination	
	complex	embedding	
main clause		relative clauses:	antecedent
subordinate clause			restrictive
superordinate clause			non-restrictive
matrix clause			sentential
finite and non-finite clauses		nominal clauses:	*that*-clause
			nominal relative
syntactic functions:	nominal		indirect question
	adjectival		
	adverbial		
	appositional		

Exercises

1 Combine the sentences in each set by means of the co-ordinating conjunctions *and* and *but*. (The sentences have been adapted from Ernest Hemingway, 'In another country'.) (**12.2**, **12.3**)

a In the fall the war was always there. We did not go to it any more.
b It was cold in the fall in Milan. The dark came very early.
c Then the electric lights came on. It was pleasant along the streets looking in the windows.
d There was much game hanging outside the shops. The snow powdered in the fur of the foxes. The wind blew their tails.
e The deer hung stiff and heavy and empty. Small birds flew in the wind. The wind turned their feathers.
f It was a cold fall. The wind came down from the mountains.

2 Combine the sentences in each set by means of co-ordination. Omit any words that make the sentence repetitive. (The sentences have been adapted from Ernest Hemingway, 'In another country'.) (**12.2**, **12.3**)

a The hospital was very old. The hospital was very beautiful.
b You entered through a gate. You walked across a courtyard. You walked out a gate on the other side.
c The machine was to bend the knee. The machine was to make the knee move as in riding a tricycle.
d 'Very interesting, very interesting,' the major said. The major handed it back to the doctor.

3 Assign each of the italicized clauses to its appropriate category. Then state its syntactic function. (**12.4**, **12.5**)

a *When she returned*, she showed me her new dress.
b I have not planned any talks *that are more important*.
c There are many ways *in which it can be helped*.
d I don't know *how this should be done*.
e Mary refused to go to the zoo *because she is allergic to animals*.
f *Why you bought that elephant gun* I can't imagine.
g They tell me *he loves snails*.
h The snails *he likes best* are expensive.
i I know *that something will go wrong*.
j *If a free society cannot help the many who are poor*, it cannot save the few *who are rich*.
k That was *what he had done for the past few days*.
l She does not think *it should be snowing at this time of the year*.
m The professor, *who had just published a book*, gave a lecture on Shakespeare.
n Peter had been invited, *but he did not show up*.

4 Combine the two sentences in each set by turning one of them into a relative clause. (**12.6.1**, **12.6.2**)

a Dr Clark will succeed Dr McLemore. Dr McLemore will retire at the close of the present school term.
b There will be a dinner Friday evening at the Denver Country Club. This dinner will precede the opening of the golf season.
c The three leaders agreed today to begin negotiations on forming a coalition government. This government is hoped to unite the war-ridden country.
d Her fiancé is with a publishing firm. He translates many books from English into Italian.
e Mr Burlingham wrote to me once about an old friend of mine, Ratcliffe. I had first met Ratcliffe in London in 1988.

f The snow emergency route plan should be strictly enforced. Under this plan, parking is banned on key streets, and cars are required to use snow tires or chains on them.

g The idea apparently has captured the imagination of countless youths. Their parents are probably more surprised by the response than anybody else.

h He brought with him the names of some people he had never met. He knew nothing about these people.

5 Identify the relative clauses in the following text and determine whether they are restrictive or non-restrictive. (**12.6.3**)

George Orwell was born in 1903 in Bengal, where his father was a government official. His real name was Eric Blair. George Orwell was a writing name, which he used also in everyday life. Like all English children in India whose parents could afford it, he came home as a small boy to go to preparatory school. He was accepted with reduced fees, which some clever boys were because they would be a good advertisement for the school. This, and his unhappiness at his prep. school, is described in a short autobiography called *Such, Such Were the Joys,* which is not yet published in England. He won scholarships to Eton and Wellington and chose Eton, which in those days indicated that his parents had some money behind them.

After five years of police service in India, he wanted to earn his living by writing. His leave pay could be eked out for a year. This gave him a year's grace in which he could bang his typewriter and see if it produced enough for food and clothes and shelter. It failed him. It has never been easy for a writer who insists on writing well to make enough money out of writing.

(Adapted from Laurence Brander's introduction to *Animal Farm.*)

6 Combine the two sentences in each set by turning one of them into an adverbial clause. Use the conjunction given in parentheses. (**12.7**, **12.7.1**)

a Many qualified young people are not going into medicine and dentistry. They can't afford the schooling costs. (*because*)

b The Hughes concern was formally declared bankrupt. Its directors indicated they could not draw up a plan for reorganization. (*after*)

c The buses cannot stop on the parkway. Land for bus stations and for parking areas nearby will be needed. (*because*)

d It could go either way. The gains for both points of view were about the same. (*since*) e Stickney could turn north in Prairie Avenue. The car spun around again. (*before*)

f You destroy confidence in banks. You do something to the economy. (*if*)

g The lease is signed. The local club will be formally recognized by Commissioner Frick. (*once*)

7 Comment on the difference in form and meaning between the members of the following sentence pairs.

a 1 I'll ask the girls who were here last night.
  2 I'll ask the girls who was here last night.
b 1 It was Alexander that she had met in Paris.
  2 It was Alexander, who she had met in Paris.
c 1 The claim that he was making was clearly untenable.
  2 The claim that he was making money was clearly untenable.
d 1 It's a pity that she refuses to accept.
  2 It's an argument that she refuses to accept.
e 1 The first speaker will be Felicia, who is sure to please everyone.
  2 The first speaker will be Felicia, which is sure to please everyone.
f 1 Peter did not say anything which could be misunderstood.
  2 Peter did not say anything, which could be misunderstood.
g 1 This is easy for the students who enjoy grammar.
  2 This is easy for the students, who enjoy grammar.

8 Identify the finite subordinate clauses in the following text and state the syntactic function of each.

Jane Tewson is the sort of charity worker who wins over the most unlikely people to her causes. It's not that the rest of us completely ignore all the homeless people we pass as we scuttle home at night: it's just that Jane Tewson's idea of charity seems to lack all sense of proportion.

First, with Four Weddings scriptwriter Richard Curtis, she founds Comic Relief, a charity which is not just successful, but so hip that fund-raisers like Billy Connolly, French and Saunders and Lenny Henry actually swear as they raise millions, which Harry Secombe and Katie Boyle never did. Then, just as Comic Relief is booming, she packs her bags and sets up a teeny new charity, Pilotlight. It has been going barely six months, but already everyone from Richard Branson to Cameron Mackintosh is keen to help.

It's not a life that leaves much free time, especially as she also dashes home to Buckinghamshire most evenings, reaching her converted barn just in time to tuck Charlie, 4, and Sam, 2, into bed. It certainly leaves her little time to sit around in her counting house, counting out her money, which may be just as well, considering that her current salary just about pays for childcare, and that her husband Charles, an Australian social anthropologist, also doesn't feature in Forbes's annual list of billionaires.

(From *The Times* – slightly adapted)

13 Clause Combinations: Non-finite Clauses

13.1 Introduction

As mentioned in **12.4**, not all subordinate clauses contain a finite verb. These are clauses in which the verb is either an infinitive or a participle construction (past participle or *-ing* participle). In addition, clauses containing no verb at all are usually classified as non-finite. In the text below the non-finite clauses have been numbered and italicized. You may note that the syntactic functions of non-finite subordinate clauses correspond to those of finite ones.

> Villagers have handed in a vital 'black box' flight recorder (1) *looted from the wreckage of a Vietnamese plane* that crashed in Cambodia (2) *killing at least 64 people*, an aviation official said Friday.
>
> The information (3) *stored inside* was expected (4) *to show* if the pilot of a Vietnam Airlines Tupolev Tu-134 (5) *landing at Phnom Penh airport Wednesday* had been off course and had failed (6) *to regain enough altitude* (7) *to correct his flight path*, officials said. The plane crashed in rice fields (8) *after hitting a stand of palm trees beyond the runway*. Two children were the only survivors of the crash.
>
> (From *The Times*)

Several of these non-finite clauses function as postmodifiers in the same way as relative clauses, namely, (1), (3), and (5). Others, (2) and (8), function as adverbials, parallel to finite adverbial clauses. Clauses (4) and (6) have a nominal function, namely, that of direct object, while (7) is a complement of the adjective *enough*.

13.2 Types of non-finite subordinate clauses and their syntactic functions

Non-finite clauses are grouped according to their form (see **12.4**, Figure 12a). English has the following categories:

- infinitive: The pilot had failed *to regain enough altitude to correct his flight path.*
- *-ing* participle: The plane crashed in rice fields *after hitting a stand of palm trees beyond the runway.*
- past participle: Villagers have handed in a vital 'black box' flight recorder *looted from the wreckage of a Vietnamese plane.*
- verbless clause: *When in Rome*, do as the Romans.

The crucial distinguishing factor is thus the form of the verb, or the lack of a verb, in the subordinate clause.

Non-finite subordinate clauses, like finite ones, can have adjectival, adverbial, or nominal functions. Examples (1) to (4) show the adjectival function, which is mostly that of postmodification. Examples (5) to (7) show the adverbial function, in which the clauses typically function as adverbials. The complementation of adjectives and adverbs may also be seen as an adverbial function. Finally, (8) to (12) show non-finite clauses in various nominal functions. Note that there is no one-to-one correspondence between the formal type of non-finite clause and the syntactic function it can fulfil.

1 The government would benefit by the views *expressed by the House.* (postmodifier)
2 The police found no evidence *to suggest that the man was guilty.* (postmodifier)
3 The number of six-year-olds *going to school on their own* has fallen. (postmodifier)
4 *Friendly as usual*, he asked them to step inside. (free predicative)
5 *While opposing a bill in the Parliament*, a member got so excited that he burnt a copy of the bill inside the house. (adverbial)
6 *Asked about his ambitions*, Thornton says: 'I'm not about to get into "being a director".' (adverbial)
7 Roger was likely *to tell his parents.* (complement of adjective)
8 *To err* is human. (subject)
9 It is exciting *to study the structure of the language.* (subject in extraposition)
10 His first job was *selling insurance.* (subject predicative)
11 She hopes *to get away with it.* (direct object)
12 They found the answer by *consulting an encyclopaedia.* (complement of preposition)

13.3 Finite vs. non-finite subordinate clauses

As non-finite verb phrases by definition lack specification of tense and modality (**2.6.4**), non-finite clauses cannot be specified for such properties either. Contrasts in aspect are also less consistently expressed than in finite clauses. Thus, in non-finite clauses this sort of information must be inferred from the context. Sometimes this is a relatively straightforward task (cf. 1 and 2), but it may also be difficult or impossible to pin down the exact meaning of a non-finite clause without the aid of context. Example (3) can yield finite counterparts with or without the progressive aspect, and in the past or in the present tense. Thus both (4) and (5) represent plausible readings of (3).

1	I saw him riding a bicycle.	I saw that he was riding a bicycle.
2	He admits to having stolen the fruit.	He admits that he has stolen the fruit.

3 The men working there are not very friendly.
4 The men who are/were working there are not very friendly.
5 The men who work/worked there are not very friendly.

Furthermore, as most non-finite clauses are not introduced by a subordinator signalling the semantic function of the clause, this meaning may be ambiguous or vague, as in (6) and (7). In most cases the intended meaning will be clear from the wider context. It should be noted that the vagueness of non-finite clauses can be exploited by speakers and writers to express two meanings at the same time, for example time and reason, as shown here.

6 Reading the book I remembered my childhood. (While/because I was reading the book I remembered my childhood.)
7 Having lived in Boston for a year, she spoke English well. (After/because/since she had lived in Boston for a year, she spoke English well.)

Compared with finite clauses, non-finite clauses can be regarded as reduced structures. In terms of meaning they are reduced in that they lack specification of tense and modality; in terms of form they are reduced in that they usually lack a subject, or even a verb in the case of verbless clauses.

13.4 Infinitive clauses

13.4.1 Form and use

Infinitive clauses can have nominal (1), adjectival (2), or adverbial functions (3):

1 I want *to go home*. (direct object)
2 She's a person *to rely on*. (postmodifier)
3 He left Kenya only *to end up as a prisoner of war in Uganda*. (adverbial)

In some contexts, infinitive clauses occur without the infinitive marker *to*. The so-called **bare infinitive** (without *to*) is typically used in *wh*-clefts containing the pro-verb *do* (5), and similar constructions such as (6). The bare infinitive is also used after verbs of perception (such as *see, hear, watch, feel*), as in (7). Here an *-ing* participle clause is often an alternative, though with a slight difference in meaning; see **13.10.2**. After certain verbs, such as *help*, the infinitive marker is optional, as in (8).

4 Stephen longed *to see Wanda again*.
5 What you should do is *sell the story to the press*.
6 All we could do was *sit down and laugh about it*.
7 Nobody ever heard *them complain about the hard work*.
8 They helped me *(to) clean out my flat*.

Furthermore, infinitive clauses may occur with or without an expressed subject. When no subject is expressed, the understood subject of the infinitive clause is the same as the subject of the superordinate clause, as in (9). Otherwise, the understood subject of an infinitive clause can be a very general one, as in (10) and (11). Note that the object form of the pronoun is used in subject position with the infinitive clauses in (12) to (14).

9 John wants to go home.
10 This is a safe place to cross the road.
11 It takes a lot of effort to go through the whole reading list.
12 For John/him to go home now would be wise.
13 What I want is for John/him to leave.
14 I want John/him to go home.

In (12) to (14) the subject of the infinitive clause is different from the subject of the superordinate clause, so it has to be expressed. As shown in the examples, this can be done in two ways, either by means of a noun phrase or by means of a prepositional phrase introduced by *for*. Generally *for* is used when the infinitive clause has the function of subject or subject predicative in the superordinate clause, as in (12) and (13). When the infinitive clause has object function, a bare noun phrase is usually preferred, as in (14).

Finite indirect questions have infinitive counterparts. Thus, *He didn't know what he should do, where he should go, or who he might turn to* may also be expressed as *He didn't know what to do, where to go, or who to turn to.* The meaning is practically the same, only the non-finite alternative lacks a subject and has less specification in the verb phrase.

Note that *to*-infinitive clauses are never used after a preposition in English. In this position an *-ing* clause must be used instead; see (15), where a Norwegian infinitive clause corresponds to an English *-ing* participle clause.

15 John blir aldri lei av å se på musikkvideoer.
John never tires of watching music videos.

13.4.2 The split infinitive

The so-called **split infinitive** is a recurrent issue in discussions of English usage. The debate concerns the placement of adverbials in infinitive clauses, as a split infinitive has an adverb between the infinitive marker and the verb, as in (1). Many people object to this usage due to a prescriptive rule often taught in schools that an infinitive verb should follow the infinitive marker directly. The adverb should then be placed either before or after the whole verb phrase, as in (2). Still, there may be cases in which the split infinitive seems to be either the only possibility or the best way to avoid ambiguity, as in (3), where any other placement of *consciously* might change the meaning of the sentence. Though split infinitives have occurred in the English language for centuries, and continue to do so, learners should be aware of these attitudes towards the construction, and avoid using it where there are alternatives.

1 The infant is unable to actively take charge of satisfying his needs.
2 The infant is unable actively to take charge of satisfying his needs.
3 He refuses to consciously start trying to remember what happened.

13.5 Form and use of past participle clauses

We can distinguish between two main functions of past participle clauses: adjectival and adverbial. Adjectival participle clauses can be viewed as reduced relative clauses with a passive meaning, as can be seen in (1) and (2) with their paraphrases.

1 The house is near a lake surrounded by beautiful hills. (... a lake which is surrounded by beautiful hills.)
2 The foreigners, treated by the rebels as guests rather than as hostages, were allowed to escape the next day. (... who were treated by the rebels ...)

Like full relative clauses, such reduced relative clauses may be restrictive or non-restrictive (**12.6.3**); i.e. they may either be needed in order to identify the referent of the antecedent (restrictive, as in 1) or offer additional or incidental information (non-restrictive, as in 2).

When past participle clauses function as adverbials, they are sometimes introduced by a subordinator, as in (3). Not all subordinating conjunctions can be used with non-finite clauses; we find particularly *when, once, until, while, if, unless*, and *(al)though* in this construction. However, the adverbial function is primarily an effect of meaning. Thus in (4) the alternative finite clause would be *When/as he was encouraged by the applause ...*

3 (When) asked to speak, she told us the story of her life.
4 Encouraged by the applause, he gave a happy smile.

13.6 Form and use of *-ing* participle clauses

Like past participle clauses, the *-ing* participle clauses can be adjectival or adverbial. In addition they can have a nominal function.

Adjectival *-ing* participle clauses can be seen as reduced relative clauses (restrictive or non-restrictive) with an active meaning; compare (1) and (2). Note that the specification of tense and aspect in the finite paraphrases has to be inferred from the context.

1 'Bed timers' is a children's chocolate drink *containing 43 per cent sugar.* (... which contains 43 per cent sugar.)
2 They avoided the radio, the morning TV news show, even the front page of the Santa Luisa Register, *resting on the kitchen bar.* (... which was resting on the kitchen bar.)

Norwegian does not have a direct equivalent of the *-ing* participle clause. It is sometimes possible to use a participle clause in Norwegian, as in (3), but a finite relative clause is a more common translation.

3 I går viste de ham den siste ære gjennom en enslig blomsteroppsats, bestående av hvite roser og tulipaner.
Yesterday they honoured him for the last time through a solitary flower decoration consisting of white roses and tulips.

When functioning as adverbials, *-ing* clauses can be introduced by a conjunction (as in this sentence). Such *-ing* clauses normally function as adjuncts of time or reason. *-ing* clauses without a conjunction may function as adjuncts, as in (4), or disjuncts, as in (5).

4 *Sipping their coffee or discussing the weather*, they avoided the radio, the morning TV news show, even the front page of the Santa Luisa Register, resting on the kitchen bar. (adjunct)
5 *Strictly speaking*, they have no chance of succeeding. (disjunct)

-ing clauses may have a nominal function, as shown in (6) to (9). Nominal *-ing* clauses occur with or without an expressed subject. A subject with specific reference is normally expressed only when it differs from the subject of the superordinate clause, as is also the case in infinitive clauses. Thus in (6) the understood subject of the *-ing* clause is *Amanda*.

6 Amanda dislikes *watching music videos*. (direct object)
7 John's hobby is *watching music videos*. (subject predicative)
8 *Watching music videos* is John's favourite pastime. (subject)
9 John never gets bored with *watching music videos*. (complement of preposition)
10 Amanda dislikes *John/John's watching music videos*.
11 Amanda dislikes *him/his watching music videos*.

As we see from (10) and (11), the subject of a nominal *-ing* participle clause can be expressed by means of either an object form or a genitive form of the noun phrase. The genitive is generally preferred in formal written English, while informal genres tend to have the object form.

13.7 Participle clauses and their subjects

As shown by (1) and (2), both past participle and *-ing* participle clauses may occur with an expressed subject. When the clause has adjectival or adverbial function, the subject never occurs with the genitive form.

1 *All their money having been spent on repairs*, they applied for a loan.
2 But neither can two great and powerful groups of nations take comfort from our present course – *both sides overburdened by the cost of modern weapons, both rightly alarmed by the steady spread of the deadly atom, yet both racing to alter that uncertain balance of terror that stays the hand of mankind's final war*.

(John F. Kennedy)

Adverbial participle clauses are like the nominal ones in that their understood subject is the subject of the superordinate clause, unless otherwise stated. We can say that the participle clause is **attached** to the subject of the superordinate clause. Thus in (3) the understood subject in the participle clause is *I*.

3 Having got my man, I didn't want him.

By contrast, an adjectival participle clause is attached to its antecedent, which thus acts as the understood subject of the participle clause, as in (4).

4 We have friends living in the countryside. (The friends live in the countryside.)

When a nominal *-ing* clause lacks an expressed subject and functions as the subject or subject predicative in the superordinate clause (see **13.6**), the participle clause is not attached to any other element in the sentence, and has no specific understood subject. In (5), for instance, the reference is to getting rich in general, not to any particular people.

5 Getting rich by dishonest means has become a common phenomenon.

13.8 Unattached participle clauses

It is a fairly common mistake to combine participle clauses and main clauses whose subjects are not identical. This often produces an unintended meaning, as the participle clause does not attach itself to the appropriate referent. The mismatch between the main clause subject and the intended subject of the participle clause accounts for the anomaly of (1) and (2). As should be evident from (3), verbless clauses are similar to participle clauses in this respect. We have suggested alternatives that better express the intended meaning. In all cases the improvement consists either in changing the subject of the superordinate clause or in converting the non-finite clause to a finite one with an expressed subject.

1 *Though newly decorated, they did not like the house.
Though it was newly decorated, they did not like the house.
Though newly decorated, the house didn't appeal to them.

2 *Being extremely popular, thousands of people tried to catch a glimpse of the supermodel.
As she was extremely popular, thousands of people tried to catch a glimpse of the supermodel.

3 *If in doubt, our adviser will assist you.
If you are in doubt, our adviser will assist you.
If in doubt, you may seek assistance from our adviser.

When participle clauses function as disjuncts, the requirement that they should be attached to the subject of the superordinate clause is not so strong. Generally, the understood subject of such disjunct participle clauses is the speaker. This is natural, since disjuncts represent the speaker's comment on a message, as in (4).

4 Generally speaking, the people concerned seemed to be in favour of the change. (I am speaking generally when I say that …)

13.9 *-ing* co-ordination

-ing participles can be combined with their matrix clauses in a way that resembles co-ordination, as in (1).

1 He walks briskly to the underground station, stopping to buy a cappuccino and a croissant outside the block where his office is located. (Cf. He walks briskly to the underground station, and stops to buy a cappuccino and a croissant outside the block where his office is located.)

Such clauses can also have approximately the same meaning as sentential relative clauses, as in (2). We have previously (**12.6.4**) noted the semantic similarity between co-ordination and sentential relative clauses.

2 The Highway Department closed U.S. 79, forcing all motorists to make a long detour.

Note that whereas co-ordination with *and* gives both clauses equal status syntactically and semantically, *-ing* co-ordination entails a certain backgrounding of the information in the *-ing* clause.

Norwegian does not have any construction parallel to *-ing* co-ordination, so translations of (1) and (2) will usually result in sentences with co-ordinated main clauses, as in (1a) and (2a).

1a Han tar en rask spasertur til undergrunnsstasjonen, og stopper for å kjøpe en cappuccino og en croissant utenfor blokken hvor kontoret hans er.
2a Vegvesenet stengte riksveg 79, og tvang dermed alle bilister til å ta en lang omveg.

13.10 Infinitive vs. *-ing* participle clauses

For the Norwegian learner it is often a problem to choose between an infinitive and an *-ing* participle clause since Norwegian does not have any formal equivalent of the *-ing* clause. In English, however, the use of the inappropriate clause type may produce unintended meaning, or simply unidiomatic language.

13.10.1 The verb selects the type of non-finite subclause (idiomatic use)

When the *-ing* clause functions as a direct object, and thus as a complement to a verb, it is the verb (in the superordinate clause) that governs the choice between infinitive and *-ing*. The complementation is idiomatic for each verb, and a good dictionary will give you this type of information. However, we have tried to outline some tendencies below.

A *-ing* after verbs of liking and disliking
dislike, enjoy, fancy, hate, love, mind

1 I don't mind doing the dishes.

But note: *like, love,* and *hate* can be followed by either infinitive or *-ing* clauses; see **13.10.2**.

B *-ing* after aspectual catenatives (cf. **6.4.4A**)
begin, start, finish, stop, keep (on), continue, cease

2 Have you finished reading the paper?

But note: *start, begin,* and *continue* may also be followed by the infinitive. *Cease* occurs more often with the infinitive than with *-ing*.

C Infinitive after speech act verbs
agree, beg, decline, offer, promise, refuse, remind, swear, threaten, warn

3 They promised to come early.

But note: *deny* and *admit* are followed by *-ing* (*admit* often by *to* + *-ing*): *He denied having taken drugs.*

D Infinitive after verbs of intention or decision
choose, decide, expect, hope, intend, long, mean, plan, resolve, want

4 Buy meat the day you intend to cook it.

But note: *consider* is followed by *-ing*: *They considered coming.*

E Infinitive with verbs of success or failure
fail, manage

5 England failed to win a place in the finals.

But note: *succeed* is followed by *in* + *-ing*: *England succeeded in winning a place in the finals.*

F Infinitive after verbs of influence or instruction
allow, ask, advise, encourage, forbid, force, get, help, instruct, learn, order, persuade, teach, tell, train, urge

6 I advise you to make the most of each day, to enjoy each one to the nth degree.

13.10.2 Difference in meaning between infinitive and *-ing* clauses

Some verbs may be complemented by either an infinitive or an *-ing* clause, in which case there is usually a difference in meaning. Broadly speaking, *-ing* clauses denote events actually taking place, while infinitive clauses denote hypothetical or future events. This accounts for the semantic difference between the pairs in (1) and (2). (Strictly speaking, *to smoke* is not a complement of the verb *stop*, but functions as an adverbial.) In (3) the difference is more subtle. The *-ing* clause indicates that the subject referent experimented with the word processor in order to find out whether she would like it or be successful with it, while the infinitive indicates that she made an attempt, but does not tell us whether she actually managed to use the word processor.

1 They stopped smoking. (They were smoking, but stopped.)
They stopped to smoke. (They were *not* smoking, but stopped in order to do so.)

2 I'd like to be a genius. (I am not a genius, but I would like to be one.)
I like being a genius. (I am a genius, and quite enjoy it.)

3 She tried using a word processor.
She tried to use a word processor.

After perception verbs, the distinction between the infinitive and the *-ing* participle corresponds to the distinction between non-progressive and progressive aspect (cf. **7.6.5**). That is, the infinitive views the action as a completed whole, while the *-ing* construction focuses on the unfolding action, with no attention to its beginning or end.

4 I heard someone coughing in the next room.
I heard someone cough in the next room.

A similar difference can be observed after verbs of remembering/forgetting, as can be seen in (5).

5 I remembered visiting my aunt in Paris. (I remembered that I visited her.)
I remembered to visit my aunt in Paris. (I did not forget to visit her.)

Sometimes the choice between the infinitive and the *-ing* construction is of little or no consequence as regards meaning. This is certainly the case in (6) and (7), where the infinitive and the *-ing* participle are in object position after the verbs *like* and *start*. In subject position an *-ing* clause is often preferred, as shown in (8).

6 I like reading. / I like to read.
7 It started raining. / It started to rain.
8 Reading books is a hobby of mine.

13.11 Verbless clauses

Since the clause is often defined as a structure with a verb and usually a subject, the concept **verbless clause** seems to be a contradiction in terms. However, when we still use the term *clause* for these structures, it is because they seem to be elliptical clauses, which are easily reconstituted into full clauses by the addition of a verb (most often *be*) and a subject which can be supplied from the context. Let us consider the example given at the outset of this chapter: *When in Rome, do as the Romans*. The first part of this sentence may be turned into a finite clause: *When you are in Rome …*

Verbless clauses may function as adverbials or as free predicatives (**9.8.3**). Free predicatives often consist of either a noun phrase or an adjective phrase, which would function as a subject predicative in a corresponding finite clause; compare (1) and (2).

1 He tumbled with Roberts, helpless and in agony.
2 He tumbled with Roberts. He was helpless and in agony.

Verbless clauses functioning as adverbials may occur with or without a subordinating conjunction. As mentioned in **13.8** they must be attached to the subject of the superordinate clause. Examples are given in (3) and (4). Corresponding finite clauses have been included in parentheses.

3 Though not actually crewel embroidery, it has that look with its overstitched raised pattern in blue, pink, bronze and gold and a sauterne background. (Cf. Though it is not actually ...)
4 A remarkably sympathetic woman, she never let her feelings interfere with her principles of integrity. (Cf. As/Though she was a remarkably sympathetic woman ...)

13.12 Non-finite clauses and style

As stated earlier in this chapter (**13.3**), non-finite clauses can be viewed as reduced structures in comparison with finite ones. For one thing, they are simply shorter, since the finite element and commonly the subject are left out. Secondly, the addressee usually has to recover information which is left out of the non-finite clause, for example tense/modality or the understood subject of the clause. Thirdly, we have seen that participle clauses with an adverbial function are often ambiguous, and the addressee has to decide on an interpretation. As a result, the density of information is often higher in a non-finite clause than in a finite one.

The compactness of non-finite clauses makes them particularly suitable for styles of writing in which language economy is important. The text given in **13.1** has been taken from a short news report. In this format it is important to give as much information as possible in as little space as possible. On the other hand, in conversation and other informal genres, this type of space-saving is usually irrelevant, and speakers may prefer finite alternatives which are easier to interpret.

Example (1) shows the condensing effect of non-finite clauses. A straightforward expansion of the non-finite clauses into finite relative clauses produces a rather inelegant sentence, so (3), where the same meaning is expressed in two sentences, may be a better finite version than (2). The Norwegian learner should, however, make a note of the use of *-ing* participle clauses with adjectival and adverbial functions, since Norwegian does not have any corresponding construction. It does, however, have a construction corresponding to past participle clauses; see (4) and (5), which are translations of (1) and the first part of the text in **13.1**, respectively. Note the translation of the example of *-ing* co-ordination in (5).

1 His 'monumental' abstraction, made up of smooth, metallic 'non-objects' acting upon each other with great tension, won Helion much acclaim during the thirties.
2 His 'monumental' abstraction, which was made up of smooth, metallic 'non-objects' that acted upon each other with great tension, won Helion much acclaim during the thirties.
3 His 'monumental' abstraction won Helion much acclaim during the thirties. It was made up of smooth, metallic 'non-objects' that acted upon each other with great tension.
4 Helions monumentale abstraksjon (*som var*) *laget av glatte, metalliske 'ikke-objekter' som virket på hverandre med stor spenning,* skaffet ham stor anerkjennelse i trettiåra.
5 Landsbyfolk har overlevert en ferdsskriver av stor betydning *som de hadde tatt fra vraket av et vietnamesisk fly* som hadde styrtet i Kambodsja, sa en representant for flyselskapet i dag. *64 mennesker ble drept i flystyrten.*

Terms

infinitive clause
-ing participle clause
past participle clause
verbless clause

unattached participle clauses
-ing co-ordination

bare infinitive
to-infinitive
split infinitive

Exercises

1 Underline the non-finite clauses in the following sentences. State what type they are, and label how they are used: subject, object, subject predicative, adverbial, complement of a preposition, or postmodifier. (**13.2**)

a Skiing in the mountains is great fun.
b From the child's point of view, adulthood is about what there is to look forward to.
c They are charged with crimes ranging from drunk driving to manslaughter.
d Getting bigger will only make him more dangerous.
e It was depressing being 20.
f The art of making a reservation is also important.
g We want to see what's new.
h The product has been judged to be better for the environment.

i To describe a visit to the barber as a male ritual or a rite of passage would perhaps be overstating its importance.
j It seems a pity to destroy it.
k I probably have a lot to learn when it comes to knowing how to eat out with style.
l Our free samples service makes it easy for you to buy from home.
m On the other side of the table you will find a student reading a newspaper while tucking into a cheese-dribbled bowl of onion soup.
n Once submerged in oil, they will keep in the fridge for several weeks, improving as they mature.

2 Identify the subordinate clauses in the following text. Determine whether they are finite or non-finite and state their type and their syntactic function. (**13.2**, **13.3**)

They say that half of all advertising is a waste of money. The problem is knowing which half. This is the kind of half-truth that explains the enormous amounts of money spent on advertising and the fact that the advertising industry boasts more millionaires than any other. If you want to get into advertising yourself, repeat this type of comment as often as you can.

3 Rewrite these sentences, turning the italicized finite clauses into non-finite or verbless ones. (**13.3**)

a Finally they showed us a grey stuffed rabbit, *which was intended for a little girl named Cheryl.*
b *Although this is one of her days off,* she is discussing the next series.
c I always write back *and tell them what I think.*
d Even the brisk weather forecast sounds more plausible *when it is delivered in her calm and reassuring voice.*
e The generation *that was born before the First World War* would be able to provide some answers.
f She smiles fondly, *as though she is recalling an elderly relative.*
g A revivified Church is required *in order that the whole world may see Catholicism in the best possible light.*

4 Rewrite these sentences, turning the italicized non-finite subordinate clauses into finite ones. Comment on any difficulty you have in thus rephrasing the sentences. (**13.3**)

a *Looking out of a window*, I was astonished to discover a wolf cub and his mother.
b *Shortly after meeting Frederic*, Kathy stopped wearing jewellery.

c Dozens of volunteers, *gathered at the church to pray*, joined hands nervously as the verdicts approached.
d The goal is *to repay all the loans.*
e In 1971 Rock Island decided *to build a rock-and-clay floodwall.*
f *Left to its own devices*, a flooding river spreads horizontally, *filling its natural floodplain and enriching it with fertile soil.*
g I asked the House a week ago *to suspend its judgement.*
h Most people would have to hire a contractor *to build this shelter.*
i *Since debuting as host of Late Night with David Letterman in February 1982*, the gap-toothed comic has rewritten the rule book for the TV talk show, *giving the form a hip, self-satirizing edge, perfectly pitched to the baby-boom generation.*
j *Being pregnant*, she was rushed into hospital.
k *Described with emotion*, they can still ring true.

5 Rewrite each sentence so as to avoid unattached participles. (**13.8**)

a After reading the book, the film remains unconvincing.
b When not going to school, my hobbies range from cooking to bungy-jumping.
c Being an old customer, we know that you are familiar with our credit arrangements.
d Before buying a house, a loan must usually be obtained.
e Drenched in maple syrup, the waiter brought us the pancakes.
f Lying in a heap on the floor, Bridget found her son's dirty laundry.
g Be careful of unattached participles writing a paper.

6 Infinitive or *-ing*? Cross out inappropriate alternatives. Explain your choice in each case. If both forms are acceptable, explain any difference in meaning. (The sentences have been taken from G. B. Shaw, *Major Barbara.*) (**13.10**)

a Oh Sir, don't try being / to be cynical, don't be ashamed of being / to be a good man.
b Lord Saxmundham has a soul being / to be saved like any of us.
c If heaven has found the way making / to make good use of his money …
d I'll do my best helping / to help him to his salvation.
e But he wants sending / to send his cheque down buying / to buy us, and go on being / to be as wicked as ever.
f That is perhaps a less questionable way of putting / to put it.
g It enables Parliament doing / to do things …
h Have you ever seen a thousand people falling/fall on their knees with one impulse to pray?

i I wish you wouldn't tell Cholly doing / to do things, Barbara.
j It is more excusable marrying / to marry him than getting / to get drunk with him.

7 Infinitive or *-ing*? Complete the following text by selecting the bare infinitive, the *to*-infinitive, or the *-ing* form of the verbs given in parentheses. (**13.10**)

(GROW) up black in the dusty township of Thaba Nchu outside Bloemfontein, David Phayane learned only part of his nation's painful history. (STUDY) the past meant (MEMORIZE) names and dates (CELEBRATE) the white colonialists. Phayane recalls a class trip to the Great Trek monument in Pretoria (COMMEMORATE) the 19th century migration across South Africa by Afrikaner settlers. 'The teacher said, "These are the men who founded the nation." Some students whispered, "These are the ones who made us (SUFFER)." But we didn't dare (SPEAK) out.'

Today he can, (BE) the principal of the Motlala Combined School in Thaba Nchu, and South Africa (BE) a multiracial democracy. (CONFRONT) the legacy of apartheid in the classroom is one way of (BRIDGE) the country's still-deep racial divide. It will be hard (STRIKE) a new balance.

8 Use the text given in exercise 7 and determine the understood or expressed subject of each *-ing* clause. (**13.7**)

9 Translate the following sentences into English. (**13.10.1**)

a Det er viktig å bevare fatningen.
b Oliver lovte å komme på møtet.
c De håper å forandre pensum.
d Å tillate røyking innendørs vil være i strid med loven.
e Han har ikke evnen til å lytte til folk.
f Sjefen prøvde å overtale henne til å bli i jobben.
g Greenpeace ville hindre fabrikken i å forurense elven.
h Michael unngikk å se henne i øynene.
i Vi ser fram til å høre fra Dem.
j Myndighetene har planer om å evakuere befolkningen i området.
k Hun bestemte seg for å ta imot tilbudet.
l Drømmer du om å reise til Australia?

10 Comment on the difference in form and meaning between the members of the following sentence pairs. (**13.10.2**)

a 1 You should try to take a few days' rest.
  2 You should try taking a few days' rest.
b 1 I did not remember to lock the door.
  2 I did not remember locking the door.
c 1 I mean to ring her at home.
  2 It means ringing her at home.
d 1 They disliked Picasso's drawing Martha.
  2 They disliked Picasso's drawing of Martha.
e 1 The visitors' smoking in the canteen makes me mad.
  2 The visitors smoking in the canteen make me mad.
f 1 She went on talking about a new book.
  2 She went on to talk about a new book.

14 Sentence Form and Communicative Function

14.1 Introduction

Language is used for a range of purposes: to make statements about things, persons, or events, to express feelings, to ask for information, to make requests, to give instructions, etc. There is a broad relationship between three basic **communicative functions** and three principal structural types of sentences:

Function:	Formal category:	Structure:
statement	declarative sentence	SV structure
question	interrogative sentence	VS structure
command	imperative sentence	V structure

A question asks for information and expects a linguistic response. A command expects some action from the addressee. A statement conveys information and just expects the addressee to listen. Example:

1 A: When *is the concert*?
B: (*It's*) at seven. *Get* ready!

However, there is no one-to-one relationship between sentence form and communicative function. A declarative sentence may be used to express a question:

2 Rand's face clouded. 'I don't understand it – a handsome, young man like you without a family? How can that be?'
'I've not had the time,' said Chance.
Rand shook his head, impressed. *'Your work was that demanding?'*
(From Jerzy Kosinski, *Being There*)

On the other hand, what is formally a question can also have other communicative functions. Compare:

3 Have you got a car? (real question)
4 Have you got a match? (request)
5 Will you be quiet! (command)
6 Isn't she pretty! (exclamation)

The communicative function of a sentence is signalled by intonation in speech and by punctuation in writing. Note the question mark in the italicized sentence in (2) and the exclamation marks in (5) and (6). The interpretation is, however, crucially connected with the speech situation. Example (4) is naturally interpreted as a request, as a match is something of little value and is usually freely given to anyone who needs one. Given the right circumstances, e.g. if someone needs transportation, (3) could also be interpreted as a request.

The range of communicative functions goes far beyond the three basic functions introduced above. We have already mentioned additional communicative functions (request and exclamation), and later in this chapter we will refer to many more (invitation, suggestion, etc.). As the concept of communicative function is expanded in this way, it becomes increasingly difficult to match grammatical categories with function.

The choice of form to express a particular communicative function is intimately connected with the formality of the speech situation, the relationship between the speaker and the addressee, and other features of the speech situation. In this chapter we will survey the main sentence types and illustrate their roles in communication.

14.2 Declarative sentences

Declarative sentences are less marked in form, less restricted in function, and more frequent in communication than the other major sentence types. They are marked by SV structure (with some exceptions; see **11.2.1–11.2.2**). When spoken with a falling intonation, they express a statement. Positive declarative sentences *affirm* the truth of the statement:

1 Oslo is the capital of ˋNORWAY.
2 Paul speaks English ˋFLUENTLY.

The speaker may emphasize the truth of the statement by stressing the auxiliary, if there is one, or else by inserting 'emphatic' *do*. Lexical *be* is treated as an auxiliary.

3 Oslo `IS the capital of Norway. } (= It is definitely true that ...)
4 Paul `DOES speak English fluently.

By changing the prosodic pattern, it is also possible to emphasize individual parts of the statement:

5 `OSLO is the capital of Norway. (not `BERGEN)
6 Paul speaks `ENGLISH fluently. (but not `GERMAN)

Sentences like these, with an early placement of the nuclear tone, usually express a contrast with something mentioned or implied in the context. They are therefore affirmative but simultaneously imply a denial.

14.2.1 Negation

In order to *deny* the truth of a statement (e.g. *I love you*) it is possible to say, for example, *If you think I love you, you are mistaken*. The simplest way is, however, to use a negative declarative sentence: *I don't love you*. There are two main types of negation.

A *Not*-negation

Not-negation consists of an auxiliary + the negative particle *not/n't*. If there is no other auxiliary, a form of *do* is inserted. Lexical *be* is treated as an auxiliary. Lexical *have* is sometimes treated as an auxiliary in British English.

1 Fred is here.	Fred isn't here.
2 He has a lot of money.	He hasn't (got) any money. (BrE) He doesn't have any money.
3 Sue knows.	Sue doesn't know.

Contracted forms are used in speech and informal written English (but, for most speakers of Standard English, *may* lacks a contracted form). Lack of contraction may signal that the negative element is especially important:

4 Fred is a Scot, but John is not.

Note that there are often two contracted forms available, one with a contracted verb, and one with *n't*:

5 She's not gone yet.	She hasn't gone yet.
6 They're not ready.	They aren't ready.
7 He'll not come.	He won't come.

On the whole, the form with *n't* is the more frequent one. It is the only alternative with *can*, *could*, *must*, *might*, *ought*, *shall* (*shan't*), *should*, and *would*. Only verb contraction is found with *am not* (*I'm not*), but *aren't I* is used in interrogative structures. *Ain't* is a non-standard form for *am/are/is* or *has/have* + *not*: *it ain't true*, *she ain't got it* (standard: *it isn't true*, *she hasn't got it*).

B *No*-negation

Alternative forms for expressing negation are frequently found with sentences containing indefinite expressions of the *any*-type. These may 'attract' the negative element:

8 There was nobody in the room. ('fantes ingen')
There wasn't anybody in the room. ('fantes ikke noen')

9 She has nothing to do. ('har ingen ting å gjøre')
She doesn't have anything to do. ('har ikke noe å gjøre')

No-negation is particularly common with *be* and *have*. Where the indefinite expression precedes the verb, *no*-negation is the only alternative:

10 Nobody knows. ('ingen')
11 No neighbours ever saw our new curtains. ('ingen')

Where both types are possible, we may find slight differences in meaning or style:

12 She's no teacher. ('noen lærer er hun ikke', 'hun er ingen god lærer')
She's not a teacher. ('hun er ikke lærer')

13 He's no lorry driver. ('han kan ikke kjøre lastebil')
He isn't a lorry driver. ('han er ikke lastebilsjåfør')

The expressions with *no* imply a judgement ('no real', 'no good'), made by the speaker/writer; the *not* expressions formulate a neutral, objective statement.

C Multiple negation

The two types of negation frequently combine in non-standard English:

14 They don't know nothing about it. (standard: They don't know anything about it.)

15 A: Do you admit that you saw him?
   B: I haven't seen nobody nowhere. (standard: I haven't seen anybody anywhere.)

Here the additional negatives do not add anything to the meaning of the sentence, except perhaps emphasis.

Multiple negation should be avoided by the foreign learner, as it is generally considered to be a sign of uneducated language use. Cases like (14) and (15) should, however, be sharply distinguished from:

16 Nobody has no pride. ('ingen mangler')
17 I couldn't not notice the way you behaved. ('jeg kunne ikke la være å')
   Normally: I couldn't help noticing the way you behaved.

In multiple negation of this kind, which is by no means non-standard, each of the negative elements separately retains its negative value. The implication is therefore positive: 'everybody has some pride', 'I noticed the way you behaved'.

14.2.2 Non-declarative functions of declarative sentences

Declarative sentences can be used to ask for information (see also example 2 in **14.1**):

1 A: What's your `NAME?
  B: Fred `SMITH.
  A: And you work in ˏOSLO?
  B: `YES.
  A: And you've lived there for a long ˏTIME?
  B: `NO.
  A: And your home ˏTOWN is?
  ...

Such SV structures, spoken with a low-rise tone, are natural in an interview situation. They often suggest that the speaker is fairly confident that he/she knows the answer. A different type is found in sentences echoing a statement by the previous speaker:

2 A: I saw an `EAGLE yesterday.
  B: You saw an ´EAGLE?

Like the echo questions dealt with below (**14.3.1**), such sentences are spoken with a high-rise tone and express surprise or disbelief.

Asking questions is a delicate matter, and the speaker may therefore choose an indirect approach:

3 That dress must have been very EX`PENSIVE. (implied: How much did it cost?)
4 I hope you received my `LETTER. (implied: Why haven't you answered?)
5 Surely we have met BE`FORE somewhere. (implied: Where did we meet?)

By using declarative sentences, the speaker can avoid asking questions which might be embarrassing. The form of the sentences (the epistemic modal *must*, the verb *hope*, and the modal adverb *surely*, respectively) suggests that the speaker is not certain and invites a response from the addressee. Another way of asking a delicate question is to use *I wonder*: *I wonder / was wondering why...*

Declarative sentences may also be used with the force of command or request, as in:

6 I order you to close the `DOOR.
7 I `LIKE this coffee. (implied: Give me some more.)

While (6) is an explicit command, (7) is an indirect request, through which the addressee is invited to infer the action desired.

Other non-declarative functions of SV structures include exclamations (**14.5**) and wishes (**14.6**).

14.3 Interrogative sentences

Interrogative sentences are marked by VS structure (with the exception taken up in **14.3.1**). An auxiliary precedes the subject. If there is no other auxiliary, a form of *do* is inserted. Lexical *be* counts as an auxiliary.

1	Where is she?	Where did she go?
2	Is she leaving today?	Did she leave yesterday?
3	Is she leaving today or tomorrow?	Did she leave today or yesterday?
4	She has left, hasn't she?	She left, didn't she?

Interrogative sentences neither affirm nor deny. They invite the addressee to:

- supply missing information (*wh*-questions, as in 1);
- indicate the truth value of the corresponding statement (*yes/no*-questions, as in 2);
- select among alternatives presented (alternative questions, as in 3); or
- indicate agreement or disagreement (tag questions, as in 4).

Four main structural types of interrogative sentences broadly correlate with four main functions, as indicated above. The traditional terms will be used in our discussion, although 'question' is, strictly speaking, a functional term.

14.3.1 *Wh*-questions

Wh-questions are introduced by a *wh*-word (**5.13**) which indicates an element to be specified by the addressee, while the rest is taken to be already known (but this is not always so, as shown by the rhetorical questions in **14.3.6**). The element to be specified could be the subject, an object, an adverbial, part of a noun or an adjective phrase, etc.:

1 Who answered the `PHONE? (subject)
2 What did you `SEE? (direct object)
3 Why did they `LEAVE? (adverbial)
4 Which book do you `WANT? } (determiner in noun phrase)
Whose book is `THIS? }
5 How big is the `HOUSE? (modifier in adjective phrase)

Note the SV order (and lack of *do*-insertion) when the question word is the subject (1).

The natural answer to a *wh*-question supplies the missing information by specifying the questioned constituent, by itself or in the context of a complete sentence (possible answers to 1 above):

6 `JOHN. } (usually)
`JOHN did. }
It was `JOHN (who answered the phone).
`JOHN answered the phone.

The nucleus is placed on the element giving the requested information. The normal intonation of both the *wh*-question and the answer is falling.

Speakers frequently follow up a *wh*-question by suggesting an answer themselves, in the form of an elliptic *yes/no*-question or an alternative question:

7 | Who answered the `PHONE? | (Was it) ˏJOHN? |
8 | What would you like to `DRINK? | ˏTEA | or `COFFEE? |

The elliptic follow-up questions have the same type of intonation as ordinary *yes/no*-questions and alternative questions (see below).

Wh-questions pronounced with a high-rise tone on the question word express an **echo question**. The question word sometimes stays in the normal position of the element which is being questioned (see also example 2 in **14.2.2**):

9 A: I saw an ˋEAGLE yesterday.
B: You saw ˊWHAT? / ˊWHAT did you see?

Such questions may express mild surprise or mild disbelief and ask for confirmation rather than information.

14.3.2 *Yes/no*-questions

Yes/no-questions are introduced by an auxiliary and are typically pronounced with a rising tone. The addressee is asked to supply a truth value, by answering *yes* or *no* alone or by giving a more fully specified answer:

1 A: Can you ˏSWIM?
B: ˋYES.
ˋYES,	I ˋCAN.
ˋYES,	I learned to swim when I was ˋFIVE.
ˋNO,	I've always been afraid of ˋWATER.

Needless to say, there are other possible answers than *yes* and *no*, indicating various degrees of certainty:

2 A: Can she ˏCOME?
B: ˋDEFINITELY. / PER ˋHAPS.
Certainly ˋNOT.
I don't ˋTHINK SO. / I don't ˋKNOW.

The initial auxiliary is often left out in informal conversation in examples like:

3 You ALL ˏRIGHT? (= Are you all right?)
4 Got what you ˏNEED? (= Have you got what you need?)

A *yes/no*-question and a *wh*-question can be combined to form an echo question:

5 A: Did you break the ˏCUP?
B: Did I ˊWHAT?

Like the echo questions illustrated previously (example 2 in **14.2.2** and example 9 in **14.3.1**), these sentences are spoken with a high-rise tone on the question word.

14.3.3 Alternative questions

An alternative question is similar in structure to a *yes/no*-question. It is marked by VS structure and rising intonation (except on the last alternative presented):

1 | Would you like ˏTEA | or ˋCOFFEE? |
2 | Do you suspect the ˏCOOK, | the ˏMAID, | or the ˋBUTLER? |

The natural answer is to select one of the alternatives supplied by the speaker.

In function, an alternative question is closely related to a *wh*-question. Both types of interrogative sentences ask for specification of an unknown element. This is represented in one case by a question word, where the answer is more or less open depending on context, and by a limited set of alternatives in the other. Compare:

3 A: Where did you ˋSTUDY?
B: At ˋOXFORD.

4 A: Did you study at ˏOXFORD | or ˋCAMBRIDGE?
B: At ˋOXFORD.

Note that what looks superficially like an alternative question could be a *yes/no*-question:

5 A: Did you study at Oxford or ˏCAMBRIDGE?
B: | ˋNO, | I took my degree at one of the ˋNEW universities. |

6 A: Would you like ˏCOFFEE or something?
B: | ˋYES, | I'd like some ˋTEA please. |

In (6) *or something* does not indicate an alternative, but rather serves to make the question less precise.

14.3.4 Tag questions

Tag questions do not constitute independent sentences but are appended or tagged on to a declarative or imperative sentence. The discussion here will be limited to tags following declarative sentences, while those in imperative sentences will be taken up in **14.4**.

Structurally, a tag question consists of an auxiliary + a personal pronoun. The former is identical to the auxiliary of the declarative sentence (if there is no auxiliary, *do* is inserted); the latter refers back to the subject. There are positive and negative tags. Negative tags usually combine with positive declaratives, while positive tags are added to negative declarative sentences. Examples:

1	Jill was right, wasn't she?	Jill wasn't right, was she?
2	You trust me, don't you?	You don't trust me, do you?

The tag can be spoken with a falling or a rising tone. Allowing for the possibility of positive and negative tags, we can therefore get a four-way contrast, as in:

	assumption	expectation
| Jill was ˋRIGHT, | ˋWASN'T she? |	+	+
| Jill was ˋRIGHT, | ˏWASN'T she? |	+	Ø
| Jill wasn't ˋRIGHT, | ˋWAS she? |	-	-
| Jill wasn't ˋRIGHT, | ˏWAS she? |	-	Ø

There are clear differences here which can be described in terms of the speaker's assumption about the truth value of the sentence and in terms of what he/she expects from the addressee. A positive declarative sentence expresses a positive assumption; a negative one, a negative assumption. Falling tones expect an answer in agreement with the speaker's assumption, whereas the expectation is neutral with rising tones, as indicated by the zero above (Ø).

Tags (especially those with rising tones) are similar to *yes/no*-questions, but there are also important differences. In the first place, there is a difference in formality; tag questions are typically informal, whereas *yes/no*-questions are found in formal as well as informal situations (as are the other types of interrogative sentences we have dealt with). Above all, there is a difference in function, which becomes clear if we translate tag questions into a language which lacks a close formal equivalent, e.g. Norwegian:

3 | You ˋTRUST me, | ˋDON'T you? |
Du stoler på meg, *ikke sant*?

4 | You ˋTRUST me, | ˏDON'T you? |
Du stoler *vel* på meg?

By inserting a tag question the speaker invites the addressee's agreement or disagreement. The primary function is not to ask for information but to maintain successful contact between the participants in the speech situation.

Although there is usually a positive/negative contrast between the body of the sentence and the tag, we do find positive declarative sentences followed by positive tags:

5 A: | I met ˋSARAH yesterday. |
B: | She's ARˋRIVED, | ˏHAS she? |
| She's ARˋRIVED, has she? |

These tags are similar in function to the Norwegian 'jaså' and can express a variety of attitudes, such as surprise or doubt (rising tones), boredom or disapproval (low tail). Frequently they just imply polite interest. Often sentences with these tags are reactions to what the previous speaker has said, and they are therefore closely related to comment questions.

14.3.5 Comment questions

Comment questions are similar to tag questions both formally and functionally, especially to the type of tag illustrated at the end of the last section. They can be positive or negative. Falling intonation implies that B acknowledges A's statement; rising intonation additionally implies surprise on B's part.

1 A: | I've bought a new ˋCAR.
B: | ˎHAVE you? |
| ˏHAVE you? |

2 A: | Jill wasn't ˋRIGHT. |
B: | ˎWASN'T she? |
| ˏWASN'T she? |

Like tags, comment questions are an important means of maintaining communication between the speaker and the listener, but whereas the usual kind of tag is a signal from the speaker that he/she wants a reaction from the addressee, comment questions are reactions from the listener indicating that he/she is paying attention to the conversation and inviting the speaker to continue:

speaker ———— tag question ————→ listener

speaker ←———— comment question ———— listener

Alternatives to comment questions are words like *oh* and *really* (in Norwegian: 'jaså, virkelig, ikke det', etc.). These expressions are often referred to as

back-channels; they show that the addressee is listening and wishes the speaker to continue.

14.3.6 Non-interrogative functions of interrogative sentences

As shown in the last couple of sections, interrogative structures can be put to other uses than asking for information, which may be signalled by an atypical intonation. Rhetorical questions have the force of statements. Note the falling intonation.

1 Does John ˋEVER tell the truth? (= John doesn't ever tell the truth.)
2 Who cares about ˋTHAT? (= Nobody cares about that.)
3 Who needs ˋSPLATTER films? (= Nobody needs splatter films.)

By using an interrogative form, the speaker can avoid making an overt statement which might be regarded as too blunt, self-evident, or categorical. The speaker *appears* to let the addressee be the judge. The skilled orator uses this device to involve the audience.

Negative *yes/no*-questions are frequently used for other purposes than asking a straightforward question. Compare:

4a Is it true?
4b Isn't it true?

5a Have your guests arrived yet?
5b Haven't your guests arrived yet?

Whereas (4a) and (5a) are genuine questions asking for information, (4b) and (5b) are more like statements ('I thought it was true', 'I thought the guests had arrived'). The speaker expresses surprise and asks for confirmation from the addressee.

Interrogative sentences, particularly those opening with the auxiliaries *can/could* and *will/would*, often express requests (see also **7.11–7.12** and **7.19–7.20**).

6 Can/Could you lend me your ˏCAR?
Will/Would you lend me your ˏCAR?

Rather than formulating an overt request, the speaker literally asks about the willingness and the ability of the addressee to do something. The use of *could* and *would* implies greater tactfulness than *can* and *will*. The appeal to the addressee's ability is, however, often completely vacuous. Compare:

7 Can you open the ˏWINDOW?
Can you turn on the ˏRADIO?

8 Can you ˏSWIM?
Can you speak ˏENGLISH?

That the sentences in (7) are requests rather than questions asking for information is shown in at least two ways: (i) *please* can be added; (ii) a *yes* or *no* answer alone, without action, is inappropriate.

Interrogative sentences with *will*, spoken with a falling tone, can express a sharp command:

9 Will you be ˋQUIET!
10 Will you do as you are ˋTOLD!

Examples of this kind express a rebuke and certainly do not invite a response:

11 How *dare* you speak to me like ˋTHAT?
12 Who do you think you ˋARE?

Interrogative sentences opening with *why don't* commonly express suggestions (13, 14), but may also have the force of an invitation (15) or a command (16):

13 Why don't you see a ˋDOCTOR?
14 Why don't we go ˋHOME?
15 Why don't you come and ˋSEE us?
16 Why don't you shut ˋUP?

Compare these with a real *why*-question:

17 Why didn't you see a ˋDOCTOR?

In (17) the speaker wants to find out the reason why some event did not take place rather than suggest a future course of action. An appropriate answer to (17) gives an explanation, whereas an answer to (13) might be something like *yes, OK*, etc.

Other non-interrogative functions of VS structures include exclamations (**14.5**) and wishes (**14.6**).

14.4 Imperative sentences

14.4.1 The form of imperative sentences

The formal characteristics of imperative sentences are (i) lack of a subject (normally), (ii) use of the base form of the verb, and (iii) absence of modals as well as tense and aspect markers. Imperative sentences are typically used in contexts where it is apparent who the addressee is; hence there is no need for a subject. They typically urge the addressee to do something (or not to do something) after the moment of speaking; hence there is no need for tense, aspect, or modal specification.

Often a **vocative** expression is used to single out the addressee:

1 | ˇJOHN, | open the ˋDOOR! |
2 | Don't drive so ˋFAST, Mary! |

Vocative expressions differ from subjects in that they may open or close the sentence. They also have special prosodic characteristics. When opening the sentence, they form an independent tone unit and carry a nuclear tone (often a fall–rise tone). At the end, they are unstressed and are included within the tail of the preceding tone unit (falling or rising). The addressee may also be singled out by *you* before the verb (in negative imperatives between *don't* and the main verb):

3 You go home and go to ˋBED!
4 Don't you let anybody ˋKNOW!

Sentences like (4) have a rude and threatening quality. To indicate that no single person is addressed, it is possible to add *somebody*, *everybody*, or the like:

5 Somebody open the ˋDOOR!
6 Come ˋON, everybody!

14.4.2 The functions of imperative sentences

The basic function of imperative sentences pronounced with a falling tone is to express a command. The command can be toned down by the use of a rising intonation pattern, often together with the softener *please*:

1	Open the ˋDOOR!	Open the ˏDOOR, please!
2	Sit ˋDOWN!	Sit ˏDOWN, please!

The force of such sentences is 'I ask you', 'I appeal to you' rather than 'I order you', i.e. they are polite requests rather than orders. Note that *please* spoken with a falling tone loses its politeness effect. When stressed and spoken with a falling tone, it gives the impression of 'I strongly plead to you':

3 | `PLEASE, | don't drive so `FAST!
4 | Sit `DOWN, | `PLEASE!

A strong appeal can also be expressed by the stressed *do*, which combines both with copular *be* and with lexical verbs:

5 *Do* come and `SEE us!
6 *Do* be `QUIET!

Tag questions, usually *will you* (less commonly *won't you*, *can you*, *can't you*), are sometimes added in imperative sentences:

7 Open the door, will you!
8 Lend me your book, can't you!

Note the difference between imperative tags and the tag questions dealt with previously (**14.3.4**). In the first place, there are only a few tags available. Secondly, there is no consistent positive/negative opposition between the tag and the body of the sentence; a positive imperative sentence may be followed by a positive or a negative tag, with little or no difference in meaning. Like ordinary tag questions, imperative tags can, however, be spoken with either a rising or a falling intonation pattern. Both types of tags also agree in expressing an appeal to the addressee. The exact effect of imperative tags is difficult to pin down. Because of the mentioning of *you*, the addressee is singled out and the command becomes more precise. When spoken with a falling tone, the command is sharpened. A rising pattern sometimes has a softening effect. Unlike *please*, imperative tags can hardly be used when speaking to a superior.

We have seen that the function of imperative sentences may vary from a command to a request or an appeal. Frequently, the effect is one of suggestion or invitation:

9 Have some more coffee!
10 Make yourself comfortable!
11 Let's have lunch!
12 Let's go, shall we!

Note especially the use of *let's* in suggestions. These can be followed by tags like *shall we*, *can't we*.

Imperative sentences are typically used in a spoken context but also occur in writing, provided that the writer and the addressee are sufficiently identified. Softeners and politeness markers are less essential here, as the addressee is not present in the coding situation:

13 Send more money. (telegram)
14 Call Bergen. (note on arrival to work)

Imperative sentences without softeners are the rule in public notices and written instructions to the general reader (e.g. *Drive slowly*, *Turn to page 50*). Note the difference between English and Norwegian in examples like:

15 Keep out of the reach of children.
Oppbevares utilgjengelig for barn.

16 Brush all over with melted butter.
Pensles med smeltet smør.

In general instructions, recipes, and the like, the English imperative often corresponds to a Norwegian *s*-passive.

In examples of the following kind, the imperative construction is equivalent to a conditional clause:

17 Go to Oslo on Easter Sunday, and you will find the place deserted. (= If you go to ...)
18 Suppose you had a million dollars, what would you do?
19 Let *x* be 10, and the answer is obvious.

With the exception of the type just illustrated, imperative sentences regularly have some kind of directive force, influencing the addressee to do something (or not to do something). However, as we have seen in the discussion above, imperative sentences are not alone in expressing commands, requests, and the like (see **14.2.2** and **14.3.6**).

14.5 Exclamations

Exclamatory sentences are a marginal sentence type. The formal features of exclamations vary, though they are all characterized by a falling intonation pattern:

1 Oh, \`DEAR!
2 Thank \`GOODNESS!

3 What a `SHAME (it is)!
4 How `AWFUL (he looks)!
5 What a lovely `DAY (we had yesterday)!

Note the structure in the last three examples. There is an introductory *wh*-word: *what* or *how* (in Norwegian: 'så' or 'for en/et/ei'). Such examples may be expanded to an SV structure as in (3) to (5) (as opposed to the VS structure of *wh*-questions; cf. **14.3.1**).

Exclamations can also be expressed by declarative and interrogative sentences:

6 It's UNBE`LIEVABLE!
7 Isn't it `WONDERFUL!

14.6 Wishes

Wishes are frequently expressed by VS structures:

1 Long live the `KING!
2 So `BE it!
3 May you live `LONG!
4 May she be SUC`CESSFUL!

In contrast to *yes/no*-questions, these sentences have a falling tone. They also have other special features which set them apart from other VS structures, in particular the use of subjunctive (*konjunktiv*) verb forms (**7.4.2**). Apart from expressions beginning with *may*, they are limited to a few more or less set phrases.

Wishes may also be expressed by SV structures:

5 God save the `QUEEN!
6 God `BLESS you!

Again, we note the use of subjunctive verb forms. In addition, wishes can of course be expressed by ordinary SV structures (*I wish ..., I hope ...*, etc.).

14.7 Sentence fragments

By sentence fragments we mean isolated words or phrases which are not integrated in a clause structure, but which – although they do not conform to the structures mentioned in **14.1** – resemble sentences in that they are formally independent and may carry a communicative function. Sentence fragments are perfectly normal in the case of **ellipsis**, where missing words and phrases can be precisely inferred from the linguistic context, e.g. in question–answer exchanges. For examples, see **14.3.1–14.3.3**.

In general, sentence fragments are closely dependent upon the linguistic or situational context for their interpretation. Given the right context we interpret the written sign *Railway crossing* as a warning and the exclamation *Slowly* as a request to slow down the driving speed.

Sentence fragments are abundant in natural discourse, particularly in informal conversation. They are common in a host of expressions which fulfil important functions as greetings, apologies, thanks, interactional signals (**16.7**), etc.

Written discourse uses sentence fragments in the **block language** characteristically found in public notices, labels, newspaper headlines, book titles, figure captions, tables, lists, and the like. In the body of a written text, sentence fragments are far less common (except in fictional dialogue). They may be employed to focus attention on a particular point or carry on a dialogue with the reader:

1 There were many children coming about the place, and he would stop for a moment and lean on his spade and watch them. Especially a small blonde girl.

2 Why not follow Lord Russell's lead? Head for the parks to enjoy the sun. Not in a foolish cause, but in a glorious one.

Sentence fragments give writing the flavour of spontaneous speech. In fiction they are often used to express the stream of thought:

3 No sense of humour, that Isaiah. He banged down the receiver. Very uncivil.

4 There was a brief-case on the back seat – and, neatly stacked beside it, a sheaf of documents tied with narrow pink tape. Not a doctor then. A solicitor. The discovery was a relief. (from a detective story)

The skilled writer does not overuse sentence fragments, as they may then lose their special effect. Students are recommended to use complete sentences in academic prose, and avoid sentence fragments and subordinate clauses which are not attached to a main clause.

Terms

declarative sentence
interrogative sentence
imperative sentence
sentence fragment

wh-question
yes/no-question
alternative question
tag question

comment question
echo question

communicative function

not-negation
no-negation
multiple negation

Exercises

1 Consider the two sentences below, where *it* stands for a specific piece of discourse/utterance. Outline briefly and generally what types of answer might be relevant in each case. (**14.1**)

What is it used for?
What is its structure?

2 Explain briefly what you understand by the form of a sentence and its communicative function. Why is it useful to operate with this distinction? In the light of your answer, comment on the following passage. (**14.1**)

> A Royal Navy spokesman instructed to explain the procedure for clearing target areas to a group of interested parties told his audience: 'Patrol launches have orders not to order trawlers away from the area. They merely inform skippers that they are in an area where bombing is about to commence. They usually co-operate by moving.'

3 What are the possible communicative functions of these declarative sentences? Try to put them into situational contexts that support your interpretations. Suggest appropriate intonation patterns and punctuation marks. The sentences have been arranged in pairs. What grammatical and/or lexical differences in each pair contribute to the difference in communicative function? (**14.2**)

a You're not working
b It's not working
c It's cold in here
d It's cold in Chicago
e Officers will wear uniforms at the ceremony

f I will wear my uniform at the ceremony
g I hereby welcome you all to this conference
h In that way he welcomed them to the conference
i You've probably sent it already
j You haven't sent it yet
k I don't mind having some more of that
l I do mind having any more of that
m Political statements are empty
n That wood basket is empty
o I think we would hear better if we were quiet
p I think he would hear better if he stopped playing loud music

4 Explain the difference in meaning between the three sentences below. Clue: Which one can mean that the speaker 'is not a professional dancer'? (**14.2.1B**)

I'm not a dancer.
I'm no dancer.
I don't dance.

5 Why is the following sentence non-standard? (**14.2.1C**)

You ain't seen nothing yet.

6 What are the possible communicative functions of the interrogative sentences below? Try to put them into situational contexts which support your interpretations. Add appropriate intonation patterns and punctuation marks. The sentences have been arranged in pairs. What grammatical and/or lexical differences contribute to the difference in communicative function? (**14.3**)

a Aren't you lucky
b Aren't you happy
c Can't you use a computer
d Can you use a computer
e Where's the salt
f Where's Salt Lake City
g Have you met my wife
h Did you meet my wife
i Had I only heard about it
j Have you only heard about it
k Whose is that filthy shirt on the floor
l Who is that man in the picture

m Will you be quiet
n Will you be my guest
o Who hasn't heard of the Beatles
p Who has heard of Bingley
q Do you want a piece of cake
r Do you want a slap in the face

7 What are the possible communicative functions of the imperative sentences below? Try to put them into situational contexts which support your interpretations. Add appropriate intonation patterns and punctuation marks. Explain what grammatical and/or lexical differences contribute to the difference in communicative function. (**14.4**)

a Have fun
b Have another helping
c Be patient
d Be a patient and get to know your local hospital
e Let's go for a walk, shall we
f Let us in, will you
g Help me with this box, please
h Help yourself to some more
i Don't be clever with me
j Don't be modest with them

8 All of the following can be used with the communicative function 'request for action' – more specifically, 'request to stop making a noise'. Describe in each case the form of the expression. (**14.1–14.4**)

a Be quiet!
b I wonder if you could be a bit more quiet?
c Could you make a little less noise, please?
d Will you stop making that awful racket?
e Hadn't you better be a little more quiet?
f I really wish you would be a little less noisy.
g Visitors are kindly requested to observe the No Noise sign.
h Silence!!
i Would it be too much to ask if you could calm down a bit?
j Please, be quiet.
k Might I be allowed to suggest that you try to be a little more quiet?
l Must you really make all that much noise?
m What a terrible noise you're making!
n This is like a kindergarten outing.
o You will stop that noise right now!

9 Go back to the examples in exercise 8. (**14.1–14.4**)

a Find a good candidate for a polite and neutral form of request.
b Find a good example of a direct and rather brusque form of request.
c Who is likely to use a form like o?
d Find an example where the speaker perhaps has gone too far in being polite.
e Only one example is such that the addressee must be present when the utterance is made in order to understand that it is a request to stop the noise. Which?
f Why do you think there are so many ways of expressing a request to stop somebody doing something the speaker finds annoying?

10 In which of the sentences below can *please* be added at the end? Justify your answer.

Will you be asking him?
Will you ask him?

11 Comment on the difference in form and meaning between the two members of each of the pairs below. (**14.1–14.5**)

a 1 How were they discouraged?
2 How discouraged they were!
b 1 Why don't you buy a car?
2 Why won't you buy a car?
c 1 What excuses did they have?
2 What excuses they had?
d 1 Have you got the time?
2 Have you got some time?
e 1 How should I know?
2 How should I proceed?
f 1 Your car blocks the driveway.
2 His car blocked the driveway.
g 1 You couldn't possibly help her?
2 I couldn't possibly have helped her.
h 1 How do you do.
2 How do you do it?
i 1 It's been nice talking to you.
2 It's been nice working with you.
j 1 How I love grammar!
2 How to learn grammar.
k 1 What a restaurant!
2 What restaurant?

15 Grammar in Written Discourse

15.1 Introduction

Discourse is a cover term for all types of language used by real people in real situations. Written discourse covers a wide variety of writing, e.g. personal letters, advertisements, prose fiction, and expository prose used for the purposes of analysis and persuasion. Formal writing differs from speech in many fundamental ways (see **16.1**).

So far we have rarely gone beyond the confines of a single sentence. In this chapter we will focus on grammar beyond the sentence. The main emphasis will be on the formal aspects that help tie sentences together into good texts.

15.2 Cohesion and coherence

Coherence in writing relies heavily on formal features of grammar and lexis, so-called **cohesive ties**. Coherence based on cohesive ties is called **cohesion.** Many cohesive ties can be explained on the basis of a more fundamental principle of information processing. This is what is called 'distribution of information' in Figure 15a. In addition, good writers create coherence by adhering to the established conventions of writing. They will write about one topic at a time, and expand on and support their arguments in sentences which closely precede or follow the **topic sentence**, which expresses the chief point to be made. In this way their thoughts on one topic are made into a coherent unit, typically a paragraph. This is what we have called 'thought organization' in the figure below. Obviously, cohesion and information distribution reflect the more fundamental controlling mechanism of thought organization.

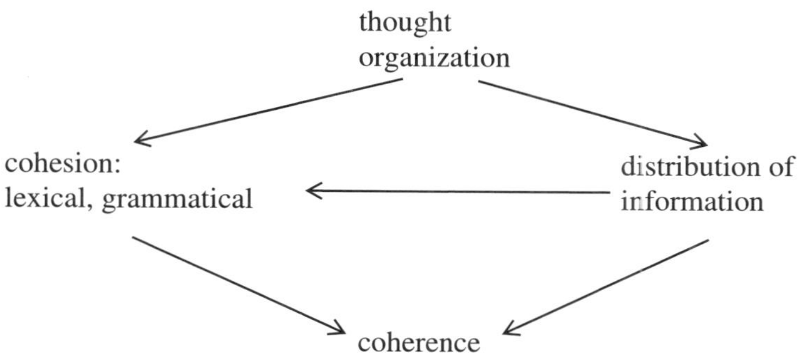

Figure 15a: Factors determining coherence

For the sake of illustration, we include an example of the well-known type which has coherence with no cohesion:

A: The lawn needs mowing.
B: I have an essay for tomorrow.

The exchange is coherent because B understands A's utterance as a request to mow the lawn and responds accordingly by explaining why he/she cannot do it. The utterances make up a coherent exchange of speech acts. However, while this type of coherence often arises in spoken dialogues, it rarely does in formal writing.

15.3 Grammatical cohesion

Most of the formal grammatical ties that we will be looking at have what is called a **textual deixis**. In the example below that means, for example, that *he* and *his* point the reader in the direction of *Tittman*, that *over the next ten years* points to *1968* and takes the reader to 1978, that *another type of treatment* points to the earlier treatment, and that *finally* makes the treatment by Dr Andrew C. B. follow those mentioned before in the text. In other words, the orientation is within the text. Compare also the remarks on chains of reference in **5.16**.

> Francis Tittman, New York contractor, broke two bones in his (i) left leg in a 40-foot fall in 1968. But the (ii) nasty fractures (iii) failed to heal. Over the next ten years (iv) Tittman (v) went to hospital more than twenty times for surgery to implant pins, nails and bone grafts, all (vi) of no avail. Finally (vii), he (viii) was transferred to Dr Andrew C. B. for another (ix) type of treatment of broken bones (x) – electricity. Tittman (xi) received

weak pulses of electric current through his (xii) leg cast each day and in less than a year (xiii) he (xiv) was back on the scaffolding (xv).

We have added roman numerals to the cohesive links and will refer to these in the following discussion.

15.3.1 Anaphoric and cataphoric expressions

A The definite article

In line 2 of the text above, *the nasty fractures* refers back to the broken bones in line 1. This is a common use of the definite article (**5.2.3**). The noun phrase is introduced in an indefinite form (*bones*); the anaphoric definite article points back to this first mention. Note that *broke two bones* is replaced by the synonymous *fractures* (**15.4**), to which the descriptive adjective *nasty* is added.

In (1) below the definite article in *the keyboard* is anaphoric, although there is no earlier mention of *keyboard*. We could say *the keyboard* has indirect anaphoric reference because we know that computers have keyboards, screens, word processing programs, etc.

1 Last summer I bought a new Compaq Presario. I am satisfied with *the* computer but I don't like *the* keyboard.

B Personal pronouns

The personal pronoun *he,* in (viii) and (xiv) in the text, obviously refers back to Tittman. This anaphoric use (**5.8.2**) avoids repetition of the same noun phrase. Example (2) contains a pronoun, *they,* which points forward to the full noun phrase *the Browns* in the following superordinate clause. This is a type of cataphoric reference. It works from an initial subordinate clause up into a following superordinate clause. This is admittedly a within-the-sentence relation.

2 When *they* had unpacked their gear, *the Browns* wanted to go to the local pub for a pint.

The use of *they* and *them* in (3) derives its effect from the fact that we are supposed to know the referents of pronouns. Here we do not, and feel temporarily at a loss. The result is that we read on in suspense to find out who *they* and *them* refer to. It is only later that we realize that *they* and *them* refer to some golfers.

3 Through the fence, between the curling flower spaces, I could see *them* hitting. *They* were coming towards where the flag was and I went along the fence. Luster was hunting in the grass by the flower tree. *They* took the flag out, and *they* were hitting.

(From William Faulkner, *The Sound and the Fury*)

C Possessive determiners

His, in (i) and (xii) in the Tittman text above, is an anaphoric possessive determiner. Its cohesive function is much the same as that of personal pronouns.

D Demonstrative pronouns and determiners

As cohesive ties, *this* and *these* can point to something which comes either before or later in the text, as shown in (4) and (5). *That* and *those* tend to refer to something that has been mentioned before. Often the demonstratives have unclear referents (6). See also **5.3**.

4 What about *this* for an enticing ad: Explore the romantic past through the peaceful and picturesque waterways of old England and Wales in a traditional narrow boat with all modern conveniences including shower and fridge.

5 He gets angry at being called 'Vicar Richard' and 'The High Priest of Pop'. – 'Do you know a lot of people think *this* is a big gimmick – that I'm not serious about it. Well, I am.'

6 Brian told me it would be wrong. He pulled out a Bible and showed me about five places where they warned against trying to contact the dead. *That* impressed me.

E Other pronouns and determiners

A similar cohesive function may be served by other pronouns and determiners, for example *some* in (7) below, and *all* (vi) and *another* (ix) in the Tittman text above. The propword *one* (**5.12A**) also marks cohesion. Whereas Norwegian uses ellipsis, English uses *one* to refer back to a countable noun in the previous sentence (8).

7 Most of the exhausted children decided to spend the night in the cabin. *Some* wanted to continue to the hotel in order to phone their parents.

8 Peter left his umbrella on the bus. Now he has to buy a new *one*. ('en ny')

F Adverbial pro-forms

Forms such as *now, then, here, there, so,* and the more formal *therefore, thus* ('in this way'), and *hence* ('as a result of this') are used to point to more precise adverbial elements used earlier in the text. The adverbial element does not have to be explicit; it may be implicitly inferred. In (11) we infer that it was because some members were ill (an adverbial of reason) that the meeting was postponed.

9 I have visited the Gaelic part of Ireland several times. I love its people, its landscape, and not least its music. However, I am not sure I want to live *there.*
10 I am convinced I made the right decision when I turned down the offer back in 1992. My situation was different *then.*
11 Some of the members had gone down with a nasty stomach ache. Therefore, the meeting had to be put off.

Now, here, and *there* can have a somewhat different cohesive function when they are used to point to places in the development within the text itself.

12 *Now* ('At this point in the text'), if we want to go ahead with our plan, we have ...
13 *Here* is where we have to stop and reconsider our position.
14 It must be very satisfying to know you're right all the time. It's a luxury I have not indulged in for many years. *There*'s a confession for you.

Then can be used as a cohesive tie, sometimes across many sentence boundaries. It refers back to some sentiment or position mentioned earlier. Note the paraphrase 'in that case', where *that* once again has rather vague reference.

15 His family does not want to have anything to do with them. Her family is equally reserved. What can we do *then*? ('in that case')

Cohesive ties like **ellipsis**, the **pro-verb** *do,* and the **pro-form** *so* are more common in speech than in writing. In face-to-face exchanges they are quickly interpreted across utterance boundaries and greatly facilitate communication. However, they also occur in writing.

G Ellipsis

Ellipsis is a term we use when some element is left out because it can be filled in from the surrounding text. In (16) there is ellipsis after *try* since the non-finite clause 'to see it our way' is recoverable from the previous sentence. Note also the elliptic subject predicative 'serious about it' at the end of (5) above. In (17) there are several possibilities with no difference in meaning.

16 We will come up with different answers to the same questions. I don't see there is any hope of your seeing it our way. I'd rather you didn't try.

17 We have tried to persuade John to take some days off. He clearly needs a break, but although he seems to be listening to our advice, he keeps saying that he can't
afford *to.* (ellipsis)
afford *it.* (pronoun)
afford *to do it.* (two pro-forms)

H The pro-verb *do*

The pro-verb *do* replaces a verb, sometimes only the verb (18), at other times the verb and predicatives or objects coming after (19).

18 He asked me if I smoked. I told him I *didn't.*
19 Now and then he will ask if he can borrow my car to visit some friends in Bergen. When he *does*, he always takes care to fill up the tank afterwards.

I The pro-form *so*

So in (20) replaces *block the road if they* ... In (21) it replaces *hanging around. Done so* in (22) replaces *divided on party lines.* There is a difference between the pro-forms *do it* and *do so*. In (22) *done it* is not likely, because the sentence is about a hypothetical situation. However, in (23), which refers to a real situation, *did so* is unacceptable. *Do it* refers directly to a real action; *do so,* more indirectly to a possible action. The difference between *said so/it* and *believe so/it* is somewhat similar. *It* refers directly to the wording of a statement, while *so* refers indirectly to the content of the statement. Note that *hope* and *think*, which point to potential situations, accept only *so*; compare *hope/think so* with **hope/think it.*

20 I have warned them that I am going to block the road if they continue to use it across my property. And *so* I will.
21 In one corner a gang of boys was assembled – some smoking, some hanging around in the hope of a smoke. The three smokers were hanging around. *So* was MacDowall.
22 The tradition would have been endangered if the committee had divided on party lines. Still, it might have *done so* if one Tory, QD, had not been determined to ...
23 They had this bet going: who dared jump from the bridge? The bridge seemed to be too high for them to try, but then suddenly Brian *did it.*

Ellipsis and all the pro-forms have one thing in common. What they point to must be clear from the co-text (see **3.1**). If they occur too far away from the material they replace, it becomes difficult to fill it in, and the text becomes difficult to understand – it becomes incoherent.

J Words expressing comparison

In this section we define 'comparison' in a rather wide sense. It includes the traditional comparative and superlative forms of adjectives and adverbs in *-er/-est* and the alternative forms with *more* and *most,* e.g. *happier, more confusing, worst, most problematic* (see **8.2**). It also includes words such as *same, similar, different, such,* and *as* expressions, to mention the most important ones. These words have a cohesive function when the basis for the comparison occurs in the preceding text. In addition to the comparative form *more shocking* in (26) we also have fronting of the subject predicative and subject–verb inversion. This takes us into word order as a cohesive principle (see **15.3.5** and **11.3.2B**).

24 A: I think John is strong enough.
B: I know John is strong, but Jim is *stronger.*

25 He knocked over a rather expensive vase when he visited us. A few days later he phoned us and said he had bought a *similar* vase, which he wanted to give us.

26 It was shocking to hear him be so critical. *Even more shocking*, I felt, was the fact that it was done in the presence of the Queen.

15.3.2 Conjuncts

Expressions like those below are called conjuncts (**10.8**). They serve to establish the logical link between sentences in a piece of written discourse. In Norwegian they are called *bindeadverb* or *bindeord.*

in the first place / to begin with	for det første/først
secondly/thirdly, etc.	for det andre/tredje, osv.
on the one hand	på den ene siden
on the other (hand)	på den andre (siden)
besides/furthermore/ moreover / in addition	dessuten/videre/dertil/ i tillegg
however	men/derimot
likewise/similarly	på samme måte / likeså
for example / for instance	for eksempel
on the contrary	tvert i mot
conversely	i motsatt fall
after all	tross alt / likevel
first and foremost / above all	først og fremst
so/consequently/therefore	så/derfor/følgelig
yet/still/nevertheless/ in spite of / despite / even so	likevel / til tross for
by way of conclusion / to conclude / to sum up /lastly/finally	som en konklusjon / for å avslutte for å runde av / til slutt

1 The tradition would have been endangered if the committee had divided on party lines. *Still,* it might have done so if one Tory, QD, had not been determined to …
2 Those cabinet Eurosceptics have been consistently wrong: wrong that …, wrong that … *So* what to do? The answer is ...
3 Aristotle's method in the Poetics, *then*, does suggest that we should isolate the work. The Chicago contingent of modern critics follow Aristotle so far in this direction that it is hard to see how they can compare one poem with another for the purpose of evaluation. But there are, *however,* several features of Aristotle's approach which open the way for the moral measure of literature. *For one thing,* Aristotle mentions that plays may corrupt the audience. *In addition,* his definition of tragedy invites our attention, because a serious and important action may very well be one that tests the moral fiber of the author of the characters. And, there is one other point in the Poetics that invites moral evaluation: Aristotle's notion that the distinctive function of tragedy is to purge one's emotions by arousing pity and fear.

(From Keith F. McKean, *The Moral Measure of Literature*)

15.3.3 Conjunctions

Conjunctions like *and, but*, *or*, although frowned upon by some prescriptivists as sentence openers, do occur in initial position. Note the underlined *but,* expressing contrast, and *and,* expressing addition, in (3) at the end of the previous section. With *nor*, sentence-initial position is the norm. See also **12.3**.

1 I do not mind at all challenging him on the consistency of his approach. *Nor* would I have the slightest qualms about confronting him with …
2 They might one day want to do what Mr F fears. *But* could they?

15.3.4 Question–answer sequences

Question–answer sequences are typical of speech, but they may also be used to good effect in writing. The question sets up expectations of an answer, which may follow directly after the question or be incorporated into the following text. In either way, the first part imposes coherence. The reader looks for the answer. Examples (1) and (2) show such sequences. The negative question in (2) is like a rhetorical question (**14.3.6**). It reveals positive assumptions on the part of the speaker. The answer confirms these assumptions. (The material in parentheses did not occur in the original.) Example (3) contains a clear rhetorical question.

1 How can this be achieved with the minimum of fuss? For one thing, we could …, but it is equally important to …
2 By why shouldn't this process apply to present members as well? (It applies to present members as well because) It would strengthen the alliance now and for the future.
3 Who is he to preach virtue to anybody? He has been through the messiest of marriage problems himself.

15.3.5 Word order

In Chapter 11 we saw that *word order* means the order of the main elements of a clause, i.e. word order is defined in terms of syntax. Clauses carry messages, in which some information tends to be given (or to be presented as if less salient) and other information is new. The unmarked tendency is for given information to precede new information (**11.1.2**).

There is good correlation between the length of clause elements, their order, and the information load they carry (**11.1.3**). Subjects tend to occur early in declarative sentences, be short, and have a definite form (pronouns, noun phrases with the definite article, etc.). Adverbials, predicatives, and objects normally follow the verb. They tend to be longer and often include indefinite elements. This is just a tendency, however, which can easily be departed from.

We rely on this ordering of information, with its accompanying linear order of clause elements, when we process texts across sentence boundaries. It is a fundamental principle of coherence. Example (1) conforms to this pattern.

1 A thrush ran out from under a shrub and started to tug a worm from the soil. *It* stood over *the worm* and tugged vertically, exposing *its speckled throat* and pointing *its beak* towards the sky. *The worm* stretched, but held. *The thrush* lowered *its head* and backed off, pulling at a more acute angle. *The worm* still held, so *the thrush* stepped in …

It is, however, noteworthy that when some clause element other than the subject begins the sentence, this non-subject element tends to contain given, or at least less salient, information. The adverbial in (2) is a good example. What is important is that the initial adverbial contains information which links the sentence to the earlier co-text and in that way creates coherence.

2 He walked round to the back of the school and crossed the strip of asphalt to the cycle shed. There were look-outs posted at either end of the shed. *In one corner of the shed* a gang of boys was assembled …

The opening adverbial in the italicized sentence in (3) below, which has inverted word order, also contains given information. The new information is *a notice: NO HAWKERS* ('dørselgere') ... In other words, the given-to-new principle of coherence is at work.

3 Billy stopped before a wrought-iron gate with spikes at the top. *On one of the gate posts was a notice: NO HAWKERS NO CALLERS.*

The same principle is at play in connection with subject–verb inversion (**11.2.2**) and many cases of fronting (**11.3.2**).

To sum up, the underlying principle which governs the distribution of information from given to new has repercussions not only for the form of given elements (e.g. pro-forms) but also for their position relative to other clause elements, both within the clause and across sentences. When it applies across sentence boundaries, it helps create textual coherence.

15.3.6 Structural parallelism

When a writer repeats the same syntactic pattern in several sentences in a row, with new or partly new vocabulary, we talk about structural parallelism. This is a rhetorical device, which also contributes to coherence. One sentence becomes an image of the previous one, and the reader senses the similarity. There may be parallels at the phrase level or the clause level. It is especially this second type which is relevant here. In (2) the parallelism is even more striking because many of the sentences have the inverted AVS order. Each fronted adverbial contains given information.

1 Like a terrible bereavement, the memory of Labour's 1983 election campaign haunts those who lived through it. They remember the divisions, with Jim Callaghan, its former leader, ripping into its non-nuclear defence policy. They remember the taunts of the defectors, with Roy Jenkins, a former Labour chancellor, ruthlessly revealing their inadequacies. Above all, they remember its titular leader, dithering impotently between party factions, until ...

2 At the back of the bed where the standard roses grew was a brick wall. It ran down the side of the garden, beyond the sunken garden, to meet a privet hedge at the bottom. On the other side of the sunken garden was an arrangement of banked flower beds, fringing the sunken garden with a long lawn on the other side of them. Growing from the long lawn were trees, their bare branches dripping. At the back of the trees, and partly screened by them, was a rubbish tip. Through the tree, lying more to the right, could be seen most of an old brick building.

(From Brian Aldiss, *Report on Probability A*)

Martin Luther King's famous speech *I Have a Dream* is well known for its structural parallelisms. Although it was spoken on that memorable day in 1963, it was based on a cleverly crafted piece of writing. Example (3) is an extract from that speech.

3 This is no time to engage in the luxury of cooling off or to take the tranquilizing drug of gradualism. Now is the time to make real the promises of Democracy. Now is the time to rise from the dark and desolate valley of segregation to the sunlit path of racial justice. Now is the time to open the doors of opportunity to all of God's children. Now is the time to lift our nation from the quicksands of racial injustice to the solid rock of brotherhood.

15.3.7 Tense choice

Tense forms locate the action, process, or state expressed by the verb with respect to the moment of coding (speaking, writing) or some other point of reference established in the text. As the time perspective normally characterizes longer stretches of text than the sentence, the choice of tense forms makes a significant contribution to textual cohesion. Notice how the shift of tense in the text below signals a transition in the narrative.

> Her voice, as she spoke, seemed to become more and more Jamaican, as though the closer she came to the memory of that day twelve years ago, the more she became the seventeen-year-old girl she then was. As they listened, the present dissolved into the past, only to become the present again – a different present, but an immediate one nonetheless; whatever had happened in that basement room so long ago seemed to be happening here and now, this instant.
>
> It is raining.
>
> She is surprised by the rain, she thinks it should be snowing at this time of the year, it's so cold outside. But it's raining instead, there is thunder and lightning. The lightning flashes illuminate the painted basement windows high on the cincer-block walls. Thunder crashes everywhere around them.
>
> They are alone in the basement room.
>
> (From Ed McBain, *Long Time No See*)

Here we progress from the conventional use of the past tense in telling a story to the historic present, which makes the narrative more dramatic and, so to speak, recreates the situation before our eyes (see **7.6.5B**). Note the explanation of the fusion of times before the tense shift.

15.4 Lexical cohesion

Lexical ties have an important cohesive function in written text (see Chapter 3). Obviously, the words chosen must be appropriate to the topic of the text. Too-frequent repetition of the same vocabulary creates a bad text. There are several ways in which good writers can vary their vocabulary while at the same time keeping their referents constant.

15.4.1 The use of synonyms or near-synonyms

Synonyms are words with the same (or approximately the same) meaning. In the Tittman text in **15.3** the writer replaced *broke two bones* by the synonymous *fractures* in the next line. In (1) below we have italicized expressions which mean 'get rid of' and underlined expressions meaning 'rubbish'. *Take away, dispose of, sling, dump, heave, shift,* and *incinerate* are all roughly synonymous with 'get rid of'. *Rubbish, refuse, muck, filth,* and the general, almost pronoun-like *stuff* are near-synonyms here. Used as in the text below, these lexical ties create cohesion and variation.

1 THE *TAKE-AWAY* RUBBISH BUSINESS

Like most aspects of living, refuse *disposal* was simpler in the old days. The peasant would just open the door and *sling* the muck out onto the earth, where it would fertilize the following year's crops or, in the case of non-biodegradable material like coins and pots, lie in the soil over the centuries until they were recycled into an archeological thesis.

With the later sophistication of city life, the practice was to open the window and *sling* it out over the passers-by, or, for the slightly more conscientious, *dump* it in the river. The Thames became rich in everything except water, and one of the smaller watercourses was completely stopped up during the 1380s. Finally faced with an outcry, London invested in twelve carts which *shifted* the stuff to dumps in the suburbs or the Essex marshes.

Still the polluters refused to co-operate. A man was nicked in 1421 for *heaving* so much filth into the street that his neighbours were forced to flee from their shops. London was not presentable until 1666 and then, briefly, during the morning after the Great Fire. This sort of *incineration* was considered an extreme method of dealing with the problem, and so the muck level continued to rise with the expanding population.

(From Valli Hazandra Despotopoulou, *Attitudes and Opinions*)

The italicized verbs in (2) have the sense component 'get hold of' in common. They are related but different in sense. Note also that coherence is achieved by the striking use of question–answer sequences (**15.3.4**).

2 Businessmen, it seems, have all the answers these days. Need to reform the tax system? *Call in* Mr T, boss of Barclays Bank. Cricket in crisis? *Send for* Lord M, the Tesco supermarkets baron. Tory party in chaos? *Grab* another grocer, Asda's AN. Want a competitive economy? *Wheel on* Lord S, the saviour of BP, a once-ailing oil giant.

The skilled writer uses lexical variation as a means of bringing out different aspects of the same thing. Thesauruses are useful when it comes to finding alternative words for the same referent!

15.4.2 The use of hyponyms and superordinate terms

In the text on rubbish disposal above, the general word *stuff* is a **superordinate term**, while words like *filth, rubbish, muck,* and *refuse* are **hyponyms** in relation to *stuff*. This means that they are included in the meaning of *stuff*, at the same time as they are more precise. The word *problem* in the last sentence is also a superordinate term. It encompasses more precise, hyponymous expressions like *sling the muck, heave so much filth, shift the stuff, take away rubbish*, in other words 'get rid of garbage'. Note that many of these words differ in level of formality.

In the example below the general word *people* finds hyponyms in *passer-by* and *crowd. Beg* and *ask for money* are synonymous expressions.

> Does he feel guilty about asking people for money? 'No', says Joe. 'Some of these people spend more money in a few minutes than I get in a week.' He doesn't do much begging in a crowd as business is usually bad, but occasionally he will shout 'spare some change' to a likely-looking passer-by.

Like synonyms, hyponyms and superordinate terms are cohesive ties at the level of lexis.

15.4.3 The use of anaphoric nouns

Anaphoric nouns are abstract nouns with definite determiners such as *that comment, this conviction,* and *this assertion* in (1) to (3) below. The definite determiner follows the rules of anaphoric reference (**15.3.1D**). However, the lexemes *comment, conviction,* and *assertion* sum up the writer's interpretation of the preceding content. Often they function as the subject of a sentence, as in the following examples.

1 'Surely, there was never a better name for a spy', you write in your obituary of Alger Hiss. *That comment* brought to mind …
2 As one of those diplomats singing the old tune that 'Italy's policies are Europe's policies, … might I be allowed to elaborate? The broad consensus in my country is that … *This conviction* stems not from starry-eyed idealism but from hard-headed analysis …
3 It is disappointing to see you parrot the conventional, but superficial, view that term limits in America 'force voters into a choice they are free to make anyway by booting the incumbent out.' *This assertion* has two problems. First …

15.4.4 The use of antonyms or near-antonyms

Antonyms are words with opposite meanings. As pointed out in Chapter 3 (**3.6.2**), it is not easy to define antonymy. One type is represented by *dead* vs. *alive*; another by *hot* vs. *cold*. In one thesaurus *dismiss, fire,* and *discharge* are given as antonyms of *engage*. Another thesaurus gives *dismiss* and *fire* as antonyms of *employ*. Both operate with a loose definition of antonymy.

If we use *employ* (or related words) for all the italicized expressions in (1), the result is a piece of coherent writing, but it becomes stylistically awkward. The difference between (1) and (2) is both extreme and artificial, but it does illustrate how the use of near-synonyms and near-antonyms help create both variety and coherence.

1 The situation is rather sad. Our market share has shrunk considerably over the last few years. We can no longer *employ* all our workers, so some, unfortunately, will have to be *made redundant*. There are, however, other companies in the area who *are hiring* people, and some of those that we have to *lay off* can probably *find work* with them. *Losing one's job* is a traumatic experience. But in this case we hope that most will be able to *find employment* elsewhere.
2 The situation is rather sad. Our market share has shrunk considerably over the last few years. We can no longer *employ* all our workers, so some, unfortunately, will have to join the ranks of the *unemployed*. There are, however, other companies in the area who are *employing* people, and some of those that we cannot *employ* can probably find *employment* with them. Becoming *unemployed* is a traumatic experience. But in this case we hope that most will be able to find *employment* elsewhere.

15.4.5 Semantic domains

A piece of writing that deals with political elections (at least in Britain) would include words like *candidate, constituency, party, polling day, votes, campaign, victory, opinion polls, majority, parliamentary, win, lose, landslide.* They belong to the semantic domain of 'political elections'. The semantic domain of 'car parts' is relatively small (at least for somebody who is not a car mechanic), whereas the semantic field of 'human feelings' is huge. When we write about a topic, we choose the relevant vocabulary and thereby impose lexical coherence of a general kind. In the Tittman text in **15.3** above, *bones, heal, Dr, fractures, surgery, implant, bone grafts, treatment, leg cast, hospital* all belong to the semantic domain of 'treatment of broken bones'. *Scaffolding* links up neatly with *contractor*. The two words create coherence within the intersecting semantic domain of 'construction', making the beginning and the end of the text hang together.

15.5 Thought organization

Some people have a focused mind and can hold on to one thought for a considerable time. At the other extreme, there are people with rambling minds. When we write, we have to discipline ourselves and give our discourse a structure. A rambling discourse is an incoherent discourse and therefore a bad discourse. A lot of bad writing, for example poor examination essays, is bad because the writer is unable to transform more or less unstructured thinking into structured writing.

Even within one genre, say, the genre called expository prose, there are many ways of organizing a piece of discourse. One typical way is to introduce the controlling idea in the first paragraph, then marshal arguments in separate paragraphs for and against the position stated in the controlling idea. The last paragraph presents the writer's synthesis or conclusion, and relates directly back to the controlling idea at the beginning. This way of moving from the general thematic idea through specific supporting details to the conclusion is called **deduction**. It is a common and well-tried method of structuring academic essays.

15.5.1 Deduction

The text below is a good example of deductive writing. This discourse has an overriding thematic idea. It is introduced in the first paragraph. Each subsequent paragraph brings in one piece of evidence or one aspect relevant to the problem, weighs it, and dismisses it in favour of something else, i.e. the writer's view, which is introduced in the last paragraph. So there is coherence within the entire text and coherence within each paragraph. This is what we mean by coherence on the level of thought organization (**15.2**).

First paragraph:	thematic idea; question to be answered later (**15.3.4**)
Second paragraph:	evidence for a tentative answer based on documentation
Third paragraph:	different type of evidence supporting the tentative answer; last sentence pointing forward in the text (*many other far more valid ways ...*)
Fourth paragraph:	criticism of those who disagree with the tentative answer
Fifth paragraph:	evidence from America against the writer's tentative answer 'interpreted' in favour of writer's view; another forward-pointing, cohesive link (*wider condition*). Note the interesting *it confirms our work* ... Is the writer a scientist with first-hand evidence?
Sixth paragraph:	further criticism of American evidence; repetition of writer's position that a 'wider context' is necessary
Seventh paragraph:	a sop to those who disagree with the writer; the last sentence (*real roots of the problem*) creates anticipation of the 'conclusive answer'
Last paragraph:	conclusion presented; televized violence given a minor role; conclusion agrees with tentative answers provided earlier, hence coherence in the text; the last sentence (*one question ...*) ties in with paragraphs three and four

Violence on TV

Complaints about violence on TV are front-page news again. Many people are concerned at what they see as a link between televized violence and violent behaviour. But how well-founded is this concern?

The Centre for Mass Communication Research has published over 200 books, reports and articles, many of them on the influence of television, including 30 on media violence, aggression or delinquency. This work indicates that in this country there is no clear evidence that television has any significant effect on the level of violence.

Studies of criminal and violent behaviour would tend to support this. We know enough to state that watching violence on television (as conventionally defined) is not, except possibly in a small number of pathological individuals, a main cause of violent behaviour. There are many other far more valid ways of accounting for violence.

We shouldn't be asking simple questions about 'the effect of television'. We rarely ask such questions about other institutions such as religion, or education. But this approach is not welcomed by those who tend to over-simplify a complex problem and seek convenient answers in simple terms of cause and effect.

American research is sometimes used to support the causal relationship, but the Surgeon-General's report on the million-dollar, 23-project research programme refers cautiously to 'a preliminary and tentative indication' of a causal relation in the short term between viewing violence and aggressive behaviour 'operating only on some children' (aggressively predisposed), and 'only in some circumstances'. It confirms our work that the viewing of violence and aggressive behaviour could be symptoms of a wider condition.

This American research has been criticized on several grounds, particularly lack of clarity and consistency in the use of concepts such as violence and aggression. But this apart, the USA is different from Britain in many ways, including the nature and amount of violence on the screen and in society. Neither television nor violent behaviour can be adequately studied outside the wider historical, economic, political and sociological context.

This is not an attempt to absolve broadcasters from their responsibilities or to ignore or dismiss the anxiety and concern. Television has influence but the process is not simple and the nature and direction are not always as commonly supposed. To focus on television and use it as a scapegoat implies a wrong definition of the problem – the real roots of the problem go unrecognized.

The source of violence is more likely to be found in the frustrations engendered by such factors as inequality, social injustice, overcrowding and modern urban living conditions. Television could add to frustration and possibly related aggression by encouraging, particularly for deprived groups, levels of aspiration and status which cannot be achieved. This is one question we might ask but the problem is not normally thought of in this way.

(From Valli Hazandra Despotopoulou, *Attitudes and Opinions*)

15.6 Analysis of grammar in written discourse

15.6.1 An advertisement

The first piece of discourse is a text printed on a package of breakfast cereal sold in the United States.

From Oregon's bountiful grain fields

High in the Pacific Northwest, in the sunshine and soil of Oregon's protected valleys, some of the nation's highest quality grains are grown. With nature's bounty all around them, it's no wonder folks in these parts are pretty finicky when it comes to their breakfast cereals. Chemical preservatives and refined sugars just won't do. It was here, many years ago, that Golden Temple started making wholesome cereals with locally grown grains to give our neighbors a pure, natural alternative to the sugar and additives in commercial brands. Words spread about our good taste and good nutrition and now we serve breakfast to smart folks like you all across America. But we're still here in Oregon, close to the fields. And we're still making natural cereals the way we always have, with the highest quality, natural ingredients. And nothing else.

Lexis and grammar together contribute to the effect of this piece of discourse. On the level of lexis, we note that colloquial words like *folks* and *finicky* co-occur with formal words with biblical connotations such as *bounty, bountiful* and (*Golden*) *temple*. *Neighbor* also has biblical connotations. The location – Oregon – is described by a series of glowing, positive words: *high* (three times), *sunshine, protected*, *natural, pure*, and of course *bountiful/bounty*.

What about grammar?

- The use of the personal pronouns *we* and *you* gives the text a personal, direct tone.
- All of the first line is taken up by place adverbials. Their length and position in front of the subject help highlight their content. In fact, the first sentence is front-heavy also because the verb phrase *are grown,* rather untypically, is light in terms of information value, which makes the first part stand out even more prominently.
- The cleft construction in line 5 highlights the element which follows *be*, in this case *here*. So once again the location stands out.
- In line 9, there are three locative adverbials in a row: *here, in Oregon, close to the fields*. The effect is to drive home to us the importance of the location.
- The partial parallelism in line 9 with the repetition of *still* highlights continuity: *But we're still ..., And we're still,* both introduced, somewhat unusually, by co-ordinating conjunctions.
- The adverbial *many years ago* in line 5 is enclosed in commas, in the focus position after *here*. Syntax and punctuation, which here suggest a separate tone unit, both give added weight to the adverbial, i.e. tradition and continuity are emphasized.
- The progressive aspect in line 9, *we're still making*, further stresses continuity.
- The sequences *just won't do* (line 4) and *And nothing else* (lines 10–11) must be read with three and two heavily stressed words, respectively. The effect is clear.

To conclude, it is fair to say that lexis, syntax, and prosody contribute to the appealing effect of this piece of discourse. Some like it; others, who particularly point to the obtrusive *smart folks like you*, do not. They find it 'overdone'.

15.6.2 Newspaper reportage

The language of the tabloid *The Sun* and that of the quality paper *The Times* differ in many ways. In the two columns below follow their reports on the same topic, The Diana, Princess of Wales, Memorial Fund, as printed on 8 September 1997. The last part of the *Times* text (on the right), which contained nothing but information on how to make a donation, has been left out. The highlighting in the text from *The Sun* appears as in the original.

Di fund will be the biggest charity ever

The fund set up after Diana's death is set to top £100million – making it the most successful charity in Britain.

Donations from here and abroad are already pouring into the Diana, Princess of Wales, Memorial Fund.

The single biggest pledge is **£3MILLION** from an unnamed British firm. The release of Elton John's Candle in the Wind could add **£10MILLION.**

Grieving members of the public are sending up to 20 sackfuls of letters daily to Kensington Palace.

Many are from children who have sent 20p or more from their pocket money.

Newspapers which donated part of their cover price from Saturday's edition – including The Sun – will contribute close to **£1MILLION.**

All the money sent to the fund will be given to more than 100 charities closely associated with the Princess.

A source at lawyers Mishcon de Reya, the fund's administrators, said: 'It will be huge.'

Fund exceeds £100m

A single anonymous donation of £3 million is understood to have taken The Diana, Princess of Wales, Memorial Fund to more than £100 million in just four days.

The donation, believed to be from a businessman, is one of the thousands ranging from children's pocket money of just a few pence to huge corporate gifts from all over Britain.

Two days after the fund was set up by Kensington Palace in response to public demand, 14 sackloads of mail, all containing donations, had been received. Experts expect the fund to become the world's biggest charity, potentially raising as much as £1 billion.

Kate Knightley-Day, from Mishcon de Reya, the Princess's former solicitors, who are helping to administer the fund, said they had been 'overwhelmed' by the number of contributions.

Anthony Julius, the Princess' former lawyer, and Michael Gibbins, her former private secretary, have both been appointed trustees of the fund. No decision has yet been made on whether it will channel money to other charities, or become an institution in its own right.

There may be typical language differences between the two papers which do not appear in the reports above, perhaps because the topic required a more sombre and responsible style than is usual in *The Sun*. Still, a few points are worth noticing.

- **Paragraphs**: *The Sun* text has 10 sentences, including the quotation in the last paragraph. These are divided into 8 paragraphs. *The Times* has 5 paragraphs and 7 sentences. With two exceptions, the paragraphs in both texts consist of a single sentence.
- **Sentence length**: *The Sun*: 20, 16, 11, 12, 17, 14, 19, 20, 11, and 4 orthographic words in the 10 sentences. *The Times*: 28, 31, 26, 17, 27, 21, and 23 orthographic words in the 7 sentences.
- **Non-finite clauses**: *The Sun*: 5. *The Times*: 8.
- **Voice in finite clauses**: *The Sun*: 1 passive (*will be given*), 11 active. *The Times*: 6 passive, 6 active.
- **Voice in non-finite clauses**: *The Sun*: 3 passive, 2 active. *The Times*: 4 active, 4 passive.

To conclude, *The Sun* has shorter sentences, fewer non-finite clauses, and fewer passives, which makes the information packaging less dense. These differences are important. They make it easier to read the text in *The Sun*. In addition, the use of bold-face type, italics, and capitalization makes particular segments stand out in the text.

15.6.3 Grammar and literary discourse

In **15.6.1** we saw that the effect of a piece of advertising depends in part on the grammatical choices that are made. In the next sample, taken from a textbook on stylistics (Laura Wright and Jonathan Hope, *Stylistics – A Practical Coursebook*), the authors suggest a correlation between a particular grammatical choice and its literary effect.

> I came in over the Pole and we were stacked up for nearly twenty minutes in a holding circuit round London before they could find us a runway and then we had to wait for a bottle-neck on the ground to get itself sorted out and all we could do was stare through the windows at the downpour and that didn't help.
>
> Sayonara, yes, very comfortable thank you.
>
> There was a long queue in No.3 Passenger Building and I was starting to sweat because the wire had said *fully urgent* and London never uses that phrase just for a laugh; then a quietly high-powered type in sharp blue civvies came up and asked who I was and I told him and he whipped me straight past Immigration and Customs without touching the sides and told me there was a police car waiting and was it nice weather in Tokyo.
>
> 'Better than here.'
>
> 'Where do we send the luggage?'
>
> 'This is all I've got.'

He took me through a fire exit and there was the rain slamming down again and the porters were trudging about in oilskins.

The radio operator had the rear door open for me and I ducked in and the driver hooked his head round to see who I was, not that he'd know.

(From Adam Hall, *The Tango Briefing*)

What is most noticeable here are the long run-on sentences with the co-ordinating conjunction *and* joining together a series of clauses, occasionally replaced by temporal connectors like *before* and *then.* Each clause reports an event in a long successive series, but since there are few full stops, the effect is that the events follow each other at what feels like a frantic pace. This is particularly the case when questions are embedded in this way, for example *and asked who I was*, and, *and was it nice weather in Tokyo*. This matches the content, too, since the words *fully urgent* show that the character is on an urgent mission. He is furthermore delayed flying into London and checking through Customs.

In the next passage the italicized passive verbs all reinforce the description of a passive and helpless child. Form and content go together.

Being a child, he is naturally helpless; everything seems *done* to him and for him, and almost nothing *is done* by him. When he *is adopted* by Mr B his workhouse clothes *are removed* and he *is dressed* in the clothes of a young gentleman, and when he *is recaptured* by thieves they promptly strip him of his new suit and give him back his old clothes. He is active in the way a ball *batted* back and forth between opposing sides is active: he *is moved* through space.

It is a fascinating aspect of stylistics to study how grammatical choices connect to and reinforce the content of a piece of writing, but we would be wary of establishing any stable one-to-one correlation.

Terms

coherence
cohesion: grammatical
lexical

thought organization
deduction
topic sentence
distribution of information

textual deixis
pro-forms

ellipsis
structural parallelism
conjuncts, conjunctions
question–answer sequences

synonyms
antonyms
hyponyms
superordinate terms
anaphoric nouns
semantic domain

Exercises

1 Identify any grammatical cohesive ties in this piece of journalistic writing. **(15.3)**

> Investigative journalism has made strides in Latin America in recent years. The new, democratically elected leaders cannot just sweep corruption and other official misdeeds under the carpet as dictators did. But some seem to wish they could. One anti-democrat is still in office to do it. Cuba, of course, allows no free press. But in recent years several underground news organisations have grown up, which put out their stories abroad or by Internet. Several of those active in them have found it wiser to go into exile. This week the head of the best known such body, Cuba Press, was arrested, in the usual early hours.
>
> More worrying, in its way, is what the governments of freer countries are up to.
>
> (From *The Economist*)

2 The sentences below are a scambled version of a text originally printed in *The People* in the late 1960s. Try to recreate the original text by putting the sentences together in the order they once had. Explain carefully what clues you rely on when you reassemble the text bits into a coherent whole. **(15.3–15.5)**

a And it was only the second time he'd 'done the pools'.

b 'If you try to become somebody different you end up by making yourself miserable.'

c As he loosened his wide leather belt and squeezed out of his gumboots last week, he looked just like the man he used to be, a £13-a-week labourer with a fertilizer firm.

d The luckiest man in Britain.

e Others may have won their thousands, some their tens of thousands, but there has been nothing to equal the £338,356 16s Percy collected last September.

f 'Money,' he said as he talked about his fortune for the first time since his big win, 'is worth having only as long as you don't let it change your way of life.'

g That's what they call Percy Harrison, the only punter to have a super scoop-the-pool win this season.

h Well, I'm able to let you into a secret.

i Ever since he won all that money, Percy has been determined not to let it change him ... and he's done it.

j Percy's luck is still holding.

(From Albert Levine (ed.), *Penguin English Reader*)

3 Explain what *the water* (line 4) refers to. What do the italicized words in line 5 refer to? In line 6 the noun phrase *each other's family* contains the cohesive tie *each other*. What two families are being referred to? Who are the candidates referred to in the definite form *the candidates* in lines 6–7? What is the referent of *it* in line 8? (**15.3**)

When 'O' and 'A' levels loom, there aren't many subjects in which parents can give direct help: except in languages. The only satisfactory way to learn a language is to be immersed in it for a while. And since just on the other side of the water, a European teenager is in the same position with *his* English as *yours* with *his* French or German, a swap seems obvious. Three weeks or so in each other's family and the candidates surely will have that part of the GCE or bac safely buttoned up. It's a simple idea and it often works well but many mistakes are made attempting it too soon. However, a well-adjusted child of 14+ should be able to cope.

4 Identify any conjuncts in the following text and translate them into Norwegian. How does the italicized material in lines 3–5 relate to and cohere with the preceding material? (**15.3.2**)

Jack Straw, the home secretary, who opposes proportional representation (PR) for Britain, is in charge of the issue. His friends cite practical barriers. *In the first place, legislation would be needed soon to register political parties and to set up the new system. Secondly, parties would have to reorganise to accommodate the new system.* So, although Mr Straw is not against PR for Europe in principle, his allies think that the odds are against it being ready for 1999. If it is not, however, many Lib Dems will be furious. They recall that Robin Cook said before the election that it was Labour's 'policy and intention' to introduce PR for Europe. This week he said that time was running out for the change. Moreover, Mr Straw is an avowed opponent of PR for Westminster. For that reason, many Lib Dems suspect that he is holding it up for Europe to avoid creating momentum for PR for Westminster.

5 Translate the following text into English. (**15.3.2**)

Dette har vært en vanskelig sak. For the første har familien stor inntekt og burde derfor ikke fått den økonomiske støtten vi har gitt. For det andre er betingelsene for tilbakebetaling (*conditions of repayment*) svært gunstige (*favourable*). Avgjørelsen er imidlertid tatt, men jeg vil si at hadde jeg vært til stede, hadde jeg stemt imot. Det er klart at jeg synes de trenger hjelp, slik som deres situasjon tross alt er, men på den annen side, kunne de gjort mer selv, for eksempel ved å kutte ned på sitt eget forbruk (*consump-*

tion). De har blant annet to biler. De er tross alt andre som trenger støtte i disse tider og vår oppgave er først og fremst å støtte dem som ikke får endene til å møtes (*make ends meet*). Dessuten har vi jo begrensende midler (*limited funds*) og må derfor se meget nøye på hver søknad. Det har videre vist seg at en del opplysninger i søknaden ikke var korrekte. Det er alvorlig. Min konklusjon er defor at vi må behandle søknaden deres på nytt (*reconsider the application*).

(From P. Lysvåg & S. Johansson, *Engelsk grammatikk og språkbruk – Øvingshefte*)

6 The following is a shortened and slightly amended letter to the editor of *The Economist.* The writer refutes claims made in a previous article in the same magazine. Explain how the writer organizes his discourse in terms of cited statements, rebuttals, and explanations. Identify specific elements in this organizational structure. **(15.5)**

Sir – Your article 'In memoriam FDR' makes a number of ridiculous assertions. Citing the Three Soldiers statue at the Vietnam Veterans' memorial, you state: 'Different interest groups petitioned to make sure that the group of soldiers was ethnically mixed.' False. As the sculptor I alone conceived of the idea of a group of three soldiers of diverse racial and ethnic characterisation because it was a true reflection of the actual participants. No one 'petitioned' or pressurised anyone.

You also assert that the interest groups petitioned to make sure that the soldiers' expressions 'suggested the perplexity the war engendered.' Nonsense. No one made any such suggestion. I chose to craft the expressions on the soldiers' faces to be faithful to the historical facts ...

You then go on to state that the 'failure of the Vietnam statue' proved that 'physical representations are beside the point.' What failure? The fact is that the Three Soldiers statue has triggered a plethora of representational monuments across the country.

7 Find one or more examples of the following types of lexical cohesion in the text below.

a repetition of the same word with the same referent
b the use of synonyms or near-synonyms
c the use of antonyms or near-antonyms
d the use of superordinate terms
e the use of hyponyms
f the use of different words from the same semantic field.

Examples in (b) to (e) do not necessarily have to belong to the same word class. What is important is that the words qualify in terms of synonymy, antonymy, etc. **(15.4)**

The torture of second class travel

With a typical business-class air ticket costing at least twice the economy fare, company accountants often wonder whether the wider seats and free champagne are really worth it. Some doctors fear that the answer is yes – for safety reasons.

Not the more obvious safety reasons like crashing into the sea or being buzzed by F-16s. Those risks are much the same at either end of the plane. No, there are other reasons for concern. Air travel gives passengers less legroom in steerage than on business class, which might make middle-aged men, at least, more likely to develop deep-vein thrombosis (DVT) – potentially lethal blood clots.

Airlines insist that the risk of flight-induced DVT is minimal. But passengers do have plausible reasons to worry. According to some medical experts, budget air travel is not harmless since prolonged pressure on the legs squeezes the veins and restricts the flow of blood. Travellers might develop clots which break off and travel from the legs to the lungs and block vital arteries there. So, the problem is not to be dismissed outright. Tourist class travellers should heed the advice of the head surgeon at a hospital in London. Don't sit still during the flight. Move about to keep the circulation moving. And if you must fly economy, don't expect to arrive in good shape.

(Based on a text in *The Economist*)

8 The text below, despite having normal cohesive ties such as *he* and *his,* might seem somewhat incoherent unless the reader is able to make a number of correct inferences. Explain how the italicized material hangs together with the preceding text. What is the referent of the definite noun phrase *the white cotton glove* in the last paragraph? What darkness is referred to in the same paragraph? Explain the use of the present tense in the italicized material. Does it have the same time reference as the present tense verbs in the rest of the first paragraph?

The commissionaire at Espinoza's restaurant seems to maintain under his particular authority all the most decrepit taxicabs in London. He is a commanding man; across his great chest the student of military medals might construe a tale of heroism and experience; *Boer farms sink to ashes, fanatical Fuzzi-wussies hurl themselves to paradise, supercilious mandarins survey the smashing of their porcelain and rending of fine silk*, in that triple row of decorations. He has only to run from the steps of Espinoza's to call to your service a vehicle as crazy as all the enemies of the King-Emperor.

Half a crown into the white cotton glove, because Simon Lent was too tired to ask for change. He and Sylvia huddled into the darkness on broken springs, between draughty windows.

(From Evelyn Waugh, 'Excursion into Reality')

9 Identify cases of faulty parallelism in these examples. Make suggestions for improvement. This material is adapted from Norwegian-produced English, so there may be unidiomatic elements here other than the lack of parallelisms. (**15.3.6**)

a The Olympics were not only good for Norway's reputation, but also to prove that we have good athletes.

b Another point which could be mentioned is that Norwegians were not the only Vikings, but Swedes and Danes as well.

c A society built on Christian values is a much better society than the Vikings.

d We have found other, perhaps more appropriate, elements in our cultural heritage to show to the world, thus attracting people to Norway.

e There was no obligation to work that prevented people from living the way they wanted. No work to destroy their free creative spirit. Work only takes people away from their children saying that they have no time to play with them.

f In this ideal society everybody cares for the elderly, helping them as much as they can.

10 In this material, also adapted from Norwegian-produced English, some pronouns have unclear or confusing referents. Identify such cases and suggest improvements. (**15.3.1D**)

a My first reaction to the cliché 'Norway – the land of the Vikings' – was that there were Vikings in other Scandinavian countries too. But Norway seems to have made the most out of this. This may be a bit strange because I believe people abroad do not think of the Vikings in positive terms.

b You should buy a computer which meets your future needs even if that is difficult to know.

c Even football supporters have adopted some of that Viking tradition. They wear helmets with horns and sometimes go berserk, especially after a win. That is unfortunate.

d How do people from other countries regard the Vikings? I think many foreigners find it very interesting. It is something which fascinates them, but I do not think it applies to Norway only. Sweden and Denmark also take part in it.

e York, a town in the North of England, is a place where they have unearthed many fascinating objects from the time of the Viking settlement.

f Even though I think 'Norway – the land of the Vikings' is a cliché, I do think it can play an important part in making people interested in Norway. By using it as 'catch phrase', they can learn other things about our country.

11 Explain the textual motivation for the cases of inverted word order and fronting in the following examples. (**15.3.5**)

a On 11 June a committee of Brussels vets turned down yet another British proposal to guarantee the safety of its meat, and Britain has issued threats to ban European beef from Britain too. Even more difficult is the question of jobs.
b On 9 June Gordon Brown went to a meeting with European finance ministers armed with a plan to stimulate job creation, including less bureaucracy and more help for small businesses. But at the centre of the Brown–Blair view on jobs lies the need for labour-market flexibility.
c 'Here's something', Carella said. He had turned to the inside back cover of the book. Pasted to it was a message in somewhat shaky longhand.
d They wanted a full-scale inquiry. This the police refused to provide.
e It was a large room. A study. The whole of one wall was covered with shelves of books from ceiling to floor. The floor, like the hallway, was covered in speckled, pale grey tiling. On the right were windows, their shutters half-closed against the light. It was very much a man's room. At the far end was an enormous leather-topped desk. Behind it sat Carlos Ferreira.

12 The passage below is from Virginia Woolf, *Mrs Dalloway*. Identify sentence fragments in the text and write them out in full sentences while preserving the basic meaning of the original. What is the difference in effect between your version and the original? (**15.6**; see also **14.7**)

For having lived in Westminster – how many years now? over twenty, – one feels even in the midst of the traffic, or waking at night, Clarissa was positive, a particular hush, or solemnity; an indescribable pause; a suspense (but that might be her heart, affected, they said, by influenza) before Big Ben strikes. There! Out it boomed. First a warning, musical; then the hour, irrevocable.

13 The following list gives advice on how not to write English. Each rule is formulated in such a way that it violates what it rules against. In each case give your own wording of the rule and explain why each example breaks its own rule. These do's and don't's are good reminders. However, native writers may occasionally break some of them, for example (b), when they write creatively.

a Don't write a run-on sentence you have to punctuate it.
b About sentence fragments.
c When one is writing, it is important to maintain your point of view.

- d Proofread your work. Do not tolerate mispellings!
- e Don't say the same thing more than once. It's redundant and repetitious.
- f Avoid the utilization of enlarged words when shortened ones will do.
- g Perform a functional iterative analysis on your work to root out third generation transitional buzz-words.
- h Make sure you hyp-henate correctly.
- i Sentences should be written in the active voice when giving instructions, so that the subject of the action can be identified clearly.
- j If the writer is considerate of the reader, he won't have a problem with ambiguous sentences.
- k Be careful of dangling participles writing a paper.
- l Each pronoun should agree with their antecedents.
- m It has come to our considered attention that in a large majority of cases, far too many people use a great deal more words than are absolutely necessary when engaged in the practice of writing sentences.

16 Grammar in Spoken Discourse

16.1 Some characteristics of speech vs. writing

Informal speech differs from formal writing in a number of respects:

A Informal speech is most typically produced in **face-to-face interaction**. A lot is communicated by body language. As the speaker and the addressee(s) are present in the same situation and can often draw on a great deal of common background knowledge, the language tends to be less explicit than in formal writing. There is more situational reference (**5.2.3**). There is an abundance of ellipsis and sentence fragments (**14.7**).

B Informal speech is typically a **joint activity**, where two or more participants are in constant interplay. Utterances need not follow each other in neat order, but often overlap. Interrogative and imperative sentences, which make a direct appeal to the addressee(s), are more common than in writing. The interchange is monitored by a range of interactive signals, such as tag questions (**14.3.4**), comment questions (**14.3.5**), and back-channels (**14.3.5**).

C Informal speech is typically a social activity, where the focus is less on the transmission of information than in writing. The term **phatic communion** has been proposed to characterize the social use of language. Typical examples are small-talk about the weather and the greeting *How do you do?*, which is not a genuine question asking for information.

D Informal speech is produced **on-line**, without the possibilities of editing which are normally found in writing. Moreover, listeners must decode at the same time as they plan their own contributions, while readers have more time at their disposal and can focus on comprehension (and can reread the text, if necessary). Syntactically, spoken discourse therefore tends to be less complex (**12.11**), and there is less variation in both structure and vocabulary. There is an abundance of stock phrases and more or less fixed collocations, which ease the on-line production of speech. Disfluencies, such as false starts, repetitions, and silent and filled pauses, are common.

E Informal speech, like spoken discourse in general, is carried by the medium of sound. While there is an obvious relationship between the graphic system and the sound system, the latter is far more flexible in the meanings it may express, particularly through the system of **intonation**. Intonation is used (i) to group words into units, (ii) to express the communicative function of sentences, (iii) to identify the most important elements in the message, and (iv) to express the emotional attitude of the speaker. The first two uses have clear parallels in the system of punctuation in writing, which is, however, more guided by purely syntactic considerations. For the last two uses, the means of expression are far more limited, at least in conventional printed text (italics, bold-face, capitalization, and the like).

16.2 Sample texts

Many of the characteristics of informal speech vs. formal writing are illustrated in the following two passages, which we will comment on in some detail later in this chapter. The passages are the same as those taken up in **12.11**, but the spoken sample is somewhat longer and is reproduced with intonation marking and with interventions from the addressee(s). The situation is this: Speaker B tells her friends c and D a story about a conflict with her mother, who was irritated by Aunt Elsie's constant knitting. The speaker had tried to defend her aunt.

Informal conversation

1	B:	| she was old and on her ˆOWN | . my auntie ˏELSIE *and* | . if she had
2	c:	*m*
3	>B:	ˏSOMETHING like ˏKNITTING | that kept her ˏHAPPY | +all+ ˏDAY | . surely that was better
4	c:	+m+
5	>B:	than sitting
6	c:	yeah .
7	>B:	doing ˏNOTHING |
8	c:	<<quite>> mild - - *yes*
9	>B:	ˋYOU ˏKNOW | she was <<a>> poor old ˏTHING *after all* | - and mother went ˋWILD with ˏME | she thought this was ˋTERRIBLE | .
10	c:	+oh gosh+

11 >B: +and that+ I couldn't see her point of ˋVIEW | at ^ALL|
12 c: +oh God <<no several sylls>>+
13 D: +| ˋYES | *siding with the ^ENEMY |+ . ^YES | . ˏYES | ˏYES | ˏYES |*
14 B: *| and of course I did see **her** point of ˏVIEW |*
15 c: **m** +oh Lord+
16 >B: + | ¯AND | . + but I didn't ˏWANT her | to ring her ˏUP | and ˏSAY | .
17 D: *and do something ^FATAL | ^YES | that's ^RIGHT |*
18 >B: | and say anything ˇAWFUL to her | because +she's+
19 c: +yeah+
20 >B: so nice and kind and ˋMILD | -
21 c: oh God
22 B: | ˋSO | - this went on for ˋWEEKS and | . I thought I'd better ring uh . my mother ˏUP | . and pretend I've ˏNEVER ˋSAID it |
23 c: m .
24 B: | I'd just ring up and ˏASK | how she's getting ˏON and |
25 c: yeah .
26 >B: | ˇSO on | . and yea-ah so I rang ˋUP | . and my ˋSISTER answered the ˏPHONE | . and she - really gave me a terrible HA ˋRANGUE |

(From the London-Lund Corpus)

The transcription is simplified and does not by any means give an exhaustive record of the speech event. The intonation is not marked for speaker c, who is a non-surreptitious speaker (aware of the recording). Some transcription conventions are:

|	tone unit boundary
SMALL CAPITALS	nucleus
ˋ ˏ etc.	nuclear tones
pairs of * or +	simultaneous speech
. and -	pauses
>	continuation
<< >>	uncertain hearing

Formal expository prose

(1) Although Faulkner was the heir in his own family to this tradition, he did not have Stark Young's inclination to romanticize and sentimentalize the planter society. (2) The myth of the Southern plantation has had only a tangential relation with actuality, as Francis Pendleton Gaines showed forty years ago, and I suspect it has had a far narrower acceptance as something real than has generally been supposed. (3) Faulkner has found it useful, but

he has employed it with his habitual independence of mind and skeptical outlook. (4) Without saying or seeming to say that in portraying the Sartoris and the Compson families Faulkner's chief concern is social criticism, we can say nevertheless that through those families he dramatizes his comment on the planter dynasties as they have existed since the decades before the Civil War. (5) It may be that in this comment he has broken from the conventional pattern more violently than in any other regard, for the treatment in his books is far removed from even the genial irony of Ellen Glasgow, who was the only important novelist before him to challenge the conventional picture of planter society.

(From the Brown Corpus)

In the discussion below, the conversation text will be referred to as CONV, and the expository prose text as PROSE. The prose text consists of five sentences only, marked (1) to (5) in the sample.

16.3 Words

16.3.1 Type–token ratio

The type–token ratio is a simple measure of the variation in vocabulary in a text. It is computed by dividing the number of different words that occur in a text (types) by the number of running words (tokens) and then multiplying by 100. In other words, it is the percentage of different words in relation to the total number of words in a text. Another measure of the degree of variation is the percentage of *hapax legomena* (a Greek expression for words that occur once only in a text). The scores for our sample texts are:

	CONV	PROSE
Running words	195	187
Different words	97	124
Type–token ratio	50%	66%
Hapax legomena	30%	58%

The figures mean that there is much less variation in vocabulary in the conversation sample.

The type–token ratio and the number of *hapax legomena* vary with the length of a text. The longer the text, the lower the score. It is therefore necessary to compare text samples of roughly equal length. Another problem is deciding what counts as a word (see the discussion of *word* in **3.2**). In our case we used a very simple definition: each orthographic sequence separated by spaces was counted as a word (with the exception that contractions like *I'd* and *couldn't* were split). In calculating different words, we counted each word form as a separate word, e.g. *do* and *did* were treated as different words for the purposes of this count, and *that* was counted as the same word irrespective of its grammatical function. The inserts (see **16.3.2**) were counted as words.

The calculation of type–token ratio can of course be refined by treating each lexeme (**3.2.1**) as a separate type, thus grouping together inflected forms as representing the same type (e.g. *do* and *did*) and splitting homographs by grammatical function (e.g. the conjunction and the demonstrative determiner *that*). However, the simple measure based on orthographic form is generally sufficient.

16.3.2 Word classes

If we go on to study the word class distribution in our two sample passages, we find some major differences (the figures below are percentages; they add up to more than 100 due to the rounding of decimals). The most notable differences have been italicized.

	CONV	PROSE
Nouns	8	*25*
Verbs	*18*	13
Adjectives	9	9
-ly adverbs	0	1
Other adverbs	*12*	4
Pronouns	*17*	8
Auxiliaries	4	6
Determiners	6	*14*
Prepositions	5	*12*
Co-ord. conj.	*9*	3
Subord. conj.	2	4
Infinitival *to*	1	2
Inserts	*11*	0

In the prose sample, the nouns outnumber the verbs. There are far more determiners (e.g. 14 occurrences of *the* in PROSE as against 2 in CONV) and prepositions. This testifies to the greater complexity of the written text at the phrase level (see further **16.4**). There is a denser packaging of information.

In the conversation sample, verbs outnumber nouns. Clauses in conversation are typically shorter and more numerous. Clause elements are very often realized by pronouns rather than by full noun phrases. First person pronouns commonly occur (10 in CONV as against 2 in PROSE). If we had examined a passage where the discourse was less dominated by a single speaker, we would also have found more second person pronouns.

Adverbs are notably more common in CONV, particularly adverbial particles like *up* and words and expressions marking the attitude of the speaker (*surely*, *after all*, *of course*). Moreover, we find many **inserts**. These are words which are not integrated in the clause structure, such as interjections (*oh gosh*), response words (*yeah*, *m*), and hesitation markers (*uh*).

As regards the distribution of co-ordinating vs. subordinating conjunctions, see **16.5** below.

In calculating the word class distribution in a text, we must of course be careful in defining what counts as a noun, verb, etc. Note, in particular, that some sequences are best regarded as **lexicalized units** (e.g. *of course*, *and so on*) and cannot be meaningfully split up into sequences of two or more word classes.

In our example above we counted each occurrence of a class as a separate occurrence. It is possible to refine the study by calculating the number of different lexemes in each category, so that the measure reflects both the degree of variation and the grammatical make-up of the text.

16.3.3 Lexical density

Lexical density is a term often used for the percentage of lexical words in a text. Again it is important to decide what counts as a lexical word vs. a function word. This may be problematic, as the same English form can sometimes be used both as a lexical word and as a function word, e.g. the verbs *be* and *have* (see **6.4.2**). The main thing is to set up criteria which can be consistently applied to the texts compared.

In our case, we can easily derive the scores for lexical density from the figures in **16.3.2**. As many adverbs which do not end in *-ly* are on the borderline of function words, we decided to exclude these from the types of words which are used in calculating lexical density. The scores are then 35 for CONV, 48 for PROSE. This means that the types of words which carry the highest information load are proportionally much less common in conversation, and the information packaging is correspondingly less dense.

16.4 Phrases

We have already seen clear indications that the conversation text is less complex at the phrase level (**16.3.2**). If we study the two text samples in more detail, we find very marked differences:

- In CONV most of the clause elements are realized by single words or phrases consisting of 2 or 3 words. The most complex phrases are 3 noun phrases consisting of 4 words and 1 adjective phrase containing 5 words:

  a poor old thing (utterance 9, noun phrase)
  her point of view (2 occurrences in utterances 11 and 14, noun phrases)
  better than sitting doing nothing (utterances 3–7, adjective phrase)

- By contrast, PROSE contains a large number of very complex phrases, including 13 noun phrases consisting of 5 words or more, 5 prepositional phrases of 6 words or more, an adverb phrase containing 7 words, and an adjective phrase consisting of 10 words. Examples:

  a far narrower acceptance as something real than has generally been supposed (sentence 4; a noun phrase with the head noun *acceptance* modified by a complex adjective phrase: *far narrower ... than has generally been supposed*)

  without saying or seeming to say that in portraying the Sartoris and the Compson families ... (sentence 4; prepositional phrase containing embedded *-ing* clauses, with further embedded clauses)

  more violently than in any other regard (sentence 5; adverb phrase with a discontinuous degree modifier).

In the PROSE text, there are often very complex patterns of embedding, with phrases and clauses nested within phrases. See the comments on complex embedding in **4.11** and **12.10**.

16.5 Clauses

The word class distribution (**16.3.2**) suggests that clauses are shorter and more numerous in conversation. Clause elements tend to be realized by single words or short phrases (**16.4**). As pointed out in **12.11** and shown by the distribution of co-ordinating vs. subordinating conjunctions in **16.3.2**, conversation is marked by co-ordination.

There is another striking difference between CONV and PROSE at the clause level. In PROSE every single word is syntactically integrated within a clause, either as a clause element (or part of a clause element) or as a clause link (conjunction). Though sentence fragments occur in writing (**14.7**), they are far more characteristic of spoken discourse.

Examples of non-integrated words and expressions in CONV are the inserts referred to in **16.3.2**, *siding with the enemy* (utterance 13), and the false start *and* (utterance 16). The non-integrated words and expressions reflect the production conditions of informal speech (**16.1**). In a text less dominated by a single speaker, the frequency of such elements could be even more marked.

16.6 Prefaces and tags

In conversation we often find elements which are very loosely attached to the clause. These include vocative expressions (**9.8.4**), tag questions (**14.3.4**, **14.4**), and noun phrase tags like the one in utterance 1 of CONV:

1 B: | she was old and on her ^OWN | . my auntie ˏELSIE *and* | ...

Here the speaker uses a pronoun in the main body of the clause, and adds a full noun phrase clarifying the reference. This type of structure is generally referred to as **right dislocation**. The opposite is **left dislocation**, as in:

2 | the man who AT`TACKED you | was he wearing ˏGLOVES |

Here the speaker first establishes the topic by the opening noun phrase, and then uses a co-referent pronoun in the following main clause.

Prefaces and tags are useful in the production of speech by breaking up a complex task and presenting the information in smaller chunks. This is a good illustration of how speech evolves (from the London–Lund Corpus):

3 | they're very nice `FRUIT | `AREN'T they | ˏCHERRIES actually |

A statement is followed by an appeal to the addressee (tag question) and an appended clarifying expression (right dislocation). The final disjunct, in the tail of the last tone unit, comments on the truth of the statement and means roughly 'this is true, in my opinion'.

16.7 Interactional signals

In conversation there is an ongoing negotiation of purpose and topic, as shown in this brief extract from a conversation between two teenage boys:

1 A: You know I was taking my jeans back?
2 B: What jeans?
3 A: You know those ones I bought on Saturday.

4 B: Why d'you take them back?
5 A: Cos all the letters have come off man. Tt!
6 B: What d'you mean letters?
7 A: You know the letters
8 B: I mean
9 A: on the back of the pocket.
10 B: No, the letters on the back of the po= pocket is plastic.
11 A: Yeah, they've come off.

(From the British National Corpus)

Note the following features: the ellipsis in the question–answer sequences; the interruption in lines 7–9; the incomplete word, the missing article, and the lapse in concord in line 10; the use of the comment clause *you know* in lines 3 and 7, signalling that speaker A expects the listener to know what he is talking about.

There are a great many more or less fixed expressions which serve important functions in the development of spoken discourse. Here is a list of examples of such interactional signals (tone unit boundaries have not been indicated):

A Openers

interrupters:	EXˇCUSE me.	Exˈcuse me for INTERˇRUPTING but . . .
	ˇSORRY.	ˈPardon me for INTERˇRUPTING but . . .
	ˇHOLD it.	ˈMay I INTERˏRUPT for a moment?
	I'd ˈlike to ˋSAY something.	ˈMay I ask a ˏQUESTION?
question openers:	I'd ˈlike to ˈknow . . . ˈCould you ˈtell me . . .	ˈCould I ˈask . . . ˈDo you ˈhappen to ˈknow . . .
casual:	ˋWELL . . . ˋLOOK . . . ˋNOW . . . Of ˋCOURSE	You ˇKNOW . . . You ˋSEE . . . ˋLISTEN . . . Now ˋREALLY . . .
digression:	ˈSpeaking of . . . ˈThat reˈminds me . . . I ˈjust ˈthought of . . . By the ˋWAY	ˋANYWAY . . . In ˋANY case . . . To ˈget ˈback to . . . ˈWhere ˋWAS I?

B Responders

agreement and disagreement:	`THAT'S ˏRIGHT. COR`RECT. `YES. E`XACTLY. You can ˈsay ˇTHAT again. ˈHear `HEAR.	`NO, I'm aˈfraid `NOT. `NOT ˏQUITE. ˈThat's RI`DICULOUS. `NO `WAY. `COME `ON. ˈBe ˎSERIOUS.
hesitation:	ˇWELL, ˈlet's `SEE. That's a ˈgood `QUESTION.	ˈWhere shall I `START? ˈHow shall I `PUT it?
disbelief:	´REALLY? ´OH?	Is ˈthat ˏRIGHT? ˈAre you ˏKIDDING?
sympathy and lack of sympathy:	ˈThat's ˈtoo ˎBAD. ˈWhat a ˎPITY. ˈOh ˎDEAR. ˈHow ˎAWFUL.	ˈServes you `RIGHT. ˈWhat did you EX`PECT. `THAT'LL ˏTEACH you. It's your ˈown `FAULT.
encouragement to continue:	`RIGHT. `YEAH. ˏREALLY?	ˏWELL? ˏYES? ˏAND?
incomprehension:	ˏPARDON? ˏSORRY? ˈCould you reˈpeat ˈthat AˏGAIN? ˈWould you ˈmind REˏPEATING that?	ˏWHAT was that again? I ˈdidn't `GET ˏTHAT. You `LOST me ˏTHERE. I'm ˈnot ˈsure I'm `FOLLOWING you.

C Closers

casual:	I ˈmust be `GOING. `SORRY to rush ˏOFF.	I `HOPE you ˈdon't ˏMIND but . . . It's been ˈnice `TALKING to you.
formal:	`THANK you for your ˏTIME. EXˇCUSE me but I ˈreally ˈmust `GO.	I ˈreally APˇPRECIATE your . . . I'd ˈbetter not ˈtake ˈup any ˈmore of your ˏTIME.

A fuller list of 'gambits' in spoken English, including remarks on conditions of use, is given in Keller and Warner (1976–77), the source of the examples above.

16.8 The speech–writing continuum

Although the comparison above has focused on two short text samples, there is no doubt that the differences we have found apply more generally to conversation vs. expository prose. Nevertheless, both speech and writing include a great deal of variation. Some types of speech, e.g. lectures and public speeches (which are monologic and often based on a written manuscript), are closer to formal writing than to conversation. Some types of writing, particularly fictional dialogue and personal letters, are close to informal speech.

A new mode of discourse which is becoming increasingly common is electronic mail. This is of course a form of writing, but it has characteristics of its own. Examples (from the *Humanist* distribution list):

1 I enjoyed RZ's recent reference to Ventura's output as 'something really sleak'. This wonderful neographism brought powerfully to mind something at once sleazy and sneaky.
Yours, ever a TeXnophile, Dominik

(Dominik Wujastyk, *Humanist*, October 1989)

2 The thing about the Mac, which I have had since 1984, nemmine the three lemons bought, chile! is its simplicity of use and friendliness to people who want to get on with it, apart from fonts and layout and better-looking MSS and ease of selection of what one wishes to do. And none of all that long engineering, retrofitted stuff for word people. Now with the large portrait screen before me in black and white and crystal clear, one can write pages and swiftly. [...] Just make the interface easy, and easier and easiest, is all one asks. Point and use, as with e-mail, and Yale's tincan modem program for getting through to all of you folks out there swiftest, or as Beckett says, 'Instanter!'
Kessler

(Jascha Kessler, *Humanist*, October 1989)

Electronic mail often seems to be produced on the spur of the moment and lacks the editing which is characteristic of other writing, perhaps because there is a feeling of immediate contact with the addressee(s) and because the message is felt to be less permanent than in traditional writing situations. We find sentence fragments, unconventional spellings, nonce-words, and in general a freedom from ordinary writing conventions.

16.9 Speech presentation

When speech is presented in ordinary writing, it differs greatly from a transcription of spontaneous speech as we have seen it in our text sample above. Three main forms of speech presentation are direct speech (**16.9.1**), indirect speech (**16.9.2**), and free indirect speech (**16.9.3**). While free indirect speech is a literary device characteristic of fiction, direct and indirect speech can of course occur both in writing and in reporting speech in conversation. Here we will focus on speech as presented in writing.

16.9.1 Direct speech

Direct speech in plays and fictional dialogue is far more orderly than natural spontaneous conversation. There is usually no overlapping speech, there are no pauses in mid-sentence, no false starts or other signs of non-fluency. These are features which normally pass unnoticed in natural discourse, unless they are very obtrusive. For the writer, they are generally superfluous, unless they are needed for some particular purpose, e.g. to express the state of mind of the speaker. Fictional dialogue gives the illusion of real conversation, but the language is subordinated to the purpose of the writer in building up a fictional world.

When something is passed off as direct speech, there has normally been some editing. The story told by speaker B in our conversation sample above will naturally be reproduced as in **12.11**, with ordinary punctuation and grammatical streamlining. Note the elimination of the back-channels and of the false start and the repetition in utterances 16 and 18. The distance in relation to the spoken utterance becomes even more marked in indirect speech.

16.9.2 Indirect speech

In reporting what somebody has said, one can opt for direct speech and present what was actually said, or indirect speech and express what was said in one's own words. The difference between direct and indirect speech is shown in:

1 a She said to me, 'I'll come and see you tomorrow.'
1 b She said (that) she would come and see me the following day.

2 a She asked him, 'What are you doing here?'
2 b She asked him what he was doing there.

The main changes in going from direct to indirect speech are:

- Quotation marks are omitted. The absence of the quotation marks means that the narrator takes responsibility for the message.
- The utterance is subordinated to the reporting verb and is converted to a *that*-clause or an indirect question. See also **12.9.2**. As regards the word order of indirect questions, see **11.2.4A**.
- Pronouns are adjusted so that they are adequate in relation to the person giving the report (*I* to *she* and *you* to *me* in 1b, *you* to *he* in 2b).
- Verb forms are back-shifted so that they are adequate in relation to the person giving the report (*'ll* to *would* in 1b, *are* to *was* in 2b). See also **7.9**.
- Deictic time and place adverbials are also adjusted to the reporting situation (*tomorrow* to *the following day* in 1b, *here* to *there* in 2b).

In other words, the deictic elements that refer to the original speech situation are changed to forms which are appropriate from the point of view of the narrator.

The relationship between direct and indirect speech is further illustrated in these examples from *The White House Transcripts*, which record conversations connected with the Watergate affair during the presidency of Richard Nixon:

3 a President: I mean, after all, it is my job and I don't want the Presidency tarnished, but also I am a law enforcement man.
3 b Mr. Nixon concluded by saying that he did not wish to see the presidency tarnished but at the same time, 'I am a law enforcement man.'

4 a Dean: I honestly believe that no one over here knew that. I know that as God is my maker I had no knowledge that they were going to do this.
4 b Dean strongly disclaimed to the President that anyone in the White House knew of the break-in in advance.

Examples (3a) and (4a) are transcriptions of the recorded utterances; (3b) and (4b) have been formulated by the editors.

In the first pair we notice that the comment clause *I mean* and the adverbial *after all* are found only in the direct version. Markers of speaker attitude are regularly omitted in indirect speech. Note also how the two forms of speech presentation are combined in this example. The passage ends with an utterance in direct speech, whereby the responsibility for the wording is clearly shifted to the original speaker.

In the second pair we find very marked differences in wording between the two versions. Note the change of the deictic expression *over here* to *in the White House* and of the demonstrative pronoun in *knew that* to *knew of the break-in*. The very strong assertion in the second sentence in (4a) is expressed through the adverbial *strongly* and the reporting verb *disclaimed.*

While example (3b) illustrates that direct and indirect speech can be combined in the same context, example (4b) shows that there are types of indirect speech which are quite distant from the original utterance, and where the narrator gives his/her interpretation rather than a record of what was actually said. No trace is left of the original wording in the case of **narrative report of speech acts**, as in:

5 She promised to come.

If we compare (5) with (1a) and (1b), we see that the narrator merely says that a particular type of speech act has occurred, in much the same way as he/she would report other actions.

16.9.3 Free indirect speech

Free indirect speech (*dekt tale, dekning*) is on the borderline between direct and indirect speech. It is often used in fiction to convey a person's stream of thought:

> Laura bent her head and hurried on. She wished now that she had put on a coat. How her frock shone! And the big hat with the velvet streamer – if only it was another hat! Were the people looking at her? They must be. It was a mistake to have come, she knew all along it was a mistake. Should she go back even now? No, too late. This was the hour. It must be.
>
> (From Katherine Mansfield, 'The Garden Party')

Free indirect speech differs from 'interior monologue' or the 'stream-of-consciousness' technique, which uses a form of direct speech. Verb forms are back-shifted and pronouns normally adjusted (*I, me* to *she, her* in the passage above). In contrast to indirect speech, there is usually no reporting clause; questions and exclamations occur as in direct speech. Because of the distancing in relation to direct speech and the subtle intrusion of the narrator, free indirect speech frequently has an ironic effect.

To conclude, there are a range of devices for the presentation of speech. They vary from direct speech, with a minimum of interference from the narrator, through free indirect speech and indirect speech to narrative report of speech acts. Moving along this scale, we see how the language is gradually distanced from the speech event and is increasingly viewed from the narrator's perspective.

Terms

phatic communion
type–token ratio
hapax legomena
lexical density

left dislocation (prefaces)
right dislocation (tags)
interactional signals

direct speech
indirect speech

free indirect speech
narrative report of speech acts

Exercises

1 Sample 1 below is an example of spoken English, more specifically an exchange between three speakers, A, B, and C. Words written in SMALL CAPITALS carry a nucleus. Nuclear tones are shown before the stressed syllable in the capitalized words. A vertical line marks the tone unit boundary. Stars mark overlapping speech. A hyphen indicates a pause; three hyphens, a longer pause. Some conventional symbols used in the original have been omitted. Sample 2 is an example of written expository prose. The two texts have roughly the same number of words.

Sample 1

A: eh it's absolutely ˋBARMY | you can hold the top --- administrative job in ˋCOLLEGE | and if you haven't got a DE ˏGREE | -
B: * ˋREALLY |*
A: *you just* can't set foot beyond a certain - you ˏKNOW |
B: but if you've got a DE ˏGREE | this is ˋMAGIC | -
C: ˋM | - ˋYES |
A: this is a battle that I'm always ˋFIGHTING | that eh a DE ˏGREE | does ˋNOT | ˋQUALIFY you | -
B: oh ˋNO I |
A: particularly for * ˋANYTHING |*
B: *well one's AˇWARE* of that | ˋYES |

(From Anna-Brita Stenström, *An Introduction to Spoken Interaction*)

Sample 2

Sinn Fein, the IRA's political wing, went to Stormont Castle this week to sign up to the so-called 'Mitchell' principles, pledging that the party will pursue its aim solely through democratic means and repudiating violence. Unionists have been demanding this for decades, but they greeted the event with a boycott of the ceremony and a picket outside. And in a confusing move, IRA immediately cast doubt over the value of Sinn Fein's gesture.

(From *The Economist*)

Questions:

a How many words are there in each text? Discuss any problems. (**3.2**, **16.3**)
b How many different words are there in each text?
c How many lexical words are there in each passage?

d How many function words are there in each?
e Which passage has the more complex phrase structure?
f Comment on the clause structure of the two texts.
g Identify and classify features that are specific to the spoken text.
h Comment on other differences in the structure of the two passages.

2 Convert the following dialogue to indirect speech. Comment on the adjustments that you have to make as regards tense and pronoun use. (**16.9.1–16.9.2**)

'Is this enough?' Matilda asked.
'Just about,' Miss Honey said. 'I don't suppose you've ever done that before?'
'Never,' Matilda said. 'It's fun. How do you get enough water for your bath?'
'I don't take a bath,' Miss Honey said. 'I wash standing up. I get a bucketful of water and I heat it on this little stove and I strip and wash myself all over.'
'Do you honestly do that?' Matilda asked.
'Of course I do,' Miss Honey said. 'Every poor person in England used to wash that way until not so very long ago. And *they* didn't have a Primus. They had to heat the water over the fire in the hearth.'

(From Roald Dahl, *Matilda*)

3 Rewrite the dialogue below as if it were a dialogue in a piece of fiction. Comment on any changes you make to the original, and on your choice of reporting verbs. Also comment on your choice between direct and indirect speech.

b: Nan went ˏOFF today | - .
a: on this B`OAT | which is
b: J`ESUS |
a: going to S`INK | or SˎOMETHING |
b: that's R`IGHT | . I think she FLˎIES | to somewhere like MARSˎEILLES | - (- yawns) before she gets the BˏOAT | -
a: and then goes WH`ERE |
b: oh G`OD knows | she does sort of quick trip of GR`EECE | -
a: who's she G`OING with |
b: a FRˎIEND | . perhaps TW`O friends | - - don't KNˎOW |

(From the London–Lund Corpus)

Appendices

Appendix 1: Irregular verbs

Base	Past tense	Past participle
A		
arise (oppstå)	*arose*	*arisen*
awake (våkne, vekke opp)	*awoke*	*awoken*
B		
be (være)	*was/were*	*been*
bear (bære)	*bore*	*borne* (båret) *born* (født)
beat (slå)	*beat*	*beaten*
become (bli)	*became*	*become*
begin (begynne)	*began*	*begun*
bend (bøye)	*bent*	*bent*
bet (vedde)	*bet, betted*	*bet, betted*
bid (by)	*bid, bade*	*bid, bidden*
bind (binde)	*bound*	*bound*
bite (bite)	*bit*	*bitten*
bleed (blø)	*bled*	*bled*
blow (blåse)	*blew*	*blown*
break (bryte)	*broke*	*broken*
breed (føde/avle)	*bred*	*bred*
bring (bringe, ta med seg)	*brought*	*brought*
broadcast (kringkaste)	*broadcast*	*broadcast*
build (bygge)	*built*	*built*
burn (brenne)	*burnt* (BrE) *burned*	*burnt* (BrE) *burned*
burst (gå i stykker)	*burst*	*burst*
buy (kjøpe)	*bought*	*bought*
C		
cast (kaste)	*cast*	*cast*
catch (fange)	*caught*	*caught*
choose (velge)	*chose*	*chosen*
cleave (kløyve)	*cleaved, cleft*	*cleaved, cleft*
cling (holde fast ved)	*clung*	*clung*
come (komme)	*came*	*come*
cost (koste)	*cost*	*cost*

creep (krype)	*crept*	*crept*
cut (skjære)	*cut*	*cut*
D		
deal (handle)	*dealt*	*dealt*
dig (grave)	*dug*	*dug*
do (gjøre) (*s*-form: *does*)	*did*	*done*
draw (tegne)	*drew*	*drawn*
dream (drømme)	*dreamt* (BrE)	*dreamt* (BrE)
	dreamed	*dreamed*
drink (drikke)	*drank*	*drunk*
drive (kjøre)	*drove*	*driven*
E		
eat (spise)	*ate*	*eaten*
F		
fall (falle)	*fell*	*fallen*
feed (gi næring til / mate)	*fed*	*fed*
feel (kjenne, føle seg)	*felt*	*felt*
fight (kjempe)	*fought*	*fought*
find (finne)	*found*	*found*
flee (flykte)	*fled*	*fled*
fling (kaste)	*flung*	*flung*
fly (fly)	*flew*	*flown*
forbid (forby)	*forbade, forbad*	*forbidden*
forget (glemme)	*forgot*	*forgotten*
forgive (tilgi)	*forgave*	*forgiven*
freeze (fryse)	*froze*	*frozen*
G		
get (få)	*got*	*got/gotten* (AmE)
give (gi)	*gave*	*given*
go (gå, reise) (*s*-form: *goes*)	*went*	*gone*
grind (male)	*ground*	*ground*
grow (vokse)	*grew*	*grown*
H		
hang (henge)	*hung*	*hung*
(henrette ved henging)	*hanged*	*hanged*
have (ha) (*s*-form: *has*)	*had*	*had*
hear (høre)	*heard*	*heard*
hide (gjemme)	*hid*	*hidden*

hit (slå)	*hit*	*hit*
hold (holde)	*held*	*held*
hurt (skade)	*hurt*	*hurt*
K		
keep (holde)	*kept*	*kept*
kneel (knele)	*knelt*	*knelt*
	kneeled (AmE)	*kneeled* (AmE)
knit (strikke)	*knitted, knit*	*knitted, knit*
know (vite)	*knew*	*known*
L		
lay (legge)	*laid*	*laid*
lead (lede)	*led*	*led*
lean (lene)	*leant* (BrE)	*leant* (BrE)
	leaned	*leaned*
leap (hoppe)	*leapt* (BrE)	*leapt* (BrE)
	leaped	*leaped*
learn (lære)	*learnt* (BrE)	*learnt* (BrE)
	learned	*learned*
leave (forlate)	*left*	*left*
lend (låne ut)	*lent*	*lent*
let (la)	*let*	*let*
lie (ligge)	*lay*	*lain*
light (tenne, lyse)	*lit, lighted*	*lit, lighted*
lose (miste)	*lost*	*lost*
M		
make (gjøre, lage)	*made*	*made*
mean (mene, bety)	*meant*	*meant*
meet (møte)	*met*	*met*
mow (klippe gress)	*mowed*	*mown*
P		
pay (betale)	*paid*	*paid*
put (sette, legge)	*put*	*put*
R		
read (lese)	*read*	*read*
ride (ride)	*rode*	*ridden*
ring (ringe)	*rang*	*rung*
rise (stå opp / reise seg)	*rose*	*risen*
run (løpe)	*run*	*run*

S

saw (sage)	*sawed*	*sawn, sawed*
say (si)	*said*	*said*
see (se)	*saw*	*seen*
seek (søke)	*sought*	*sought*
sell (selge)	*sold*	*sold*
send (sende)	*sent*	*sent*
set (sette)	*set*	*set*
sew (sy)	*sewed*	*sewn, sewed*
shake (riste)	*shook*	*shaken*
shine (skinne)	*shone*	*shone*
shoot (skyte)	*shot*	*shot*
show (vise)	*showed*	*shown*
shrink (krympe)	*shrank*	*shrunk*
shut (lukke)	*shut*	*shut*
sing (synge)	*sang*	*sung*
sink (synke)	*sank*	*sunk*
sit (sitte)	*sat*	*sat*
sleep (sove)	*slept*	*slept*
slide (gli)	*slid*	*slid*
slink (luske)	*slunk*	*slunk*
smell (lukte)	*smelt* (BrE)	*smelt* (BrE)
	smelled	*smelled*
sow (så)	*sowed*	*sown, sowed*
speak (snakke)	*spoke*	*spoken*
spell (stave)	*spelt* (BrE)	*spelt* (BrE)
	spelled	*spelled*
spend (bruke)	*spent*	*spent*
spill (søle)	*spilt* (BrE)	*spilt* (BrE)
	spilled	*spilled*
spin (spinne)	*spun, span*	*spun*
spit (spytte)	*spat*	*spat*
	spit (AmE)	*spit* (AmE)
spoil (ødelegge)	*spoilt* (BrE)	*spoilt* (BrE)
	spoiled	*spoiled*
spread (spre)	*spread*	*spread*
spring (hoppe)	*sprang*	*sprung*
	sprung (AmE)	
stand (stå)	*stood*	*stood*
steal (stjele)	*stole*	*stolen*
stick (feste, sitte fast)	*stuck*	*stuck*
sting (stikke)	*stung*	*stung*
stink (stinke)	*stank, stunk*	*stunk*

swear (banne, sverge)	*swore*	*sworn*
sweep (feie)	*swept*	*swept*
swim (svømme)	*swam*	*swum*
swing (svinge)	*swung*	*swung*

T

take (ta)	*took*	*taken*
teach (lære bort)	*taught*	*taught*
tear (rive i stykker)	*tore*	*torn*
tell (fortelle)	*told*	*told*
think (tenke, synes)	*thought*	*thought*
throw (kaste)	*threw*	*thrown*
thrust (presse, stikke)	*thrust*	*thrust*

U

understand (forstå)	*understood*	*understood*
undertake (foreta)	*undertook*	*undertook*
upset (velte, forstyrre)	*upset*	*upset*

W

wake (vekke)	*woke, waked*	*woken, waked*
wear (ha på seg)	*wore*	*worn*
weave (veve)	*wove*	*woven*
weep (gråte)	*wept*	*wept*
win (vinne)	*won*	*won*
wind (trekke opp)	*wound*	*wound*
wring (vri)	*wrung*	*wrung*
write (skrive)	*wrote*	*written*

Appendix 2: Nationality words

Country / continent	Adjective	Persons		The people
		Singular	Plural	
Africa	African	an African	(the) Africans	the Africans
Albania	Albanian	an Albanian	(the) Albanians	the Albanians
Asia	Asian	an Asian	(the) Asians	the Asians
Australia	Australian	an Australian	(the) Australians	the Australians
Austria	Austrian	an Austrian	(the) Austrians	the Austrians
Belgium	Belgian	a Belgian	(the) Belgians	the Belgians
Belarus (Belorussia)	Belorussian	a Belorussian	(the) Belorussians	the Belorussians
Bosnia and Herzegovina[1]	Bosnian	a Bosnian	(the) Bosnians	the Bosnians
Brazil	Brazilian	a Brazilian	(the) Brazilians	the Brazilians
Bulgaria	Bulgarian	a Bulgarian	(the) Bulgarians	the Bulgarians
Canada	Canadian	a Canadian	(the) Canadians	the Canadians
China	Chinese	a Chinese	(the) Chinese	the Chinese
Croatia	Croatian	a Croatian / Croat	(the) Croatians / Croats	the Croatians / Croats
the Czech Republic	Czech	a Czech	(the) Czechs	the Czechs
Denmark	Danish	a Dane	(the) Danes	the Danes
Egypt	Egyptian	an Egyptian	(the) Egyptians	the Egyptians
England	English	an Englishman	(the) Englishmen[2]	the English
Estonia	Estonian	an Estonian	(the) Estonians	the Estonians
Europe	European	a European	(the) Europeans	the Europeans
Finland	Finnish	a Finn	(the) Finns	the Finns
France	French	a Frenchman	(the) Frenchmen	the French
Germany	German	a German	(the) Germans	the Germans
Greece	Greek / Grecian[3]	a Greek	(the) Greeks	the Greeks
Holland / the Netherlands[4]	Dutch	a Dutchman	(the) Dutchmen	the Dutch
Hungary	Hungarian	a Hungarian	(the) Hungarians	the Hungarians
Iceland	Icelandic	an Icelander	(the) Icelanders	the Icelanders
India	Indian	an Indian	(the) Indians	the Indians
Indonesia	Indonesian	an Indonesian	(the) Indonesians	the Indonesians
Iran	Iranian	an Iranian	(the) Iranians	the Iranians
Iraq	Iraqi	an Iraqi	(the) Iraqis	the Iraqis
Ireland / Eire / the Irish Republic[5]	Irish	an Irishman	(the) Irishmen	the Irish
Israel	Israeli	an Israeli	(the) Israelis	the Israelis
Italy	Italian	an Italian	(the) Italians	the Italians
Japan	Japanese	a Japanese	(the) Japanese	the Japanese
Latvia	Latvian	a Latvian	(the) Latvians	the Latvians
Lebanon	Lebanese	a Lebanese	(the) Lebanese	the Lebanese
Lithuania	Lithuanian	a Lithuanian	(the) Lithuanians	the Lithuanians
Mexico	Mexican	a Mexican	(the) Mexicans	the Mexicans
New Zealand	New Zealand	a New Zealander	(the) New Zealanders	the New Zealanders

Norway	Norwegian	a Norwegian	(the) Norwegians	the Norwegians
Pakistan	Pakistani	a Pakistani	(the) Pakistanis	the Pakistanis
Palestine	Palestinian	a Palestinian	(the) Palestinians	the Palestinians
Poland	Polish	a Pole	(the) Poles	the Poles
Portugal	Portuguese	a Portuguese	(the) Portuguese	the Portuguese
Romania	Romanian	a Romanian	(the) Romanians	the Romanians
Russia	Russian	a Russian	(the) Russians	the Russians
Saudi Arabia	Saudi	a Saudi	(the) Saudis	the Saudis
Scotland	Scottish / Scots / Scotch[6]	a Scot	(the) Scots	the Scots / Scottish
Serbia	Serb / Serbian	a Serb	(the) Serbs	the Serbs
Slovakia	Slovakian	a Slovak	(the) Slovaks	the Slovaks
Slovenia	Slovenia	a Slovenian	(the) Slovanians	the Slovanians
South Africa	South African	a South African	(the) South Africans	the South Africans
South Korea	South Korean	a South Korean	(the) South Koreans	the South Koreans
Spain	Spanish	a Spaniard	(the) Spaniards	the Spaniards / Spanish
Sweden	Swedish	a Swede	(the) Swedes	the Swedes
Switzerland	Swiss	a Swiss	(the) Swiss	the Swiss
Turkey	Turkish	a Turk	(the) Turks	the Turks
(the) Ukraine	Ukrainian	a Ukrainian	(the) Ukrainians	the Ukrainians
the United Kingdom / Britain[7]	British	a Briton[8]	(the) Britons	the British
the United States of America[9]	American	an American	(the) Americans	the Americans
Wales[10]	Welsh	a Welshman	(the) Welshmen	the Welsh

1 The official name of the country is *Bosnia and Herzegovina*. Normally the word *Bosnian* is used as an adjective and with reference to people who live in Bosnia and Herzegovina.

2 To avoid the sexual bias in the general *Englishman/men,* we can use *English people* or, more precisely, *Englishwoman/women* if required. The same applies to *Frenchman/men*, *Dutchman/men,* and *Irishman/men.*

3 The adjective *Grecian* is used about ancient Greece.

4 Both *Holland* and *the Netherlands* are used.

5 Ireland has two official languages, English and Irish. The official name for *Ireland / the Irish Republic* in Irish is *Eire.*

6 *Scottish* and *Scots* are common as adjectives. *Scotch* is used primarily about whisky. *Scots* is used about the regional dialects of Scotland.

7 *Britain* includes England, Scotland, and Wales. *The United Kingdom* additionally includes Northern Ireland. We should not use *England* or *English* if we want to refer to all of Britain or the United Kingdom. In such cases *Britain / British / the UK* are the correct forms. *The British Isles* also includes Ireland.

8 *Brit* or *Britisher* are informal, typically American, variants of *Briton.*

9 *The United States*, *the USA*, and *the US* are all current names. Remember the article. US can also be used as an adjective: the US involvement in the Gulf.

Many citizens of countries in South and Central America resent being lumped together as (South or Central) Americans. It would be more correct to refer to those who live in e.g. Bolivia, Chile, and Nicaragua as Bolivians, Chileans, and Nicaraguans, respectively.

10 The Welsh name for Wales is *Cymru.*

Appendix 3: Numerals

Cardinal numerals	Ordinal numerals	Fractions
1 one	1st first	
2 two	2nd second	1/2 a/one-half
3 three	3rd third	1/3 a/one-third
4 four	4th fourth	1/4 a/one-quarter
5 five	5th fifth	1/5 a/one-fifth
6 six	6th sixth	1/6 a/one-sixth
7 seven	7th seventh	1/7 a/one-seventh
8 eight	8th eighth	1/8 a/one-eighth
9 nine	9th ninth	1/9 a/one-ninth
10 ten	10th tenth	1/10 a/one-tenth
11 eleven	11th eleventh	...
12 twelve	12th twelfth	2/3 two-thirds
13 thirteen	13th thirteenth	3/4 three-fourths
14 fourteen	14th fourteenth	4/5 four-fifths
15 fifteen	15th fifteenth	
16 sixteen	16th sixteenth	
17 seventeen	17th seventeenth	
18 eighteen	18th eighteenth	
19 nineteen	19th nineteenth	
20 twenty	20th twentieth	
21 twenty-one	21st twenty-first	
30 thirty	30th thirtieth	
40 forty	40th fortieth	
50 fifty	50th fiftieth	
60 sixty	60th sixtieth	
70 seventy	70th seventieth	
80 eighty	80th eightieth	
90 ninety	90th ninetieth	
100 a/one hundred	100th hundredth	
101 a/one hundred and one	101st (one) hundred and first	
110 a/one hundred and ten	110th (one) hundred and tenth	
200 two hundred	200th two hundredth	
225 two hundred and twenty-five	225th two hundred and twenty-fifth	
1,000 a/one thousand	1,000th (one) thousandth	
1,020 a/one thousand and twenty		
1,200 a/one thousand two hundred		
2,000 two thousand		
2,500 two thousand five hundred		
10,000 ten thousand		
10,020 ten thousand and twenty		
10,200 ten thousand two hundred		
100,000 a/one hundred thousand		
1,000,000 a/one million		
2,000,000 two million		
1,000,000,000 a/one thousand million, one billion (especially AmE) (corresponds to Norwegian 'milliard')		

A 0 ('null') is usually written and pronounced *nought* /nɔ:t/ in British English and *zero* /ˈzi:roʊ/ in American English. *Zero* is generally used in measurements, e.g. in connection with temperature. *O* /əʊ/ is used in numbers where each digit is pronounced by itself, e.g. in phone numbers. In connection with scores and sports results, we find *nil* (football) and *love* (tennis and similar games).

Arsenal won by 2–0 / two goals to nil.
What's the score? – It's 40–0 (forty love).

B *Half* is used as a noun (with the plural form *halves*) or as a determiner. Note the word order:

half an hour (AmE also: a half hour)
half the time
half a dozen etc.
But: two and a half years

C Decimals are written with a full stop and are pronounced, as in: *2.05, two point nought/O five* (BrE), *two point zero/O five* (AmE). A comma is used to mark off thousands (see the list above).

D There are different ways of pronouncing high numbers. For example, 350 can be pronounced *three hundred and fifty* or *three fifty*; and 3,500 can be pronounced *three thousand five hundred* or *thirty-five hundred* (commonly used with round numbers). Each digit is usually pronounced by itself in phone numbers, account numbers, and the like.

E Numbers that can be written as one or two words (*twenty, twenty-five, two thousand*, etc.) are usually written with letters, and others with digits. Avoid using a digit at the start of a sentence (except in a list).

F Note that numerals are treated as nouns and receive plural endings in expressions like:

hundreds of times
millions of people
a lady in her forties (also: a girl in her teens = a teenager)
in the thirties/30's/30s
in the mid-seventies
three-fifths
two-thirds majority

G To express approximate numbers it is possible to use expressions like:

She is about ninety / ninetyish / ninety or so / ninety or thereabouts.
We'll come about nine / at ninish / at nine or so / at nine or thereabouts.

Appendix 4: Spelling rules

A Final consonants before endings beginning with a vowel

The final consonant in monosyllabic words is doubled in front of endings which begin with a vowel (1–3). Forms which end in a silent *-e* are exceptions (4). If the final consonant is *w, x,* or *y,* or if there are two vowels before the final consonant, it is not doubled (5–6).

If the stress falls on the final syllable in a word of two or more syllables which ends in a consonant, the consonant is doubled (7–11). The * marks a stress shift, which explains why the consonant is not doubled.

A final *-l* in words of one or more syllables is doubled in British English (BrE) (12–13), but generally not in American English (AmE). There are exceptions (14).

	Base form	***-ed***	***-er***	***-ing***	**Other**
1	beg	begged		begging	beggar
2	drop	dropped		dropping	
3	slim	slimmed	slimmer	slimming	slimmest
4	hope	hoped		hoping	
5	tax	taxed	taxer	taxing	
6	heat	heated	heater	heating	
7	admit	admitted		admitting	
8	confer	conferred		conferring	conference*
9	occur	occurred		occurring	occurrence
10	prefer	preferred		preferring	preference/ preferable*
11	regret	regretted		regretting	regrettable
12	travel	travelled traveled	traveller traveler	travelling traveling (AmE)	
13	marvel	marvelled marveled		marvelling marveling (AmE)	marvellous
14	parallel	paralleled		paralleling	

The final *-l* is not doubled if the ending begins with a consonant (15–16).

15	expel	expelled		expelling	expulsion
16	fulfil	fulfilled		fulfilling	fulfilment

Note that a final silent *-e* is dropped in many cases in front of the *-able* ending (17), but there are also many exceptions (18). If the final silent *-e* precedes an ending which starts with a consonant, the *-e* is normally kept (19).

17 adorable, advisable, desirable, forgivable, movable
18 changeable, likeable, manageable, noticeable, sizeable
19 careful, hopeful, accurately, achievement, excitement, *but* argument, acknowledg(e)ment, judg(e)ment

B Final *-y* before endings

The main rule is that a final *-y* changes to *-i* in front of endings if the *-y* is preceded by a consonant, but is kept if it is preceded by a vowel. This rule is observed in a series of inflectional endings.

1 plural of nouns: *baby-babies, city-cities, sky-skies,* but *key-keys, play-plays*
2 third person present tense: *try-tries, carry-carries, dry-dries*, but *buy-buys, employ-employs*
3 past tense endings: *try-tried, carry-carried,* but *play-played, employ-employed*
4 comparison of adjectives: *easy-easier/easiest, merry-merrier/merriest*, but *grey-greyer/greyest*
5 the formation of adverbs: *hasty-hastily, pretty-prettily*

In front of the *-ing* ending, there is no change from *-y* to *-i*: *carry-carrying, try-trying, say-saying, employ-employing.*

Note that *-ie* changes to *-y* in *die-dying, lie-lying,* and *tie-tying.*

C Double or single *-l*

1 *All, full, well* are spelt with two *l*'s. However, if they are part of a compound word, one *l* is regularly dropped: *almost, already, always, fulfil, skilful, welcome. All right* should be written as two words.
2 When *-ful* is the last part of a word of two or more syllables, it is spelt with one *l*: *careful, painful, useful, wonderful, mouthful.*
3 If the adverb ending *-ly* is added to a word which ends in *-l*, the result is an adverb with two *l*'s. Otherwise, we get only one *-l*: *actually, gradually, occasionally, really, usually;* but *completely, quickly, stupidly.*

   If the base form ends in *-ic,* the adverb ending is *-ally: basically, critically, tragically.* The notable exception is *publicly.*

   Note *truly, duly, wholly,* and *fully.*

D *-ise* or *-ize*

This verb ending is spelt *-ize* in AmE, and *-ise* or *-ize* in BrE. Since *-ize* is acceptable in both varieties, it is probably the safer spelling: *italicize, nationalize, summarize.*

Note, however, that there is no choice in the following: *advise, advertise, comprise, exercise, revise, surprise, supervise.*

E *-ie-* or *-ei-*

Words which are pronounced with a long /iː/ are generally spelt *-ie-* except after *c-*: *achieve, believe, brief, chief, field, grief, niece, relief, retrieve, yield.* After *c-* we tend to find the *-ei-* spelling: *ceiling, conceive, deceive, preceive, receive.*

The spelling *-ei-* is used in *either, neither, seize, height,* and *weird.* The same spelling is used in *eight, freight, heir, neighbour, weigh,* and *weight.* Here the pronunciation is consistently /eɪ/.

F Some systematic differences between BrE and AmE

Words that end in *-our* in BrE are normally spelt *-or* in AmE (1–2). Some words that end in *-re* in BrE are spelt *-er* in AmE (3–4). There is a tendency for some words to end in *-ogue* in BrE, but *-og* in AmE (5). See also **A** and **D**.

	BrE	AmE
1	colour	color
2	harbour	harbor
3	theatre	theater
4	centre	center
5	catalogue	catalog

G Differences between BrE and AmE in some individual words

	BrE	AmE	meaning
	alu'minium	a'luminum	aluminium
	centenary	centennial	hundreårsdag
	cheque	check	sjekk (betalingsmiddel)
	defence	defense	forsvar
	jail/gaol	jail	fengsel
	jewellery	jewelry	smykker
	offence	offense	forseelse
	pyjamas	pajamas	pyjamas
	plough	plow	plog, pløye
	practise (verb)	practice	praktisere, øve
	programme	program	program
NB!	(program	program	dataprogram)
	speci'ality	'specialty	spesialitet
	tyre	tire	bildekk

Appendix 5: Punctuation

The two (somewhat strained) versions of the letter below show that punctuation matters.

Dear John,
I want a man who knows what love is all about. You are generous, kind, thoughtful. People who are not like you admit to being useless and inferior. You have ruined me for other men. I yearn for you. I have no feelings whatsoever when we're apart. I can forever be happy. Will you let me be yours?

Gloria

Dear John,
I want a man who knows what love is. All about you are generous, kind, thoughtful people, who are not like you. Admit to being useless and inferior. You have ruined me. For other men, I yearn. For you, I have no feelings whatsoever. When we're apart, I can forever be happy. Will you let me be?

Yours,
Gloria

Rules

A The Comma

1 Compound sentences
There is some variation in the use of a comma in compound sentences, i.e. two or more clauses combined by a co-ordinating conjunction (*and, but, or, for*, or *nor*). Generally, if the second clause is long and introduced by *but*, there is a clear tendency to use the comma (1). At the other extreme we have a short second clause with an ellipted subject (and possibly an auxiliary) introduced by *and*. In such cases a comma is less common (2).

1 We are thinking of buying a car, but we haven't made up our minds yet.
2 The job seemed interesting enough and well worth applying for.

2 Initial adverbial elements
A comma should be used after initial adverbial clauses (3–4). Americans also tend to set off shorter initial phrases by a comma (5). There is more variation in British English, but generally, the longer the phrase, the stronger the reason for a comma. The comma helps to show where the following subject begins.

3 If you're ever in London, you must come and visit us.
4 Having looked through our files, I am convinced we have nothing on Mr X.
5 Within a week, Apple's shares had fallen back to their earlier price.

3 Final adverbial elements

The tendency is not to use a comma when the adverbial element comes at the end (6), unless it clearly belongs to a separate information unit (7).

6 This lady came in two days a week while I dashed off to the library between feeds.
7 Most of the activity was concentrated around the church, as it still is in many parts of the United States.

4 Enumerations

A comma should be used to separate a series of parallel phrases or clauses (8). In lists of single words, there is more variation (9–10). A writer who puts in commas gives more weight to each word. In British English there is normally no comma in front of the *and* which introduces the last element in the series. American practice is to include the comma. If there are only two premodifiers in front of the head noun, the comma is usually dropped (11).

8 She left the room in a huff, ran down the stairs, slammed the front door(,) and got into her car.
9 My kisses were met by small warm rubbery unrejecting cheeks.
10 She had a soft, timid, undetermined note in her voice.
11 She walked with long deliberate strides.

5 Parenthetical elements

Parenthetical or final elements which represent separate information units such as non-restrictive relative clauses (12), comment clauses (13–14), appositions (15), and final *-ing* participle clauses (16) should be set off by commas.

12 We drove down to meet Bixby, who had agreed to show us the flat.
13 Crocodiles, I've been told, do not actually like human flesh.
14 We can't allow you in here on your own, I'm afraid.
15 John Marshall, our present director, has announced his resignation.
16 She accompanied me downstairs in the lift, telling me en route about the party and how she had met Joe there.

6 Disjuncts and conjuncts

Disjuncts tend to be set off by commas (17). Single-word disjuncts like *probably* and *possibly* in mid-position are the exceptions (18). Conjuncts should be marked off by commas (19).

17 It was, understandably, not a pleasant sight.
18 Could you possibly meet me a little later?
19 The real reason, however, was that his girlfriend had come on a surprise visit.

7 Numerals

In numbers with four or more digits, a comma should be used to separate any three digits (20).

20 We've agreed to buy it at a price of £150,000.

8 Vocatives and inserts

Inserts like *yes, no, really, please* (21) and noun phrases of direct address (22) should be marked off by commas. Commas are often dropped around a *please* in mid-position.

21 (Please,) Could you (, please,) stop on your way home tomorrow (, please)?
22 Thomas, would you mind playing it once more?

9 Reminders for Norwegians

Norwegians must remember not to put a comma between the subject and the verb (23–24). They must observe that restrictive relative clauses, unlike the corresponding Norwegian ones, are not set off by commas in English (25). No commas must be used in front of a *that*-clause, no matter what its function (26a). However, if there is a co-ordinating conjunction before *that* a comma should be put in (26b).

It is not correct to use a comma to separate two or more independent main clauses. The correct punctuation is a full stop, or at least a semicolon (27a). Alternatively, one can put in a comma and a co-ordinating conjunction (27b).

23 People with a steady and an average income can now afford to move up in the housing market. (NOT ... income, can now ...)
24 What he said at the meeting comes as no surprise to me. (NOT ... meeting, comes ...)
25 The house we looked at last month has still not been sold. (NOT ... month, has ...)
26a Eventually they had come around to accepting that there were no two ways about it. (NOT ... accepting, that ...)
26b He claimed that he knew nothing about it, and that he had no way of finding out unless he checked some confidential files.
27a A complete silence fell. I suddenly felt quite overcome with weakness and misery. (NOT ... fell, I ...)
27b A complete silence fell, and I felt quite overcome with weakness and misery.

B The Semicolon

The semicolon can in most cases be replaced by a full stop. It should be used to link two independent main clauses which are not connected by a co-ordinating conjunction (28). The choice between a full stop and a semicolon is often quite subjective. A semicolon indicates that the material in the two independent main clauses is part of one idea or thought. A full stop shows that the connection in content is not made explicit by punctuation, but must be left to the reader to infer.

28 I was relieved a little; he surely could not expect me to leave before next Thursday.

C The Colon

The colon should only be used to help the reader understand that what follows is a further explication of something. Most commonly, what follows the colon is not a complete clause, but a list of phrases (29). The colon should be used sparingly.

29 Please send the stipulated items: namely, your birth certificate and your passport.

D The Apostrophe

The apostrophe is required to form the genitive of singular (30) and plural nouns (31) (see **5.5**). The apostrophe **must not** be used with possessive determiners, for example *his, yours*, and *its* (32).

Norwegians often confuse contracted forms with similar-sounding possessives (33). The contracted forms in (33) are common in informal writing, but should be avoided in more formal types of written discourse, for example in academic essays.

The apostrophe is furthermore used to form the plurals of letters, numerals, and citation forms of words to avoid misunderstanding (34). If no misunderstanding is likely, a straightforward plural *s* is now becoming more common (35).

30 Tom's car, my friend's reaction, my doctor's advice, yesterday's paper
31 my parents' future, the students' marks, the children's clothes, men's behaviour
32 his advice, these books are yours, the committee had given its recommendations

33 Contracted forms:	Possessives:
it's (= it is, it has)	its publications (possessive determiner)
you're (= you are)	your exam (possessive determiner)
he's (= he is, he has)	his problems (possessive determiner)
they're (= they are)	their expenses (possessive determiner)
who's (= who is, who has)	whose support (possessive relative)
there's (= there is)	the prize is theirs (possessive pronoun)

34 Quite a few of your s's should have been capitalized.
35 In the 1930s, the depression hit most countries in the industrialized world.

E Inverted Commas

Use inverted commas to mark quotations from other writers or speakers. The inverted commas should point inward and, unlike in Norwegian, be placed above the line. Any punctuation marks which are part of the quotation should come before the inverted commas. These points are illustrated in (36).

Inverted commas are used to mark citation forms (37) and choice of words which somehow stand out from the style of the rest of the text (38).

36 'Do you ever drink that type of wine?' he asked.
37 The word 'boy' is a regular plural noun.
38 I wouldn't exactly call him a 'wally'.

F The Hyphen

There is considerable variation in the use of the hyphen. However, a few general points can be made. Compounds consisting of words from different word classes tend to be hyphenated (39). Hyphens are the rule in word sequences which premodify nouns (40).

Norwegians should note in particular that compound nouns, which are spelt as one word in Norwegian, are often spelt as two words in English (41). But there is a lot of variation, so consult your dictionary (see also **4.8.1**).

Hyphens at the end of lines should be avoided, since the rules for end-of-line hyphenation are complicated. But note that monolingual English dictionaries often indicate hyphenation points for their head words. See the examples in **3.9.2**.

39 passer-by, runner-up, brother-in-law, T-shirt, make-up, washing-up, dry-cleaning
40 a ten-year-old boy, a well-to-do family, a would-be climber, this do-it-yourself stuff, 17th-century architecture
41 'morgenavis' = morning paper, 'vaskemaskin' = washing machine, 'veggteppe' = wall-hanging, 'kredittkort' = credit card, 'historiebok' = history book

Appendix 6: List of grammatical terms with Norwegian translations

active voice	aktiv
adjectival	adjektivisk
adjective	adjektiv
adjective phrase	adjektivfrase
adjunct	predikatsadverbial
adverb	adverb
adverbial	adverbial
adverb phrase	adverbfrase
affected	'berørt' (semantisk rolle)
agent	agens
alternative question	alternativt spørsmål
anaphoric	anaforisk (som peker tilbake på noe tidligere i teksten)
anaphoric reference	referanse til noe tidligere i teksten
antecedent	korrelat
anticipatory *it*	*it* som foreløpig subjekt eller objekt
anticipatory object	foreløpig (direkte) objekt
anticipatory subject	foreløpig subjekt
antonym	antonym (ord med motsatt betydning)
antonymy	antonymi
apposition	apposisjon
article	artikkel
aspect	aspekt
attributive	attributiv
auxiliary	hjelpeverb
auxiliary equivalent	verb(frase) som har samme funksjon som et hjelpeverb
bare infinitive	infinitiv uten *to*
case	kasus
cataphoric reference	referanse til noe lenger framme i teksten
catenative	'kjedeverb' med status mellom hjelpeverb og leksikalsk verb
classifying genitive	bestemmende genitivsledd
classifying modifier	bestemmende adledd/beskriverledd
clause	setning
clause element	setningsledd
clefting	utbryting
coherence	koherens
cohesion	kohesjon
collective noun	substantiv med kollektiv betydning
collocation	kollokasjon
comment question	kommentarspørsmål
common noun	fellesnavn, appellativ
communicative function	kommunikativ funksjon
comparative	komparativ
comparison	komparasjon (bøying av adjektiv/adverb)
complement	utfylling

complementation	utfylling
complement of preposition	utfylling til en preposisjon
complex sentence	helsetning med leddsetning
complex transitive verb	treverdig verb med objekt og objektspredikativ
compound noun	sammensatt substantiv
compound sentence	to eller flere helsetninger som er ordnet parataktisk
concord	samsvar/kongruens (oftest mellom subjekt og verbal)
conditional clause	betingselsessetning
conjunct	bindeadverbial
connector	bindeord
connotation	konnotasjon
co-ordinating conjunction	sideordnende konjunksjon
co-ordination	sideordning
copular verb	uselvstendig verb
countable	tellelig
declarative sentence	fortellende setning
definite article	bestemt artikkel
demonstrative determiner	påpekende bestemmerord
demonstrative pronoun	påpekende pronomen
derived noun	avledet substantiv
descriptive grammar	deskriptiv grammatikk
determiner	bestemmerord
direct object	direkte objekt
direct speech	direkte tale
discourse	diskurs (tekst i sammenheng)
disjunct	setningsadverbial som viser hvordan taleren stiller seg til ytringen
ditransitive verb	treverdig verb med to objekter
do-insertion	omskrivning med *to do*
double genitive	dobbel genitiv
dummy *it*	ikke-referensielt 'det'
dynamic passive	*bli*-passiv
dynamic verb	dynamisk verb
dysphemism	nedsettende omskrivning
echo question	ekkospørsmål
effected object	resultatobjekt (semantisk rolle)
ellipsis	ellipse
embedding	underordning, innføyning
empty *it*	'det' som formelt subjekt
end position	plassen etter de obligatoriske leddene i en setning
end weight principle	vektprinsippet
epistemic modality	epistemisk modalitet
euphemism	eufemisme, forskjønnende omskrivning
exclamation	utrop
existential *there*	*there* i presenteringssetninger
extraposition	ekstraposisjon

false friends	ord som har formelle likheter uten å bety det samme
finite (subordinate) clause	finitt (ledd)setning
finite verb	finitt verb
free indirect speech	fri indirekte tale, dekt tale
free predicative	fritt predikativ
fronting	framflytting
function word	funksjonsord
fuzzy category	kategori uten klare grenser
gender	kjønn
genitive	genitiv
gradability	graderbarhet
grammatical auxiliary	grammatisk hjelpeverb
grammatical concord	grammatisk samsvar/kongruens
head	kjerne (i en frase)
homonymy	homonymi
hyponym	hyponym
hyponymy	hyponymi
imperative	imperativ
indefinite article	ubestemt artikkel
indefinite pronoun	ubestemt pronomen
indicative	indikativ
indirect object	indirekte objekt
indirect question	avhengig spørresetning
indirect speech	indirekte tale
infinitive clause	infinitivsetning
infinitive marker	infinitivsmerke
information principle	informasjonsprinsippet
-*ing* co-ordination	sideordning av helsetning og en -*ing*-setning
-*ing* participle	presens partisipp
-*ing* participle clause	presens partisippsetning, -*ing*-setning
initial position	plassen til det første leddet i en setning
insert	interjeksjon
instrumental	instrumental
interactional signals	konvensjonelle ord og uttrykk som er typiske for konversasjon
interrogative sentence	spørresetning
intransitive verb	intransitivt verb
inversion	inversjon, omvendt ordstilling
irregular verb	uregelmessig verb
it-cleft	utbrytingssetning med *it*
left dislocation	venstre-dislokering
lexeme	leksem
lexical teddy bear	kjent ord som blir brukt for mye av en fremmedspråkbruker
lexical verb	leksikalsk verb
lexical words	innholdsord

loan translation	oversettelseslån
long passive	passivsetning med uttrykt agens
main clause	hovedsetning, helsetning
main verb	hovedverb
matrix clause	hovedsetning minus leddsetning
medial position	adverbialplass mellom subjektet og hovedverbet i en setning
metalanguage	metaspråk
modal auxiliary	modalt hjelpeverb
modality	modalitet
modification	forhold mellom kjerne og modifiserende ledd
modifier	adledd, beskriverledd (i en frase)
monotransitive verb	toverdig verb med direkte objekt
mood	modus
morpheme	morfem
morphology	morfologi
multi-word verb	flere ord som utgjør et verballeksem
negator	nektingsledd
nominal	nominal, nomen-
nominalized adjective	substantivert adjektiv
nominal relative clause	nominal relativsetning
nominal subordinate clause	nominal leddsetning
no-negation	nekting med *no* og ord som begynner med *no-*
non-finite	ikke-finitt, infinitt
non-finite subordinate clause	ikke-finitt leddsetning
non-restrictive	ikke-restriktiv
non-restrictive relative clause	ikke-restriktiv/unødvendig relativsetning
notional concord	kongruens med betydning (ikke form)
notional subject	egentlig subjekt
not-negation	nekting med *not*
noun	substantiv
noun phrase	nomenfrase
numeral	tallord
obfuscation	'tåkelegging'
object predicative	objektspredikativ
obligatory	obligatorisk
oblique object	preposisjonsobjekt
optional	fakultativ, ikke obligatorisk
participle	partisipp
passive voice	passiv
past participle	perfektum partisipp
past participle clause	ikke-finitt setning med perfektum partisipp som verbal
past tense	preteritum
perfective aspect	perfektivt aspekt
personal pronoun	personlig pronomen

phatic communion	fatisk kommunikasjon
phrasal verb	partikkelverb
phrase	frase
plural-only nouns	substantiv som bare forekommer i flertall
polysemy	polysemi
positive	positiv
possessive determiner	bestemmerord som uttrykker eiendomsforhold
possessive pronoun	eiendomspronomen
postmodifier	etterstilt attributt
postponement	det å sette noe lengre bak i setningen
pragmatic function	pragmatisk funksjon
pragmatics	pragmatikk
predicative	predikativ
premodifier	foranstilt attributt
preposition	preposisjon
prepositional phrase	preposisjonsfrase
prepositional verb	preposisjonsverb
prescriptive grammar	preskriptiv/normativ grammatikk
presentative construction	presenteringskonstruksjon
present tense	presens
principle of end weight	vektprinsippet
pro-form	proform
progressive aspect	samtidsform
pronoun	pronomen
proper noun	egennavn, proprium
prototype	prototyp (typisk eksempel på noe)
proximity concord	kongruens med nærmeste ledd
quantifying determiner	kvantor
recipient	mottaker (semantisk rolle)
reciprocal pronoun	resiprokt pronomen
reference	referanse
referent	referent
referential *it*	det personlige pronomen *it*
reflexive pronoun	refleksivt pronomen
regional variation	regional språkvariasjon
register	register
regular verb	regelmessig verb
relative clause	relativsetning
restrictive	restriktiv
restrictive relative clause	restriktiv/nødvendig relativsetning
reversed *wh*-cleft	utbrytingssetning med *wh*-setningen til slutt
right dislocation	høyredislokering
root modality	ikke-epistemisk (optativ) modalitet
semantic domain	semantisk felt
semantic role	semantisk rolle

semantics	semantikk
sense	betydning
sentence	uavhengig setning, periode
sentence fragment	setningsemne
sentential relative clause	relativsetning med (en større del av) en setning som korrelat
short passive	passiv uten uttrykt agens
simple sentence	helsetning (uten leddsetning), særsetning
situational reference	referanse til noe utenfor teksten
social variation	sosial språkvariasjon
specifying modifier	beskrivende adledd/beskriverledd
speech act	talehandling
split infinitive	infinitiv med et ledd mellom *to* og verbet
split modifier	delt adledd/beskriverledd
stative passive	*være*-passiv
stative verb	statisk verb
structural parallelism	parallellisme i ordstilling
subject	subjekt
subject–auxiliary inversion	inversjon av subjektet og et hjelpeverb
subject predicative	subjektspredikativ
subject–verb inversion	inversjon av subjekt og verbal
subjunctive	konjunktiv
subordinate clause	leddsetning
subordinating conjunction	underordnende konjunksjon (subjunksjon minus relativpronomen)
subordination	underordning
superlative	superlativ
superordinate clause	oversetning
superordinate term	overordnet begrep
synonym	synonym
synonymy	synonymi
syntax	syntaks
tag question	halespørsmål, tilhengerspørsmål
tense	tempus, (verb)tid
textual deixis	referanse til noe i den øvrige teksten
that-clause	*at*-setning
to-infinitive	infinitiv med *to*
topic sentence	setning som uttrykker emnet for et avsnitt
transitivity	transitivitet
type–token ratio	forhold mellom antall forskjellige ord i en tekst og det totale antall ord
unattached participle clause	partisippsetning uten forankring i oversetningen
uncountable	utellelig
unit noun	substantiv som brukes for å gi tellelig referanse
valency	valens
verb	(1) verb (ordklasse); (2) verbal (setningsledd)
verbless clause	setning uten verbal
verb phrase	verbfrase

vocative	vokativ
voice	diatese
wh-cleft	utbrytingssetning med *wh*-ord
wh-determiner	*wh*-ord som fungerer som bestemmerord
wh-pronoun	*wh*-pronomen
wh-question	spørsmål med spørreord
yes/no-question	*ja-/nei*-spørsmål (spørsmål uten spørreord)

Works Consulted

Grammars

COBUILD – English Grammar, Collins, London 1990

Faarlund, Jan Terje; Svein Lie, and Kjell Ivar Vannebo, *Norsk referansegrammatikk*, Universitetsforlaget, Oslo 1997

Givón, Talmy, *English Grammar, A Function-Based Introduction*, John Benjamins Publishing Company, Amsterdam 1993

Halliday, Michael, *An Introduction to Functional Grammar*, Edward Arnold, London 1995

Johansson, Stig and Per Lysvåg, *Understanding English Grammar,* Parts 1 and 2, Universitetsforlaget, Oslo 1986 and 1987

Lysvåg, Per and Stig Johansson, *Engelsk grammatikk og språkbruk – Form og funksjon,* Aschehoug, Oslo 1990

Lysvåg, Per and Stig Johansson, *Going for Grammar*, Aschehoug, Oslo 1995

Quirk, Randolph; Sidney Greenbaum, Geoffrey Leech, and Jan Svartvik, *A Comprehensive Grammar of the English Language*, Longman, London 1985

Woods, Edwards and Nicole McLeod, *Using English Grammar – Meaning and Form,* Prentice Hall, London 1990

Dictionaries and thesauruses

Cambridge International Dictionary of English, Cambridge University Press 1995

Collins COBUILD English Language Dictionary, Collins, London 1987

Longman Dictionary of Contemporary English, 3rd ed., Longman, London 1995

Longman Language Activator, Longman, London 1993

Merriam-Webster's Collegiate Dictionary, 10th ed., Merriam-Webster, Inc., Springfield, MA 1993

Oxford Advanced Learner's Dictionary, 3rd ed., Oxford University Press, 1974

Pocket Roget's Thesaurus, Longman, London 1986

Roget's Student Thesaurus, HarperCollins, New York 1994

Urdang, Laurence, *The Macmillan Dictionary of Synonyms and Antonyms*, London 1995

Other works

Björk, Lennart and Christine Raisanen, *Academic Writing*, Studentlitteratur, Lund 1996

Bolinger, Dwight, *Language – The Loaded Weapon, The Use and Abuse of Language Today*, Longman, London and New York 1980

Carter, Ronald, *Vocabulary, Applied Linguistic Perspectives*, Routledge, London 1994

Endresen, Rolf Theil, Hanne Gram Simonsen, and Andreas Sveen, *Innføring i lingvistikk,* Universitetsforlaget, Oslo 1996

Green, Georgia, *Pragmatics and Natural Language Understanding*, Lawrence Erlbaum Associates, London 1989

Hasselgren, Angela, 'Lexical Teddy Bears and Advanced Learners: A Study into the Ways Norwegian Students Cope with English Vocabulary', *International Journal of Applied Linguistics,* Vol. 4, No. 2, 1994

Hayakawa, S. I., *Language in Thought and Action*, 3rd ed., Harcourt Brace Jovanovich, New York 1972

Hurford, James and Brendan Heasley, *Semantics – A Coursebook*, Cambridge University Press, Cambridge 1983

Jackson, Howard, *Words and Their Meaning*, Longman, London 1988

Keller, E. and S. T. Warner, *Gambits 1: Openers* (1976), *Gambits 2: Links* (1976), *Gambits 3: Responders and Closers*, Public Service Commission, Language Training Branch, Ottawa 1977

McKinnon, William, *Aspect of Modern Business Style*, Universitetsforlaget, Oslo 1983

Rudska, B., J. Channell, Y. Putseys, and P. Ostyn, *The Words You Need*, Macmillan Press, London 1981

Stenström, Anna-Brita, *An Introduction to Spoken Interaction,* Longman, London 1994

Svartvik, Jan and Randolph Quirk, *A Corpus of English Conversation*, Gleerup, Lund 1980

Ungerer, Friedrich and Hans-Jörg Schmid, *An Introduction to Cognitive Linguistics*, Longman, London 1996

Wright, Laura and Jonathan Hope, *Stylistics – A Practical Coursebook*, Routledge, London 1996.

Sources of examples

Aldiss, Brian, *Report on Probability A*, Sphere, 1977

Amis, Kingsley, *One Fat Englishman,* Penguin Books, 1966

Brown, Mick, *American Heartbeat*, Penguin, 1994

Bryson, Bill, *Bizarre World,* Warner Books, 1995

Caroll, Lewis, *Alice in Wonderland*, Wordsworth Classics, 1992

Chesterton, G. K., *Father Brown*, Wordsworth Classics, 1992

Dahl, Roald, *Boy: Tales of a Childhood,* Penguin Books, 1986

Dahl, Roald, *Matilda,* Jonathan Cape, 1988

Faulkner, William, *The Sound and the Fury*, Penguin, 1964

Hall, Adam, *The Tango Briefing*, in Laura Wright and Jonathan Hope, *Stylistics – A Practical Coursebook*, Routledge, 1996

Hazandra Despotopoulou, Valli, *Attitudes and Opinions*, Macmillan, 1980

Hemingway, Ernest, 'In another country', in *The Essential Hemingway*, Granada, 1977

Hughes, Langston, *The Dream Keeper and Other Poems,* Knopf, 1932

Kosinski, Jerzy, *Being There*, Bantam Books, 1972
Mansfield, Katherine, *The Garden Party and Other Stories*, Penguin Books, 1951
McBain, Ed, *Long Time No See,* copyright by Hui Corporation, reproduced by permission of Hamish Hamilton
McDermid, Val, *An Unsuitable Job for a Woman*, HarperCollins, 1995
Morrison, Toni, *Sula*, Knopf, 1973
Murdoch, Iris, *The Bell*, Longman, 1990
The Norton Anthology of American Literature, Shorter Fourth Edition, Norton, 1995
Opie, Iona and Peter, *Children's Games in Street and Playground*, Oxford University Press, 1984
Orwell, George, *Animal Farm*, Longman, 1960
Pile, Stephen, *The Book of Heroic Failures*, Futura, 1980
Sacks, Oliver, *The Man Who Mistook His Wife for a Hat*, Pan Books, 1986
Salinger, J. D., *The Catcher in the Rye*, Penguin, 1984
Shaw, George Bernard, *Major Barbara*, Constable, 1913
Simmonds, Posy, *Very Posy*, Fontana/Collins, 1985
Townsend, Sue, *The Queen and I*, Mandarin, 1993
Waugh, Evelyn, 'Excursion into Reality', in *Present Laughter – An Anthology of Comic Writing*, Malcolm Bradbury, ed., Phoenix Giants, 1994
Weldon, Fay, *The Heart of the Country*, Arrow Books, 1987
The White House Transcripts, Bantam Books, 1974

Individual examples have been drawn from electronic text corpora: the Brown Corpus (a million-word collection of printed American English texts), the London–Lund Corpus (half a million words of educated spoken British English), and the British National Corpus (a 100-million-word corpus of written and spoken English texts).

Index